THE BIN LADEN PAPERS

NELLY LAHOUD is an associate professor of security studies in the Department of National Security and Strategy at U.S. Army War College. She is also a senior fellow in New America's International Security program. She is the author of three books, including *The Jihadis' Path to Self-Destruction*.

Further praise for *The Bin Laden Papers*:

"A remarkable book which transports readers to bin Laden's residence."
Tim Willasey-Wilsey, *International Affairs*

"In terms of understanding al-Qaeda between 2001 and 2011 this book is indispensable ... A revelation on nearly every page."
Jim Motavalli, *New York Journal of Books*

"A narrative that illuminates Bin Laden's character and style . . . The corrective insights contained in this excellent readable book merit careful attention."
Aspects of History

"The definitive and original account of the trajectory of al-Qaeda from 2001 to the death of Bin Laden."
Martha Crenshaw, coauthor of *Countering Terrorism*

"A masterful analysis and riveting story ... *The Bin Laden Papers* clarifies a man and his movement that confused and confounded much of the world for decades."
General (Ret.) Stanley McChrystal, former commander of
United States Forces Afghanistan

NELLY LAHOUD

THE BIN LADEN PAPERS

How the Abbottabad Raid Revealed the Truth about Al-Qaeda, Its Leader and His Family

YALE UNIVERSITY PRESS
NEW HAVEN AND LONDON

For information about this and other Yale University Press publications, please contact:
U.S. Office: sales.press@yale.edu   yalebooks.com
Europe Office: sales@yaleup.co.uk   yalebooks.co.uk

Set in Adobe Garamond Pro by IDSUK (DataConnection) Ltd
Printed in Great Britain by Clays Ltd, Elcograf S.p.A

Library of Congress Control Number: 2023934615

ISBN 978-0-300-26063-2 (hbk)
ISBN 978-0-300-27042-6 (pbk)

A catalogue record for this book is available from the British Library.

10 9 8 7 6 5 4 3 2 1

At the age of 14 or thereabouts, I decided that the curriculum of the school Baccalaureate in my native city, Beirut, Lebanon, was going to be a waste of my time. I assembled the household and presented my case—"What's the use of studying Rousseau, al-Mutanabbi, and pre-Islamic poetry?!" I posited. With impeccable reasoning, I elucidated how dropping out of school and pursuing computer science at a technical college would be far more advantageous. By the time I was done, everyone was on board. Well, almost everyone. My mother, who was not fortunate to have received an education herself, merely rolled her eyes and dismissed my proposition outright.

Today, my computer skills are way below mediocre, and I so much enjoy reading Rousseau and Arabic poetry.

This book is dedicated to the memory of my late mother, Reda—one of the smartest people I've ever known.

CONTENTS

CONTENTS

ILLUSTRATIONS

ACKNOWLEDGMENTS

I am deeply grateful to individuals and institutions who made it possible for me to complete this project. Writing a book that chronicles al-Qaeda's post-9/11 history based on nearly 6,000 pages of the group's internal communications is challenging, but feasible. However, getting to this starting point required going through nearly 100,000 files of Arabic materials—a daunting undertaking. But a fortuitous meeting with Peter Bergen at a conference in Beirut in 2018 made this book possible. Peter had interviewed Usama bin Laden long before I heard the name of al-Qaeda's leader, and he encouraged me to study the Bin Laden Papers in their entirety. The support of Peter and New America allowed me to work with two capable research assistants—Rana Choueiry and Muhammad al-Ubaydi—and go through nearly 100,000 files to identify the 6,000 pages of relevant materials. Throughout the process of writing this book, Peter's mentorship, including his feedback, was invaluable; and he generously used his contacts to advance and promote my research at every opportunity.

I was exceedingly fortunate to have the support of the great historian of Islam Michael Cook during the journey of writing this book. Michael read and commented on all the draft chapters and spinoff articles. Thanks to his input, I grasped obscure historical elements which allowed me to have a richer understanding of the letters. Michael also read several letters to help me trace some technical references. The feedback of this most learned—intimidatingly so—scholar immeasurably improved the content and style of the book. I hope that this final draft pleases him.

ACKNOWLEDGMENTS

I was also fortunate that my friend Gary Apple enthusiastically and patiently read the full manuscript and spinoff articles. Gary read the materials from a general reader's perspective, but the feedback of this brilliant playwright went far beyond generality. On many occasions, I revisited the letters to address Gary's poignant probing, and the book is better and clearer because of his numerous insightful suggestions about structure, style, and more.

I am grateful to members and former members of the U.S. military who helped me along the way. On many occasions—too many to count—I reached out to Colonel (Ret.) Liam Collins with queries, advice, and requests, and his support was critical to advancing my work on the book. It is thanks to Liam and the broader West Point family that I had the first opportunity to work on the Bin Laden Papers when the first seventeen documents were declassified in 2012. Lieutenant Commander Kurt Albaugh helped me navigate and analyze some themes that required technical knowledge of the maritime domain. General (Ret.) Joseph Votel took the time to shed light on the potential operational impact of Bin Laden's planned maritime attacks and the military response they would likely engender. Admiral (Ret.) William H. McRaven kindly shed light on the additional length of time the SEALs spent in the Abbottabad compound to recover the electronics on which the Bin Laden Papers were saved.

I am also grateful for the input of a community of friends and colleagues with whom I discussed or shared parts of the manuscript: Mia Bloom, Stuart Caudill, Cliff Chanin, Thomas Hegghammer, Monica Khouri, Katrina Lee Koo, Stephen Menn, Debra Morgan, Ragnhild Nordas, Beryl Radin, Roland Rich, William (Bill) Roebuck, David Sterman, Marin Strmecki, Rebecca Stringer, and Heba Taha.

All my scholarly endeavors are an extension of what I have learned from my Ph.D. supervisors—Barry Hindess (d. 2018), Anthony H. Johns, and Tony Street. I am forever their student.

I am most thankful to the supportive team at Yale University Press, particularly to my editor, Joanna (Jo) Godfrey. Not only did I benefit from Jo's rigorous edits and meticulous attention to detail, but her professionalism and dedication to various aspects of the book project were beyond exceptional.

ACKNOWLEDGMENTS

My thanks also to two peer reviewers, whose feedback was most valuable. One of them turned out to be the superb scholar of al-Qaeda Anne Likuski (née Stenersen), whose report immeasurably improved what was supposed to be a final draft.

Of course, all the book's shortcomings are my own.

Last but not least, I am fortunate to enjoy the love and support of family and friends on several continents. I am especially grateful to those among them who have absolutely no interest in my research.

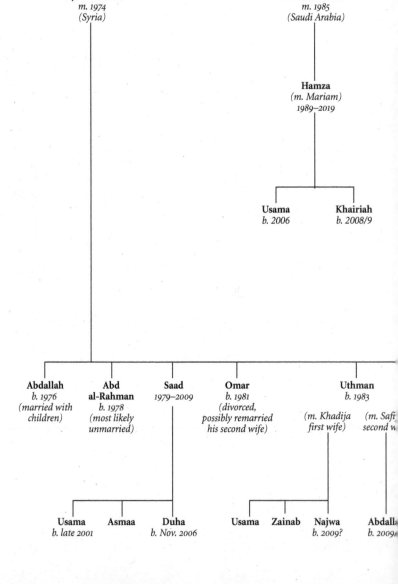

Usama bin Laden

Wives, children, and grandchildren on May 1, 2011

Najwa Ghanem
m. 1974
(Syria)

Khairiah Sabar
m. 1985
(Saudi Arabia)

Hamza
(m. Mariam)
1989–2019

Usama
b. 2006

Khairiah
b. 2008/9

Abdallah
b. 1976
(married with children)

Abd al-Rahman
b. 1978
(most likely unmarried)

Saad
1979–2009

Omar
b. 1981
(divorced, possibly remarried his second wife)

Uthman
b. 1983

(m. Khadija first wife)

(m. Safi second w

Usama
b. late 2001

Asmaa

Duha
b. Nov. 2006

Usama

Zainab

Najwa
b. 2009?

Abdall
b. 2009

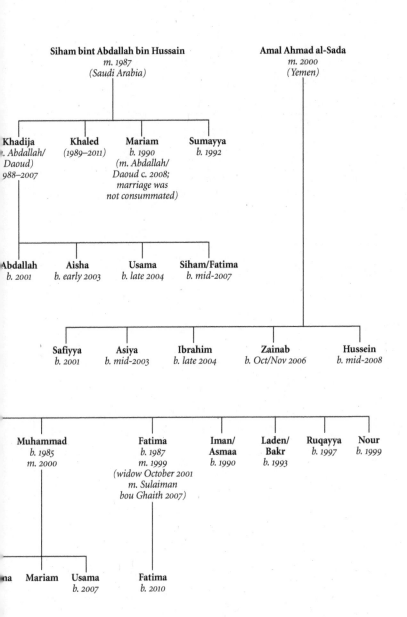

Siham bint Abdallah bin Hussain
m. 1987
(Saudi Arabia)

Amal Ahmad al-Sada
m. 2000
(Yemen)

Khadija
*. Abdallah/
Daoud)*
988–2007

Khaled
(1989–2011)

Mariam
b. 1990
*(m. Abdallah/
Daoud c. 2008;
marriage was
not consummated)*

Sumayya
b. 1992

Abdallah
b. 2001

Aisha
b. early 2003

Usama
b. late 2004

Siham/Fatima
b. mid-2007

Safiyya
b. 2001

Asiya
b. mid-2003

Ibrahim
b. late 2004

Zainab
b. Oct/Nov 2006

Hussein
b. mid-2008

Muhammad
b. 1985
m. 2000

Fatima
b. 1987
m. 1999
*(widow October 2001
m. Sulaiman
bou Ghaith 2007)*

**Iman/
Asmaa**
b. 1990

**Laden/
Bakr**
b. 1993

Ruqayya
b. 1997

Nour
b. 1999

na

Mariam

Usama
b. 2007

Fatima
b. 2010

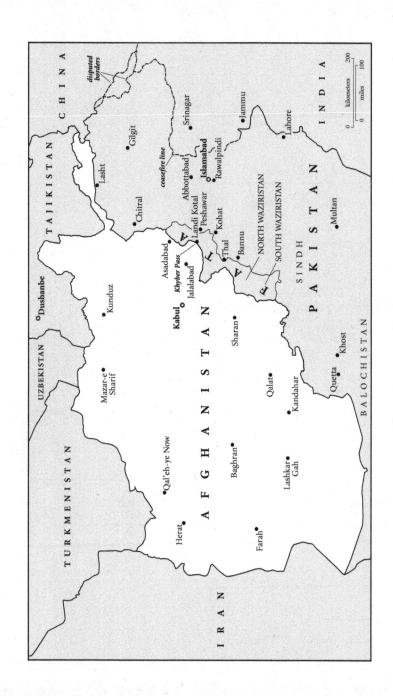

PROLOGUE
EIGHTEEN MINUTES

"We have to get this done in thirty minutes," said Admiral William H. McRaven to Captain Pete Van Hooser, as they planned the raid on Usama bin Laden's compound in Abbottabad, Pakistan. The Admiral had tasked Van Hooser with overseeing the technical execution of the operation,[1] which included being in direct communication with the Navy SEAL ground commander to update McRaven in real time on how the mission was unfolding.[2]

Speed was of the essence. McRaven's studies, combined with his lengthy and decorated experience, had taught him that most successful operations "were completed in thirty minutes."[3] Long before President Barack Obama entrusted McRaven with planning and overseeing the Abbottabad raid, the Admiral had conducted a historical study that examined eight Special Operations missions. The study had concluded that speed was critical to the achievement of "relative superiority" by a small attacking force over its larger and well-defended enemy.[4] The success of Special Operations missions, McRaven deduced, hinges on relative superiority, which is achieved "at a pivotal moment in an engagement"; "any delay will expand your area of vulnerability."[5]

The Navy SEALs are part of the U.S. Special Operations Forces (SOF) community and take pride in being trained to "achieve the impossible."[6] Those selected to carry out the Abbottabad raid were the *crème de la crème* of the SEALs. McRaven observed that "all were handpicked" and "had extensive combat experience."[7] The same was true for the aviation crews of the two Black Hawks and two MH-47 Chinooks transporting the SEALs to Usama bin Laden's doorstep.[8]

On April 30, 2011, hours before the SEALs departed on the mission, McRaven assembled his team: "Gentlemen," he addressed them, "each of you has done hundreds of missions just like this one. . . . Just play your game like you always have and we will be successful."[9] Completing the mission within thirty minutes was critical, because "minutes and seconds spell the difference between success and failure."[10]

Later that night, the SEALs set out to get Bin Laden and the mission was under way. They were in the compound and, nearing their allotted time window for the raid, Van Hooser alerted McRaven: "Sir, the SEALs are requesting some additional time on the ground." After McRaven enquired about the holdup, Van Hooser explained: "Sir, they say they found a whole shit-ton of computers and electronic gear on the second floor."[11]

Minutes earlier, the ground commander had communicated on the radio: "For God and Country, Geronimo, Geronimo, Geronimo!"—the code for "*We had gotten bin Laden*"—and McRaven had confirmed that "Geronimo" was "EKIA" (Enemy Killed in Action).[12] "[T]he plan called for thirty minutes on the ground—no more,"[13] but McRaven immediately recognized the potential intelligence value of Bin Laden's hard drives. Since the start of Operation Enduring Freedom in Afghanistan on October 7, 2001, every mission carried out by SOF has involved sensitive-site exploitation (SSE) when feasible, in the form of seizing data that could yield invaluable intelligence.[14]

Though McRaven's "gut" told him "to stick with the plan,"[15] he gave the "go-ahead" to recover the electronics. At forty minutes, he decided that they had pushed the envelope far enough and told them "to wrap it up," and "about eight minutes later—or so—we took off."[16]

Over subsequent years, select documents recovered by the SEALs were declassified, but the bulk of it remained under the exclusive purview of the intelligence community. By November 2017, over six years after the raid, "nearly 470,000 additional files" were declassified. Among these items are nearly 6,000 Arabic pages of internal communiqués that were never intended for public consumption. We would not have the Bin Laden Papers had it not been for the SEALs courageous efforts during those perilous additional eighteen minutes.

INTRODUCTION

This book owes its existence to the Special Operations Forces (SOF) who carried out the raid on Usama bin Laden's compound in Abbottabad, Pakistan, on May 1, 2011. It is a study of al-Qaeda's declassified internal correspondence and documents that SOF recovered from Bin Laden's "computers and electronic gear" on the second floor of the compound[1]—nearly 6,000 Arabic pages.

I have had the privilege of working with members of the SOF community during my work at the Combating Terrorism Center (CTC) at West Point (2010–15) and since, and, based on my limited experience, I appreciate why they are *Special*. At West Point, there is a large concentration of unassuming heroes whose accomplishments are not readily apparent to civilians like me with limited knowledge of military vernacular and uniform decorations. One of them, Liam Collins, was my boss, and it was whispered to me that he is a "rock star" in the SOF community. I was told that he was called "Lucky" by his teammates to mark the many dangerous encounters he had survived while on active duty. During Liam's retirement ceremony from the Army in 2019, I had a glimpse of his bravery through the speeches of those who had served with him and witnessed his valor.

I learned from Liam that leaders are those who make decisions under extraordinary conditions by knowing when to lead and when to be team players, which also defined his role as director of the CTC. During his tenure, the U.S. government declassified and released through the CTC seventeen out of thousands of documents recovered from Abbottabad. Liam entrusted me with taking the lead in the study that accompanied their release, and I learned from him how and why SOF conduct sensitive-site exploitation (SSE),[2] as the SEALs did in Abbottabad to recover the electronics on the second floor.

Days before the CTC released the seventeen documents and the Abbottabad report, a group of SOF aviators visited West Point. One of them had taken part in the Abbottabad raid, and I was overwhelmed when he walked into my office with Liam in tow. There were limits to what I could ask about the mission. Typical of SOF, he went on to downplay the danger that he and his team went through to recover the documents and thanked me for my work on them. I told him that his SOF team would be the first readers of the CTC study when it was finalized. The CTC of course mailed the report to the appropriate address before it was bound and publicly released.

I learned more about the SOF world through another hero, Kent Solheim, when he was a CTC fellow. Kent is a member of the 3rd Special Forces Group; he was wounded in Iraq and his injuries resulted in the loss of one of his legs. He requested a waiver to remain on active duty and was subsequently deployed several times. Kent's Silver Star never came up in our conversations. The medal was awarded for having "single-handedly thwarted an enemy assault by exposing himself to enemy fire to kill a rocket propelled grenade gunner and enemy gunman maneuvering on his comrades."[3] I found out about Kent's injuries when I noticed his prosthetic leg while he was riding his bike at West Point.

In 2014–15, Kent decided that Special Forces and other military units should learn about the CTC's research on the Islamic State before deploying to Iraq to "advise and assist" the Iraqi army. During our travels to various Forts across the United States to present our research, I was introduced to a community of critical thinkers who were eager to consume dispassionate analysis. As usual with SOF and other Army communities, we, the civilian researchers, were made to feel part of the team. In fact, Kent often introduced me as a member of the 3rd Group to gain entry to the SOF gym (with functional equipment) when I tagged along.

My precious possessions include Kent's Green Beret to mark my official honorary membership of the 3rd Group, and Liam's blood chit, which he carried during his deployment in Afghanistan in 2001. The blood chit is a numbered note that military personnel carry in case they are shot down or isolated during their deployment. It identifies them as Americans and encourages the local population to assist them.[4] The note displays the text in the language(s) spoken in the geographical zones of their deployment. The English version reads:

I am an American and do not speak your language. I will not harm you! I bear no malice towards your people. My friend, please provide me food, water, shelter, and necessary medical attention. Also, please provide safe passage to the nearest friendly forces of any country supporting the Americans and their allies. You will be rewarded for assisting me when you present this number to American authorities.

I have been painfully mindful throughout my research that the SOF's road to Abbottabad started in New York on September 11, 2001, when nearly 3,000 people lost their lives. On the ground floor of the 9/11 Memorial & Museum that was built at the site of the Twin Towers is the In Memoriam gallery whose four walls display the photographs of all those killed on 9/11. It viscerally reminds the visitor that she is standing at the site of a massacre.[5] It is beyond regrettable that the chain of events that led to the Bin Laden Papers' existence occurred in the first place, and that this book had subsequently to be written.

For many years, I have taught in the yearly executive education program on counterterrorism run by the New York City Fire Department (FDNY), which suffered major fatalities on 9/11. The course was conceived after 9/11 by Chief (Ret.) Joseph "Joe" Pfeifer. Joe was the first FDNY chief at the World Trade Center and lost his brother, Kevin, also a firefighter, in the attacks. After he retired from the FDNY, Joe wrote a book, *Ordinary Heroes*, about this harrowing day. Joe and his FDNY colleagues have sensitized me to the pernicious impact of terrorism on first responders and to the extraordinary challenges they face even on days that are so ordinary to the rest of us.

Throughout the journey of writing this book, I sought to assemble the narrative that is revealed in the Papers and bring to light what Bin Laden and those in his covert orbit were doing, thinking, communicating, and planning. It is as if the narrative is a tapestry, and the Bin Laden Papers are the threads that must be rewoven to display its design.

Initially, I considered writing a book that reviewed the existing literature about Bin Laden and al-Qaeda, including material that drew selectively on a subset of the Papers themselves, to revisit key assumptions on the subject. My concern was that such an approach would produce a book that mostly focused on *what did not happen*, as opposed to the more compelling and untold story of *what actually happened*.

Instead, I chose to build on my academic background in language and textual analysis to read and analyze the Bin Laden Papers in a way that had not yet been attempted. Over the years, my Ph.D. supervisors and other mentors have impressed upon me the importance of what philologists describe as "the art of reading slowly."[6] Guided by their wisdom, I endeavored to understand what is explicit in the Bin Laden Papers and, when possible, to surmise what is implicit.

My goal is to present the reader with a contextual understanding of the Papers and to include as much of the raw materials as I can. It is my hope that you, the reader, can partake in the analysis, and also in the challenges, the riddles, and the revelations that I encountered during my research. Together, we shall inhabit a zone that allows us to observe the world of the players whose correspondence we are reading.

Keep in mind that everything in this book flows from the Bin Laden Papers themselves. We shall see, through al-Qaeda's eyes, an "afflicted" organization whose international terrorism was halted following the fall of the Taliban regime in December 2001. We shall experience first-hand the devastating effects of drones as a counterterrorism weapon against al-Qaeda and other militants. We shall witness Bin Laden's unwavering commitment to the political cause for which he sacrificed his personal fortune and understand why his ideas continue to mobilize people today. We shall encounter Bin Laden's methodical mind through his plans to mount large-scale attacks "the effects of which," he wrote, "will far exceed 9/11." We shall observe how al-Qaeda struggled with the unintended consequences of the activities of the jihadi groups it inspired. The letters will take us into Bin Laden's household where we shall meet his wives and daughters who effectively co-authored the public statements he delivered over the years, and also listen in on negotiations to find a bride for his son Khaled. Unexpectedly, we shall discover in the letters the identity of the *real* courier whose capture likely allowed the CIA to uncover Bin Laden's Abbottabad hideout.

I noted earlier that this book is like an exercise in reweaving threads to expose the design of the tapestry that Bin Laden and others in his orbit had woven. The tapestry, however, is missing some threads, and I have only been able to produce an incomplete narrative. Though many of the Bin Laden Papers are unambiguous in their expression, some were not recovered or had been destroyed by Bin Laden, while others were deliberately written in coded language, almost Delphic in their riddles. Some missing letters I could partially reconstruct from those that were recovered, others may be lost forever. Some riddles I could solve, others defeated me.

Notwithstanding the missing threads, the nearly 6,000 Arabic pages recovered allow us to put together a chronological account of the key events that defined al-Qaeda in the decade between 9/11 and its founder's demise in 2011. They lay bare al-Qaeda's secrets and serve as a corrective to existing narratives about the group. I did not turn to secondary sources to complete the narrative and risk contributing to the existing literature that does not fit with the reality revealed in the Bin Laden Papers. I did, however, draw on secondary sources to illuminate and provide context for issues raised in the papers and that other scholars had studied.

To appreciate the invaluable information al-Qaeda's internal communications reveal, it is helpful to understand how Bin Laden and his associates communicated, and why their correspondence was intrinsic to the activities of al-Qaeda under Bin Laden's leadership.

In Abbottabad, the Bin Laden family adhered to strict security measures to avoid being tracked by the CIA or the Pakistani government. The letters make it abundantly clear that the Bin Ladens did not have access to the internet or a phone at the compound, and all communications between Bin Laden and his associates were made through electronic letters delivered by couriers. Some letters had been handwritten, then scanned and saved as JPG files, but most were typed and saved as Word documents. One letter discloses the mechanics involved: The electronic letters were saved on "SIM cards" and then placed in an "envelope." Upon reaching their intended destination, the letters had to be "extracted." In case the files fell into the wrong hands, Bin Laden and his associates penned their letters using aliases that they changed periodically. Sometimes, they did not even sign or date their respective letters.

With this in mind, some remarks on how to read the letters are in order. To state the obvious, chronicling al-Qaeda's history post-9/11 requires analyzing the letters according to their authorship and the chronological order in which they were composed. But these matters are not always clear-cut, and the reader often has to determine the authorship and estimate the date on the basis of clues provided in the content of the letters.[7] Importantly, there is a marked difference between the awkward Arabic writing style of the Bin Laden Papers and the polished public statements of al-Qaeda's leaders. It bears repeating that the letters were not written for public consumption and were often composed in haste. Accordingly, the authors prioritized content over style and often jammed in information in a form that assumed knowledge on the part of their small inner-circle readers. For example, a seemingly vague sentence will be understood only after reading the letter in its entirety—e.g., in the course of composing a letter, the author remembered a detail which they later added arbitrarily on a different page of the same letter, knowing that the reader could easily connect the dots.

Often, a close reading of several letters is required to understand cryptic references. For example, an issue may be explicitly stated in an earlier letter, and then, in subsequent letters, will be addressed, now seemingly more vaguely, in a series of back-and-forth communications. The reader has to connect the dots between this ensemble of letters and, only then, an "Aha!" moment will follow. Also, the nearly 6,000 Arabic pages of internal communications include several versions of the same letters. Some are duplicates, while others are drafts composed at various stages of the writing process. For instance, the same letter exists at page 4 of the drafting process, then at page 9 of the drafting process, then at page 18, and so on. Often, an earlier incomplete draft includes important information that did not go into the final version of the letter.

Thus, understanding the letters often involves assimilating information and details outside a given passage, either from the same letter and/or from several others. For these reasons, when I translated passages from the letters, I limited the use of brackets—"[. . .]"—to designate what is implicit but does not directly appear in the text. Otherwise, it would have been unwieldy and distracting for the reader.

Beyond connecting the dots between the letters, understanding the Bin Laden Papers also entails discriminating between the kinds and sources of information therein. The Papers represent an incontrovertible account of al-Qaeda's inner workings, dynamics, and worldview. As such, their content is by far more authoritative than all existing literature, including publications based on interviews with, and autobiographies of, those involved with al-Qaeda. The Bin Laden Papers reveal the post-9/11 history of al-Qaeda as it was being made by its chief players, whereas other accounts were written with the benefit of hindsight and often with an agenda (e.g., many participants seem to have discovered their inner nonviolent dispositions in the wake of the global "war on terror").

But, at the risk of stating the obvious, not everything in the letters is equally authoritative. For instance, the perceptions of Bin Laden and his associates about world politics should be taken with a grain of salt. When the leaders of al-Qaeda posit collaborations between Iran and the United States, or between Iran and Pakistan, etc., to undermine jihadism, we should of course not treat their accounts as truth. However, we can surmise from their consistently expressed suspicions, fears, and paranoia in relation to these state actors that al-Qaeda was not a creation of the CIA—as some conspiracy theorists would like us to believe—nor was it advancing Iran, Saudi Arabia, and Pakistan's political objectives, as some analysts are convinced.

Also, it will become very clear in the course of this book that Bin Laden and his associates, including those based in North Waziristan—one of seven agencies or districts that make up Pakistan's Federally Administered Tribal Areas (FATA)—went to great lengths to hide. As such, their understanding of their own milieu may be deficient at times. For instance, though we should accept that their fear of some of the Afghan and Pakistani Taliban is real, we should not assume that al-Qaeda's correspondence represents the truth about the inner dynamics of these groups. The same is true about al-Qaeda's perceptions and assessments of regional jihadi groups in Iraq, Yemen, Somalia, and North Africa.

The files recovered by the SOF from Usama bin Laden's compound and subsequently declassified can be accessed on several websites. In 2012, the Office of the Director of National Intelligence declassified the first batch of al-Qaeda's internal correspondence through the CTC at West Point.[8] More of al-Qaeda's internal correspondence was subsequently declassified and released directly on the Office of the Director of National Intelligence (ODNI) website in May 2015, March 2016, and January 2017.[9] The ODNI provided English translations for all the documents it declassified, including those on the CTC website. I found the ODNI translations to be inadequate, sometimes incomplete, and occasionally unintelligible. Presumably, the translation provided by the U.S. government prioritized actionable intelligence (e.g., identifying the names of militants who might pose an immediate security threat) over content analysis. In November 2017, the CIA declassified "nearly 470,000 additional files," which can be accessed directly on its website, but no translation has been provided.[10] The files consist of "audio,[11] document,[12] image,[13] video,[14] and software operating system files."[15]

In addition to these files, the SOF also recovered a 220-page handwritten document, available as a PDF file.[16] According to the CIA, the importance of this notebook was immediately apparent to the SEALs team, and photographs of its pages were taken "in the urgent hours after the raid" to allow U.S. intelligence analysts to review it "in search of clues that would reveal ongoing al-Qa'ida plots."[17] The CIA description of this document as "Bin Ladin's journal" is inaccurate. A close reading reveals that it consists of transcriptions of family conversations that took place on one of the top floors of the Abbottabad compound during the last two months of Bin Laden's life. The notebook is a unique document, not least because it allows the reader to be a fly on the wall and observe the dynamics between Bin Laden and most of the adult members of his family in Abbottabad.

The files released by the CIA are by far the most comprehensive. Out of the nearly 6,000 pages of al-Qaeda's internal correspondence, about 4,500 pages were declassified by the CIA. Based on my research, al-Qaeda's internal correspondence is to be found in the 24,168 Microsoft Office files that were converted into PDFs, the 72,195 images (IMGs), and the 220-page handwritten document. With the help of two research assistants, I went through more than 96,000 files. Most of these consist of materials that are publicly available—e.g. newspaper articles, ideological treatises, jihadi videos, and recorded lectures. During the process of mining these files, we extracted and put together what has been described as a "treasure trove" of intelligence, namely al-Qaeda's internal communications: nearly 6,000 Arabic pages (including those released by the ODNI). I read each of them closely, often multiple times. I also randomly clicked on hundreds (most likely thousands) of audio and video files. Among them, I discovered some audio recordings featuring Bin Laden's grandchildren elocuting poetry, and even some videos that were recorded in the compound.

According to the CIA website, files that included pornography were recovered from Bin Laden's compound, but these were of course not released. Based on my research, it is highly doubtful that such materials were Bin Laden's. In none of the letters are such materials mentioned or requested. To appreciate why this is extremely unlikely, the reader should go to Chapter Seven, which reveals the extensive deliberations by al-Qaeda's leaders concerning the permissibility of masturbation. However, some of the files I examined and which were released by the CIA consist of images of dating websites and salacious pictures.

But it is not difficult to reconcile these seemingly contradictory issues. As noted earlier, the Bin Ladens did not have access to the internet. Yet, the letters indicate that the electronic files on which Bin Laden saved his correspondence often had viruses when they reached their destination. Invariably, viruses infect computers through the internet. Obviously, the Bin Ladens were not shopping at the local Apple store and had to make do with poorly refurbished computers that had been infected with viruses. As much as some would like to believe otherwise, the said pornography as well as the salacious pictures recovered were likely deleted files that existed on the computers before their purchase for use by the Bin Ladens. It is possible for technicians to retrieve these files.[18]

Throughout this book, translations of the Bin Laden Papers are my own. I benefited from the suggestions of the great historian of Islam and inimitable Arabist Professor Michael Cook. The chief players' names have been truncated for readability, and for the most part they are referred to by their first names (see Appendix Two for a fuller explanation of the naming conventions). As far as I am aware, this is the first study that is based on a systematic reading of all the declassified Arabic internal communications recovered from Bin Laden's compound. According to the CIA, some "materials that are sensitive such that their release would directly damage efforts to keep the nation secure" remain classified.[19] As such, and as with all research, this book is the first but certainly not the final word on the Bin Laden Papers.

PART I
"AFFLICTED"
AL-QAEDA
(2001–2011)

1

"THE BIRTH OF THE IDEA"

*Our affliction and trouble following the fall of the Islamic Emirate
[i.e., Taliban regime] were heartrending, and the weakness, failure, and
aimlessness that befell us were harrowing. . . . This all happened especially
after you both disappeared from the scene out of necessity, and due to your
inability to experience our painful reality and to meet and converse with us.*

Letter from Tawfiq, second-tier al-Qaeda leader, to Usama bin Laden
and Ayman al-Zawahiri, September 8, 2004[1]

When, in 1999, Usama bin Laden came up with the idea of attacking the
United States by crashing planes into buildings, he envisaged a decisive blow
that would lead to the withdrawal of U.S. military forces from the Middle
East. He was convinced that such large-scale attacks would so terrorize
Americans that, to regain a sense of security, they would put pressure on their
government to change its Middle East policy.

Usama, however, miscalculated. Badly.

While he eventually translated his idea into the deadliest foreign attack on
U.S. soil, far from cowering, Americans rallied behind their President. They
supported a war that swiftly brought the collapse of the Taliban regime, and
the crushing of Usama's own al-Qaeda organization. We learn from the Bin
Laden Papers that Usama was forced to "disappear from the scene out of necessity" to ensure his security as well as that of those in his orbit. For nearly three
years, between late 2001 and early 2004, even though he released several

statements to the world at large, Usama had no command over the global jihadi landscape.

During that time, a certain Abdallah Khan was in charge of al-Qaeda's military affairs. When Usama eventually reconnected with associates in his organization, he learned that Abdallah Khan was "self-absorbed and insolent," and his leadership style divided al-Qaeda and alienated it from individuals and groups who had previously supported it. He also learned that Pakistan had launched a campaign of arrests in its major cities, capturing "around 600 brothers," and, as a result, al-Qaeda's "external work," i.e., international terrorism, was halted. As to the Afghan Taliban, Usama's associates assessed that "90 percent" of them had been "lured by the shiny dollars" and turned against al-Qaeda.[2]

In the wake of the Taliban's fall, al-Qaeda was effectively crushed.

How could the same group that attacked the world's greatest power find itself shattered so swiftly? The road to 9/11 and the subsequent collapse of the Taliban regime all started with Usama being inspired by a news report.

"The Birth of the Idea of September 11"

Scribbled on a sheet of paper torn from a spiral notebook are a few handwritten lines that Usama composed in September 2002 under the heading "The Birth of the Idea of September 11."[3] It was meant to be the first in a series of seven papers detailing his reasons for "making the decision" to carry out the 9/11 attacks. He titled and numbered the page accordingly: "Making the decision—1." But Usama stopped halfway through when he realized that he was recording too much information, and started anew on a different page.

Still, the two short paragraphs on this lone piece of paper are invaluable, not least because Usama chose not to include them with the other pages. Though the handwriting of some words is poor, it is decipherable. We learn that it was on October 31, 1999 that Usama conceived the idea of the 9/11 attacks. On the first line we read that "the idea [of 9/11] was conceived when I heard the news of a plane crash by its pilot, al-Batouty." Usama was referring to the plane (EgyptAir Flight 990 from New York to Cairo) that crashed off the

16

New England coast on October 31, 1999, killing 217 people. The initial media reports mentioned several possible causes behind the crash, including pilot Gameel al-Batouty's vengeful motives against his employer, which was eventually confirmed.[4]

Upon hearing the news, Usama continues, "I turned to the brothers who were with me at the time" and lamented: "Why didn't he crash it into a financial tower?" He was clearly disappointed that al-Batouty did not put his thirst for vengeance to better use. In Usama's mind, a plane crashing into a financial tower would have delivered an unignorable message of anti-Americanism.[5]

The second paragraph cuts right to the chase: "This is how the idea of 9/11 was conceived and developed in my head, and that is when we began the planning." At the time, we learn that "nobody knew of this idea except Abu Hafs and Abu al-Khair." In 1999, Abu Hafs was Usama's second-in-command, and Abu al-Khair was another highly trusted member of al-Qaeda.[6]

The 9/11 Commission Report credits Khaled Sheikh Muhammad (KSM) as the architect of the 9/11 attacks. KSM is not mentioned in Usama's notes, although he may have been instrumental in other ways later on when Usama's idea seemed to be going nowhere. But it is evident from the notes that it was al-Batouty who accidentally and posthumously provided the initial inspiration for the 9/11 attacks. Usama's notes go on to expose the incompetence of at least two of the hijackers:

> We sent some men to study English in America, Rabia Nawwaf al-Hazmi and Khaled al-Mihdar. They spent a year there without accomplishing anything. They used to send us letters to tell us that they were not successful at learning English. Khaled al-Mihdar despaired and returned to Mecca. He was too embarrassed to return to Afghanistan to tell me in person. But Rabia stayed there while Khaled al-Mihdar

Usama stopped writing in the middle of the sentence, and the reader is left guessing how these two seemingly hopeless men, al-Hazmi and al-Mihdar, ultimately made the list of nineteen hijackers chosen to fulfill Usama's idea.

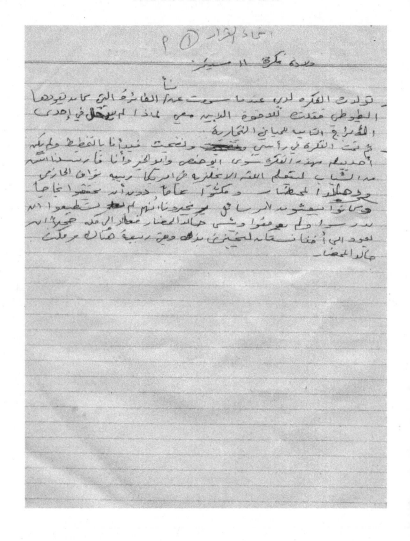

After two such enticing paragraphs, why did Usama stop writing his account of the birth of the idea of 9/11? He was composing his notes in September 2002, a year after the attacks, and likely envisaged sharing them with his associates. The notes were more candid than their author was usually comfortable with being. Doubtless, he did not want to admit how little he had thought of at least two of the hijackers. It must be difficult for a religious man to reconcile how God could guide these young believers to take on the world's superpower, but not firm up their abilities to learn English.[7] Usama must have realized midway through that page the vast gap between how he truly felt about two of the hijackers, and how he should be celebrating their deeds. When he publicly spoke about the hijackers months after he composed his notes, he proudly described them as "knights" made up of "a group of young believers"; "God had guided them, [and] firmed up their belief"; and they "were able to prove to the world that it is possible to resist and to fight the so-called superpowers."[8] Other letters composed much later reveal that most of the hijackers had not been privy to the details of the 9/11 attacks until very late in the preparations. "Except for Muhammad Atta and Ziyad al-Jirahi," Usama wrote in one letter, "all the other brothers were made aware of the operational details within a very short period prior to the attacks."[9]

The remaining pages that Usama developed and numbered 1 to 7 were dictated and do not mention the nineteen hijackers or the "birth of the idea." Instead, they are titled "What Led to the Decision" and "Why I Made It," disclosing the problems Usama had had with the Taliban as he pursued his global jihad from Afghanistan.[10]

"What Led to the Decision" and "Why I Made It"

When Usama conceived of the 9/11 attacks, he was living in Afghanistan.[11] Within months of his arrival in 1996,[12] the Taliban, a group of religious students led by Mullah Omar, took control of the capital, Kabul, which had been under the control of the Northern Alliance led by Ahmed Shah Masoud.[13] Despite their victory, the Taliban failed to defeat Masoud, who was able to retreat to the Panjshir Valley with his followers.[14]

In the post-9/11 letters that he composed in Abbottabad, Usama shared with his associates that he had experienced Afghan factionalism first-hand during the 1980s, and had concluded that Afghan leaders "care only about their chieftaincy." With the exception of a few of them,[15] he thought, "their personal interests are always prioritized over the political cause."[16] Perhaps it was out of necessity that Usama chose to side with the Taliban. But he clearly appreciated their religious model, which, if combined with his global jihad agenda, had the potential to be replicated elsewhere.

Usama's ambitions to make al-Qaeda a force on the world stage preceded the Taliban's rise to power. In his 1996 "Declaration of Jihad," or the "Ladenese Epistle," as it has come to be known, Usama presented himself as the champion of Muslim causes across the globe, sermonizing about the plight of Muslims in Palestine, Lebanon, Tajikistan, Burma, Kashmir, Ogaden, just to name a few.[17]

It soon became clear that he was ready to back his words with deeds. In May 1998, in an interview with the then NBC journalist John Miller, Usama threatened that "every day the Americans delay their departure" from Saudi Arabia (and other Muslim lands) "they will receive a new corpse."[18] Weeks later, on August 7, 1998, al-Qaeda carried out two simultaneous terrorist attacks against U.S. embassies in Nairobi and Dar es Salaam, killing 224 people and wounding more than 4,000.[19] In the lengthy autobiography (1,156 pages) that he posted online in 2009, al-Qaeda's lead planner for the attacks, Fadil Harun, recalled that the 1998 bombings transformed al-Qaeda into a "giant" in the jihadi landscape, and resulted in a flood of Muslim youth traveling to Afghanistan to train and partake in the global jihad.[20] The attacks also jolted U.S. intelligence, and the National Security Advisor at the time, Sandy Berger, described them as a "watershed event in the level of attention given to the bin Laden threat."[21]

Was this "watershed event" orchestrated from Afghanistan without the knowledge of the Taliban and other jihadi groups based there at the time? To appreciate the revelations in the Bin Laden Papers, it is helpful to get a sense of the widely reported portrait of Usama's decision-making, especially his relationship with Mullah Omar before 9/11.

Some of those who had been involved with al-Qaeda in one way or another conveniently publicized their opposition to international terrorism in the wake of the global "war on terror," invariably blaming Usama (and his deputy, Ayman al-Zawahiri) for acting unilaterally.[22] One of Usama's closest advisors, Abu al-Walid al-Misri (Mustafa Hamid), laid sole responsibility for al-Qaeda's terrorist attacks at Usama's feet, and claimed that Usama's decisions did not receive Mullah Omar's permission.[23] Even the former head of al-Qaeda's Legal Committee, Abu Hafs al-Mauritani, blasted Usama for the ruin that befell the Islamic Emirate of Afghanistan. After his release from Iran in 2012, Abu Hafs claimed that he had told Usama that "you are following a path that contradicts *sharia*, reason, and logic,"[24] and when his counsel wasn't heeded, he left al-Qaeda because he did not want to be part of something that "threw Afghanistan into the abyss."[25]

But the more we learn first-hand about Usama's consultative approach to running al-Qaeda, we cannot help but question the veracity of the claims of his (jihadi) critics who discovered their inner nonviolent dispositions post-9/11.

Not surprisingly, the Bin Laden Papers do not change our ideas about Usama's intentions; if anything, they reveal more about his unwavering commitment to international terrorism. But they do paint a portrait of a man who placed a high premium both on consultation and on fulfilling promises in his decision-making. As such, it is inconceivable that he alone bears responsibility for the tragic decisions that he supposedly made unilaterally. Time and again, we read in the letters that Usama did not just seek the counsel of his associates, but he was also ready to change course if they disapproved of his plans and vision.[26] We learn from the documents that, in Abbottabad, Usama even solicited and counted on the support of his wives and daughters to draft his letters and public statements.

How much, then, did other jihadi leaders in Afghanistan, including the Taliban, know in advance about al-Qaeda's international terrorism plots?

According to the letters, the specifics of al-Qaeda's terrorist operations were planned in the utmost secrecy. Typically, only al-Qaeda's leader of international terrorism (*al-'amal al-khariji*) and those involved in the planning were privy to the operational details of the attacks.[27] But al-Qaeda clearly signaled its intentions in advance. Usama's seven pages of handwritten notes reveal that consultation with other groups, including the Taliban, preceded the international attacks al-Qaeda orchestrated from Afghanistan.

At that time, al-Qaeda and other militants seem to have operated on the basis that consultation (*shura*) between groups was obligatory, and a Shura Council (*majlis al-shura*) was set up for that purpose. The leader was bound to accept the counsel he was given (*al-shura mulzima*). This is not a premise drawn from classical Islamic texts;[28] presumably it was implemented in Afghanistan during the 1980s to prevent leaders of jihadi groups from acting unilaterally. This likely continued under the Taliban. The leader of one of the jihadi groups, Abu Musab al-Suri, relates that, by 2000, the number of Arab and non-Arab jihadi groups in Afghanistan had reached fourteen, all officially recognized by the Taliban's ministries of defense, interior, and intelligence.[29]

Many years later, Ayman recalled in one of the Bin Laden Papers to Usama that the consultative process is an agreement between "jihadi groups [to fight] to establish Islamic rule," obligating groups to consult about "serious" matters before acting. This, according to Ayman, was what drove his own Egyptian Jihad Group to merge with al-Qaeda and, "with God's Grace, we found you [i.e., Usama] to be someone who consults with, respects, and submits to the opinions of the Shura Council's members about most if not all matters."[30]

In keeping with this consultative process, the seven handwritten pages divulge that the "Nairobi attacks"—as Usama referred to the 1998 East Africa bombings—were "supported by everyone." Usama recalled that "there was no opposition from the Taliban, or at least it wasn't clear." All members of the Shura Council gave their support, even though it was suggested that if the United States retaliated, al-Qaeda would exist only "in the past tense."[31]

Usama's private musings corroborate his public statements at the time. In the wake of the 1998 East Africa bombings and in his first and lengthy interview with Al Jazeera, Usama publicly endorsed the Taliban for carrying the banner of Islam, and called on Muslims worldwide to support them.[32] After all, Mullah Omar was not just the leader of the Taliban, but also ascribed to himself the title "Commander of the Faithful" (*amir al-mu'minin*).[33] In Islamic parlance, this title also designates the leader of the *umma*, the global community of Muslims.

Mullah Omar indeed appeared to be supportive of a global agenda befitting his title. He refused to hand over Usama to the United States and did not change his mind even after U.S. missile strikes were launched on al-Qaeda bases in Afghanistan on August 20, 1998, in retaliation for the East Africa bombings.

On October 12, 2000, al-Qaeda rammed a small boat filled with explosives into the Navy Destroyer USS *Cole* as it was refueling in the Yemeni port of Aden, killing seventeen U.S. Navy personnel.[34] While this strengthened al-Qaeda in the global jihadi landscape, the deliberations that led to the attack were far from harmonious. We learn from Usama's notes that when he first proposed it, he did not receive the same unanimous support of members of the Shura Council as he had for the East Africa bombings.[35] Some members raised concerns over the international media campaign against the Taliban, while others feared U.S. retaliation. Though there was no "serious opposition" to the USS *Cole* attack from senior members of al-Qaeda on the Shura Council,[36] "the Taliban," Usama recalled, "had begun to feel the weight of the [international community's] pressure" and "became more vocal in their opposition." Presumably, those who opposed the attack were not persuasive enough.

Following the USS *Cole* attack, at a large gathering attended by journalists, Usama came across as cavalier about his group's achievement. When a journalist asked Usama, "Is it true that America is seeking to negotiate with you" to avert another attack, al-Qaeda's second-in-command, Abu Hafs, couldn't contain his laughter. Abu Hafs was sitting to the right of his leader, who also couldn't maintain his usual poised manner. Their joint laughter and Usama's subsequent words reflected their cockiness about taking on the world's greatest superpower. Usama noted that he had received "indirect" messages that he believed were from the American government, querying whether al-Qaeda would stop its attacks if the United States withdrew its forces from Saudi Arabia. But he, Usama continued, consistently let it be known that "the issue is far bigger than Saudi Arabia, it concerns the entire *umma*'s destiny."[37]

In private, however, Usama was struggling to win the support of other groups in Afghanistan, especially the Taliban. The opposition he encountered over the USS *Cole* attack made it clear to him that the Taliban were not as dedicated to the *umma* as he had hoped and expected. Usama's private notes disclose in great detail the challenges he faced. He came to realize that the Taliban were focused on one local enemy, namely Ahmed Shah Masoud, who had managed to fortify his base in the Panjshir Valley. By contrast, Usama was concerned with the "enemy" that threatened the entire *umma*, namely the United States, Western Europe, and Israel, and sought to broaden the Taliban's outlook:

> I used to tell them that Afghanistan is less than 2 percent of the Muslim world. The Crusader alliance was seeking, through concentrated efforts, to paralyze the entire Muslim world in order to possess its resources. The real great war is that between Muslims and this Crusader alliance. But in your mind, and for the past five years, you reduced this real great war to just a minor battle over 5 kilometers in the Panjshir Valley. You advance a few kilometers, then you retreat some.[38]

Usama repeatedly explained to the Taliban that "the Northern Alliance is but one soldier [in the enemy's] army," and that the bigger enemy is "the Crusader-Zionist alliance that dominates the world." He was patently frustrated by those who were content with "disabling the capability of this soldier [i.e., Ahmed Shah Masoud] and abandoning more than 98 percent of the *umma* to be defiled by the Crusader-Zionists."[39]

With planning for 9/11 under way, Usama's time was being consumed by legal arguments with those who, in his mind, "lacked sufficient awareness of the formidable threat" that faced the *umma*. The disputes concerned who had the legal authority to declare jihad and who got to decide which terrorist operations were lawful from an Islamic legal standpoint. There was a technical dimension to the debates, and the extent of the ruler's authority—in this case, Mullah Omar—was in dispute. Usama argued: "When the Imam declares a call to arms (*istanfara*), jihad ceases to be a communal obligation (*fard kifaya*) and becomes an individual obligation (*fard 'ayn*). But if jihad had become an individual obligation, the Imam does not have the authorization to make it a communal obligation."[40] Usama was referring to the legal doctrine of jihad as developed by the early Muslim jurists. *Grosso modo*, under normal circumstances, the ruler has the authority to launch an offensive jihad (*jihad al-talab*). Since the decision to go to war is a choice, some Muslims can fulfill the obligation of jihad on behalf of others—that is what communal obligation means. But when a territory under the sovereignty of Islamic rule is invaded, the circumstances are exceptional, and it is automatically presumed that this is a defensive jihad (*jihad al-daf*). In this case, a call to arms (*nafir 'amm*) follows. Muslims who would have otherwise gone about their business while others fought on their behalf, cease to have that option. Instead, defensive jihad renders the obligation of jihad incumbent upon every Muslim regardless of whether the ruler explicitly authorized it.[41]

What stood between Usama's 9/11 plan and its execution was the support of Mullah Omar. Usama's notes reveal that while he accepted that it was the prerogative of the ruler to declare jihad, he stressed in his debates that the ruler's powers are subject to oversight. He narrated his legal disputes with the Taliban and other jihadi groups as follows:

> [I told them] that it is agreed that declaring jihad comes under the authority of the ruler, but he is subject to oversight. This issue was the cause of the dispute:
>
> [They said that] God commanded us to obey the ruler, and went on citing Qur'anic verses and sayings (Hadiths) attributed to the Prophet Muhammad to support their position.
>
> I argued that God commanded us to fight the infidels, and cited other verses and *ahadith* to support my position.
>
> They excused me [on account of my good intentions], and I excused them [on account of theirs].
>
> This dispute had a major adverse effect on the work; it took away from the energy needed to be dedicated to prepare for the [9/11] strike. . . .
>
> The situation was very difficult for me, too many issues to cover here, but it was of the utmost seriousness.[42]

It is clear from Usama's notes that Mullah Omar was not part of these debates. Usama did not succeed in convincing senior members of the Taliban and other groups of the merit of his legal justifications. The latter had no time to get into the minutiae and told him that, as far as they were concerned, the matter was settled—it is only "the Commander of the Faithful . . . who gets to decide which battlefront to declare open and which to close."[43]

While Usama was having these legal debates, an international campaign against the Taliban was already under way. In 1999, the UN had imposed sanctions against them. The international community had also mounted a campaign against the Taliban barring girls' education, and widespread condemnation followed the Taliban's destruction of the two monumental ancient standing Buddha statues in the Bamiyan Valley in March 2001.[44] Perhaps Usama was thinking about these and other considerations when he recalled in his notes that he developed a sense of urgency about doing something before it was too late: "We knew for certain that Afghanistan was already a target, and that America was determined to bring down the Taliban and the invasion was inevitable. And everything that happened [after 9/11] was going to happen even if we did not strike the head of the false god." Usama's reasoning reeks of repressed Arab guilt rather than foresight. His recollections sound suspiciously like special pleading after the event—i.e., it was going to happen anyway, so it wasn't our fault.[45] Indeed, we learn from other letters recovered from Usama's compound that al-Qaeda and other militants had not anticipated a full-scale war on Afghanistan. The worst they had envisaged was "limited U.S. airstrikes," and that "the Americans would go on to lend military support to Ahmed Shah Masoud's Northern Alliance" in its power struggle against the Taliban.[46]

As he went on to justify his decision *a posteriori*, Usama claimed that only a large-scale attack could deliver his intended "decisive blow" against the United States and jolt Muslims from their "mindlessness."[47] Thus:

One of the important issues that influenced reaching the [9/11] decision is the reality that the entire Muslim world is subjected to the reign of blasphemous regimes and to American hegemony. This American idol has imposed itself on the Muslim world and its influence has even penetrated the minds of Muslims. . . .

It was therefore necessary to do something to break the fear of this false god and destroy the myth of American invincibility that has taken over the hearts of Muslims. It was necessary to do something so that Muslims may wake up from their mindlessness and overcome their weakness and start thinking more about the *umma*.[48]

According to his notes, there was another strategic factor that played into his decision. He listed "the importance of drawing the enemy to Afghanistan so that we could subject him to a war of attrition that will damage his economy, morale, human resources."[49] Once again, this was likely a *post factum* line of reasoning, which failed to take into account that, in the same notes, he claimed to have thought that the U.S. invasion of Afghanistan was "inevitable" anyway.

As he was dictating his recollections, it was as if Usama were delivering a monologue. "He who tells you that yoghurt is licit and wine is forbidden is no expert (*faqih*)," he ruminated.[50] "The true expert," he indulged, "is he who, when what is licit is mixed with what is forbidden, is able to teach you which is which by looking into the circumstantial evidence . . . and by giving more weight to what is in the interest of the general good."[51] Usama clearly saw himself as the "expert" pursuing the "interest of the general good," while the Taliban's narrow jihad blinded them from seeing the "general good."

Notwithstanding Usama's frustration, his notes reflect the respect he had for the leader of the Taliban, Mullah Omar. Unlike the leaders of Muslim-majority states whom he often accused of defrauding their populace, of stealing the *umma*'s wealth, and of serving U.S. interests, Usama recognized that Mullah Omar was a different kind of Muslim leader. "The Taliban," he admitted, "have a good leader, a mujahid, the head of an Islamic State, and he had been fighting jihad for five years." He conceded that this was "quite delicate for the Taliban . . . how could they disobey such leaders[?]"[52]

At any rate, Usama was convinced of the righteousness of his cause and of the necessity to expand the fight for the soul of the *umma* beyond the borders of Panjshir. His notes reveal that he recognized that the Taliban would not consider any form of jihad that did not prioritize ridding Afghanistan of Masoud's Northern Alliance. This meant doing what was necessary to remove any obstacle from his path of pursuing global jihad for the *umma*. On September 9, 2001, two days before the 9/11 attacks, Masoud was assassinated. It is widely believed and documented that al-Qaeda was behind his assassination.[53] Usama's notes neither confirm nor counter its role in the operation.

Was the timing of Masoud's assassination a mere coincidence? Doubtful. The events are suspiciously close. If al-Qaeda was indeed behind the assassination, why did Usama decide to eliminate Masoud, whom he considered to be but one insignificant "soldier"? He must have realized that the war against the United States had to pass through Panjshir. Was this part of a *quid pro quo* with Mullah Omar? We shall return to this question later in this chapter.

The Calamity of an "Idea"

Within less than two years of conceiving the idea, Usama put it into action. On September 11, 2001, and on Usama's orders, nineteen terrorists hijacked four commercial airplanes, crashing two into the Twin Towers of the World Trade Center in New York City and a third into the Pentagon in Arlington, Virginia. A fourth, United Flight 93, is believed to have been destined to burst through the U.S. Capitol, but was forced to crash into an empty field in Pennsylvania after passengers learned of the other attacks and overpowered the hijackers.[54] The three coordinated attacks killed 2,983 individuals.[55]

Afghanistan's neighbor Pakistan sought to persuade the Taliban to hand over Usama to the United States and so avoid a war on its border. According to President Pervez Musharraf, who had seized power in a coup in 1999, he sent three missions to meet with Mullah Omar, the first within days of the attacks. The primary objective of Musharraf's envoy, General Mahmoud, was to convince Mullah Omar to deliver Usama to the United States, and thereby spare the Afghans the cruelty of war. Mullah Omar, Musharraf related, repeatedly asked for proof of Usama's responsibility for the attack,[56] but Pakistan did not have tangible evidence to convince him. On one occasion, Mullah Omar purportedly showed "a little bit of flexibility" when he and General Mahmoud were alone. He agreed to let Usama be tried by an Islamic court made up of religious scholars, but that was as far as he was prepared to go.

Was Mullah Omar sincere about subjecting Usama to a trial in an Islamic court? Or was he buying time? Probably the latter, because he must have known, based on prior experience, that his proposal would be rejected. According to the political memoirs of the Taliban's ambassador to Pakistan at the time, Abdul Salam Zaeef, the Taliban had proposed the same thing after the 1998 East Africa bombings, and the United States had rejected their offer, insisting that they should either hand over Usama or deport him to another country.[57]

When Musharraf failed to deliver Usama to the United States, he knew that war could no longer be prevented. He entered into close cooperation with the United States, which included the "use of our airspace, logistic support and intelligence cooperation, information exchange."[58]

On October 7, 2001, on the orders of President George W. Bush, Operation Enduring Freedom began. This saw the U.S. military (and other coalition forces) launch strikes against al-Qaeda and Taliban targets in Afghanistan. In his address to the nation, Bush indicated that he had chosen this course of action after the Taliban refused to meet a series of his demands, which included handing over the leaders of al-Qaeda.[59]

Initially, we learn from the letters that al-Qaeda militants took to fighting to repel the invasion. Before long, however, the Taliban forces were collapsing around them. Al-Qaeda's fighters were at Kandahar airport, "facing American soldiers and the apostate soldiers of the atheist Gul Agha militia." When the Taliban's final collapse was near, al-Qaeda fighters received "a short and encrypted message: 'Withdraw.'" On December 6, 2001, "the collapse was a *fait accompli*." The letters reveal that Usama later learned that when the Taliban forces were defeated, Mullah Omar came "under severe pressure from the tribes, the Pashtun leaders, and all the people and their representatives, to hand over Kandahar to the tribal council. This was due to the ugliness of the American aggression which the people could not bear."[60]

"The Americans' response was beyond anyone's expectations," one al-Qaeda leader assessed in a letter years later. "The Crusader campaign was very severe," he explained, and it was "followed by confusion, scattering, and an overwhelming chaos. Many people perished, a lot of money was lost, and more!"[61] Al-Qaeda's second-tier leader at the time, Tawfiq, whose letter is cited at the head of this chapter, lamented that "all jihadis" were shocked and felt "inept, feeble, and scattered."[62] The jihadi leader and strategist Abu Musab al-Suri, who was "a witness to the war," bemoaned that it was nothing short of a "cataclysmic catastrophe" for the jihadis. He estimated that the real number of jihadis and their supporters who were killed "is larger by far than the official number of 3,000–4,000." Among the fallen, he believed, were "almost 400 Arab jihadis who heroically fought on various battlefield fronts and were martyred defending Afghanistan."[63]

We learn from the letters that, despite the "colossal consequences of the 9/11 attacks," all jihadi groups reasoned it was necessary "to come to terms with the painful reality" that now beset them.[64] They had no intention of surrendering. Rather, they determined that they should take shelter, "be patient and remain steadfast," until the moment came when they could resume the jihad.[65]

Mullah Omar could not travel back in time and hand over Usama to spare his people a ruinous war. When it became evident that the Arabs, i.e., al-Qaeda and other Arab jihadis, were the primary target of the air campaign, he decided to prioritize the security of his fellow Afghans. We learn from former detainees who were forced to seek refuge in Iran that Mullah Omar sent a clear order: "It was necessary for the Arab brothers to evacuate Afghanistan, including the border strip with Pakistan, to ease the pressure on the mujahidin and the Muslims in those areas."[66] The letters reveal that only a "very few [Arab] brothers" stayed to continue fighting; the rest, with their women and children, obeyed the order of the man to whom they had given their allegiance, the Commander of the Faithful, Mullah Omar.

We read in the Bin Laden Papers that Usama "disappeared from the scene out of necessity."[67] Trusted companions who were by his side later related that he said little about the U.S.-led war, maintained a positive outlook, spoke of "auspicious signs and urged patience."[68] They chose not to discuss the implications of the war with him, let alone get into any discussion about whose fault it was. "It was not the time," they concluded.[69] They last saw Usama after escorting him to Tora Bora in eastern Afghanistan.[70] At least one person stayed with him. This must have been Abu Ahmed al-Kuwaiti. He and his brother—who was either with them or joined them later—were the two "security guards" who were killed during the SOF raid that killed Usama. Abu Ahmed was a Pakistani national, and not of Kuwaiti origin, as his alias suggests. His real name was Ibrahim Saeed Ahmed. Abu Ahmed and his brother lived in a separate house in the same compound, and we know from one of Usama's letters composed in January 2011, that he and the two brothers had "been treading this great path [i.e., God's path] for longer than eight years together."[71]

Musing on Mullah Omar's Legacy

One is left to wonder why Mullah Omar, faced with the prospect of such devastating destruction, still refused to hand over Usama to the United States. He purportedly told a journalist: "I don't want to go down in history as someone who betrayed his guest. I am willing to give my life, my regime. Since we have given him refuge I cannot throw him out now."[72] Mullah Omar's alleged statement, which could only be construed as irrational, if not outright stupid, has been justified, *ad nauseam*, as an extension of his religious devotion, and much ink has been spilled on exploring a litany of Islamic edicts to support this unlikely explanation.

To start with, notwithstanding the importance of protecting one's guest in Afghan culture, the relationship between Arabs and the Taliban in Afghanistan was not based on guest-and-host dynamics. When Voice of America interviewed Mullah Omar ten days after the 9/11 attacks and asked him whether he would give Usama up, he replied: "No. We cannot do that. If we did, it means we are not Muslims, that Islam is finished. If we were afraid of attack, we could have surrendered him the last time we were threatened."[73]

Mullah Omar's response was about something much deeper than being a good host. It was about the fraternal (and sororal) bond that unites believers in Islam.[74] In Islamic parlance, and using the terminology consistently employed in the Bin Laden Papers and in jihadi literature, Usama and other Arabs considered themselves to be *muhajirun*, "emigrants," and referred to the Afghans as *ansar*, "helpers."[75] These relationship dynamics echo those that developed between the first generation of Muslims during the seventh century. In 622, the Prophet Muhammad and his followers—consisting of men, women, and children—performed the *hijra*, "emigration," from Mecca to Yathrib in modern-day Saudi Arabia, escaping religious persecution. In support of their faith, these emigrants or *muhajirun* left their homes and properties behind. In Yathrib, they were welcomed by the *ansar*, who embraced the new religion. Muhammad went on to establish the first Islamic community in Yathrib, and it has since acquired the name "Medina," the Arabic for "city."[76]

The Afghan Taliban referred to the Arabs and non-Afghan fighters as *ansar*,[77] since the term *muhajirun* is associated with those who have precedence in jihad. Still, they did not use terms such as "guests" and "hosts," for these would diminish the religious brotherly bond that unites believers. When, on one occasion, al-Qaeda heard that some among the Pakistani Taliban (TTP)—whose letters show them to be lacking in basic understanding of Islamic law—used the term "guests" in reference to al-Qaeda, two of Usama's associates wrote to the TTP leader to protest: "It has reached us that some people are referring to us as guests in some political contexts. We should like to make it known to you that such a designation has no basis in Islamic law. Rather, believers are brothers in religion."[78] Crucially, it does not compute that Mullah Omar's deep religiosity would have prevented him from handing over his "guest" Usama to the Americans, while at the same time it permitted him to order the Arabs, including women and children who had nowhere else to go, to leave Afghanistan, as documented in several letters. Therefore, what might have stopped him from handing over Usama was far more likely a rational consideration: namely, he had agreed to let Usama carry out the 9/11 attacks in return for the assassination of Masoud.

Mullah Omar may have given Usama his blessing for reasons other than his elimination of Masoud. Despite the Taliban's control of most of the country, the United Nations (UN) did not recognize them as the legal government of Afghanistan. The UN was not just "condemning" and "deploring" the Taliban for providing "safe haven to Usama bin Laden,"[79] it also rejected the Taliban's Islamic form of governance and violations of international human rights.[80] Any hope of international recognition and relief that Mullah Omar might have had was probably thwarted in February 2001 when the United States closed the Taliban's New York office, depriving them of access to appeal to the UN.[81]

The international community's political and economic embargo worsened the suffering of the Afghans as they were facing an unprecedented drought. Months before the 9/11 attacks, in June 2001, the scholar of Afghanistan's politics Gilles Dorronsoro warned that the destruction of the Bamiyan statues was not a religious act, but rather an expression of the Taliban's defiance of the international community.[82] Perhaps it was an extension of this same outrage that led Mullah Omar to give Usama his blessing for the 9/11 attacks.

Other clues point to a closer relationship between al-Qaeda and Mullah Omar specifically before the 9/11 attacks. An undated letter recovered by the U.S. military from one of al-Qaeda's houses in Afghanistan in 2001 suggests that Usama was in the habit of informing and consulting with Mullah Omar about al-Qaeda's activities before 9/11. In this letter, Usama wrote about, among other things, the training that al-Qaeda had conducted with "Tajik brothers" and requested to meet and consult with Mullah Omar to discuss potential media interviews about the situation in Saudi Arabia.[83]

There are other pointers in pre-9/11 jihadi literature that suggest that it wasn't Mullah Omar who was opposed to Usama's international terrorism, but rather other Taliban leaders in his circle, perhaps the same ones to whom Usama referred in his 2002 private notes. Writing in 1998, in the immediate aftermath of the August 20 U.S. missile strikes on Afghanistan in retaliation for the East Africa bombings, the jihadi leader Abu Musab al-Suri narrates the following:

The world shook by America's violent debauchery after it launched cruise missiles, targeting Arab and Afghan training camps. In his public response, Mullah Omar stated that he would never hand over Usama bin Laden and other Arab jihadis, even if he had to fight until the last drop of blood. After Mullah Omar refused to hand over Abu Abdallah [i.e., Usama], America threatened to use nuclear and biological weapons against Afghanistan. In the wake of this, all the Taliban ministers met at Mullah Omar's house for three days to reach a decision concerning this looming threat. We all expected them to ask Abu Abdallah and the Arabs to freeze all their activities and close down their training camps. I rushed to meet with some of the Taliban ministers to learn first-hand about their decision. I was amazed to hear one of them relate that Mullah Omar rebuked those among his ministers who admitted their fear of America and lectured them on the importance of putting their trust in God. He reminded them that the Afghans, with God's support, had defeated those who were more powerful than America, none other than their neighboring Russians.[84]

Al-Suri's testimony of Mullah Omar's support of Usama's activities is particularly valuable, not least because it features in a book that provides a critical and candid assessment of the politics of both the Taliban and Arab jihadis in Afghanistan.

The cockiness of Mullah Omar in the face of the United States is also recorded by none other than Abu Hafs al-Mauritani, whom we met earlier (in a post-9/11 garb, conveniently denouncing Usama for opposing Sharia and disobeying Mullah Omar). On November 30, 2001, at the height of the U.S.-led invasion of Afghanistan, an Al Jazeera journalist asked Abu Hafs if al-Qaeda, rather than the Taliban, was in effect ruling Afghanistan. Abu Hafs categorically stated:

The Commander of the Faithful (*amir al-mu'minin*), Mullah Omar, is the leader who rules over Afghanistan, including al-Qaeda and all the jihadi groups and individuals based there. . . . America is feared by all states and by global military alliances, [but not by Mullah Omar] who said: "America promised us defeat, and God promised us victory. We will see which of the two promises will be fulfilled." When Mullah Omar addressed the *umma* to incite Muslims to take up jihad, he clearly stated: "I am not calling on you to take up jihad to protect my rule and my government. Had I been motivated by such goals, I would have followed the path of Arab rulers and knelt to the [will of the] Americans, who would have supplied me with money, men, and weapons. But a dignified death is far greater than a life of servility."[85]

In light of these accounts of Mullah Omar, combined with Usama's 2002 private notes, it is logical to ask: Had Usama indeed betrayed Mullah Omar by carrying out the 9/11 attacks, as many would have us believe, shouldn't we expect that their relationship would at least sour post-9/11? This did not happen. Far from it. Instead, the Bin Laden Papers show that Usama and his associates continued to count on Mullah Omar's "trustworthiness" and, unlike some of the Taliban "traitors," he was "steadfast on the path of jihad." When Usama resumed contact with his associates in 2004, he instructed them to "send his greetings" to Mullah Omar, whom "we consider to be trustworthy," and also to send him a "lump sum."

Al-Qaeda's leaders later strove to forge good relations with those Taliban who remained "steadfast," but even they became fewer by the day. "Confirmed reports" reached al-Qaeda that in May 2007 most of them "had joined forces with the Americans to kill Mullah Dadullah," a Taliban leader who was known for his uncompromising views against the United States and Pakistan.[86] When this happened, Usama counseled his associates to be vigilant, warning that most of the Taliban leaders "have no qualms about being led by the intelligence agency of apostate states," a reference to Pakistan's intelligence agency, the ISI. "Those Taliban leaders," he continued, "accept establishing only that part of the religion that the despot allows, and have turned their backs on making God's religion Supreme." What alarmed Usama the most was the prospect that "if our friend [i.e., Mullah Omar] disappears, they would succeed him." Clearly, Usama saw Mullah Omar as a bulwark against those on the payroll of intelligence agencies. Were Mullah Omar out of the picture, Usama warned his associates, the other Taliban leaders

> would want to drag us with them in their path of error, and we must be cautious concerning them. Accordingly, any request on their part that might lead to suspending or weakening the obligation of jihad on the individual (*al-jihad al-muta'ayyin*) should be rejected. They must also be told that they are not authorized to enter into any agreement on our behalf, especially with states that are involved in the war against Muslims. Otherwise, we risk unknowingly falling into one of the circles that are led by state intelligence agencies. Beware not to share your secrets with them.[87]

We learn from other letters that Taliban leaders whom al-Qaeda trusted included Mansur Dadullah, the Haqqanis, and Mullah Omar. Those whom al-Qaeda did not trust included Mullah Baradar,[88] Mullah Obaidullah,[89] and Mullah Akhtar Mansour.[90] It is noteworthy that Mullah Obaidullah was reported captured by Pakistani authorities in 2007 and "was released under mysterious circumstances." The letters insinuate that he was collaborating with Pakistani intelligence against Mullah Dadullah.

Nowhere do the letters suggest that Usama and his associates ever doubted Mullah Omar's unwavering commitment to jihad. By 2010, al-Qaeda's fears of the Taliban had deepened. In a letter to Usama, we find Ayman expressing his alarm that the Taliban were "psychologically prepared" to enter into an agreement with the United States that would render al-Qaeda impotent. But, like Usama, Ayman made a clear distinction between the trustworthy Mullah Omar and the other "hypocrite" Taliban leaders: "Due to their arrogance, fear, and paranoia, the Crusaders [i.e., Americans, in this case] are too reluctant to enter into an agreement with Mullah Omar and those like him. Instead, they would rather negotiate with the traitors, spies, and hypocrites among those who claim to be moderate Taliban."[91] Therefore, al-Qaeda's enduring trust in Mullah Omar post-9/11 lends itself to the musing that he had given his blessing to the 9/11 attacks. Also, considerable weight is given in Islam to fulfilling one's agreement (*'ahd*),[92] an issue that Usama repeatedly stressed in his letters.[93] So important was this for Usama that he even admonished fulfilling one's agreements with al-Qaeda's enemies, including the Americans. It would be inconceivable for Usama to be preaching this in his private communications after having himself supposedly lied to Mullah Omar, of all people.

If Mullah Omar therefore had preapproved the 9/11 attacks, it would have been both Islamically unlawful and politically irrational to violate his agreement after the fact. It is possible that Mullah Omar, like al-Qaeda's leaders, took a calculated risk that, just as the Americans had not invaded Afghanistan after the 1998 and 2000 attacks, they would refrain from invading after 9/11. If that was indeed his rationale, he was obviously wrong in his assumptions, but it is doubtful that he was a stupid "host."

Usama and Ayman's predictions concerning the "hypocrite" Taliban were not far off the mark. Mullah Omar died in 2013, but the Taliban did not report the fact until 2015.[94] This was probably because his closest associates, the very Taliban leaders that Usama mistrusted, wanted to pursue negotiations with the United States. In 2019, Mullah Baradar, who had been reported to be in close contact with Mullah Omar, "turned his back on religion" and led the U.S.–Taliban talks in Qatar. On February 20, 2020, even Sirajuddin Haqqani, one of the Taliban leaders most trusted by al-Qaeda, was part of the same negotiations and wrote an op-ed for *The New York Times* which recognized that the "killing and maiming must stop." And on February 29, 2020, an "Agreement for Bringing Peace to Afghanistan" was concluded between the United States and the Taliban.[95]

From a post-August 2021 vantage point, following the U.S. withdrawal from Afghanistan and the return to power of the Taliban, the Agreement is also telling. The United States accepted a deal that excluded the internationally recognized Afghan government led by President Ashraf Ghani. What's more, the Taliban leaders who negotiated it in Qatar insisted that they were not representing a group, but that they were there on behalf of an emirate/state, as if the whole territory of Afghanistan was under their jurisdiction. Thus, the full title of the deal was: "Agreement for Bringing Peace to Afghanistan between the Islamic Emirate of Afghanistan which is not recognized by the United States as a state and is known as the Taliban and the United States of America." This title features in every clause, a total of sixteen times in the four-page document.[96] If the U.S. negotiating team had been unaware of the implications of this title at the time of signing it, its significance was plainly illustrated when the Taliban marched on Kabul in August 2021.

2

JIHADIS BETWEEN BORDERS

With the fall of the Islamic Emirate, and Mullah Omar subsequently ordering Arabs to withdraw from Afghanistan, chaos, confusion and the scattering of brothers ensued. . . . A large number of brothers, many of them with their families, flooded into Pakistan, especially to Karachi. The Pakistanis' campaign of arrests of the brothers followed, and so many terrible things happened . . .! Then others headed to Iran, and similarly terrible things happened to them.

Letter from Atiya, al-Qaeda's point of contact with regional jihadi groups, to his intermediary in Saudi Arabia, January–February 2007[1]

Jihadis reject the legitimacy of nation-states and seek to make God's Word supreme on earth. In keeping with that spirit, when the Taliban established their Islamic Emirate of Afghanistan, Arab jihadis traveled there to live in the "newborn abode of Islam and the only one on earth." Like the early believers— the seventh-century *muhajirun* who emigrated *en famille* with Muhammad in support of their faith—modern jihadis had traveled with their families in tow to Afghanistan. They had emigrated from far and wide—especially from Muslim-majority states that had suppressed jihadism through imprisonment, torture, and persecution. But in early December 2001, Mullah Omar ordered Arabs to evacuate Afghanistan. Having given him their allegiance, the Arabs had no choice but to comply with his order. Accordingly, those who had arrived as *muhajirun* in Mullah Omar's Islamic Emirate departed as *muhajjarun*, "displaced persons," once he ordered their evacuation.

Usama bin Laden disappeared into "the mountains of Tora Bora" before Mullah Omar issued his order,[2] and others had to shoulder the burden of displacement. Many of those he left behind had multiple wives (up to four) and numerous children, making them conspicuous and vulnerable.

What happened to Arab jihadi families in the aftermath of the Taliban's fall?

The Bin Laden Papers reveal that they found themselves in a grim predicament. Evacuating Afghanistan was, as one letter put it, a "major problem we faced . . . an enormous responsibility that would test even those who are most forbearing." What had started off in the late 1990s in optimism as a religious journey abruptly descended into despair in the aftermath of the Taliban's fall. In December 2001, jihadis found themselves at the mercy of the states whose borders and legitimacy they had rejected.

Displaced

To appreciate the enormity of the challenges that are graphically depicted in the Bin Laden Papers, we must first get a glimpse of the influx of Arabs into Afghanistan during the years that preceded the Taliban's fall. The period 1996–2001 was coeval with the rule of the Taliban in Afghanistan. Even as the international community intensified its campaign against the Taliban through a political and economic embargo, the Afghan arena was growing with "émigrés" (*muhajirun*) of the jihadi variety. The jihadi leader Abu Musab al-Suri wrote wistfully about those years in his 1,600-page book, a *magnum opus* in the jihadi library:

> With the Taliban's welcoming of and good neighborliness to the incoming vanguards,[3] the Afghan arena began to attract jihadis, including those who wanted a more conducive environment to pursue their jihad ambitions. When the Taliban proclaimed the implementation of Islamic law, and achieved control of nearly 94 percent of the territories, Afghanistan became the newborn abode of Islam and the only one on earth.[4]

Al-Suri recounts that, by 2000, Arab guesthouses and training camps had sprung up in the main cities of Afghanistan, e.g., in the capital Kabul, Kandahar, Khost, and Jalalabad. The international economic and political embargoes against the Taliban did not deter more *muhajirun* from traveling to the "newborn abode of Islam." Al-Suri estimates that the number of those who traveled in and out of Afghanistan during the period 1996–2001 reached several thousand men:

> Those who settled in Afghanistan numbered nearly 350 families or thereabouts, and almost 1,400 Arab men from various nationalities. In addition, Afghanistan was home to hundreds of households from Central Asia, most notably Uzbekistan and Tajikistan—the last stronghold of communism where Islamic movements are subjected to oppression. There were also *muhajirun* from East Turkestan, which is occupied by China and where Muslims have been subjected to all sorts of torture and humiliation.[5]

In effect, the Taliban's Emirate was growing into a microcosm of the *umma*—i.e., the global community of Muslims. Those years, which held much promise for jihadis, came to a sudden and forceful end when Operation Enduring Freedom was launched on October 7, 2001. One of al-Qaeda's leaders soberly reflected: "The American response to the 9/11 attacks was colossal, way beyond our expectations. We also did not imagine that the Taliban Emirate would collapse so rapidly. The reason of course is due to the thrust of the shock, and the ugliness of the bombing and its destruction."[6]

By December 6, 2001, the Taliban's collapse was complete, and al-Qaeda fighters received Mullah Omar's order to stop fighting, to withdraw from Kandahar, and to evacuate Afghanistan.

Al-Qaeda was left without even a Plan A. The group had anticipated U.S. targeted strikes on Afghanistan in response to the 9/11 attacks, but had not prepared for a war. Its "afflictions" were compounded after Mullah Omar ordered Arabs to evacuate Afghanistan. By the time he issued his order, Usama had "disappeared" into the "mountains of Tora Bora," and his second-in-command,

Abu Hafs al-Misri, had been killed in an airstrike. Ayman al-Zawahiri, who went on to become one of the most prominent public faces of al-Qaeda and Usama's successor, had also "disappeared"—probably with Usama initially. Consequential decisions were left to second-tier leaders in al-Qaeda, sometimes in coordination with other Arab jihadi groups. One of those second-tier leaders at the time, Atiya, who, in 2010, became al-Qaeda's leader in Afghanistan and Pakistan (Af-Pak), narrated the following:

> After the fall of Kandahar, we headed to Khost that same night, where a large group of Arab jihadis had endured horrors in the valley. . . . We spread in the cities of Khost and Gardez. Meetings and coordination began: There were differences of opinion as to what we should do next. There were those who favored withdrawing to Pakistan, while others preferred that we continue to fight to the death. After a few days of deliberations, most people reached the view that it was best to withdraw to Pakistan. And indeed, we withdrew in several batches to Waziristan, then to other areas in Pakistan, and only a very small group of Arabs and another group of Uzbeks from Turkestan remained.[7]

The remaining groups to which Atiya was referring were most likely part of the foreign fighters' unit Liwa' al-Ansar. It was set up by Mullah Omar in June 2001, and non-Afghan fighters fought under its banner.[8] Initially, it was led by Uzbeks,[9] and one of the recovered letters suggests that al-Qaeda was still funding the unit as late as November 2002.[10] But a 2004 letter from Ayman to Usama relates that "a big problem" had emerged between its leaders and Ayman didn't understand what was truly going on.[11]

All things being equal, fleeing to Pakistan was the logical choice for al-Qaeda. It was familiar terrain to those who had fought against the Soviets in the 1980s. Peshawar, in particular, was home to guesthouses set up by groups from different countries and with different ideological leanings and that were affiliated with training camps in Afghanistan.[12] Years earlier, in a 1998 interview with Al Jazeera, Usama celebrated the support of Pakistanis for the jihadi cause, noting:

We found a sympathetic and generous people in Pakistan who exceeded all our expectations. . . . The people in Pakistan gave a clear measure of the extent of their hatred at American arrogance towards the Islamic world. . . . There are groups that are sympathetic to Islam and to the jihad against the Americans. There are also a few groups that are unfortunately still cooperating with the enemies of our *umma*, the Americans.[13]

When the journalist pressed him on whether al-Qaeda had support at the official level in Pakistan, Usama confirmed that he could indeed count on the backing of "elements within the government."[14]

Al-Qaeda had not fully processed the extent to which its fortunes had changed after Pervez Musharraf became president in a 1999 coup. It had hoped that the "large number of brothers, many of them with their families, [who] flooded into Pakistan, especially to Karachi," in late 2001, would be given shelter there. But the Pakistani leader had forged a close collaboration with the CIA following the 9/11 attacks,[15] and Atiya bemoaned that "so many terrible things happened . . .!" The letters reveal that Pakistan launched a "campaign of arrests that went on in the major cities, such as Karachi, Lahore, and even in the small ones,"[16] and that "around 600 brothers, perhaps even more, were captured."[17] It was also reported in the media that some Pakistanis sought to profit from the situation, luring Arabs to their dinner tables only to "sell them to the Americans," as "bounties ranged from $3,000 to $25,000."[18]

In October 2002, Ayman publicly accused the Pakistani regime of "betrayal," for it "provided intelligence, military bases, and all kinds of support to the American forces."[19] Pakistan's campaign against al-Qaeda was unrelenting and, for several years after 9/11, al-Qaeda's ability to operate in Pakistan was halted

because of the difficulty of carrying out work in Pakistan due to the stringent security measures the government has taken against us. . . . The mere act of renting a house, or bringing a brother from another country, or organizing the travel of a brother, or moving a brother from one place to

43

another inside Pakistan, or making a phone call, now requires enormous efforts. The financial, logistical, and security efforts required to perform any of these things is probably comparable to the efforts we needed to plan and prepare for a [terrorist] operation in the past.[20]

By early 2002, Arab jihadis were no longer welcome in Afghanistan, and certainly not in Pakistan, where they would risk capture and most likely rendition to CIA custody.[21]

The Tyranny of Borders

Besides Pakistan, the states bordering Afghanistan are Turkmenistan, Uzbekistan, and Tajikistan to the north, China to the northeast, and Iran to the west. The three Central Asian states to the north and China to the northeast were not considered escape destinations by al-Qaeda. Though many militant groups from those states were operating in Afghanistan, they had been training and preparing to eventually wage jihad against their own governments. Turkmenistan's borders were the most difficult for jihadis to cross. Back in the late 1980s, they had tried to pass through the country to get to Azerbaijan and assist the Azeris in their conflict with Armenia, but were met with dismal failure.[22] In the jihadi literature, we read that the regime in Turkmenistan "was strong and did not allow any infiltrations into its territories . . . and the Arab presence was very limited."[23] Turkmenistan's impenetrable borders forced jihadis to seek an alternative illegal route through Iran, which "became the principal route for jihadis who wanted to go to Azerbaijan."[24] Besides, most of the border areas to the north were controlled by the Northern Alliance, whose leader, Ahmed Shah Masoud, al-Qaeda is reported to have assassinated days before the 9/11 attacks.[25]

Escaping west was fraught with problems for al-Qaeda. The group's hostility toward Iran is palpable throughout the Bin Laden Papers. Al-Qaeda saw it as an expansionist Shia power infringing on Sunnis and, in one letter, Usama recalled that he had been warning publicly about the "Rafida threat"—a reference to the Shia regime of Iran—as early as 1987.[26] Similarly, letters by other al-Qaeda leaders stress that while the United States was the "current enemy," Iran was the "postponed enemy." Al-Qaeda also learned from the "failed and bitter experience" of some of the Egyptian Islamic Group members who had fled to Iran, hoping to receive support. However, some jihadis, including those within al-Qaeda, had contacts with Sunni militants in Iran, the "Baluch brothers," who actively opposed the regime. Thus, when borders to the north, east, and south of Afghanistan were closed to them, the jihadis headed west.

We learn from Atiya, who entered Iran in early 2002 and managed to evade arrest, that the first wave of jihadis who escaped to Iran did not include members of al-Qaeda, but consisted of groups of "different nationalities and types."[27] Some, Atiya explains, "obtained visas from the Iranian consulate in Karachi" in the hope that this would facilitate their travel onward from Iran. Others crossed into Iran without a visa, opting for the illegal route "through smuggling and border crossing, which is not difficult to do."[28] Jihadis of the first wave settled in the eastern Iranian city of Zahedan, where "a few Kurdish or Sunni Baluch brothers" helped them forge IDs and find housing. Before long, however, "they were betrayed" by some "Sunni brothers" and were arrested.[29]

The Iranian authorities' initial response was to process the passage of jihadis out of Iran safely, swiftly, and quietly. Iran could not have been thrilled to have in its midst jihadis—men, women, and children—who refer to Iran as "Rafida," a derogatory sectarian term. But it could not hand the jihadis over to the United States either, as anti-Americanism had been a staple of Iranian foreign policy since the 1979 Revolution. It was during that revolution when Ayatollah Khomeini, Iran's first Supreme Leader, designated the United States as the "great Satan," a phrase that his successor, Ayatollah Khamenei, continues to cite to spice up his sermons.[30] The 1979 Revolutionaries had also held U.S. embassy personnel hostage for 444 days (November 4, 1979–January 20, 1981), prompting the United States to cut off diplomatic ties in April 1980. Following the 9/11 attacks, the United States did not consider using Iran's hostility toward al-Qaeda to its advantage. Instead, President George W. Bush's "axis of evil" foreign policy branded Iran as one of the evils, along with Iraq and North Korea.[31]

Thus, notwithstanding its ideological enmity with jihadism, it would have been inconceivable for Iran to hand over the jihadis to the United States. Such a move would have essentially repaid the U.S.'s "evil" designation with a good-will gesture, and the Iranian government's legitimacy would have been threatened in the eyes of a sizable segment of its populace. Indeed, when jihadis of the first wave were captured in Iran, they were hailed as "heroes who struck a blow to America" by "low-ranking individuals in the Iranian intelligence, the Basij [a division of Iran's Revolutionary Guards] and others." Some related in letters to Usama that "when we were in Iran, we found books about you in Persian with your photograph on the cover."[32]

Iran chose to put the first wave of jihadis up in hotels until their safe passage could be arranged. The letters reveal that the authorities allowed "the brothers to choose their onward destination, but only after taking their photographs and fingerprints."[33] According to Atiya, "most Saudis and Kuwaitis and those from the Gulf generally" were allowed to leave, sometimes "with the assistance of the Saudi embassy in Tehran." Other countries that helped included "Malaysia, China, Indonesia, and Singapore."[34] It wasn't clear to al-Qaeda's leadership if these countries "purposely turned a blind eye" or whether they simply did not know the militant background of the jihadi returnees.[35]

In return, the Iranian authorities demanded that jihadis should "refrain from any activities, movements, or assemblies that would attract attention," and instructed them not to communicate by phone "because America monitors all forms of communication."[36] Iran seems to have tried to recruit some "brothers" to advance its own anti-American agenda, but was unsuccessful. One of Atiya's letters, intended for the attention of Saudi sheikhs, relates:

> With respect to the Saudi brothers specifically, the Iranians proposed to a very few of them—specifically those who had recently become jihadis, and whom the Iranians judged to be ideologically malleable—that they would be prepared to support them and train them in Hizbullah training camps in Lebanon, if they so wished; that they would support them with money

and other kinds of assistance if they wanted to hit American targets only in Saudi Arabia and the rest of the Gulf. . . .

I did not hear that the Iranians proposed to anyone to attack the local governments, like the Saudi regime for example, or others. I am also not aware that any of the brothers accepted any of these proposals. These kinds of propositions were only made to low-ranking newly enlisted brothers. As far as I know, they did not make such proposals to jihadi veterans.[37]

It does not appear that Iran exerted any additional pressure on the jihadis of the first wave. It was likely put off by their behavior. As Atiya put it, the arrivals were "anarchic" and violated the "security conditions" Iran had set. They used mobile phones, formed groupings, and, "in a short period of time, they set up guesthouses." Atiya was sure that the "Americans listened in on these calls," and perhaps Iran could not usher them beyond its borders fast enough.[38]

In the meantime, Pakistan was intensifying its arrests, and al-Qaeda reasoned that crossing into Iran was a risk worth taking. In late February 2002, a second wave of jihadis, including members of al-Qaeda and their families, illegally entered. Among them were members of Usama's family: his second wife, Khairiah, their son Hamza, and six children by his first wife, Najwa. They settled in several cities such as "Zahedan, Shiraz, Mashhad, Tehran, and Karaj,"[39] assisted by the "Baluch brothers," who were most likely the Iranian group Jundallah,[40] whose leader we shall meet again in Chapter Nine.[41]

Soon after the jihadis reached Iran:

Everyone began to rent houses through trusted Sunni brothers. Many of them, may God reward them, rushed to help their jihadi brothers, urged by the righteous scholars and sheikhs who are loyal to and supporters of the Taliban and Al-Qaeda. Each group of jihadis was assisted by a few Kurdish or Sunni Baluch brothers who worked with them to rent houses for families and bachelors alike. In many instances, the brothers forged documents and used fake IDs to rent houses. This is a simple matter in Iran.[42]

47

For almost a year, most members of al-Qaeda and their families evaded the authorities.[43] They adopted stringent security measures, refraining from meeting or sharing one another's addresses, "except on rare occasions out of necessity." They also avoided mobile phones, minimized their internet use, and limited their interactions with the Sunnis of Iran.

Eventually, the letters reveal, the Iranian authorities figured out an efficient way of tracking the jihadis in their midst. Though they were unable to police their porous borders with Afghanistan and Pakistan, the authorities began to monitor the "Baluch brothers." In December 2002, they launched a swift and comprehensive campaign, arresting most of the jihadis of the second wave, including al-Qaeda's senior leaders and their families.

Iran's policy of processing jihadi detainees out of the country was halted in March 2003, after the United States invaded neighboring Iraq, toppling Saddam Hussein's regime. Among the last to be processed was Abu Musab al-Zarqawi, who initially headed to Iraqi Kurdistan with members of his group. When Iran released al-Zarqawi, little did it know that he would go on to wage jihad in Iraq not just against the Americans, but also against the Shia and their holy shrines, which are popular pilgrimage destinations for the majority Shia Iranians. And when the United States invaded Iraq, little did the Americans know that al-Qaeda's flame of jihad in Afghanistan and Pakistan was nearly extinguished. While the United States swiftly put an end to Saddam's regime and the chemical weapons he did not have, it was also igniting another flame of jihad that continues to burn today.

Detention in Iran

When the second wave of jihadis headed to Iran, they had hoped that their journey would be some sort of a *Stairway to* a safe haven, and certainly not *The Road to Hell* that they found themselves treading. The detainees were not charged and were not provided access to legal representation. Their detention was not even officially acknowledged by Iran. According to the letters, the women and children were initially placed in two houses without security guards, and Iranian female security personnel "would stop by to check on their needs." We learn from Usama's son Saad, who escaped in 2008, that he and the other men who were arrested in December 2002 were initially placed "in a secret prison underground near the airport in Tehran. We were there for five months. We went on hunger strikes to protest our conditions."[44] In response, the Iranian authorities moved the men to another location and allowed family visits.

The prison officials soon realized that the family visits compromised the security measures they had in place. The visits necessitated the removal of male security guards to prevent mixing between the sexes, and "a few brothers managed to escape." Later, the Iranian authorities discovered that the women had been sneaking "some mobile phones and laptops to their husbands"; in response, they "struck some of the sisters with an electric cane." The authorities then reasoned that it was more efficient if the families were all detained together. Saad recounts: "After the third hunger strike, the authorities moved us into a detention compound with the rest of the families. . . . We were held in the compound at all times, except in cases of severe medical emergencies that required hospitalization." Their housing consisted of "a large oblong-shaped secret prison [in Tehran]. In the middle was a corridor with rooms on the right and left. Each room was divided up into a bedroom, a bathroom, and a kitchen. Some had two bedrooms. The actual prison was surrounded by three high security gates."[45] Another letter by a former detainee adds that these were "bastioned detention centers that were run by three government bodies, possibly more, including the intelligence service, the Iranian Revolutionary Guards, and the judiciary."[46]

The prisoners suffered from numerous medical conditions that were repeatedly ignored by the prison authorities, and Saad rued that "the calamities piled up, and the psychological problems increased." When his wife was in her ninth month of pregnancy and needed induced labor, the prison authorities kept postponing her transfer to the hospital. It was only after "the fetus stopped moving" that they took her to the hospital "to deliver him after he died."

The Iranians, Saad wrote, "were masters at making us lose our nerve and took pleasure in torturing us psychologically." He was convinced that the authorities' methods were intentionally designed "to make us kill ourselves or to drive us crazy, which is what happened to most of the women." Among those whose mental health suffered were Usama's daughters Iman and Fatima by his first wife, Najwa.

What the letters do not explicitly state, simply because it was assumed, was that segregation between the sexes was observed in the compound. This would have placed additional limitations on the movement of women to avoid mixing with men who were not their *mahram*, a blood relative to whom it is unlawful to get married, such as a brother, a father, or a son. This may well have exacerbated the women's psychological problems.

The poor conditions took their toll on others as well. One of the former detainees, a Libyan jihadi named al-Subay'i, described detention in Iran as being "exiled from religion" in a land where the "greatest Satan" reigns. He was, of course, referring to the Supreme Leader of Iran, Ayatollah Khamenei, whom he regarded as worse than the President of the United States. He cursed him for what he inflicted on "God's worshippers, the jihadis, their families, and their children." An embittered al-Subay'i found the Iranians to be "closer to the Jews and the hypocrites based on our experiences with them."[47]

In Qur'anic parlance, the "hypocrites" are those who appear to be God's friends when they are in fact serving His enemies. The great scholar of Islamic thought Michael Cook explains that the Qur'an assures believers that God knows what is in the hypocrites' hearts, and they "face a fearsome prospect" in the hereafter: "God is wroth with them, and has cursed them, and has prepared for them Gehenna—an evil homecoming!" (Qur'an 48:6).[48] But the hereafter seemed too far away for al-Subay'i, who prayed to God to exact His punishment as soon as possible: "May He disgrace the Iranians both in this world and in the hereafter."[49] So desperate were the detention conditions in Iran that al-Subay'i even begged to be "deported to any other country, even to Israel." He told the Iranian guards that "Israel has more honor than you."[50]

We shall learn much more about al-Qaeda's presence in Iran in Chapter Nine.

From "Knights of Jihad" to a "Bargaining Chip"

Within a short period, the same organization that had produced the "knights of jihad" who brought down the "Towers of New York" was unable to determine the fate of its own members and their families. As the Iranian intelligence service pursued their "psychological torture" of the detainees, al-Qaeda's second-tier leaders ascertained that "[w]ith the American invasion of Iraq—the fall of Saddam, the beginning of jihad and resistance there, the salient and rapid rise of Abu Musab al-Zarqawi, the emergence of the name of al-Qaeda, and the rapidly unfolding events, the Iranian authorities decided to keep our brothers as a bargaining chip."[51] There is merit to that supposition. A handwritten letter recovered from Usama's compound reveals that, in July 2004, Iran sent an intermediary to meet one of the leaders of al-Qaeda. It is not clear how this meeting was organized or whether it took place in Iraq or Iran. It might have been arranged by a unnamed "brother" described in one of Atiya's letters:

> He is one of those highly talented individuals, both socially and diplomatically. He can perform miracles wherever you send him. . . . This brother had managed to establish some connections in Iran to the extent that he even entered the city of Qom under the pretense that he wanted to study Persian literature—as far as I could remember. There, he got to know some [Sunni] Arabs who had become Shia and were pursuing their studies in Iran. He forged friendships with them, and used to engage them in conversations and debates. This brother had a unique quality—he gained friends with every conversation and debate in which he engaged, and benefited from their help. Indeed, they helped him a lot, and they facilitated his studies and housing and introduced him to some senior and influential people there.[52]

Though we cannot be certain that the meeting was arranged through this "talented brother," the possibility is not far-fetched. At any rate, Iran's intermediary reached out to al-Qaeda in July 2004, following attacks in Baghdad and

Karbala on Shia holy sites. The group led by Abu Musab al-Zarqawi was suspected of being behind those attacks, and was assumed to be affiliated with Usama and al-Qaeda.[53]

Iran reasoned that this was the time to use the detainees as a "bargaining chip." If Usama wanted to ensure the safety of the detainees, including his family, he had to accede to Iran's demands. A handwritten letter by Hafiz, who was one of al-Qaeda's second-tier leaders at the time and who met with the intermediary, sums up Iran's overture. Some words in the letter are coded:[54]

The Iranians are interested in connecting with someone from the side of the chief [i.e., Usama] and their interest is not limited to the issue of the sick people [i.e., Usama's family]. Rather, in the first place, they are interested in the situation in Iraq, for they believe that the brothers there, specifically al-Azraq [i.e., Abu Musab al-Zarqawi] and his group, are behind the attacks on the holy Shia sites. That is why the Iranians are keen to meet with a representative from the side of the chief to discuss this issue, seek clarification, and look into the possibility of cooperating.

The intermediary went on to insist that:

The Iranians need at the very least a letter signed by the chief in which he gives assurance that the Shia holy sites are not the target of our jihadi brothers. . . . They also want the *chief* to make it public that what is happening in Iraq is the result of some erratic behavior on the part of al-Azraq, and that he, the chief, and his people [i.e., al-Qaeda] are not pleased with these attacks and disapprove of targeting such places.[55]

Hafiz had no contact with Usama at that time. He told the intermediary that a letter from Usama was not possible, although he might be able to arrange for a letter from one of his representatives. But before proceeding, Hafiz insisted that he wanted more reliable information about Usama's family: "Until now, we are still not confident and do not have any knowledge of the situation of the sick people, and it is therefore difficult to agree to the terms set by the Iranians under these conditions."[56] If Iran was serious, he informed the intermediary, it would have to release "one of the sick people so that we can assess the situation."[57]

As we discover later in this book, Iran had no intention of releasing Usama's family or any members of al-Qaeda at that time. Likewise, al-Qaeda never seriously entertained the idea of cooperating with Iran. For a few years, it continued to use Iran as a passageway to move money and smuggle people. Those who were trusted to carry out such risky missions were urged to study an Islamic legal treatise on the permissibility of committing suicide—which is generally prohibited in Islam—before setting out.[58] In the event that the Iranians captured them, they were advised to carry a "tool" that would allow them to commit suicide rather than disclose al-Qaeda's secrets to its enemy under duress.[59]

For years, Iran did not officially acknowledge that it was detaining members of al-Qaeda and of Usama's family; it was as if they did not exist. Although Iran was unable to use the detainees as a "bargaining chip" to tame Abu Musab and put an end to his ruthless attacks against the Shia in Iraq, it probably imagined that by keeping them, it was exerting pressure on al-Qaeda to refrain from attacking it. Iran was unaware that al-Qaeda had been crushed and lacked the wherewithal to carry out any international attacks. It was also unaware that had al-Qaeda been able to do so, it would have prioritized attacking the United States, and not Iran. In an ironic and fortuitous twist, Iran's detention of senior members of al-Qaeda ensured that the group remained crippled, thereby preventing it from attacking the United States. It also saved the United States the expense and trouble of incarcerating an additional large group of people in Guantanamo, and compounding the condemnations of international human rights bodies.

With its senior leaders detained in Iran, and the rest "afflicted" in the border area between Afghanistan and Pakistan, al-Qaeda's international terrorism was halted. As we shall see in the following chapter, al-Qaeda looked on as terrorist attacks in the name of jihad continued to claim casualties around the world, giving Usama the opportunity to bless them *post factum*.

GLOBAL JIHAD ON AUTOPILOT

Usama bin Laden was not consulted before the attacks in the Arabian
Peninsula. . . . What I know is that the brothers acted on their own during a
very difficult period and at a time when communications with al-Qaeda were
very difficult and virtually absent, etc. The brothers were being persecuted,
arrested, and harmed by the Saudi authorities, and concluded that it was
necessary to do something in response.

Letter from a "trusted intermediary" in Saudi Arabia to
Atiya, February 19, 2007[1]

For nearly three years after the fall of the Taliban, Usama did not have operational command over al-Qaeda. He had one or two security guards by his side,
most likely those who were later killed during the Abbottabad raid. He
managed to reunite with his fourth wife, Amal, either in late 2002 or early
2003, and they conceived their second child, a girl they named Asiya,[2] which
means "afflicted." It is the same name given by Qur'anic commentators to the
wife of Pharaoh who adopted Moses. The commentators named Pharaoh's wife
"Asiya" to denote the cruelties she endured at the hands of her husband, who,
according to the Islamic tradition, lashed her to death because of her faith in
the One God. But thanks to Moses' prayers, she felt no pain.[3] For observing
Muslims, the afflictions of Pharaoh's wife are part of God's plan—it was Asiya
who saved Moses, who later delivered the Israelites from servitude. By naming
his daughter Asiya, Usama probably wanted to draw parallels between the

afflictions of Pharaoh's wife and his own, no doubt to console himself and strengthen his resolve.

Terrorist attacks continued even after al-Qaeda was crushed. In 2002, jihadi terrorist operations took place in Tunisia, Pakistan, Yemen, Kuwait, Bali, and Moscow. Though Usama was isolated, he managed to release public statements in the form of tapes that were delivered to Al Jazeera or letters posted on websites,[4] ensuring that his own location could not be traced.[5] Usama boasted that the terrorist assaults were a continuation of the 9/11 attacks and were carried out by the "zealous sons of Islam in defense of their religion."[6] In 2003–04, terrorist attacks reached Usama's native country, Saudi Arabia.

We learn from the 2004 letters exchanged between Usama and his associates that the senior leaders of al-Qaeda had either been eliminated or arrested, and second-tier leaders were scattered and in disarray.[7] Usama's involvement during 2002–04 was limited to the news he was getting on "satellite television," and he asked his associates to keep track of all the events in Saudi Arabia to get "a comprehensive understanding of the situation" there.[8]

Global jihad was on autopilot.

A Sanguine Usama Reconnects

The letters recovered by the SEALs suggest that Usama hadn't been in command of al-Qaeda for three years following the fall of the Taliban. The 2004 letters show his associates informing him about events that had occurred three years prior. One of them recounts what had happened to al-Qaeda after Usama "disappeared from the scene out of necessity," and his "inability to experience our painful reality."[9] Another letter relates al-Qaeda's activities "during the past three years."[10] Ayman al-Zawahiri had also "disappeared," but he seems to have established contact with second-tier leaders of al-Qaeda before Usama. Judging by the contents of Ayman's October 2004 letter to Usama, the two had not been in contact for nearly three years. Ayman assured Usama that "I am doing well and I live in a secure place (*makani jayyid*)" and also shared that God had "blessed me with a girl." Ayman had been prolific in his writings, and his letter covered the publications he had produced, including "eighteen statements, twelve of which had been released." The long list he enumerated matches his 2001–04 output.[11]

More tellingly, in one of his first 2004 letters, Usama assessed, for the first time, events that had occurred in 2002. We do not know how Usama's circumstances changed and why it was that contact was re-established with his associates in 2004. In one of the letters, Usama refers to a "person in Peshawar" who had provided shelter to his son Muhammad back in 2002.[12] It is possible that after Usama emerged from the Tora Bora mountains, he hid in the same place.

At any rate, in 2004, Usama was eager to renew al-Qaeda's international terrorism. One of his first letters was addressed to Hamza al-Rabia, soon to be appointed the leader of al-Qaeda's "external work," i.e., international terrorism.[13] It was brimming with energy and filled with ambitious plans to replicate the terror that the 9/11 attacks had engendered.[14] Though Usama included a tally of the attacks that had occurred during his "disappearance," his letter reveals that he only had prior knowledge of the Mombasa attacks of November 28, 2002. On that day, two terrorist operations were carried out simultaneously. The first targeted the Israeli-owned Paradise Hotel, killing fifteen people; the second fired two missiles that narrowly missed an Israeli El Al jetliner as it was taking off from Mombasa Airport.

The other attacks, however, inspired Usama. The 2002 Bali bombings had killed 202 people, most of whom were Australians. Usama saw the potential for more operations in Southeast Asia:

> The political opposition in those countries is strong, and their public is calling for their military forces to be withdrawn [from Iraq and Afghanistan]. Therefore, any kind of attack in those countries would be effective, even a small one would do, such as planting a booby trap at the bottom of one of their diplomats' cars. The attack needn't target the ambassador's car, a junior diplomat's car would do.[15]

Usama advised Hamza to connect with the "brothers in Indonesia + Abu Sayyaf" in the Philippines to pursue such attacks in the region. But if these were to proceed, he wanted "members of other groups to cease all other organizational ties at least until our work is completed."[16] At this point, Usama wanted to guard his al-Qaeda brand.

How did al-Qaeda pull off the simultaneous Mombasa attacks in 2002 if the organization had been "afflicted" and its leader incommunicado?

We learn more about al-Qaeda's involvement thanks to Fadil Harun, one of the operatives who planned the Mombasa attacks. Harun had been the lead planner of the 1998 East Africa bombings and, in 2000, al-Qaeda dispatched him to the region to prepare for the Mombasa operations. After the 2002 attacks, Harun was on the run in East Africa; he was killed in 2011. Though he maintained an absolute loyalty to Usama, he disapproved of most jihadi groups acting in the name of al-Qaeda. He vented his frustrations in his autobiography, which he posted online in February 2009 without first clearing it with al-Qaeda's leadership. Several Bin Laden Papers bemoan that Harun's "tell-all" account provided the "enemy" with sensitive information about al-Qaeda and its activities.[17]

Usama's 2004 letter states that "we thank brothers al-Zawl and al-Dawsari for the two Mombasa attacks, both of which were excellent." Al-Zawl was Harun's alias, while al-Dawsari was the alias of another operative, Abu Talha al-Sudani.[18] In his autobiography Harun recounts that Usama had authorized the Mombasa attacks in 2000 and had dispatched him from Afghanistan to East Africa in December of that year to get a head start.[19] Due to his "disappearance" from the scene, it was not until 2004 that Usama could comment on the Mombasa attacks. Though the two missiles targeting the El Al jetliner had missed, Usama was nonetheless impressed by the simplicity of the attack and its potential: "The [attempted] attack on the jetliner was especially superb, it could easily be replicated on any of the planes of other enemies, such as those affiliated with Britain, Australia, Japan, Poland, Italy, or any of the occupying countries [in Iraq and Afghanistan]."[20]

Usama went on to advise the operatives

to mount similar attacks, using basic anti-aircraft guns such as DShK or Zikuyak,[21] to avoid being intercepted by modern technology. Multiple weapons should be used to fire bullets that could penetrate the wings of the plane and set it ablaze. This should be done when the plane has just taken off—not when it is landing—because the pilot needs a long time to turn the plane around in the air. This way the plane would be burned by the time the pilot gets to land it.[22]

To assure that Hamza and others in al-Qaeda appreciated the impact of attacks of this nature, Usama continued:

You and the brothers should be mindful of the potential positive impact and the lasting effects of such attacks, especially in the current circumstances. For example, the material losses America incurred as a result of the attack on its Nairobi embassy [i.e., the 1998 East Africa bombings] were probably around one million dollars. The same attack, however, forced America to spend billions of dollars not just to rebuild its embassy, but also to fortify the security of its embassies and consulates worldwide. In addition, the Nairobi attack successfully weakened the Americans' morale.[23]

In other words, Usama was educating his operatives about the value of using simple weaponry to produce spectacular results.

The rest of Usama's 2004 letter was forward-looking. Not surprisingly, the plans he charted were primarily devoted to new attacks in the United States to be "put into action at the earliest opportunity." His preference was to target airlines, because the "New York attack [i.e., 9/11] inflicted a deep injury, leaving an open wound in the psyche of the people in the West in general." He reasoned that "even a touch of threat, however light, would generate a loud scream."[24]

Usama was mindful that the increased security at airports made aviation attacks more challenging. He suggested "hiring private planes," which he believed were subject to relatively lax security measures. He proposed filling passenger seats with explosives, and carrying out "martyrdom operations" akin to the "9/11 New York attack": "It is important that the size of the private plane should be relatively large, and it would be even better if it were a jet because speed plays a crucial role in the success of the operation, particularly when it crashes into a building."[25]

In the event that using airplanes proved difficult, Usama methodically charted alternative plans, targeting rail lines:

> In view of the vast distances in America, for we are talking about very long and critical railway tracks, I propose removing part of the steel rail, the length of a full piece, or around 12 meters. This would be done using strong manual jacks that are simple to operate, and it would be easier especially if several air compressors are available, for they are strong and fast. Otherwise use the iron smelting tool used by blacksmiths and welders, and mount it on a solid piece of iron to stabilize it.
>
> Note that if cement is used to anchor the railroad spike to a railway sleeper, it is unlikely that an average-size hoisting crane would be strong enough to lift up 12 meters of steel rail. But it is possible to use a powerful hydraulic jack that could lift up to 100 tons. They are widely available in stores, mostly used by drivers of large trucks. Note that the lifting should be either at the beginning or at the end of the steel rail to be removed.
>
> The sabotage of the railroad tracks should take place in a remote area, near a river or a deep valley, as far away from the cities as possible.[26]

The "Afflicted" Respond

The letters reveal that, by 2004, most of al-Qaeda's senior (*kibar*) leaders had either been eliminated or arrested. Al-Qaeda's second-in-command, Abu Hafs al-Misri, was killed in November 2001. The leaders of al-Qaeda's military and operational activities, Saif al-Adl and Abu Muhammad al-Misri, were detained in Iran in late 2002. So was Abu Hafs al-Mauritani, who was the leader of al-Qaeda's Legal Committee. Other than Usama, the only surviving senior leader was Ayman al-Zawahiri, whose Jihad Group had merged with al-Qaeda in 2000. He too had "disappeared" after the fall of the Taliban.

In 2004, Usama's remaining associates were second-tier leaders. They had reluctantly sought refuge in the FATA, an autonomous area run by local tribes in northwest Pakistan, a region bordering Afghanistan. Some members of al-Qaeda stayed in Afghanistan to fight alongside "trusted" Taliban. We shall learn more about al-Qaeda's presence in the FATA in Chapter Five.

Those who corresponded with Usama in 2004 were clearly trusted and, later that year, Usama elevated them to senior leadership positions to improve their standing in al-Qaeda and in relation to other jihadi groups, including the Taliban. They inhabited a different universe to the one featuring "al-Qaeda attacks" that Usama was watching on "satellite television." Their responses to Usama's letter fell short of saying "What planet are you living on?," but were jammed with accounts of the group's calamities and operational impotence. They did not even comment on Usama's plans to wage more attacks in the United States. One of them, Tawfiq, addressed his letter to the "two Sheikhs," Usama and Ayman. He sensed that "the rest of the brothers" were restrained in their letters out of concern for the two Sheikhs' feelings, "not least because of the severe affliction that surrounds you two in particular."

Tawfiq, however, was not going to "play with the truth." His handwritten letter was filled with morbid news, giving the two Sheikhs a raw account of al-Qaeda's affairs during their three years of absence:

Our afflictions and troubles following the fall of the Islamic Emirate were heartrending. The weakness, failure, and aimlessness that befell us were harrowing. We Muslims were defiled and desecrated, and our state was ripped asunder. Our lands were occupied, our resources were plundered. . . . This is what happened to jihadis in general, and to us in al-Qaeda in particular. Unfortunately, this tragic state of affairs is known to all Arab jihadis and Afghans after the fall of the Islamic Emirate. This all happened especially after you both disappeared from the scene out of necessity, and due to your inability to experience our painful reality and to meet and converse with us.

Tawfiq relayed to the two Sheikhs that "everyone misses" them, and "we even dream of seeing you both and conversing with you like before." He bemoaned that al-Qaeda was not just "afflicted" by the sophisticated weapons of its "enemies," but also by "leadership roles being taken up by people who are unfit." He lamented that the organization that had been based on "by-laws" and whose leaders were expected to be consultative had been impaired by its own mistakes and had all but ended. In early 2004, Tawfiq and others set up a Legal Committee to coordinate with other militants in the Af-Pak theater of operations. But their efforts were hindered because a certain Abdallah Khan, who was "self-absorbed and insolent," had "appointed himself as the military commander of al-Qaeda."

Who was Abdallah Khan? One of the letters reveals that "the Taliban are the ones who appointed Abdallah Khan as military commander."[27] An Afghan by that name features in the "Guantanamo files" as the "former Taliban Commander of Kandahar Airfield." According to the WikiLeaks files, one of the Guantanamo detainees was mistaken for Abdallah and was captured after he "left Chawchak village for Khandahar [*sic*] to sell goods at a bazaar" on January 29, 2003.[28] The other possibility is that Abdallah Khan is an alias for Abd al-Hadi, the Arab leader of the foreign fighters' brigade, Liwa' al-Ansar, a unit that Mullah Omar had set up in June 2001.[29] At any rate, Tawfiq proceeds:[30]

I do not wish to criticize the military commander to belittle him. But Abdallah Khan's messiness, his lack of clarity, the many unilateral decisions he took, and his overreach, all harmed al-Qaeda both internally and externally. In fact, his conduct caused many individuals and groups that traditionally supported al-Qaeda to stop dealing with us.

Tawfiq summed up the internal problems that al-Qaeda was facing as follows:

First: Responsibilities are not properly assigned or clarified. Those in charge are not known to the members of the organization and the scope of their responsibilities is not clearly designated.

Second: Lack of clarity concerning the organization's by-laws and the orders issued by the general leader of the organization. . . . It goes without saying that the by-laws are the basis and cornerstone of the organization.

Third: The absence of legal and bureaucratic regulations for the organization. If they exist, they are not made known to the members. Regulations should serve as arbiters to resolve the problems I mentioned.

Fourth: The role of the Legal Committee (which was formed nearly eight months ago) is yet to be activated. It should be empowered and given its due standing in all sectors and areas. This way it would serve both the *ansar* [i.e., local militants in Afghanistan and Pakistan] and the *muhajirun* [i.e., Arab militants] to resolve problems and remove illnesses before they spread.

Fifth: This is the most important one. The absence of any legal constraints on those in charge. As it stands, consultation is not believed to be binding on the general military commander. I repeat that this is especially serious in view of your absence and inability to experience our painful reality in the organization. Also, this is especially serious because Abdallah Khan lacks basic legal knowledge. When I approached him and explained to him that his role carries certain obligations, and that these are an extension of his allegiance to you [Usama], he did not care. He considers that most matters require unilateral decisions,[31] and that he alone gets to decide, so much so that his conduct reached a level of blatant lies and deception to which I was a witness.

If Usama had hoped that other letters might bring some glad tidings, he would have been disappointed. The words of Khaled al-Habib, a loyal member of al-Qaeda and a second-tier leader at the time, were equally dispiriting. Al-Qaeda lacked any "achievements" of its own, he said, only being able to lay claim to a few joint operations with the Taliban:

As for our battlefield achievements, they are negligible: some very modest operations, mostly with PM [*sic*] rockets, and from a distance. Also a few ambush-style operations, but they are nowhere near what is needed or desired, considering the large number of the Taliban. Also, of these, only three operations were carried out during the past three years. This slackness in the work can be attributed to numerous reasons. They include the fact that the Afghans' fear is extreme, and more than 90 percent of them have deviated from the path of jihad. They did so both due to their extreme fear of the air campaign's bombings and because they have been lured by the shiny dollars [that the Americans dangled in front of them].[32]

Khaled's letter was filled with "negative outcomes." Al-Qaeda's "afflictions" were not limited to the group's losses in Afghanistan, they also included the "martyrdom of some twenty-two brothers and the capture of more than 600, among them Khaled Sheikh Muhammad [KSM], in Pakistan." This "horror movie," Khaled lamented, "is ongoing."[33]

The Taliban were also putting a different kind of pressure on al-Qaeda, because their "financial situation was very difficult." Wakil Khan, likely an alias for Atiya or Tawfiq at the time, informed Usama that the Taliban "appointed Zia-ur-Rahman Madani, the former governor of Logar province," to raise money. They wanted Usama to recommend him in writing,[34] no doubt to elevate his standing and attract donations from the Gulf.[35] Wakil's letter also stressed the "Pakistani pressure" on al-Qaeda's movements and complained that the "work," i.e., international terrorism, had been halted as a result.[36]

What are we to conclude about al-Qaeda's role in the global jihad that burgeoned after 9/11?

There is nothing in the letters that suggests that Usama authorized the jihadi attacks in various countries during that time. But Usama (and Ayman) publicly endorsed, *post factum*, terrorist attacks, especially those against countries that had joined the U.S.-led wars in Afghanistan and Iraq. On one occasion, happenstance worked in al-Qaeda's favor, specifically Ayman. In September 2004, within days of him releasing a public statement, several tourist hotels in Sinai, Egypt, were bombed by terrorists. In an October 2004 letter, we encounter Ayman congratulating Usama on the attacks, but instead of describing how al-Qaeda pulled it off, we find him attributing the success to divine fortune. Referring to himself in the third person, he wrote: "Our thanks to God for favoring us, the operation was carried out six days after Ayman al-Zawahiri released a public statement about Palestine." What's more, he added, "Israel accused al-Qaeda of being behind the attack."[37]

The fact that post-9/11 terrorist attacks around the world were carried out in the name of jihad made it easier for countries to suspect that they had been orchestrated by the mighty al-Qaeda that had struck the deadliest foreign attack on U.S. soil. For a while, this served al-Qaeda just fine. Usama probably convinced himself that the collapse of the Islamic Emirate in Afghanistan ultimately served the "general good" and awakened Muslims "from their mindlessness," just as he had intended.[38]

Given the group's "afflictions," it is no surprise that the letters exchanged during 2004 do not reveal any al-Qaeda involvement in the 2002–04 international terrorist attacks, except the 2002 Mombasa attacks for the reasons noted earlier. There is also no reference to the March 2004 Madrid train attacks, which saw terrorists detonate bombs on four commuter trains, killing 191 people and wounding 1,841 others.[39]

Was this the end for al-Qaeda? The "brothers" were convinced that God would not abandon those who fought in His path. So, "when God knew of our afflictions and helplessness," Khaled al-Habib consoled his leader, "he opened the door of jihad for us and the entire *umma* in Iraq." He was of course referring to the rise of jihadism there in the aftermath of the 2003 U.S. invasion.

Al-Qaeda's "afflictions," combined with its leaders' mistrust of most of the Taliban and the unremitting pressure from Pakistan, led Khaled to urge Usama:

> We should move all the brothers to Iraq. This would bring numerous benefits to the external work [i.e., international terrorism], and also to the internal work. We would leave one brother in Pakistan to organize the activities of those who are sincere about their commitment to fight against

the leaders of unbelief inside Pakistan. We would also leave two other brothers to maintain communications with you and collect donations, and another brother to liaise with the cousins [i.e., the Taliban] on the work in Afghanistan. I have already explained to you earlier in my letter about our relationship with the cousins. That is why I believe that sending the brothers to Iraq would ensure their safety.[40]

Wakil concurred. He also shared with Usama that the Pakistani authorities were interrogating some Taliban leaders, and expressed his fear that they might betray al-Qaeda.

On the Iraq front, Usama's associates had something tangible to report other than "God knew of our afflictions." The leader of the most powerful jihadi group in Iraq, Abu Musab al-Zarqawi, had sent an envoy, Jaafar, to meet with Usama's associates either in late 2003 or early 2004.[41] The missives exchanged between Abu Musab and al-Qaeda are undated, short, and deliberately esoteric. Abu Musab's group, al-Tawhid wa-al-Jihad, had been operating in Iraq since 2003. In April 2004, it claimed responsibility for some of the deadliest attacks, including the killing of Sérgio Vieira de Mello, the UN Secretary-General Special Representative for Iraq, on August 19, 2003.[42]

Notwithstanding his own "accomplishments" in Iraq, Abu Musab was eager for his group to merge with al-Qaeda. He wanted the world to know that "we are the sons of the Father [i.e., Usama]" and that "we are a branch of the original" al-Qaeda.[43] He stressed that the two Sheikhs, Usama and Ayman, should know "that we are as we have always been, and they shall always be pleased with everything they hear about us."[44] Abu Musab was not only keen to keep the al-Qaeda brand in the business of terrorism, he was also prepared to contribute to its financial upkeep. "On another matter," he concluded his missive, "should you need any money, we are doing relatively well out here, and we could send you some of what we have."[45]

Usama's associates reported that Abdallah Khan was planning to go to Iraq to take over as the leader of al-Qaeda there, and warned that unless he was stopped, he could squander the opportunity offered by this seemingly divine intervention. All three associates feared that Abdallah could "divide the ranks of the jihadis" in Iraq.

Usama's Decisions

In late 2004, Usama realized that it was impossible for his associates to follow through with the plan of attacks he had charted. Instead, he made several swift decisions in response to their suggestions. First, he instructed everyone in his circle to hide (*kumun*). "With respect to your security conditions," he wrote to his associates, "it is best that you stay invisible." As to those whose work necessitated meeting with others, he advised that "they should do so through letters and by relying on a very limited number of couriers (we propose two or three at most)."

Usama assessed that al-Qaeda's relationship with the Taliban, as described by Tawfiq, was not viable, and "it was inconceivable to continue to be part of such a grouping on that basis."[46] In other words, he wanted to free al-Qaeda and its leaders from having to operate under the premise that consultation was binding (*al-shura ghayr mulzima*). He appointed Tawfiq as the general operational leader of al-Qaeda in Afghanistan and Pakistan. This was a new senior position, and Usama wanted it known to the Taliban that he was back in charge of al-Qaeda's affairs and that Tawfiq reported directly to him. He replaced the Taliban's appointee, Abdallah Khan, with Khaled al-Habib, who was to report to Tawfiq. He also declined the Taliban's request to recommend Zia-ur-Rahman Madani as a fundraiser.[47]

By the same token, Usama wanted to reconnect with those whom he trusted in Afghanistan and to support them financially, as al-Qaeda's own resources permitted. At the top of his list was the leader of the Taliban, Mullah Omar:

Send my greetings to Hajji Salim Khan [i.e., Mullah Omar], we consider him to be trustworthy, even though he lost his sight. Send him a lump sum of about 100,000 Kaldar [around US$2,325], depending on your financial situation. Also send my greetings to Younis Khalis and his son, and give his son a similar amount.[48]

Usama clearly continued to trust Mullah Omar, but was wary of those who surrounded him. The other Afghan leader, Younis Khalis, had engineered Usama's move to Afghanistan in 1996, when Sudan was exerting pressure on him to leave.

On the Iraq front, though he had not been in the loop during the initial discussions between al-Qaeda and Abu Musab al-Zarqawi's group, Usama nevertheless blessed the arrangement that his associates had reached. "The merger with the group al-Tawhid wa-al-Jihad is tremendous," he wrote to Ayman and Tawfiq, and urged them "to give this matter considerable attention, for it is a major step toward uniting the efforts of the jihadis."[49] In December 2004, Usama publicly admitted Abu Musab's group into al-Qaeda. While he neither ruled out nor approved moving al-Qaeda to Iraq, he agreed to sending Hamza al-Rabia, whom he appointed as leader of the "external work":

> After Hamza liaises with Abu Musab al-Zarqawi to ensure his safe travel, it would be fine for him to go to Iraq on his own. Hamza should explain to Abu Musab that he wants to set up an independent unit for international operations, taking advantage of personnel who could travel with ease to carry out such missions.[50]

He wanted Hamza to prioritize attacks in America, but only in those states that had voted for George W. Bush in 2004.[51] Usama had given his "pledge of security" (*aman*) to Americans who voted against Bush and the war in Iraq when, days before the election, he publicly promised that "whichever *state* does not encroach upon our security thereby ensures its own [my italics]."[52] Usama's letter reveals that he was prepared to uphold his pledge of security. As we shall see, the plans to set up an "independent unit" in Iraq were thwarted, and Hamza was killed in Pakistan in 2005.

Usama also took a decision concerning Iran. As noted in the previous chapter, Iran had sent an intermediary to propose an arrangement: If Usama wanted to ensure the safety of al-Qaeda detainees in Iran, he should pressure Abu Musab to refrain from attacking the Shia and their holy sites in Iraq. Usama determined:

> As to the people of the west [i.e., the Iranians] and their desire to establish contact with us, we propose that you send them either a verbal or a written communication asking them to release Ahmad Hasan or al-Zayyat so that we may have some clarity about the situation and the people they are detaining. . . . Any further contact has to be conditional on this.[53]

Ahmad Hasan and al-Zayyat are referred to in the letters as "*al-kibar*," i.e., the "senior ones," in al-Qaeda and, as late as 2010, they were still detained in Iran.[54]

Jihad in Saudi Arabia, 2003–04

The letters do not corroborate claims that it was on Usama's orders and instructions that al-Qaeda fighters left Afghanistan to carry out attacks in Bali, Moscow, Saudi Arabia, etc.[55] Furthermore, they make it clear that there was no way that Usama's son Saad and al-Qaeda's military commander, Saif al-Adl, could have orchestrated the attacks from Iran, as the Saudi newspaper *al-Sharq al-Awsat* alleged.[56] Though the Bin Laden Papers do not provide a full picture of how the terrorist campaign unfolded in Saudi Arabia, they nevertheless point to jihadis acting independently of Usama.

Jihadi zeal was not lacking in the kingdom, but it was not predominantly of the al-Qaeda variety. We learn from a letter addressed to Usama, predating the Bin Laden Papers, that as late as June 2000, al-Qaeda was not well known in Saudi Arabia. The author of the letter, Abu Hudhayfa, notes that though Usama "was one of the symbols of jihad" in the kingdom, "he was not the most prominent." He urged Usama to develop a media strategy to win Saudi supporters, because "it is deeply regretful that the [al-Qaeda] movement suffers from political and media visibility deficit" in the kingdom. Al-Qaeda's shortcomings, Abu Hudhayfa lamented, "makes one pity" that "its blessed journey" is not sufficiently known to the "brothers" in Saudi Arabia.[57]

The Bin Laden Papers reveal that Saudi returnees were among jihadis who fled to Iran after Mullah Omar ordered Arabs to evacuate Afghanistan. According to the Papers, Iran coordinated their travels with the Saudi embassy in Tehran. References in the letters to "brothers" making phone calls from Iran to "Chechnya"[58] suggest that some of the Saudi returnees may have been the followers of Khattab, another jihadi leader from Saudi Arabia. Some contend that Khattab was more popular than Usama in the kingdom. Whereas Usama began his journey in Afghanistan against the Russians before he turned his terrorism against the "American idol," Khattab's jihad was consistently against the Russians. Like Usama, he fought the Soviets in Afghanistan, then rose to fame in Chechnya, where he was eventually assassinated by the Russians in 2002.[59]

On May 7, 2003, the Saudi Ministry of Interior put out a statement announcing that it had foiled a large terrorist attack in Riyadh and confiscated a sizable quantity of explosives and ammunitions. It included the names and photographs of nineteen men "wanted" by the authorities.[60] No. 10 on the list was Yousef Saleh Fahd al-Uyayri, who became known as the "leader of al-Qaeda in the Arabian Peninsula" before he was killed in June 2003. Days after the Ministry posted the names, suicide bombers attacked residential compounds, resulting in thirty-five people being killed, including nine bombers. For almost two years, the jihadis' campaign in the kingdom was sustained through a series of clashes with security forces and bombings.[61]

Usama and Ayman had to wait until 2007, when Atiya established contact with a "trusted intermediary" in Saudi Arabia, to get a more reliable understanding of those events. The intermediary's letter included the views of one of the few clerics who supported al-Qaeda in Saudi Arabia, Bishr al-Bishr, who was under house arrest at the time. The intermediary disabused Usama and Ayman of some of the fake news they had been getting either from "satellite television" and/or unreliable jihadi publications. "It seems to me," the Saudi intermediary wrote, that the father and the doctor [i.e., Usama and Ayman] lack reliable information about some issues. This was especially noticeable to me after listening to a recent public statement by the doctor—May God protect him. It appears to me that important information about events in [Saudi Arabia] does not reach them accurately. Some of what they believe is imagined, and it is incumbent upon us all to address their shortcomings and inform them—with God's help.[62]

One of the issues that Usama and Ayman lacked reliable information about was the so-called "al-Qaeda in the Arabian Peninsula" and its leader. The "trusted intermediary" categorically stated that "Sheikh Yousef al-Uyayri was never in his life the leader of al-Qaeda in the Arabian Peninsula [i.e., Saudi Arabia], and never supported the 2003 bombings, because he did not deem them to be lawful." Another intermediary, "Abu al-Tayyib from the Arabian Peninsula," confirmed this a year later:

> Sheikh Yousef used to say that no good could come of starting work in the Arabian Peninsula, because we consider it as a supply line for money, men, and the backing of many religious scholars. The people would oppose us, not to mention that we do not have the power or capacity to bring down the regime.[63]

According to the letters, far from spearheading the terrorist campaign, Yousef tried to stop it. After the Ministry of Interior posted its list of nineteen "wanted" jihadis, Yousef released a public statement rejecting the accusations and denying any involvement in the attacks that followed. He passionately affirmed that "we have not raised the banner of jihad to kill the believers."

Usama and Ayman also learned from the "trusted intermediary" that there was no organized "al-Qaeda in the Arabian Peninsula" group. Instead: "The brothers acted on their own during a very difficult period and at a time when communications with al-Qaeda were very difficult and virtually absent, etc. The brothers were being persecuted, arrested, and harmed by the Saudi authorities, and concluded that it was necessary to do something in response."[64]

Abu al-Tayyib recalled that, back in 1997, Usama disapproved of jihad in Saudi Arabia and had urged restraint. When someone asked him about this issue, Usama responded that "if we decide to work [i.e., attack] there, those with beards [i.e., clerics] would be the first to oppose us." It was understood that such an endeavor would be doomed to failure, because it would not receive the support of the clerical establishment, which Usama knew to be critical.[65]

We can be confident then that the 2003–04 terrorist campaign in Saudi Arabia was not launched at Usama's behest. It is also unlikely that the "brothers" who "acted on their own" were veteran members of al-Qaeda.

Did the Saudi authorities' campaign of arrests provoke the jihadis? It is likely that Saudi returnees from Afghanistan were closely monitored by the authorities, and eventually many were imprisoned, as we shall see below. But the approximate date when the authorities began to imprison and torture jihadis is not evident from the Bin Laden Papers. According to Yousef al-Uyayri, the arrests began soon after the 9/11 attacks. He and his brethren, he claimed, were wrongfully persecuted "on the orders of America," and he insisted that, following the fall of the Taliban, "America sent the Saudi authorities a list of 141 names and aliases collected through interrogations of detainees at Guantanamo."

A variation on Yousef's claims is latently echoed in some U.S. literature on the subject. In his *Desert Diplomat*, Robert W. Jordan, the U.S. Ambassador to Saudi Arabia (2001–03), remarked positively on the promptness with which the Saudi Minister of Interior responded to requests by U.S. intelligence agencies. Jordan wrote fondly of Muhammad bin Nayef, the "Saudi point man in the war on terror," and praised him for having "turned over the material to the FBI almost immediately."[66] Yousef's claims are also echoed in the Senate Committee's report on the CIA's "enhanced interrogation techniques." In a footnote in the highly redacted report, we read that from "information collected 'subsequent to the application of enhanced measures,' the CIA 'learned more in-depth details' about operational planning, 'to include ongoing operations against both the US and Saudi interests in Saudi Arabia.'"[67]

Did U.S. intelligence agencies pressure the Saudi authorities to launch a campaign of arrests in the kingdom, as Yousef claimed?[68] If the Saudi authorities had indeed begun arresting jihadis on their return from Afghanistan, as the "trusted intermediary" reports in his letter, it is likely that the "brothers" were provoked into accumulating ammunition in preparation for a showdown. It follows that the Ministry of Interior's publication of a list of "nineteen wanted men" served as the precipitant that the jihadis had feared, or perhaps wanted. The "trusted intermediary," who did not support the attacks, explained that the "brothers" were "persecuted," and they "concluded that it was necessary to do something in response."[69]

Though he may have disapproved of jihad in Saudi Arabia in 1997, Usama was pleased with the 2003–04 attacks. In December 2004, he released a public statement addressed to "Muslims in Saudi Arabia in particular." He sermonized that "love for the Hijaz is deep in my heart, but its rulers are wolves." He included the Saudi regime among the "oppressive, traitorous ruling families in the region," accusing them of being subservient to "America and its allies."[70] In the same month, he wrote to his associates, asking them

> to contact the brothers in the Peninsula [i.e., Saudi Arabia], if that is at all possible, to communicate to them his greetings and to notify them that the attacks they recently carried out had a great effect, with God's help. We would like for them, if it is at all feasible and their conditions permit, to assassinate the regime's chief figures, namely Sultan, Nayef, Salman, and Abdallah. We also would like for them to set up a secret unit under the name "Muhammad bin Maslama" to eliminate the hypocrites and apostates who sided with the local and international unbelievers . . . such as writers, and the clerics—who issue legal opinions in defense of the tyrants, all of whom serve the American aggression in Iraq and in the broader region.[71]

We might want to reflect for a moment on the historical import of the name of the secret unit that Usama wanted to set up in the kingdom.

Muhammad bin Maslama was a seventh-century figure who led a group to assassinate Ka'b ibn al-Ashraf, a poet who satirized the Prophet Muhammad. He was the first to volunteer after Muhammad prayed to the Lord to deliver him from Ka'b "for the evil he declareth and the poems he declaimeth."[72] When Muhammad declared war against Ka'b's tribe, Bani Nadir, he was up against rhymed stanzas that penetrated deeper than the sword. In the words of the historian Martin Lings, "a gifted poet was like a multitude of men, for his verses were repeated from mouth to mouth" among the Arabs.

Usama understood the lessons of this historical episode for his own times, for, as he put it, "the media occupies the greater portion of the battle today" and the scholars and journalists "are worse than the satirical poets of the pre-Islamic era."[73] When he wrote his letter, he wanted the "brothers" to follow Muhammad bin Maslama's lead. At that time, Sultan (Bandar bin Sultan) was the Saudi Ambassador to the United States; Nayef (Muhammad bin Nayef) was the Minister of Interior; Salman (most likely Salman bin Abd al-Aziz) was the Governor of Riyadh (and became King in 2015); and Abdallah (Abdallah bin Abd al-Aziz) was the King.

Usama was too late to influence the terrorist campaign in Saudi Arabia. By the time he had a chance to compose his instructions to the "brothers" in Saudi Arabia, the Saudi authorities had managed to suppress the jihadi campaign in the kingdom. It is unlikely that his letter reached them.

ON SAUDI ARABIA AND AL-QAEDA

Saudi Arabia is widely reported to have supported al-Qaeda. Reports ranged from accusing the royal family of involvement in the 9/11 attacks to insisting that the Saudi clerical establishment fathered al-Qaeda's ideology. Bandar bin Sultan, who was on Usama's hit list in 2004, is one of two members of the royal family named in a long-running U.S. lawsuit relating to his alleged support of the 9/11 attacks.[74] As the 2004 letter just cited confirms, al-Qaeda's hostility toward Bandar, and the Saudi regime as a whole, is incontestable, as is Usama's disdain for most Saudi clerics, whom he believed were tools in the hands of the regime.

The hostility was mutual. The letters reveal that the Saudi authorities managed to subdue support for al-Qaeda in the kingdom and, by 2007, even discussing al-Qaeda could get a person arrested. The "trusted intermediary" related in his letter that "recruiting for Usama has become even more dangerous than going to be with Usama." The clerics, he lamented, were equally hostile to al-Qaeda. Though they are "as numerous as the grains of sand," he rued, those "who fully support you [i.e., al-Qaeda] are probably three or four at most."[75]

We learn from another Saudi intermediary that political prisons had proliferated in the kingdom and, by 2008, the authorities had arrested more than 5,000 political prisoners of the jihadi variety.[76] The jihadis' feelings of persecution were aggravated by the authorities' approach to de-radicalization. The "trusted intermediary" recounted:

I have ascertained that Saudi intelligence met with some jihadis both inside and outside prisons. They discussed with them the issue of the Rafida [i.e., Shia in Saudi Arabia and the Iranian regime] and what position the jihadis would take in the event that a war with Iran broke out. The authorities want to use the brothers as donkeys [i.e., stupid people] to realize the objectives of both the American and Saudi governments.[77]

The "trusted intermediary" was referring to a specific incident that he had learned about from a "brother" inside 'Ulaysha prison, who "wrote to us the following":

A few days ago, an incident occurred in 'Ulaysha prison. One of the officials, a lieutenant general, called in one of the veteran brothers. On his return, this brother related: "I was taken into a building where I found jihadis from the Ruways and Hayer prisons. Then the lieutenant general took me by the hand and walked me into an office and told me, 'The state did not hold grudges against you when it imprisoned you. It is rather out of concern for you, you the people of this country, and such things.' Then the lieutenant general said, 'I am going to confide something serious and highly secretive to you: We have reliable information that Iran is planning attacks in the east of Saudi Arabia against the Rafida [i.e., an area mostly populated by Shia]. They want to give the appearance that the Saudi state carried out attacks against its Shia population, and accuse it of sectarianism.'"

The brother asked: "So what are you actually asking?" The lieutenant general responded: "We would like for the al-Qaeda organization to carry out terrorist attacks inside Iran, and to claim responsibility for them. To this end, we would support you with money and weapons." Then this brother said: "This is somewhat difficult, but let me think about it." Then the lieutenant general said: "The Rafida in Qatif are all armed, and the government knows that." The brother said: "Leave those in Qatif to us, and we will have them slaughtered in three months. You go on devising your strategies and do not worry about the Rafida in Qatif." At this point the lieutenant general implored God earnestly, stood up, and said: "Good on you. That is what we need," before he left the room. That same day, at night, the same brother was called in again and was taken to a resting area with other jihadis. They were given a lecture about the Rafida threat, their ambitions, and their malice against Islam. Two days after this incident, they took this brother, and we don't know where he is now.[78]

The letters do not suggest that the Saudi government actually funded and weaponized the kingdom's jihadis against Iran. If the incidents described here are true, we might surmise that the authorities most likely wanted to test the jihadis' anti-Shia and anti-Iran credentials. The Saudi authorities were clearly under the impression that the kingdom's jihadis were all members of al-Qaeda. Given that Khattab, who marshaled support among jihadis in the kingdom, was killed in 2002, the rest probably wanted to be part of al-Qaeda. They were likely proud that their government referred to them as "al-Qaeda," whose support the lieutenant general was pretending to solicit.

We also learn from the letters that sectarianism was embedded in the de-radicalization program that the Saudi authorities developed to "reform" their political prisoners. Abu al-Tayyib described the program in detail in his 2008 letter. "During their interrogations and torture," he recounted, the security forces paid more attention to those "who leaned toward engaging in domestic work" than those who "leaned toward engaging in external work." He described the interrogators' techniques as follows:

The interrogators have acquired some knowledge of the religious sciences to avert being entrapped by prisoners who use Islamic legal argumentations to justify their actions. The authorities have also recruited interrogators who specialize in [terrorism] financing [through] charity donations. They now follow sophisticated interrogation techniques. These are:

The interrogators pose a series of different questions and at different times. The questions are all about the same thing, but they are posed in different ways to verify if the prisoner's responses are consistent and if he is telling the truth. If the interrogators do not succeed using this technique, they stamp "dishonest" on the prisoner's file and refer him to another section, where he will be flogged and tortured!

Some of the young men are tricked by this form of interrogation technique. The authorities then start to think well of them [and the potential to de-radicalize them]. Then comes the role of Muhammad bin Nayef [i.e., Minster of Interior at the time], and he is more deceitful than his father. . . . He uses the Ministry's budget to give the young men money and cover their debts. He then says to them [reprovingly]: "You used to show patience and forgiveness toward the polytheism of the Taliban state and its transgressions, yet you won't do the same for this blessed state, which implements Islamic law?! Sure, this state has some transgressions that we are trying to fix!" Then he adds: "By God, like you, I am unhappy with some of the conduct, politics, and transgressions of which our Sharia disapproves." He goes on with more such deceitful language to brainwash the young men. He is skillful at that, and has an impressive education . . . and he also says: "We need our young men to defend this country against the threat of the Rafida."[79]

We can't be sure if Abu al-Tayyib is telling the truth, but it is difficult to think of reasons that would cause him to falsify these accounts.

During 2002–04 then, the "afflicted" al-Qaeda could at most watch global jihad from a distance. As an organization, it was all but ruined. But as we shall see in the following chapter, after reconnecting with his associates, Usama revived al-Qaeda with a new ensemble of leaders in an attempt to resume "the work after it had been halted."

4

AL-QAEDA "HIDES"

With respect to your security situation, the default position for all the brothers should be to hide (kumun). . . . (This instruction should be understood as an obligation, and not as an advice.)

Draft letter by Usama bin Laden, late 2004[1]

In late 2004, Usama bin Laden was back at the helm of al-Qaeda's affairs—insofar as his dependence on couriers permitted. We don't know where he was living then, but we learn from one letter that, around that time, he had reunited with his third wife, Siham, and their children Khaled, Mariam, and Sumayya. Their eldest, Khadija, and her family were likely in North Waziristan. Far from being just a family reunion, the contributions of Usama's family to al-Qaeda will become apparent in subsequent chapters.

Usama's first order of business was for his "afflicted" associates to go into hiding. More precisely, he instructed that "hiding should be the default position (*al-asl al-kumun*)" for members of his organization, fearing that they would be betrayed by Taliban leaders with suspected ties to Pakistani security forces.

Usama assumed that *kumun* would be a temporary measure, and al-Qaeda would regain momentum and resume the "work after it had been halted." He also envisaged that as its "work" went into suspended mode in the Af-Pak region, al-Qaeda could pursue international terrorism in Iraq, the new arena of "amazing jihadi victories," as described in one of the letters.

Notwithstanding Usama and his associates' resolve and determination, things did not go according to plan. As to relaunching international terrorism from Iraq, this was challenging, as will become apparent as we learn more, later in the book, about the complex relationship al-Qaeda developed with jihadi groups there and elsewhere.

"New Phase" and New Leaders

With much resolve and determination, Usama launched a "new phase" in late 2004, instructing his associates to adopt *kumun* as their default position. This applied to all,

> particularly those whose work does not require movement, such as those who work in the jihadi media. As to those whose work necessitates movement and meetings, they should do so through letters and by relying on a very limited number of couriers (we propose two to three at most)—our correspondence shall follow the closed-circle model. Otherwise, they should not move from their hideouts, unless it is absolutely necessary.[2]

The "closed-circle model" echoes that illustrated by Colonel Mathieu in *The Battle of Algiers* (1966), which depicts the Algerians' struggle for independence against the French. In the film, the phlegmatic colonel draws on a blackboard a series of triangles that form a large pyramid to highlight the challenges facing the French military. The ensemble of triangles illustrate that the French are up against an organization made up of small cells, and that each militant in a given cell might at most compromise the security of three others, if captured.

The closed circle of couriers that Usama put in place was even tighter, and we will learn more about his own network in Chapter Eleven. He gave zero latitude, stressing that his instructions were in the nature of commands, which meant that they were "obligations" to be carried out by his associates. Usama also saw *kumun* as an opportunity to rebuild al-Qaeda by promoting second-tier leaders to senior positions, mapping out a chain of command, and instituting an internal reporting culture.

Deputy Leader

Usama needed a new deputy to replace Abu Hafs al-Misri, who was killed in a U.S. airstrike on Afghanistan in November 2001. In the aftermath of the Taliban's fall, Ayman al-Zawahiri became the face of al-Qaeda, ardently inciting Muslims to take up jihad, including giving an interview to the jihadi media on the second anniversary of the 9/11 attacks. Because of this visibility, the media took it for granted that Ayman was Usama's deputy.

Usama may have designated Ayman as his deputy when the two of them "disappeared out of necessity" in late 2001. But it is more likely that Usama was inspired by the media's designation, because it was not until late 2004 that he officially named Ayman as his deputy to his associates. Usama could think of two or three others who would have been equally fitting for the role, but it is not as if there were many senior leaders left to choose from: "As you know, the senior and experienced brothers have either been killed or captured. . . . Since you are able to reach the doctor, consult him regularly, for he is the deputy leader."[3] Thus, "with respect to the doctor [i.e., Ayman]," he wrote to Tawfiq, "he is the best and finest of the remaining jihadi brothers that we have known during the past decades." While Usama ordered everyone in al-Qaeda to hide, he urged that Ayman should hide even more:

As to brother Abu Fatima [i.e., Ayman], we should like for you to arrange a secure location for him. It should not be known to any of the brothers—particularly those who are wanted by the authorities and whose photographs have been published—unless they hide in the same place with him, and agree to refrain from any movement outside his hideout. Correspondence with Abu Fatima should be through trusted couriers who are not wanted by or known to the authorities.[4]

Usama also authorized that Ayman should always have a budget of 50,000 euros at his disposal.[5] At the time, Usama's preference was to use euros, since the U.S. dollar was trading at a low rate.[6] Considering the circumstances,

Usama felt it necessary that he and Ayman should be away from their base and in a secure place. He believed that the mere survival of experienced leaders was sufficient to "inflict harm on the enemy."

General Leader of al-Qaeda

Since he could only lead *in absentia*, Usama appointed Tawfiq as the "general leader of al-Qaeda." This was a new senior position, and Tawfiq reported directly to Usama. But when it was not possible to reach Usama in a timely fashion, Tawfiq was authorized to make decisions, after consulting with his trusted associates and subordinates:

Brother Tawfiq should carry out all his responsibilities without being restrained by other brothers, including those who are older and who have longer experience in jihad. On this basis, it should be known to all the brothers with leadership responsibilities, especially those in the military domain, that Tawfiq is the most senior in the [Af-Pak] district. . . .[7] Brother Tawfiq should liaise with the military commander Khaled al-Habib through exchanging letters delivered by couriers, and discuss with him the complete structure of the group. The two should agree on having at least two deputies for Tawfiq. In other words, Tawfiq and his deputies should coordinate and work in concert, especially in running military affairs. Such coordination helps with cultivating the cadres.

Tawfiq should emphasize to Khaled al-Habib and the other brothers in positions of responsibility that they should consult regularly with [subordinate] competent brothers. They should give them the opportunity to maximize their potential and capabilities, especially when it comes to innovating ways that would vex the enemy.

Usama determined that positions of responsibility should be rotated. Al-Qaeda had adopted, or at least had envisaged, this rotation model in its early days in the 1980s. It was designed to give leaders the time "to pursue knowledge," a sabbatical of sorts, and to "give opportunities to their deputies to assume responsibilities of their own."[8] Of course, conditions had changed, but Usama was strategizing for the long term, and was eager to develop new cadres who would move al-Qaeda's plans forward:

> The morale should be uplifted, and the cadres must be made to feel the importance of the new project. They should be asked to present in writing their proposals on how they plan to spite the enemy. You [i.e., Tawfiq] should empower Khaled al-Habib and those who would eventually replace him, and your subordinates should be given the opportunity to innovate new methods. Let them hold their positions for a year, unless we decide to renew them.[9]

Usama prepared Tawfiq for the challenges awaiting him, not least the "short-comings of managing from a distance." He explained that regular visits to the battlefield allow leaders to take decisive measures to keep in check the inflated egos of platoon commanders. But with al-Qaeda's survival depending on *kumun*, such visits were not feasible. Thus, Usama urged "avoiding harsh decisions" and advised "pursuing one's goal gradually." For instance, if a "brother" is not up to standard, "it would be sensible to thank him for his work, give him some time off, and then assign him to another position suited to his skills." In other words, "dismissal is not an option under current conditions."[10]

Disengagement . . . "Gently"

Tawfiq was thirty-one, and much was expected of him in his new role. Perhaps to lift his morale, Usama shared that he believed himself to be blessed with *firasa*—an intuition that allows one to be a good judge of men based on their conduct, conversation, and physical features[11]—and he had determined that "you are the right person to be leading the work in these difficult conditions."[12]

Usama imparted a stream of advice, drawn from both his own past experiences and from those of legendary Muslim figures, to coach Tawfiq. "I was two years younger than you," he wrote, "when I led Ma'sadat al-Ansar against the

Soviets in 1986" a reference to the first entity that Usama founded in Afghanistan. He recalled the challenges he faced, including those that made it necessary for him to extricate himself from those who were closest to him:

> I should like to illustrate this with a personal example. When Sheikh Abdallah Azzam and I began working together in Peshawar, everything proceeded smoothly. This changed when new brothers joined and disrupted what had been a great relationship. Though founding the Services Bureau (*maktab al-khidamat*) was my idea, and my relationship with Sheikh Abdallah was as good as one could imagine, the new brothers' gossip and bickering cast a negative shadow on the work. I decided to let them have the Bureau, without getting into any altercations with them, while I continued to maintain a solid and fond relationship with Sheikh Abdallah.[13]

Sheikh Azzam was Usama's mentor and, in 1984, he had established the Services Bureau, which hosted Arabs who wanted to support the Afghan cause.[14] This meant that the Services Bureau facilitated and supported the work of Usama's al-Ma'asada.[15] The two entities worked closely together, until Usama decided that it was no longer productive to maintain this collaboration.

Usama was walking down this specific memory lane because he wanted Tawfiq to do something similar. He wanted al-Qaeda to disengage from other jihadi groups, including the Taliban, just as he had done with the Services Bureau—amicably.

August 20, 1988 Revisited

It is necessary to pause at this juncture and travel back in time to revisit the events to which Usama refers in his 2004 letter. To do so, we should return to August 20, 1988, and meditate long and hard on the document that supposedly describes the "birth" of al-Qaeda. This and other internal al-Qaeda documents were recovered from Bosnia in December 2001 as part of an investigation into a charitable organization, the Benevolence International Foundation (BIF), and its connections with al-Qaeda.

It is assumed by many that al-Qaeda was born following a long meeting that concluded at 2:00 a.m. on August 20, 1988, having started at sunset the day before. The handwritten document that records this protracted meeting has been described as the "founding minutes of al-Qaeda." On its own, it is not helpful, because it does not actually detail what happened and what was discussed. Instead, it includes the names of those who attended the meeting, and refers to "a new division in Peshawar" and to "al-Qaeda" as a distinct "organized Islamic group."[16]

In what looks like an addendum to the document, it is recorded that the meeting covered "forty points" that "Sheikh Usama summed up under two headings: (1) *al-mazalim*, and (2) poor management and ill-treatment." In Islamic parlance, "*al-mazalim*" is an institution responsible for dealing with complaints and dispensing justice, much like a Human Resources department. Other 1988 documents in Usama's handwriting mention specific complaints about Sheikh Azzam and his Bureau, such as "Is the Services Bureau set up to serve the governments or Arab [volunteers]," and "Sheikh Abdallah Azzam should clarify whether he has [political] positions other than those he espouses in the Consultative Council; and if so, is it reasonable for the Council to bear such comportment[?]"[17] These clearly point to Usama having profound and irreconcilable differences with Azzam and his Services Bureau which necessitated parting ways.

It is likely that on August 20, Usama made a convincing case to support his disengagement from the Bureau, because the meeting "resulted in [allowing] the Sheikh [i.e., Usama] to do as he sees fit tomorrow." The same document states that "on Saturday morning, 8/20/1988, the plaintiff brothers arrived." The key phrase is "plaintiff brothers," making it clear that the meeting had been about a complaint brought forward by Usama against the Services Bureau. In light of Usama's 2004 letter, we now understand that this was not a meeting about the birth of a new group, it was more like a court case that allowed an existing group, al-Ma'sada, that had been operating for "a year and a half," to separate from the Services Bureau, and develop its own charter and membership under a new name.[18] Accordingly, August 20, 1988 is a date that marks a *divorce* between two existing entities. Other documents indicate that the newly independent entity was meant to be based in Kabul. It must have taken a while to get used to the new name, "al-Qaeda," because as late as October 12, 1988, it was referred to in some internal documents as "the new Ma'sada"[19] (*al-ma'sada al-jadida*).

Usama hoped that a variation of the August 20, 1988 divorce could be repeated in 2004, this time a disengagement from other jihadi groups, including the Taliban. He advised Tawfiq "to clarify the situation to the leaders and the scholars in the region where you are located." More specifically:

> What is required is to let the leaders and the scholars in the region know gently that it was the Taliban who appointed Abdallah Khan as the military commander. But you should also let them know that the author of this letter [i.e., Usama] is the one who appointed you, Tawfiq, as the general leader to oversee all the brothers in al-Qaeda.[20]

Usama hoped that the removal of Abdallah Khan would be welcomed by the leaders in the region since Abdallah's reputation was tainted. At the same time, he was making it clear to the same leaders that his appointee, Tawfiq, was acting, and indeed leading, on his behalf.

But Usama also wanted to do things differently moving forward. He wanted al-Qaeda's decision-making to proceed on the basis that the fruits of any consultation should, at most, inform (*mu'lima*) the leader, without obligating him to accept the counsel (*ghayr mulzima*). He wasn't just thinking of his own standing as leader, but also of all those in leadership positions. In Usama's view, leaders could not afford to be indecisive. While he instructed that all those in leadership positions should embrace a culture of consultation (horizontally and vertically), he did not want them to be at the mercy of others' opinions. Otherwise, the result would be chaos.[21]

This was a sensitive issue, to say the least. Internal al-Qaeda documents from the 1980s show that since 1987–88, al-Qaeda had been operating on the basis that the leader's decisions (i.e., Usama's) could be overruled if the majority of the Shura Council (i.e., consultative body) disapproved.[22] These early documents include a hand-drawn chart of al-Qaeda, with Abu Abdallah (i.e., Usama) at the helm; above is written "consultation is obligatory" (*al-shura mulzima*).[23] Judging by the discussions in the Bin Laden Papers, it is likely that the Shura Council had consisted of members of other jihadi groups.

Usama wanted to change this arrangement. He sought to convince Tawfiq (and himself) that al-Qaeda had been operating on the basis that the decisions of the Shura were not binding on the leader (*ghayr mulzima*). This issue irked Usama whenever he raised it in the letters, which suggests that his own position had changed over time. At any rate, in 2004, Usama did not want to feel obligated to keep Abdallah Khan in his position to please the Taliban, not least after learning that al-Qaeda was at risk of being betrayed by a large segment of the Afghan Taliban. Reaching out to Mullah Omar directly was not possible. The letters make it clear that messages to Mullah Omar had to go through Taliban leaders whom al-Qaeda did not trust.

Nonetheless, pushing for disengagement from other jihadi groups and the Taliban was bad optics for al-Qaeda, considering that it was supposed to be part of the same community (*jama'a*). Usama was publicly calling on Muslims to unite behind jihadis, yet he was asking Tawfiq to proceed in the opposite direction. Usama assured Tawfiq that such a disengagement "does not violate any of the legal texts that exhort union among Muslims":

> The concept of *jama'a* is not simply about bringing people together, but it is for the sake of worshipping God. It is through unity that the height of this worship could be realized. But when unity becomes an obstacle, then this is absolutely not the kind of unity that the legal texts exhort.[24]

The concept of *jama'a* is a cornerstone of Islam, and it is a maxim of al-Qaeda. The term designates a small "group," a "society," or even a larger "community" of like-minded fellows. Inherent to the *jama'a* is order, without which people would fall into anarchy. "There is no jihad without *jama'a*" is a common adage in the jihadi literature; a more elaborate version adds that "there is no *jama'a* without a leader, and there is no leader unless his commands are heard and obeyed."[25] Notwithstanding his appeal to legal texts, Usama was effectively advancing a *realpolitik* reasoning. From a religious perspective, the disengagement he was proposing was terribly complicated: It was akin to believing in the sanctity of marriage, but still calling for divorce because it was better for the kids.

Tawfiq had the unenviable task of moving this disengagement forward. His earlier letter discussed in previous chapters showed that he was clearly unafraid to speak his mind, and Usama went on to augment his self-esteem:

> With God's thanks, you are earnest, and you have men and weapons. . . . Proceed, and do not hesitate. Should some people start complaining about you, be nice to them, and say the truth, which is: "All that we want is to reactivate the work after it had been halted. . . ." Always treat people well, regardless of their conduct, for such an approach is likely to minimize conflict. . . . Do not waste your time arguing with those who do not like what you're doing. Instead, respond with "May God support us and you so that we may all defend His religion."

Usama was mindful of the challenges awaiting Tawfiq. He reminded him that "God will count your deeds on the Day of Judgement" (*Allahu hasibuka*), and counseled that he should fortify himself with "patience and piety." When times are tough, he continued, "always remember that our Prophet's Companions, who led the great early Islamic conquests, were younger than you." (No pressure!) Perhaps in the spirit of the *Advice for Rulers* tradition, Usama imparted a few prescriptions drawn from both the Qur'an and realpolitik that he believed were important for all leaders:

1. Be patient, and if you run out of patience, turn to perseverance.
2. Be lenient with all the brothers, and if you run out of leniency, turn to forbearance.

3. Consult, abundantly if you can. Then make your decisions resolutely and decisively.

4. Be empathetic, and always smile at your brother. Sometimes smiling amounts to almsgiving.

5. Delegate affairs to those in whose capability and trustworthiness you have confidence. Do not cut your links with those who fall a bit short of such qualities. Those whom you cannot accommodate, beware not to turn them into your enemies.[26]

So, as Usama and Ayman loudly proclaimed jihadi unity on the world stage, disengagement from the Taliban and other groups had to proceed quietly. It is worth noting that even when Usama was not in operational command of al-Qaeda, there was no hiatus in al-Qaeda's presence in the media. The group's top two leaders maintained a regular stream of public statements, cheering jihadis around the world, as if they were in charge.

Al-Qaeda's presence in the media, a priority for Usama, allowed its leaders to make their political case, which centered on the plight of Muslims at the hands of their "apostate rulers" and the West's support of Muslim autocrats. It also allowed them to project a strength that in reality they lacked. Usama did not think highly of jihadi media and preferred to have his missives broadcast by mainstream outlets. He asked Tawfiq "to find a secure line of communication with any American TV station to release our statements, we propose CBS." He wanted Americans to learn about "Bush and his administration's lies, and that our war of attrition is succeeding. . . . It is important for us that the American public understand that our attacks have their justifications."

Usama also did not want to give up on having an al-Qaeda presence inside Pakistan. He urged Tawfiq and Hamza al-Rabia, who was in charge of international terrorism, to "entrust some Pakistani brothers, who believe in our program, to set up an al-Qaeda branch in Pakistan." Usama was eager for the Pakistani branch "to recruit personnel to carry out work [i.e., terrorism] both inside and outside Pakistan."[27]

Al-Qaeda Rebuilt

The letters reveal that Usama rebuilt his organization with new leaders and instituted an internal reporting culture that complied with the chain of command he had mapped out. He managed to do so under conditions of *kumun*, mistrust of the Taliban, and the global "war on terror."

Tawfiq's tenure likely ended after a year. Next time we meet him, he was using the alias Jargh al-Din, communicating Usama's December 2004 guidance to Abd al-Rahman al-Maghrebi, who oversaw the jihadi media. The two were clearly fond of each other, and Abd al-Rahman wanted to connect in person. "With respect to your request that we should meet," Tawfiq regretfully informed his friend, "I should very much like to see you and kiss you, but the Teacher [Usama] instructed that we should postpone all in-person meetings."[28] The same letter reveals that members of al-Qaeda were being taught to use encryption, and Tawfiq indicated that Usama "also instructed that all encryption and [media] studies should be pursued through correspondence."[29]

Not much was written by or about Tawfiq in subsequent years. Usama may have moved to his Abbottabad compound in 2005 (according to U.S. intelligence), which might explain why there were fewer letters when Tawfiq was in charge. During that year, it is possible that Khaled al-Habib succeeded Tawfiq.[30] In 2006, second-tier leaders were reporting to Hajji Uthman, who took over as the general leader of al-Qaeda. We last hear of Tawfiq in December 2007, when Usama's son-in-law Daoud reported "the lion's death."[31] The letter does not indicate that Tawfiq was "martyred," and mainstream media reported that he died of hepatitis.[32] His reported illness may have had something to do with his short tenure.

Hajji Uthman's appointment as the general leader of al-Qaeda is somewhat bizarre. Though Usama considered him to be "virtuous" and competent in finance, he had advised Tawfiq to keep him away from running military and political affairs. In 2005–06, the most capable operative was Atiya, whose acumen arguably exceeded that of Usama and Ayman. However, he was busy liaising with and mediating between jihadi groups in Iraq and making contacts with trusted intermediaries in various countries. And in his spare time, he was reviewing and editing Ayman's voluminous writings. Also, Atiya was around thirty-five at the time, while Hajji Uthman was fifty, and that probably counted in the latter's favor. (Hajji Uthman continued to be the general leader of al-Qaeda in the Af-Pak district until he was killed in a drone strike in May 2010. He was replaced by Atiya.)[33]

What about the rest of the "brothers"? The letters suggest that some of Usama's "brothers" continued to fight alongside trusted Taliban, while most of them were concentrated in the mountainous FATA of Pakistan, which proved its utility in the immediate aftermath of the Taliban's fall. According to one letter, one of the FATA's tribal leaders, Mufti Sulaiman, was "a very good man with a white beard and helped the [Arab] brothers after they left the Tora Bora mountains. He gave them shelter, and set them up with [fake] IDs and passports."[34]

Eventually, the leaders of al-Qaeda took up residence in North Waziristan. The FATA leaders did not form a unified front; each had his own interests and agenda. A 2004 handwritten letter warned of al-Qaeda's involvement with the Waziri tribes: "Even if the tribes asked, it is best that you [i.e., al-Qaeda] do not get involved or lend them military and financial aid. No good can come of this."[35]

It is not clear whether al-Qaeda took part in the fighting alongside the tribes, but it at least volunteered to train militants in the FATA. The leaders of al-Qaeda maintained that their allegiance to Mullah Omar allowed the group to exercise independence. Their survival depended entirely on "brothers" opposed to the Pakistani state, and the FATA was the place to be. The historian Brian Glyn Williams observes that the FATA is "the wildest and most undeveloped part of Pakistan . . . a world unto itself."[36] Long before the emergence of al-Qaeda, Williams explains, the inhabitants of the FATA had resisted British rule and maintained a virtual autonomy over their own affairs. When Pakistan gained its independence in 1947, the government did not alter the FATA's autonomous status and neglected to invest adequate resources to improve the lives of its inhabitants.[37] According to one journalist who grew up in the FATA,

Pakistan's military and political establishment considered Waziristan's residents "as if they were tribes that were living in the Amazon."[38]

Following the launch of the "war on terror" in 2001, the FATA became home to domestic militants opposed to the Pakistani state, and harbored a spectrum of foreign militant groups of the jihadi variety.[39] Pakistan's decision to lend its support to the "war on terror" served its own interests. Steve Coll reports that, in 2002, Pakistan's President, Pervez Musharraf, agreed to allow the CIA to fly drones over the FATA, where militants threatening the Pakistani state were based.[40] The arrangement served the CIA, whose priority was to track al-Qaeda and, by extension, the militants who sheltered its members.

Usama's hopes of resuming the "work that had been halted" did not materialize. Targeted strikes on al-Qaeda leaders in Pakistan made sure that the "work" did not advance. One of those eliminated by such a strike was Hamza al-Rabia, who had been authorized to travel to Iraq to set up a secret international terrorism unit. Hamza's death in December 2005 must have halted al-Qaeda's international terrorism aspirations again.[41]

However, al-Qaeda continued to use jihad on autopilot to its advantage. On July 7, 2005, four Muslim suicide bombers of Pakistani origin—three of whom were born in the United Kingdom—carried out simultaneous attacks on London's transit system, killing fifty-two commuters. Two months later, Ayman al-Zawahiri publicly blessed the attacks in a montage of video clips that featured the last testament of one of the suicide bombers, Muhammad Sidique Khan. In between Ayman's speech and Siddiq's testament, we watch clips of planes crashing into the Twin Towers alongside clips of ambulances jamming London's streets in the aftermath of the 7/7 attacks. The soundtrack for this montage is a *nashid* (a piece of cappella chanting): "Terrorist, indeed I am; the enemies of religion I terrorize." In his testament, Siddiq said that he was inspired by "today's heroes, like our beloved Sheikh Usama bin Laden, Dr. Ayman al-Zawahiri, and Abu Musab al-Zarqawi, and all the brothers and sisters who are fighting in God's path."[42]

Ayman did not take credit for the attacks, but he cheered that they were "as glorious as those that preceded them in New York, Washington, and Madrid for having moved the battle to the land of the enemy whose armies had been occupying our land in Chechnya, Afghanistan, Iraq, and Palestine." The content of Siddiq's testament does not suggest that he had coordinated his speech with that of Ayman, and there is nothing in the letters that points to al-Qaeda having planned or contributed to the attacks.

In fact, everything in the Bin Laden Papers indicates that al-Qaeda could not have been behind the attacks. We get some insight into al-Qaeda's workings during that period from an intriguing letter that includes the group's itemized expenses. In March 2006, Hajji Uthman reported to Usama that al-Qaeda had a total of 176,000 euros:

> Expenses during that period totaled 178,000 euros (75,000 euros toward military expenses; 40,000 euros in surety bonds (*kafalat*) toward families in Peshawar for six months; 20,000 euros toward similar surety bonds; 25,000 euros toward administrative expenses; 6,000 euros toward jihadi media expenses; 1,200 euros toward legal expenses; and 10,800 euros toward miscellaneous expenses.
>
> Remarks about expenses:
>
> A- The military budget decreased to 15,000 euros during the past two months.
>
> B- The Peshawar families' six-month surety bonds are due on March 27 [i.e., within twenty-six days].
>
> C- Administrative expenses have increased due to the marriages of eight brothers during this period. This means that the additional expenses went toward marriage assistance (which used to be $1,000, then $700, then $500). The assistance includes setting up their homes and their surety bonds. We are in an awkward position concerning this kind of assistance: On the one hand, we are considering doing away with this assistance in view of our financial situation. On the other hand, we are mindful that marriage is important for the men and to ensuring that they remain steadfast.[43]

Noticeably absent are expenses on "external work," i.e., international terrorism. It is also clear that al-Qaeda had a minuscule military budget to cover the salaries of its fighters and the cost of the group's weaponry. The "surety bonds," a considerable part of its budget, went to the families of its fallen and captured fighters.

Judging by al-Qaeda's finances in 2006, and the letters exchanged between 2004 and 2007, it is inconceivable that it had the wherewithal to mount international attacks, as was widely reported. For instance, nowhere do the letters discuss the Madrid and London bombings, which were attributed to al-Qaeda. Nor do they refer to the August 2006 failed plot to use liquid bombs to blow up several transatlantic airliners, also attributed to al-Qaeda.[44]

Nonetheless, in 2006, al-Qaeda was clearly hoping to move forward on the international terrorism front, and its only possible path was through setting up a secret unit in Iraq. This did not materialize. "With respect to the external work," Atiya reported to Usama and Hajji Uthman, "we have discussed it with the brother," a reference to Abu Musab in Iraq. But Atiya lamented that "on the practical level, it does not escape you that there is nothing . . .!"[45]

Though al-Qaeda failed to set up a unit in Iraq, it persisted with its attempts to plan attacks from the Af-Pak region. The "brothers" had nothing to do with the 2006 transatlantic plot, but they were nevertheless inspired by it; as late as August 2009, they were still experimenting and trying to replicate it.[46]

Nonetheless, it was no small feat for Usama to rebuild a shattered organization in less than two years, and to do so while he and the other leaders were hiding. But as we shall see in the next chapter, hiding became al-Qaeda's *modus operandi*. Until Usama's death, despite the group's operational impotence, al-Qaeda continued to be perceived, falsely it turned out, as a Leviathan in the jihadi landscape.

We don't know how Tawfiq proceeded with his disengagement assignment. Subsequent letters reveal that the extent to which consultation (*shura*) with other groups was binding on al-Qaeda's leaders remained unresolved. It was too challenging from an Islamic legal perspective. Usama, who in practice regularly consulted his associates and deferred to their opinions, continued to argue strongly—too strongly in fact—in support of the view that *shura* means merely the requirement to inform (*al-shura mu'lima*) the leader. Hence, after hearing what members of the Shura have to say, it is for the leader to make up his mind what to do.[47] Ayman, who admired Usama for his consultative leadership, argued the opposite. He insisted that the "brothers" who endured "bitter conditions" in God's path deserved to be part of the decision-making process and should not be treated as mere followers.[48] Differences did not arise between al-Qaeda's leaders as a result of these opposing views. But with growing differences between al-Qaeda and other jihadi groups, including the Afghan Taliban, the process of consultation became more of a burden than a bond between like-minded groups.

With respect to the Afghan Taliban specifically, the letters reveal that Usama and his associates never really trusted them as a group again. In 2007, al-Qaeda's relationship with the Taliban reached breaking point. In May, the leaders of al-Qaeda received "confirmed reports" that some Afghan Taliban "had joined forces with the Americans to kill Mullah Dadullah," a senior Taliban military commander.[49] In other words, they believed they had collaborated with the Pakistani intelligence service, who, in al-Qaeda's eyes, worked for the CIA. The Taliban leaders involved in his killing, according to one letter, included Mullah Baradar, Mullah Obaidullah, and Mullah Akhtar Mansour. We cannot be sure who was behind Dadullah's killing, but one thing is clear—al-Qaeda's mistrust of some of the Taliban was growing.

The killed commander's younger half-brother, Mullah Mansur Dadullah, captured two of those who had participated in the assassination. We learn from one letter:

They confessed that they had been tasked by their leaders to assassinate Mullah Dadullah. They said that their leaders justified the killing on the basis that "Mullah Dadullah operates on his own and doesn't listen to us. He opposes any initiative on our part to negotiate with the Americans and the Karzai government, even if this is in the interest of the Taliban." News of their capture and confessions reached their leaders, and signs of divisions are now emerging among the Taliban.[50]

Mullah Mansur Dadullah wanted Usama's advice and, at his insistence, the leaders of al-Qaeda heard the confessions of those who slew his half-brother directly. They were of course disturbed by what they heard and advised Mansur to raise the matter directly with Mullah Omar, leading Mansur to lament that the only available link to Mullah Omar was via the same Taliban leaders who had been responsible for his half-brother's killing.

Usama was alarmed by the events and warned his associates that most of the Afghan Taliban leaders "have no qualms about being led by the intelligence agencies of apostate states." He feared that "if our friend [i.e., Mullah Omar] disappears, they would succeed him," and would want al-Qaeda to comply with their wishes. He instructed his associates to make it known to those Taliban leaders that "they are not authorized to enter into any agreement on our behalf, especially with states that are involved in the war against Muslims."[51]

Perhaps to halt the divisions that ensued following Dadullah's killing, the Afghan Taliban sent representatives to North Waziristan, hoping to persuade al-Qaeda of their shared goals. But the killing seems to have been a turning point. According to Atiya, rumors were rife "that forces within the Taliban are distancing themselves from al-Qaeda to evade the terrorism accusation." He met with the Afghan Taliban's representatives to investigate these rumors:

We found people who appear to be good, God knows best. . . . They assured us that these rumors are false. . . . They explained what they actually mean in their public statements when they say: "We would negotiate with the Karzai government only after all foreign occupying forces are withdrawn from Afghanistan. . . ." They told us: "We say such things to gain a political advantage, and this is wise. . . ." And they also said: "You know us too well, you have lived with us, we sacrificed together, we are like one body," and a plethora of such beautiful words.[52]

Atiya clearly had his doubts, and Usama wasn't buying any of it. In May 2008, he wrote to Ayman to alert him:

This is not just the assassination of one man [i.e., Mullah Dadullah]. . . . It is the beginning of the elimination of the entire sincere jihadi movement that refuses to be cajoled into compromising God's religion. You, the al-Qaeda brothers, and the leaders of the Mehsud [tribe] should be wary of this compromising movement. Many of them will not abstain from shedding your blood.[53]

Usama's associates had indicated to him that their strategy was to think well (*husn al-zann*) of the suspected Afghan Taliban leaders, unless they did things that forced them to think the contrary. But Usama was adamant that they had shown their true colors when they sought "to free those accused of Mullah Dadullah's killing." He insisted: "It is important that we strengthen the sincere Taliban movement, and weaken the movement that compromises God's religion and represents Pakistan's intelligence agency [ISI]. This is but a continuation of the war that began in Afghanistan to curb and banish al-Qaeda."[54]

Ayman concurred with Usama that it was crucial to win the trust of the "sincere Taliban leaders" and to assure them that "al-Qaeda's activities are in their best interests, first as Muslims and also as rulers of an independent state that will not succumb to servility." But by May 2010, Ayman assessed that the Afghan Taliban were "psychologically prepared" to accept a deal that would see them rein in al-Qaeda in return for reclaiming power. When he admitted his fear in a letter to Usama, Ayman consoled himself that "the Lord is helping us fend off this blow through the impossible conditions the Crusaders are imposing."

Still, he considered possible scenarios. "Had I been advising the Americans," he wrote, "and thank God that I am not," I would advise them "to negotiate directly with Mullah Omar and demand that he should agree to keep al-Qaeda impotent in Afghanistan and its members as political refugees, because most Taliban would agree with these terms." But "what if," Ayman asked, "this were to happen?" His trust in Mullah Omar was unshaken. He was confident that the "Crusaders are too fearful to reach an agreement with Mullah Omar and would rather negotiate with the traitors, spies, and hypocrites, who present themselves as the moderate Taliban."[55]

Usama maintained his loyalty to Mullah Omar. It also seems that Mullah Omar counted on Usama's collaboration. We learn that, in June 2010, Mullah Omar sent an intermediary to North Waziristan to discuss a matter of "the utmost importance" with him. Usama was confined to his compound in Abbottabad, adhering to the most stringent security measures to evade the authorities. So Atiya politely informed Mullah Omar's intermediary that meeting with Usama "was not possible."[56] Eventually, Usama received a letter from Mullah Omar. This has not been recovered, but Usama's response has. In September 2010, Usama wrote to Mullah Omar that "we hear and obey every-thing you stated. We are your soldiers, heart and soul, together defending God's great religion."[57] He didn't divulge specifics, no doubt fearing that the letter was likely to be read by "traitors" in Mullah Omar's immediate circle.

It is evident from the Bin Laden Papers that not all the Afghan Taliban were equal in the eyes of al-Qaeda. But it is also clear that al-Qaeda continued to be bound to the Taliban through a consultative association. This created a strain on al-Qaeda, and perhaps also on those Afghan Taliban who wanted to break their association with al-Qaeda. Ayman was certain that the Taliban were "burdened" by their "legal and psychological" association with al-Qaeda.

Mullah Omar died in 2013, although the fact was only reported in 2015. A few years later, Usama and Ayman's nightmare came true when Taliban leaders who had been in close contact with Mullah Omar participated in the peace process that culminated in a U.S.–Afghan Taliban ceremony on February 29, 2020. Even the Haqqanis, who were trusted by al-Qaeda, took part in the process. According to the resulting agreement, the Taliban committed "to prevent any group or individual, including al-Qa'ida, from using the soil of Afghanistan to threaten the security of the United States and its allies."[58]

Will the Taliban deliver on their promise to the United States to rein in al-Qaeda? A 2020 UN report speaks of divisions within the Afghan Taliban and of ongoing consultation between their top leaders and al-Qaeda.[59] Judging by the Bin Laden Papers, the Taliban's factionalism may prove an intractable problem for the United States. But the same factionalism may also complicate matters for al-Qaeda and other terrorist groups seeking refuge in Afghanistan. Though al-Qaeda celebrated U.S. troop withdrawal and "congratulated the umma on God's victory in Afghanistan" in an August 2021 statement,[60] we can easily imagine the anxiety of its leaders in their deliberations behind the scene.

It is doubtful that the Afghan Taliban involved al-Qaeda in a meaningful way in their negotiations with the United States. Ayman's letter had predicted almost verbatim the terms of the agreement as early as 2010, and he and his associates were undoubtedly devastated that those "who turned their back on religion" returned to power. He was mindful then that there was nothing that al-Qaeda could do to stop the U.S.-Taliban rapprochement. This did not stop him, however, from releasing a public statement, "warning the Islamic *umma* of the danger of the United Nations," soon after the Taliban nominated a U.N. envoy seeking international legitimacy. Though Ayman's November 2021 statement was in the form of "advice," he was implicitly warning the Taliban that their policies amount to being in apostasy of Islam. He was at pains to stress that "the U.N. Charter patently contradicts Islamic law" and went on to highlight Article 1(3) that promotes human rights without distinction as to gender and religion.[61]

Thus, the reported "ongoing consultation" between some Afghan Taliban and al-Qaeda may very well be a continuation of the deep mutual mistrust that the two entities have harbored since the fall of the Islamic Emirate of Afghanistan in December 2001.

5
THE "CALAMITY"

After careful and precise examination, we have concluded that the demise of all the brothers who were killed by drone strikes resulted from their own mistakes. The enemy's success is not due to their brilliance or modern superior technology, but rather, it has to do with the brothers repeatedly neglecting to comply with basic security measures that should be clear to everyone by now.

Al-Qaeda's Security Committee, 2010[1]

Back in 2004, when Usama bin Laden commanded that "hiding" (*kumun*) should be the default position of members of his group, he was concerned about enemies of the *homo sapiens* variety. Specifically, he feared that his men would be betrayed by the Afghan Taliban who had "turned their back on religion," and were prepared to collaborate with Pakistan and ultimately the CIA. Usama, however, did not anticipate that *kumun* would become al-Qaeda's *modus operandi*. That same year, the CIA launched its drone campaign over the FATA of Pakistan where al-Qaeda had sought refuge,[2] and, according to Bob Woodward, the Agency "stepped-up Predator drone strikes on al Qaeda leaders and specific camps" in 2008.[3]

Nothing in al-Qaeda's training or ideological tools had prepared its members for the drones, and its leaders discovered that this kind of predator was nothing short of "a calamity with which we have been afflicted." Ironically, as we shall discover, jihadism's greatest asset—namely, the enthusiasm of men who do not fear death racing to meet their Creator—proved to be a liability in the face of drones.

Al-Qaeda's Af-Pak Milieu

To appreciate the astounding effects of the drones, it is helpful to understand al-Qaeda's Af-Pak environment, including its struggle against Pakistan as well as its tenuous relationship with the Pakistani Taliban (TTP), one of the most active militant groups opposed to the Pakistani state.

Af-Pak

The Bin Laden Papers reveal that, by the time Usama was killed, al-Qaeda had a battalion of about seventy fighters spread between Nuristan (eastern Afghanistan) and Kunar (northeastern Afghanistan).[4] It also had some men stationed in the provinces of "Ghazni, Paktia, Paktika, Wardak, and Zabul," most likely fighting in battalions led by "sincere" Afghan Taliban, i.e., those who refused to be "cajoled into compromising God's religion." The attack on the U.S. Bagram Air Base in May 2010 is mentioned as a joint operation, with the group led by Siraj Haqqani of the Taliban. The letters report that one of al-Qaeda's men, Abu Talha al-Almani, was "martyred" during the operation. Abu Talha was a German convert who had joined al-Qaeda in 2006 or 2007 on condition that he would be assigned a "martyrdom operation." The leaders of al-Qaeda saw in him a great candidate for international terrorism,[5] and "tried their best to put off his martyrdom." But they ultimately changed their minds. According to one letter, "the man's desire to achieve martyrdom reached a very high level that could not be stopped."[6] Abu Talha had been married to another German convert, Elisabeth Anna Windischmann, who was equally zealous. One of the letters recovered by the SEALs was by Elisabeth, who described herself as an orphan, "not because my parents are dead, but because they are infidels." She beseeched Usama, whom she considered to be "like a father to me": "If you want to remind people of God's Message, repeat the 9/11 attacks. May God grant you success."[7]

Al-Qaeda's leaders, operatives, cadres, and their families were hiding in the FATA.[8] The letters reveal that they were all "confined to North Waziristan,"[9] and indicate that they had training facilities in the area, mainly in "explosives."

The area was by no means a safe zone for al-Qaeda, but it was a stronghold for militants, local and foreign, opposed to the Pakistani state. Al-Qaeda's leaders also counted on the loyalty of "brothers" in the provinces of Sindh and Baluchistan,[10] where some Arab widows and children lived. Also, women in Waziristan could seek medical treatments there, mostly in the city of Karachi, in Sindh.

Elsewhere in Pakistan, al-Qaeda was highly constrained. We discovered in previous chapters that when Usama proposed to set up an al-Qaeda branch "to recruit personnel to carry out work [i.e., terrorism] both inside and outside Pakistan,"[11] his associates thought it was impossible. But when, in July 2007, Pakistani troops besieged and then stormed the Lal Masjid (Red Mosque) in Islamabad, resulting in the deaths of 100 people, Usama saw an opportunity to rally Pakistanis in support of al-Qaeda. It is reported that the mosque and its adjacent seminaries had served as a center of "radical Islamic learning," and when Pakistan's President, Pervez Musharraf, lent his support to the "war on terror" in 2001, the Lal Masjid was "the center of calls for his assassination."[12]

Within a month of the bloody siege, Usama released a public statement calling "on Muslims in Pakistan to take up jihad to rid themselves of Pervez, his government, his army, and all those who support him."[13] Usama's call soon backfired when militant Pakistani groups mounted terrorist attacks that targeted civilians indiscriminately. Atiya urged Usama to moderate his rhetoric:

If only, our dear Sheikh, you could clarify the issue of jihad in Pakistan and how it fits into our policy and strategy. Since your public statement calling on Pakistanis to rebel and to take up jihad against the apostate Pervez government, etc., a new situation has surely arisen. In my view, this requires more precision and clarification. The Pakistani brothers who are with us are asking a lot about this, and also relayed to us the concerns of other Pakistani elites, Islamists, and others.[14]

Atiya wanted Usama to convey publicly that "we only fight Pakistan because it is a tailpiece and a helper to the Americans."[15]

Al-Qaeda's leader in Af-Pak, Hajji Uthman, also recognized that al-Qaeda must differentiate itself from others operating in Pakistan:

> The Pakistani brothers who joined us advised us to have an official spokesman in Pakistan. They recommend that we should make clear what the objective of our work [i.e., attacks] is inside Pakistan, claim responsibility for the attacks that we carry out, and make it known which attacks are not our responsibility. The latter are exploited by enemies to alienate Muslims from supporting us.[16]

It appears that by 2008, the number of Pakistani "brothers" operating under the command of al-Qaeda had grown. Hajji Uthman proudly informed Usama that the Pakistani group headed by Ilyas Kashmiri "is considered to be one of the largest groups with us," and that Ilyas "always sends his regards to you."[17]

Ilyas is widely credited for terrorism in India,[18] including being tied to the 2008 Mumbai attacks that left 166 people dead.[19] And yet, the Bin Laden Papers reveal that, as late as 2010, Ilyas was still itching "to work inside India." He desperately wanted "to pull the rug from under those who do [so-called] jihad to benefit Pakistani intelligence" and "to demonstrate to the *umma* what is the true duty of those who are doing jihad."[20]

Others who flocked to work with al-Qaeda included "a group that counts a [medical] doctor among its members." Hajji Uthman reports that "this doctor also studied strategy and planning and has a good vision on how to operate inside Pakistan." He and others in al-Qaeda met with the doctor several times, and "we asked him to write down his vision."[21] The Pakistani doctor responded with an essay entitled "Jihad in Pakistan," contending that jihad is necessary because:

> 1. Pakistan played a principal role in the fall of the Islamic Emirate in Afghanistan.
> 2. The Pakistani regime arrested nearly 800 foreign jihadis and handed them over to America. . . .

3. When the tribal Pakistani areas welcomed the jihadis, Pakistani forces launched military operations in those areas to eliminate them.

Pakistan had engendered conditions that "severely weakened" jihadis, preventing the people of Pakistan from being "mentally prepared to take up jihad." The doctor proposed a strategy that focused on strengthening the "tribal belt" in the FATA and on unifying the jihadis:

Despite the dominance of the British, they could not control the FATA like they did other regions in Pakistan. . . . [But] Pakistani jihadis, of all levels—be they Taliban in the local tribal areas, jihadi groups or organizations outside those areas—lack a unified and clear theory of war. They are all intellectually divided. Even members of the same entity have different views about current events and espouse divergent visions of the enemy. . . . That is why it is necessary for the jihadi leadership to put together a clear theory of war. It should then bring together all the Pakistani groups and the local Taliban leaders and engage in long deliberations with them. And if the leaders of all Pakistani jihadi groups begin to see eye to eye on political conditions, and agree on a common program, more than half of our mission will have been accomplished.[22]

The doctor's vision seems to have influenced al-Qaeda. In June 2008, a delegation went on a ten-day trip "to forge ties with the leaders of jihad" in the districts of Kurram, Orakzai, and Khyber in the FATA. The trip was facilitated by a certain "Mullah Abd al-Manan." If this was the same Mullah Abd al-Manan who was Afghan Taliban military chief for the southern Helmand province,[23] he probably lent al-Qaeda some of his contacts in the FATA.

The internal report that sums up the trip reveals that, in the FATA, al-Qaeda was in contact with thirty-six important "personalities," who are identified by numbers (e.g., "Personality 1," etc.).[24] Fortunately, the SEALs recovered a separate document that lists all thirty-six corresponding names.[25] We learn that al-Qaeda wanted to assess the jihadi commitment of these "personalities" and determine if they were prepared "to receive us in their areas—as families or individuals—and to allow us to establish some training centers." The trip also allowed the delegation "to get to know the road well" to these districts, and to identify the side roads to avoid checkpoints on the way from Mir Ali in North Waziristan.

In all likelihood, all the "personalities" they met were local tribal leaders, some of whom had units fighting in Afghanistan. One whom they met in Kurram was Hajji Mahmoud, who appeared to be among the keenest supporters of al-Qaeda in the area. He stood out because one of his sons, Mawlawi Mehboub, used to study in the Lal Masjid and "harbors a lot of enmity against Pakistan." In the "rugged, mountainous" Orakzai, where the delegation gazed at the "breathtaking views," they also met several commanders who expressed their willingness "to prepare houses to receive" al-Qaeda. Khyber was less promising, and the report reveals that "we did not find a single sincere commander [there] with whom we could forge ties." Some of the "personalities" in that district were suspected of "receiving aid supervised by the Americans," while others were believed to have ties with the Pakistani government.

Though it was reported that the leaders of the TTP were "loosely in control of more than 30 militant groups operating in Pakistan's north-west,"[26] al-Qaeda did not view matters this way. The report noted: "The people in Kurram and Orazkai were particularly bothered by the conduct of Baitullah and his group led by a young man called Hakim. The latter is vulgar and has no clue about God's religion, not even about the most basic matters." This is a reference to the TTP leader, Baitullah Mehsud, and his second-in-command, Hakimullah, whom we will meet again later in this chapter.

Ultimately, the trip was not productive for al-Qaeda. The report concludes that though "much progress has been made" in those areas, "caution is necessary." The delegation observed that "people in those areas were not as fearful as they once were" and "jihadis are noticeably visible," but surmised that they wouldn't put up a fight if the Pakistani government were to attack. People in the two districts, the report concludes, "are not like the Waziris" with regard to their willingness to fight and endure hardship. The report expressed additional concerns. Some of the people in the region were divided along rigid theological lines. Also, "some of them cultivate cannabis, and some even cultivate opium." The report warns that "whoever moves to this area must have a solid legal understanding of this matter."[27]

It does not appear that al-Qaeda ended up moving any of its members to these districts. Thus, al-Qaeda militants remained confined to North Waziristan, which may have made it easier for the CIA to hunt them down.

The Pakistani State Problem

Steve Coll reports that, in 2002, Pakistan's President, Pervez Musharraf, agreed to allow the CIA to fly drones over the FATA on condition he received "precision weapons and night operating capabilities" from the Bush Administration.[28] This arrangement permitted the CIA to track down al-Qaeda militants, and by extension served Pakistan in its war against local militants in the FATA. It bore fruit for Musharraf when the first reported CIA drone attack in 2004 killed Nek Muhammad, who had been fighting the Pakistani military.[29] Pakistan was also conducting its own military operations in the FATA, and according to Islamabad's Institute of Strategic Studies, the Pakistani army launched "at least five major military operations between 2001–2010."[30]

Bob Woodward's 2010 book, *Obama's Wars*, reports that the CIA "stepped-up Predator drone strikes on al Qaeda leaders and specific camps" in 2008.[31] We glean from the letters that around the same time al-Qaeda was under growing pressure in the FATA. The letters reaching Usama were increasingly reporting the "martyrdom of brothers" as a result of "spying attacks" (*darabat bi-al-jasusiyya*), that is, drone strikes that hit their targets through the help of local spies.[32]

The letters make clear that al-Qaeda believed that the spies were on the CIA's payroll and were recruited by Pakistani intelligence. In December 2008, al-Qaeda set up a Security Committee to find ways to counter the drones. It consisted of eight people—four Arabs and four non-Arabs. It was headed by a certain Abu al-Wafa, who had served in the Saudi Army before joining al-Qaeda. His deputy, al-Zubayr al-Maghrebi, had previously been a member of the Libyan Fighting Group, and joined the Committee in 2009 after his release from Iran.[33]

From the outset, the Committee recognized, as the internal report put it, that "our war with the enemy is an intelligence war, not a military one." Its members advised that "our intelligence capabilities must be commensurate with the weight of the global war waged against us."[34] To that end, the Committee developed an elaborate framework for its work to cover: (1) intelligence gathering; (2) recruiting and training security personnel; (3) combating spies through surveillance, interrogations, and arrests; (4) countering the "enemy's" (i.e., CIA's) narrative/propaganda; and (5) assassinations. The non-Arabs on the Committee "worked mostly to combat spies through arrests, interrogation, and imprisonment."[35]

When members of the Committee took their proposal to Hajji Uthman, he initially allocated a mere 40,000 rupees (around $480) to cover their work. "This sum is not sufficient to feed the personnel associated with the Committee," they protested. He increased the budget to 50,000 rupees and instructed them to focus on combating spies, insisting that al-Qaeda could not afford to spend more. Other letters by Hajji Uthman confirm that al-Qaeda was struggling financially at the time. In fact, al-Qaeda's finances had dwindled to the point that he had "to apologize for not giving permission to brothers who wanted to get married." (Married fighters received an extra stipend, and when they died, al-Qaeda supported their widows and children.)[36] Members of the Security Committee made it clear to Hajji Uthman that the elements of their proposal were interrelated, and that they could not proceed until all were funded. Eventually, the budget was increased to 200,000 rupees ($2,380).

Al-Qaeda needed Pakistan to ease its pressure in the FATA. To that end, in September 2008, it kidnapped an Afghan diplomat shortly after he had been nominated as ambassador to Pakistan. It is reported that the $5 million ransom that al-Qaeda received came from an Afghan government fund that received monthly payments from the CIA.[37] This might explain the additional funds al-Qaeda's Security Committee received.

Al-Qaeda also launched a media offensive against the Pakistani state. In May 2009, Usama called on Pakistanis to unite against their new President, Asif Ali Zardari, who maintained his predecessor's military campaigns in the FATA. He accused him of taking his orders from President Obama and of launching a war against his own people. Usama called on

Muslims everywhere in Pakistan to unite and defy Zardari and his army, for he threatens their religion, security, unity, and economy. They should continue to work together to get rid of him and bring him to justice. The great harm that Pakistan suffered at the hands of Pervez notwithstanding, the harm that Zardari is causing is even greater given how he is carrying out America's demands in Pakistan. . . . The only way to put an end to his sedition and that of his army is through jihad in the path of God.[38]

A month later, Ayman assailed Pakistan's entire ruling establishment. "The American-Crusader is playing with Pakistan's destiny," he said, and "the only hope to save it from this catastrophic fate is jihad":

The current ruling class in Pakistan aligns itself under the cross of the contemporary Crusader campaign and competes for American bribes. That is why the true ruler of Pakistan is the American ambassador, who pays the bribes and issues orders. That is also why he expects the Pakistani ruling class to fight Muslims and jihadis and to sacrifice Pakistan and the soul and dignity of its people to achieve America's greedy and disgusting objectives.[39]

Usama and Ayman's campaign had no impact on Pakistan's policy in the FATA. The drones were unrelenting, and al-Qaeda continued to lose "brothers" by the dozen.[40] In May 2010, al-Qaeda's Af-Pak leader, Hajji Uthman, was killed in a drone strike, along "with his Egyptian wife, three of his girls, and his granddaughter."

What was al-Qaeda to do? Usama had reached the decision that it should focus all its capabilities on attacking "the Americans," as we shall see in the next chapter, and was prepared to make a truce (*muhadana*) with Pakistan. In June 2010, Atiya reported that he had sent messages to the Pakistani authorities through intermediaries to inform them:

Our war is against the Americans in Afghanistan. If the Pakistani govern-ment and its army leave us alone, we will do the same. Otherwise, if they continue to attack us and support the Americans in their drone war against us, they shall suffer attacks that will shock them in Islamabad, Bindi, and other areas.[41]

Pakistan's ISI did not respond. Soon after, Atiya disclosed:

We leaked information (through Siraj Haqqani and with the help of some of the Mehsud brothers and others) that al-Qaeda, and also the TTP, are preparing large-scale seismic operations inside Pakistan. Al-Qaeda's leader-ship, however, stopped them in an effort to calm the situation with Pakistan. However, if Pakistan were to launch military attacks in Waziristan, the operations would be carried out. They are large-scale attacks, ready to hit the heart of Pakistan![42]

It is clear from the letters that al-Qaeda did not have any concrete plans to carry out such attacks. But according to Atiya, this time the threats drew an indirect response from the ISI:

In the wake of this, Pakistan's intelligence agency contacted us through the so-called Pakistani "jihadi" group of which they approve, Harakat al-Muja-hidin, led by Fadl al-Rahman Khalil. Their messenger informed us that the leaders of the ISI, such as Shuja Shah [ISI general], want to talk to us directly.[43]

The "brothers" who met with the ISI messenger reiterated al-Qaeda's commitment to a truce with Pakistan. Three weeks later, the ISI sent the same messenger again. "What is most interesting this time," Atiya remarked, is that he was "accompanied by Hamid Gul," a former ISI general, who reportedly had ties with al-Qaeda before 9/11:[44]

> He attended along with Fadl al-Rahman Khalil as an advisor! They told us: Give us some time, a month or two. We are currently trying to convince and pressure the Americans to negotiate with al-Qaeda. We are trying to persuade them that negotiating with the [Afghan] Taliban without including al-Qaeda is useless. Because we, the Pakistanis, don't object to negotiating with you.[45]

We don't know if Hamid Gul and Fadl al-Rahman were in fact representing the ISI. At any rate, Atiya reported that "the brothers on our side told them that we shall let our leadership know. That's all."[46] Atiya himself wasn't convinced of the ISI's sincerity. "As you can tell," he wrote to Usama, "it's nothing more than mere talk!!" and he surmised that "the Pakistanis are playing tricks on us."[47]

The TTP Problem

While al-Qaeda was sending out conciliatory messages to the ISI, the TTP were mounting terrorist attacks in different parts of Pakistan. Their leader, Baitullah Mehsud, was killed in a drone strike in August 2009, and his successor was none other than Hakimullah—the "vulgar" man who "has no clue about God's religion"—whom we met earlier in this chapter.

Judging by the letters, the TTP were out of control, giving Pakistan more reasons to maintain its pressure in the FATA. Under Hakimullah's leadership, the group launched attacks that targeted mosques and other public places throughout Pakistan, shedding the blood of hundreds of Muslim civilians. In a passionate letter to his leaders, the American convert and al-Qaeda media advisor Adam Gadahn wrote of the "embedded ignorance" in the TTP's ranks and enumerated a long list of the group's "unlawful" attacks. Writing in excellent Arabic, Gadahn urged his leaders to take a public stance to put an end to the TTP's campaign of bloodshed.[48]

Rather than toning down their attacks, the TTP took steps to go global. On May 1, 2010, without first consulting al-Qaeda, the TTP attempted an attack on New York City. The assailant, Faisal Shahzad, parked a car loaded with explosives in Times Square but, fortunately for New Yorkers, could not detonate it. He was arrested two days later at John F. Kennedy International Airport while attempting to flee to Dubai.

Usama watched the trial and was underwhelmed by Faisal's understanding of Islamic teachings. Faisal had become a citizen of the United States, which meant that he had sworn an oath to defend the Constitution and laws of the United States during his naturalization ceremony. When asked about his oath during his trial, Faisal brazenly responded that he had lied. This infuriated Usama, who wrote to Atiya:

> It does not escape you that Faisal's lie amounts to betrayal (*ghadr*) and does not fall under permissible lying to [evade] the enemy [in wartime]. Perhaps the brother does not understand this Islamic legal matter or was confused. Please ask our Pakistani Taliban brothers to address this matter in a public statement that makes it clear that *ghadr* is unlawful. . . . Also draw their attention to the fact that brother Faisal Shahzad appeared in a photograph alongside Commander Hakimullah Mehsud. I would like to verify whether Mehsud knew that when a person acquires an American citizenship, he takes an oath and swears not to harm America. He should be informed of the matter, in case he is unaware. The negative consequences of this issue are known to you. [We must therefore act swiftly] to remove the suspicion that jihadis violate their oaths and engage in *ghadr*.[49]

To be clear, Usama was not objecting to attacks in the United States. Far from it. But he distinguished between tricking the enemy in wartime and violating one's oath. The former is permissible in Islamic law, but not the latter. Usama noted in his letters that he wanted attacks in the United States to be

carried out either by Muslims born in the United States or those visiting on a
U.S. visa—i.e., those who had not taken the oath of citizenship.

The TTP's *ghadr* was just one of their many unlawful acts in the eyes of
al-Qaeda. Atiya and Abu Yahya al-Libi, al-Qaeda's legal scholars, threatened
Hakimullah that al-Qaeda was going to dissociate itself publicly from the TTP
unless they changed their ways.[50] In a joint letter, they explained that his group's
indiscriminate attacks did not qualify as *tatarrus*—i.e., when collateral damage
is deemed lawful under special circumstances—and pointed out the numerous
Islamic legal mistakes in the TTP charter that Hakimullah had drafted. The
charter declared that Hakimullah was "the sole leader (*amir*)," and anyone who
did not pledge allegiance to him would be considered a rebel (*baghi*) who should
be fought. Atiya and Abu Yahya pointed to the pretentiousness of such a claim,
which, in their words, "neglected to differentiate between the position of a
leader of jihad and that of the great Imam," i.e., the leader of the global community of Muslims (*umma*).[51]

Hakimullah seems to have been just as unhappy with al-Qaeda. We glean
from the letters that he spread rumors that members of al-Qaeda were "guests"
in Waziristan. He probably did so either to cut al-Qaeda down to size or out of
religious ignorance, or both. Atiya and Abu Yahya bluntly stated:

> We should like to clarify to you that we, in al-Qaeda, are a global jihadi
> Islamic organization. We are not bound by a nation or race, and we, in
> Afghanistan, have given our allegiance to the mujahid and Commander of
> the Faithful, Mullah Omar, the leader of the Islamic Emirate of Afghanistan.
> We are authorized by the Commander of the Faithful to carry out general
> jihad. It has reached us that some people are referring to us as guests in some
> political contexts. We should like to make it known to you that such a desig-
> nation has no basis in Islamic law. Rather, believers are brothers in religion.[52]

In light of the letters, we might surmise that the TTP's conduct compounded
al-Qaeda's losses to the drones, particularly if Pakistan was indeed supporting
the CIA by infiltrating the area with spies, as al-Qaeda believed. Ironically, it

was probably due to the TTP's ambitions to mount international attacks from the FATA that led some to conclude, erroneously it turned out, that al-Qaeda's operational capabilities had endured.

The Spies–Drones Nexus

We learn from the Security Committee's May 2010 report that, despite its limited budget, much had been accomplished by its members:

> We managed to dismantle and destroy many of the spying networks. We were also able to uncover the enemy's plans, its methods of recruiting spies, and how it conducts its espionage. About thirty to forty spies were killed. We were able to put together a network to connect information between most of the groups present in the area, and intelligence was shared in an effective way. We have also gained the trust of many people. . . . Had the financial support been sufficient or at least comparable to the military budget, we would have had a greater effect and accomplished more because the work of intelligence is intertwined with social reform, with bringing people together and gaining their trust.[53]

More of the Committee's specific findings are included in Atiya's letter to the leaders of jihadi groups in Yemen and Somalia.[54] To avoid repeating the "bitter" experience of al-Qaeda in North Waziristan, he shared in great detail the Security Committee's findings:

> —The bombing of this evil [spying aircraft] is very precise.
> —In general, the drones are not meant to miss their targets. Still, they made some rare mistakes here [i.e., North Waziristan].
> —This evil cannot do anything without "eyes" on the ground, and that is the human element.
> —That is why they [i.e., the CIA] need time to build a network of spies on the ground. The length of time depends on the reality with which they are

dealing. They do so in collaboration with the local apostate regime [i.e., Pakistani intelligence in the case of North Waziristan], which serves as the [CIA's] agent and collaborator.

—To this end, they spend large amounts of money. Their *modus operandi* is to throw dollars at purchasing people's loyalties.

—The types of candidates who would play the role of spies (network leaders and despicable associates who sell their loyalties) should generally be known to you in your social setting. . . .

—The work of this evil [i.e., drones] relies on identifying the target by means of human collaborators on the ground. They use a variety of tools, we call them *shariha*, consisting of an electronic ringlet/circle. We believe that it is simple. It relies on disseminating either specific proper waves or specific rays (light) below infrared or above it. . . . It is possible that they rely on another tool, a liquescent indicator, consisting of a phosphoric or similar color that the collaborator places on the roofs of houses, cars, or the like, and it is possible that they use GPS to identify the coordinates of the target. They may rely on identifying the target by way of taking images (similar to Google Images), or something else. But for this to happen there must be a collaborator on the ground (spy) who would inform them either by phone or other communication method that their target (the individual or individuals) is at the location where the sign was placed (depending on the tools we just enumerated).

—The drone missiles are small but powerful, but do not penetrate the ground or sturdy barriers. That is why ditches are effective, God willing.

—But they may use larger missiles if they know that the real target is hiding in a place that could not be reached by a small missile. Their missiles range in sizes.

—All drone types emit a unique sound. A drone can therefore be distinguished by its sound at night and/or during the day, as we have come to learn.

—Based on our numerous experiences, a single drone does not carry out a bombing (it is as if it does not have the capacity to do so). Rather, when the drones intend to strike, they usually have several of them roaming in the area, all close to each other. It is as if some of them identify the target from different angles for precision, while others deliver the missile.

—That is why if you happen to see three of them in close range of each other roaming in an area, know that they are about to hit a specific target. At this point, it is necessary to take decisive security measures to resist them: Leave the area or change your location—even if only slightly, by entering ditches that have been secretly dug in advance for this purpose— and cancel all meetings to avoid any gatherings.[55]

Atiya's points about surveillance, reconnaissance, and precision airstrikes corroborate publicly available information. U.S. government websites describe a drone as an "Unmanned Aerial Vehicle" that is "remotely piloted," allowing the remote pilot/operator to access imagery thousands of miles away in real time and to execute targets in those distant places. The family of drones includes the RQ-1 Predator, designed to provide the remote pilot with "surveillance and reconnaissance" in real time; the MQ-1 Predator is similar, but has the additional capability of being used for "armed reconnaissance and interdiction," meaning that it carries a missile that can be used to "execute targets"; and the MQ-9 Reaper Hunter/Killer UAV is designed "for precision airstrikes," meaning that it has the more sophisticated capability to "perform strike, coordination, and reconnaissance against high-value, fleeting, and time-sensitive targets."[56] Understandably, the role of spies does not feature in government literature, but it is alluded to by some analysts.[57]

The drones were roaming almost constantly over North Waziristan, and al-Qaeda was clearly overwhelmed. Usama was alarmed by "the cumulative [reconnaissance] data the Americans have been collecting of the area over the years." He warned Ayman of the danger of individuals visiting the same house, not just by car but also on foot, "for the Americans are capable of discerning that men are frequenting a specific house more than usual."[58] He advised Atiya that he and the "brothers" should plan to hide over the long haul and to arrange for a regular supply of food:

Rather than storing wheat, it is my opinion that you should find two capable local brothers who have a knack for trade. Better still, they should already work in this domain. You would ask them to include trading in wheat, sugar, legumes, and similar essential nutrients in their commercial activities. They would need to have a solid and durable storehouse resistant to water infiltration. It should be located away from rivers and above the valleys so that it is not vulnerable to floods. You would contribute to their trade through buying the food quantities you and the brothers need, knowing that this should include reserves for at least one year. The stockpile should be replaced with fresh products on a regular basis, and you would have an understanding with the trading brothers that, in the event of a crisis, they would sell exclusively to al-Qaeda. . . . The storehouse should be located in an area that would permit moving the wheat to the brothers when necessary.

Atiya had suggested amassing a stockpile of food instead, but Usama thought that it would be difficult to move the food if they needed to relocate. But if this was the most convenient way, Usama suggested

buying clean barrels with sturdy lids—ones that would have been used to store food, such as fizzy drinks or vegetable oils, but not chemicals. The barrels would need to be washed then dried in the sun for a day. The lids of such barrels must have a rubber ring to prevent air infiltration. This allows legumes to last for seven years if they are stored the same year they were produced, and if they are clean of mites, insects, and the like.[59]

Bob Woodward's book *Obama's Wars* was published in September 2010, and it covered the evolution of the CIA drone campaign under the Bush and Obama administrations.[60] Excerpts from it are cited in a letter that reached Usama. Most alarming for al-Qaeda was the information Woodward reported about some 150 Taliban training facilities that the CIA had identified in the FATA. Al-Qaeda was also concerned about the ties that Woodward reported between the ISI and the Haqqanis, who feature in the letters as trusted partners of al-Qaeda.[61]

After reading Woodward's account, Usama gave up on the FATA altogether. "It appears to me that the area is highly exposed," he wrote to Atiya, and suggested that "the best solution is to evacuate the area altogether." He proposed moving all the "brothers" to other cities in Pakistan, to be housed away from the densely populated areas with trustworthy security guards—much like his own arrangement in Abbottabad. He also wanted Atiya to counsel the Taliban about their movements, and let them know that their training camps had been exposed.[62]

In late January 2011, Atiya informed Usama that the men preferred to die in the FATA rather than risk moving to cities where they could be captured by the ISI. Atiya was resigned to the fact that the only remaining option was to endeavor to hide as much as possible. As to the TTP, Atiya despaired:

> We counsel them a lot, but they are like the Afghans, they do not care much. To be fair, they are not all the same, some of them care and are eager to develop and learn, while others don't. Overall, all of them are now targets [i.e., of the drones], and they understand that the enemy is targeting everyone. Many of their fighters and commandants have been killed. The [bitter] reality teaches best![63]

Atiya describes an intractable problem. North Waziristan is "crowded with groups, and our control over their affairs is limited," and "our familial burden weighs upon us." He meant that the men could not freely move to safe zones because they had to ensure the safe movements of their families. Al-Qaeda's future looked bleak:

> It is inevitable that we shall endure great suffering, and many of us will be killed, because the jihadis in the area are conspicuous, visible, and their movements in the open are excessive. As a result, we have become an organization that is almost 90 percent overt. This is undoubtedly unhelpful in

such an environment, in view of the regional and international conditions against us!! The numbers are large, much greater than this arena can absorb. The political, economic, security, and administrative environment cannot handle such numbers (add to all this the effort required to advance those people, educate them, cultivate them, edify them). The large number of *muhajirun* [i.e., foreign fighters] simply cannot be demographically or socially absorbed. It is not just us Arabs who are present in this arena, others are present in much greater numbers, e.g., Turks, Uzbeks, those of Russian stock (Bulgarians, Azerbaijanis, Dagestanis, etc.). This kind of presence is unorganized, lacking in forethought and proper control, and everyone tries to influence everyone else. Our affairs suffer from a signifi-cant degree of chaos, and we shall not be able to improve our conditions at all. This is my opinion, in brief. . . . That is why, not long ago, I advised that we change our discourse concerning mobilizing people [to join the jihad].[64]

Atiya had indeed written on this issue when he responded to questions that were posted online under the heading "Responses Concerning the Departure for Jihad" (*ajwiba fi al-nafir*). He delicately stated that Afghanistan needed no additional fighters, and Muslims would do better to send money to support jihadis who were already there. But if their jihad calling was irresistible, Atiya added, then they should head to arenas other than Afghanistan, such as Somalia.

Drones: The Insurmountable Challenge

Judging by the Security Committee's findings, countering the drones was not just feasible, but simple. It required jihadis to comply with security measures, i.e., to hide when the drones were roaming above the area, and to be watchful and limited in their movements to evade spies. Yet the Committee's report painted a despairing picture. Its members determined that all the deaths could have been easily prevented had the "brothers" complied with basic security measures. Instead, they kept repeating the same mistakes that had become familiar to all, such as "leaving the car without a guard," or "the Arab brother decides to take his car to the mechanics himself" instead of via his security guard.[65]

These measures did indeed seem feasible, so why did they prove impossible to implement?

Jihad vs Kumun

The drones presented an ideological challenge for the jihadis, and those who oversaw the work of al-Qaeda's Security Committee were mindful of that. Four out of eighteen pages of the Committee's report are devoted to a legal justification of their work, highlighting verses in the Qur'an that stress the importance of "security" (e.g., 2:126; 106:4), the virtue of "watchfulness" (e.g., 4:71, 102), and contending that watchfulness goes hand in hand with departing for jihad (*nafir*).

Notwithstanding the report's rich Qur'anic citations, the security measures the Committee sought to enforce are alien to jihadi culture. For decades, jihadi leaders and ideologues have reminded Muslims of the religious obligation of fighting/jihad and condemned those who neglect it. Thus, regardless of their differences, all jihadis believe that they have a covenant with God, they fight (*qital*) to make God's Word supreme on earth and, in return, God rewards them with eternal life in Paradise (Qur'an 9:112).

How could jihadis reconcile the obligation to fight with the necessity to hide? Al-Qaeda militants were facing an *unmanned* enemy that *watched* them from the sky, tracking them far away from the battlefield, and recording their routine daily movements, interminably if necessary. Once the intended target was identified, a missile followed, rarely missing. The predator they were facing necessitated hiding, and not fighting. This was hardly the kind of action promoted by the ideological literature that motivated them to join the jihad in the first place. This shift did not just disorient ordinary jihadis, it unsettled their leaders too. The Committee's report notes that many leaders set a bad example, refusing to comply with sensible security measures. "It is a malady for which we have not found a cure," the authors of the report bemoaned.

The Spying Dilemma

The challenge of hiding instead of fighting was compounded by another ideological impasse, namely spying. Though the jihadis' enemy was unmanned, it saw them through the "eyes" of spies, i.e., those who posed as their friends and allies on the ground. On the theoretical front, it was easy to condemn spies, since spying is unlawful in Islam and even intruding on fellow Muslims' privacy is censured.[66] In 2009, al-Qaeda's legal scholar-in-residence, Abu Yahya al-Libi, published a treatise about spying in Islamic law. Drawing on what constitutes a spy (sing. *jasus*; pl. *jawasis*) in the Qur'an (cf. 49:12), Abu Yahya highlighted God's punishment that awaits them (cf. 22:19–22; 14:15–17), and the importance of combating them to protect jihadis.[67] Ayman wrote the Foreword to the treatise, endlessly praising Abu Yahya's erudition concerning the "calamity" (*al-nazila*) that had befallen jihadis.

But at the practical level, spying posed a problem of a different order. How could the Security Committee counter espionage effectively without intruding on fellow Muslims' privacy? Not surprisingly, members of the Committee were themselves accused of spying, which adversely affected their work. For instance, some leaders did not respond to the Committee's requests for information, and some jihadi groups even warned their members against working with al-Qaeda. Though the leader of the Committee was noted for his good relations with Waziri groups, important information was kept from him. For example, the report notes that al-Qaeda had no prior knowledge of Abu Dujana al-Khurasani's operation that killed seven CIA officers.[68]

The perception that al-Qaeda was spying also engendered what might be considered a psychological problem for jihadis. Many of them joined the jihad to rebel against their rulers whom they deemed to be tyrants (*tughat*), and the jihadi ideological literature incessantly calls on Muslims to fight against the policing regimes that persecute and spy on them, even in their mosques. This must have been a charge the Security Committee faced on a regular basis, and its report takes pains to differentiate al-Qaeda's work from that carried out by tyrants:

Our surveillance is the opposite of that carried out by tyrants. While they destroy, we build. While they violate God's Word, we obey Him. The tyrants' surveillance is farthest from God's wishes, ours is intended to bring us closer to God. Their surveillance covers the believer and the infidel, our surveillance is limited to the infidel enemy and his collaborators.[69]

The defensive tone is sufficient to explain why the drones turned out to be a "calamity" that confounded al-Qaeda and its members. The Committee had no hope that jihadis would change their ways and adopt the necessary security measures, and bemoaned the lack of funds that prevented al-Qaeda from outbidding the CIA to buy/gain the loyalty of the locals: "That is why money is important so that we could enrich people with what is lawful, [drawing them] away from that which is unlawful, and this is the most annihilating weapon against the enemy. We have succeeded in spreading and countering the enemy's rumors only partially, given our limited budget."[70] Al-Qaeda's Security Committee was losing the intelligence war because it did not have the CIA's money to cheat or, in its own parlance, to "enrich people with what is lawful."

Whither Jihad?

The U.S. response to the 9/11 attacks put an end to the ability of Usama and his al-Qaeda to mount international terrorism.[71] Though Usama rebuilt his organization after he reconnected with his associates in 2004, outside the Af-Pak region al-Qaeda did not "reactivate the work that had been halted" after the fall of the Taliban.[72] In short, when the drone missions were stepped up over the FATA, al-Qaeda's "afflictions" gave way to "calamities."

Distant from his organization, Usama lacked empathy. Though he repeatedly counseled his associates to hide, he couldn't quite fathom his group's operational impotence. In 2009, while the drones were overwhelming al-Qaeda in North Waziristan, he complained about "the weakness of the brother in charge of external work," and suggested that Atiya should "replace him." Hajji Uthman advised against it, and Atiya noted the "difficult conditions" that prevented the group from pursuing its "work." Atiya promised that he would personally "follow up on the work, and endeavor to encourage and advise the brother through ongoing consultation and reflections,"[73] and consoled Usama:

> On the research and planning front, the brothers have manufactured materials that could pass through airport security and gates undetected (explosive materials that are hidden in specific ways). These materials have been successfully produced, and we will soon be moving to the trial phase, and we hope to transport some of the materials to Europe. Early experiments are promising and positive. May God grant us success.[74]

Atiya was likely referring to the August 2006 attempted plot to use liquid bombs to blow up several transatlantic airliners, and was hopeful that al-Qaeda could develop such materials. Al-Qaeda's "research and planning" failed to graduate to the implementation stage. As al-Qaeda pursued its "research," other jihadi groups in the FATA were clearly ahead of them. Within a month of Atiya's letter, a plot to bomb the New York City subway system using hydrogen peroxide and acetone products was foiled. According to the FBI, Najibullah Zazi, who pleaded guilty for planning the attacks, had received "detailed bomb-making instructions in Pakistan."[75] It is clear from the letters that the leaders of al-Qaeda in the FATA were wary of partnering with enthusiasts who "lacked focus" to conduct international terrorism. For example, we learn that Atiya and Ayman refused to fund Muhannad al-Abyani (referred to as "brother Tufan") whose seven-page manifesto, entitled "Terrorize Them" *(arhibuhum)*, consists of rambling sentences that reflect his lust to shed blood indiscriminately. Without proposing any methodology, his plans called for "killing thousands of Americans and Europeans" using a kitchen sink approach that included "HHO bombs," "cyanide," and "hydrogen peroxide synthesis." It appears that "brother Tufan" also fancied himself to be knowledgeable in medicine and when he started writing about the inflammation of the spleen, Ayman—a physician by training—could not resist telling him that even butchers and cooks have more intelligent things to say about this abdominal organ. When Usama reviewed

Tufan's credentials, he briefly and categorically noted that "with respect to working [i.e., attacking] inside America, brother Tufan is not suitable."[76]

In January 2010, Hajji Uthman found himself having to spell out the problem to Usama, as if he were explaining it to a new recruit:

> External work [i.e., international terrorism] is undoubtedly very important. But it is also the case that the phase we're going through is different. Though we have not succeeded in mounting a special attack during the past few years, we are nevertheless achieving our objective, namely: terrorizing and deterring the enemy, and engaging them in a war of attrition. Indeed, the enemy are spending much money on their security and are terrorized on an ongoing basis. They do not feel secure at all, they admit this and are certain of it. . . . The lack of success in carrying out external work—meaning the success of large attacks, or even small ones, in the enemy's territory—can be attributed to many reasons, including individuals as well as our circumstances, which do not permit us to spend money on external or internal work. What I am trying to say is that we are advancing, even if we do not succeed in carrying out a specific attack, because we are succeeding overall.[77]

It is likely that Usama did not agree that achieving nothing constituted overall success. The drones continued to overwhelm al-Qaeda and, in June 2010, Atiya reported that the group's main objective was to survive.[78] Circumstances did not improve and, in late 2010, Atiya wrote that "we purchased some explosives, and we put together some simple plans," but "our situation is difficult, because of a severe shortage in our cadres, and the spies are like a pandemic in our area, may God help us."[79]

As we shall discover in the following chapter, Usama did not give up on his goals. During his final year, while the drones were raining devastation on his organization, Usama was planning for the future. He decided to move some of his more promising operatives outside the FATA, and drafted plans for operations "the effects of which far exceed the 9/11 attacks" against "the Americans."

"THE AMERICANS"

We want to force the enemy to end his aggression and fighting against us. God willing, this would be achieved by focusing on the leaders of kufr *(infidel), namely America. It is well known that in America, power and authority are of the people and by the people, represented by Congress and the White House. It is necessary to focus our fighting on the American people and their representatives.*

Letter from Usama bin Laden to Hajji Uthman and Atiya, 2010[1]

In late 2009, around the time Usama bin Laden was complaining about his group's operational impotence, an energetic young member of al-Qaeda, Younis al-Mauritani, wrote to Ayman al-Zawahiri, proposing to reactivate al-Qaeda's international "work." Younis did not expect that his letter would reach Usama, let alone that Usama himself would take an interest in his proposal and write to him to discuss it.[2] By then, Usama had had nine years to reflect and conclude that the 9/11 attacks had not produced the "decisive blow" that he had intended. They had failed to force the United States to withdraw its military forces from Muslim-majority states, and so he decided to change al-Qaeda's strategy. Usama wanted his group to focus on the "the original source of power" in the United States, namely "the American people," who should be made "to feel the great suffering of our people."

Though Usama's letters show a restrained admiration for the American people, he had no intention of changing his *métier*. The correspondence with Younis reveals Usama's plans for "large-scale operations the effects of which would far exceed the 9/11 attacks" to force Americans to change their government's policy toward the Middle East.[3] Usama's most critical letter "To the honorable Sheikh Younis" opened: "This is addressed specifically to you, top secret, do not share it with anyone." Arabic script cannot be capitalized, but the line was typed in red and in a large bold font to deliver an arresting effect.

Usama tasked Younis with leading a team of operatives to carry out large coordinated maritime attacks. The details of the plans were highly technical and so were the ramifications if the attacks had been carried out, as we will explore later in this chapter.

Why Change al-Qaeda's Strategy?

Since the American people are center stage in Usama's strategy, it is helpful to explore the ways they featured in the evolution of his thinking over the years. We shall therefore first probe *why* Usama decided to change al-Qaeda's strategy, before we delve into the new strategy and how he intended to implement it.

In transcribed conversations with his daughter, we find Usama recalling that it was in 1986 that he first suggested that "we ought to strike inside America" in order to address the plight of the Palestinians.[4] For Usama, the Palestinian grievance was real, and he considered it to be "the reason we started our jihad."[5] But it was also a convenient theme to adopt. The jihadi strategist Abu Musab al-Suri observes that, by "adopting the Palestinian cause" in his media campaigns, Usama "advanced jihadism to a new level."[6] In doing so, Abu Musab explains, Usama made foreign occupation of Muslim-majority states a staple grievance of Muslims worldwide.[7]

In 2010, Usama assessed that jihadis were losing sight of the true purpose of global jihad. He lamented that regional groups (in Iraq, Yemen, Somalia, and Pakistan) who took up the mantle of jihad had become local and a "liability to [global] jihad." Usama's associates in North Waziristan spent much of their energy counseling the leaders in those regions, but had little influence on their conduct. We shall learn more about al-Qaeda's complex relationship with these groups in the next chapter.

By this time, Usama had decided to revive global jihad as he understood it. In a letter to Hajji Uthman and Atiya, he reminded them of what al-Qaeda stood for:

> I should like to start my letter by stressing the necessity of being mindful, always, of the basis of our war with America lest we gradually deviate from our goal. . . . Our goal is summed up in the oath (*qasam*) we swore after 9/11. . . . The fight that we seek is that which will force the enemy to cease its attacks against us.[8]

The oath (*qasam*) is a reference to an ultimatum that was recorded in anticipation of the U.S.-led war on Afghanistan in response to the 9/11 attacks. The video was released on the day Operation Enduring Freedom was launched, October 7, 2001. "I have only a few words for America and its people," Usama pronounced in an exigent tone before delivering his ultimatum: "I *swear* by God Almighty Who raised the heavens without effort that neither America nor anyone who lives there will enjoy safety until safety becomes a reality for us living in Palestine and before all the infidel armies leave the land of Muhammad."[9]

This ultimatum has come to be known as the "*qasam*" in jihadi literature. It features in many of al-Qaeda's videos and, long after Usama's demise, continues to mobilize those with a jihadi inclination. On December 6, 2019, the *qasam* was put into action on U.S. soil when Mohammed al-Shamrani, a second lieutenant in the Royal Saudi Air Force, carried out a deadly shooting in Florida at the Naval Air Station in Pensacola, killing three U.S. sailors and injuring eight others.[10] Al-Shamrani left behind a letter addressed to the American people that had the unmistakable imprint of Usama's *qasam*. "Security is a shared destiny," al-Shamrani wrote, and Americans "will not enjoy safety before we experience it as a reality in Palestine and U.S. forces withdraw from our lands."[11]

As he reflected on the state of global jihad, Usama saw al-Qaeda's operational impotence as an extension of the failure to make progress on the Palestinian front. He expressed this using the following analogy:

The example of Palestine is analogous to a vessel with a huge crane in the Mediterranean Sea. Mounted on the ropes of the crane is a large elephant that got dropped inside the small courtyard of our home, destroying walls and injuring people. In response, the people began to hit the elephant with sticks to expel it. They have been doing so for longer than sixty years, and to no avail. . . .

The right response should have been to strike the vessel that holds the ropes to which the elephant is attached. This way, the vessel has no choice but to lift the elephant and remove it from our courtyard. The vessel is analogous to America. . . .

The same is true with the rest of Muslims elsewhere. They endure great suffering at the hands of their rulers—the agents of America. The solution to their suffering is also through striking America to force it to abandon the apostate rulers and leave Muslims alone.

For example, if the power of jihadis in Egypt exceeds that of the apostate regime, and if jihadis proceed to establish God's Law, everyone knows that America will immediately deploy its military forces, starting with the Sixth Fleet, to save the Egyptian regime.[12]

As he reflected on al-Qaeda's record, Usama had other sobering thoughts. Global jihad itself, he came to realize, had been ill-conceived, and we find him articulating his regret through another of his analogies:

The conflict between the Muslim world and America is analogous to a large river dam. On the two banks of the river are numerous small villages with houses built with clay. Some evildoers opened some of the walls of the levee structure, causing the water of the river to overflow its banks unto the villages, destroying houses and injuring people. Some courageous men rushed to help the elderly, the women, and the children, diligently working night and day and risking their lives to save them and provide them with a secure shelter.

What these courageous men needed to do instead was to think more and do less to alleviate the ongoing suffering that consumed their energy.

A few of these knights should have simply punished the evildoers who had opened the walls of the levee structure and expelled them from the area. Then, they should have proceeded to close the walls to stop the water's overflow. That is the only way that a suffering so great could come to an end.[13]

We can assume that Usama saw himself and his followers among the "courageous men" and "knights" who were "risking their lives." For decades, and long before the 9/11 attacks, he and other jihadi leaders called on Muslims worldwide to emigrate (*hijra*), to train (*i'dad*), and to gather together (*ribat*) to fight (*jihad*) against foreign occupation in Afghanistan, Iraq, and Somalia. It took Usama several decades to realize that the global jihad "energy"—which he and his fellow "knights" had been "consuming," culminating in the 9/11 attacks— had been wasted. In other words, their global jihad was not effectively designed to undermine the security of all Americans in a meaningful way, as his *qasam* had threatened. And unless he and his fellow jihadis were going to "think more and do less," he concluded, they would never be able to deliver "security as a reality in Palestine," or elsewhere for that matter.

It is clear from the letters that Usama himself was re-evaluating his own thinking even when he was seemingly stating the obvious to his associates. "It is critically important," he wrote in one letter, "to study the culture and history of one's enemy,"[14] and focus on "the way the enemy thinks and on his weaknesses and strengths." Only then, Usama assessed, "and after God's support, could one make more sensible decisions."[15]

Usama browsed through the history of the United States and concluded that the "principal factor" that led to a decisive resolution to end the U.S.'s foreign wars was "when popular anger and domestic opposition increased." On his mind in particular was the Vietnam War, which engendered the kind of domestic opposition that Usama had hoped to achieve through the 9/11 attacks. This was not a new idea. Usama had publicly invoked the Vietnam War in an interview soon after 9/11, stating:

I demand the American people to take note of their government's policy against Muslims. They described the government's policy against Vietnam as wrong. They should now take the same stand that they did previously. The onus is on Americans to prevent Muslims from being killed at the hands of their government.[16]

Some nine years later, in 2010, Usama had to concede that the Vietnam War and the 9/11 attacks were not comparable. After he meditated on the "astronomical number" of "57,000 American soldiers killed" in Vietnam,[17] he wrote to his associates:

> You already know that the population of America is 300 million [*sic*].
> Around 1,000 American soldiers were killed in Afghanistan during eight years, and around 4,000 were killed in Iraq. This means that only a small segment of the American population has been directly affected, and this is far from sufficient to affect the American people *en masse* and cause them to exert pressure on their politicians to end the war.
> The number of American deaths in Afghanistan is 3.3 out of a million. It is so minuscule compared to their losses in Vietnam, which was . . . 380 out of a million, bearing in mind that the population of America at the time was 150 million [*sic*].[18]

Usama went on that "when their President Nixon [*sic*] erred and ordered a conscription for military service—[i.e., the draft]—to continue the war," his decision affected "the security of every individual American." That is when, he added, "the American people, in particular university students, took to the streets, organizing large protests against the war and forcing their government to withdraw its forces from Vietnam."[19]

Usama's reflections should not be assessed on their historical (in)accuracy.[20] He understood the importance of the anti-war protests during the Vietnam War,[21] and wanted to replicate them under the conditions that al-Qaeda would create.

As we will discover in more detail later in this chapter, Usama's plan called for large operations that would "thrust the United States into a severe economic crisis," adversely affecting the "income of every American citizen." Only then, he reasoned, could al-Qaeda "influence directly all the American people, or most of them," predicting that they would take to the streets, replicating the Vietnam anti-war protests, and demand that their government change its foreign policy. It was a change that al-Qaeda would force out of the barrel of a gun (or explosives), and Americans would bring about through a torrent of votes.

The New al-Qaeda Strategy

Usama determined that al-Qaeda needed to achieve a "balance of terror" with the United States. Failing that, he shared with his associates, al-Qaeda was in "decline" and "risked dying as an organization." The new strategy is of course inspired by the political doctrine of the "balance of power"—how modern states manage peaceful and/or hostile relations with each other. As a non-state actor, al-Qaeda lacked power, but Usama understood the importance of "balance" in the equation between jihadis and their enemies. Thus, he wanted al-Qaeda

to put the White House, Congress, and Pentagon under direct pressure through a balance of terror between us and them. This would be achieved when we could directly influence the American people, or most of them, by carrying out large-scale operations inside America, stripping them of their security. We would also carry out large-scale attacks targeting countries that export oil to America, thereby adversely affecting the income of every American citizen when his salary ceases to meet his cost of living, especially his fuel.

Such large-scale operations should go hand in hand with launching an intensive media campaign, part of it to be broadcast via American media outlets, if feasible. Our media campaign would justify our operations against America and oil-exporting countries on the basis that we are denied security in our own countries, particularly in Palestine, Iraq, Afghanistan, Pakistan, and Somalia. The wording would be similar to our *qasam*, such as *America shall not dream of enjoying security before we get to live it as a reality in Palestine.*[22]

In the course of his strategizing, Usama received a letter from the Pakistani operative working under al-Qaeda, Ilyas Kashmiri, whom we met briefly in the previous chapter. Ilyas was impatient to "work inside India" and "to pull the rug from under those who do [so-called] jihad to benefit Pakistani intelligence." To that end, he sought Usama's advice. "How do you propose that we do that, may God reward you?" Ilyas enquired.[23] He did not get the response he had hoped for. Instead, Usama tasked him with targeting President Obama and General Petraeus, who was the United States Central Command at the time, during their trips to Afghanistan.[24]

A year earlier, before Younis had come into the picture, Usama's answer to that question might have been different. He had written to Ayman that "after the Mumbai events and their repercussions in the region," it was important for al-Qaeda to release a statement "to assure Muslims in Pakistan that we stand by them in their jihad against India and its ambitions. We should also warn India of the outcome if it attacks Muslims in Pakistan . . . that we would target its economic joints to deplete its economy until it collapses."[25] By 2010, Usama saw al-Qaeda's strategy entirely differently. He instructed that al-Qaeda should concentrate all its resources exclusively on "the Americans, the original source of power that could swiftly halt this aggression." To ensure that those in his orbit appreciated the specificity and urgency of this point, Usama explained it in plain and simple terms:

Every spear and every booby trap at our disposal must be put to use to target Americans only. Our resources should not be wasted on others, such as on those who are part of the NATO alliance. For example, if we lie in wait for the enemy on the road between Kandahar and Helmand [Province] and we see military vehicles passing by, if the first vehicle is transporting Afghan soldiers, and the second is transporting NATO soldiers, while the third is transporting American soldiers, we should attack the third, even if the number of soldiers in the first two is greater.[26]

Indeed, in April 2011, al-Qaeda entertained reaching a "suitable arrangement" with the United Kingdom in order to concentrate on the United States.

Atiya learned that British intelligence told "some of the Libyan brothers in Britain" to relay to al-Qaeda that "Britain is prepared to withdraw from Afghanistan if al-Qaeda commits explicitly not to carry out any attacks against Britain or its interests."[27] There is no reason why Atiya would lie about this, but most likely by making this offer British intelligence was testing who in its midst had contact with al-Qaeda.

Usama's new strategy did not appeal to all the leaders of al-Qaeda. It is common in the letters for Usama to consult with his associates and for them to share candidly their opinions with him. On this occasion, Ayman was blunt in questioning Usama's new strategy. Of course, he agreed that international terrorism is "important and useful," but could not fathom why it was necessary for al-Qaeda to focus exclusively on the Americans:

> The difference between the Americans' losses in Vietnam and those they suffered in Iraq and Afghanistan does not mean that the American public is indifferent to their government withdrawing from Afghanistan. This comparison is somewhat simplistic and inaccurate.
>
> The American government has already announced the date when it plans to withdraw its forces from both countries, despite the strategic problems this withdrawal poses for America. The number of soldiers killed is not the only or even most important factor in America's decision. The economic and psychological factors are likely more important and decisive.
>
> By psychological factor, I am referring to the critical juncture during a war when the superior military power despairs about achieving victory. This occurs when this power realizes that the situation on the ground will not improve even if the fighting continues for years to come. Thus, it loses the enthusiasm to fight and picks up its belongings and leaves. That is what happens when great powers and their organized armies confront multiple moving armed groups.
>
> I agree and support the importance of striking inside both America and Europe, but it is also critical to be cognizant that the battle in Afghanistan and in Iraq is also very important.

It is true that striking inside America and Europe has a significant psychological effect, but remember that Russia was defeated in Afghanistan, a poor and wretched place, without the Afghan striking inside Russia. France was defeated in Algeria without the Algerians striking inside France [*sic*], and America was defeated in Vietnam without the Vietnamese striking inside America.[28]

Ayman was also concerned that Usama's change of course would be embarrassing for al-Qaeda. He reminded Usama of the public statements that they both had delivered over the years about the importance of fighting in Iraq and Afghanistan. Ayman's differences with Usama do not appear to have continued beyond this letter, however.

"Top Secret, Do Not Share it with Anyone"

Prior to the Abbottabad raid, little was known about Younis al-Mauritani. "Our brother Sheikh Younis is multi-talented," Hajji Uthman lauded him in one letter. Younis "is truly impressive and capable of serving in many areas. He is learned, and blessed with a virtuous personality and a mature mind," he added.[29] We learn from Younis's letters to Usama that he received his jihadi formation in the Islamic Maghreb with the group led by Khaled Abu al-Abbas, also known as Belmokhtar, who had sent Younis as his envoy to al-Qaeda, probably in 2007. The purpose of Younis's visit, according to Belmokhtar, was to share "our reality and the history of our group," in the hope of achieving a closer relationship with al-Qaeda, perhaps even a merger.[30] Younis was enthusiastic about his mission and wrote a detailed study of the history of Belmokhtar's group and a geopolitical assessment of northwest Africa,[31] but "the brothers in al-Qaeda were not interested."[32] Younis did not return to North Africa, most likely because he impressed al-Qaeda's leaders in North Waziristan. He was assigned a role on al-Qaeda's Legal Committee, and eventually became the deputy of Abu Yahya al-Libi, the head of the Committee.[33]

Younis was in awe of Usama. "We are in a state of worship," he wrote, quoting a line from Usama's speeches. He averred that the two shared the same belief that "our time is not wasted," that the jihadis were in this fight for the long run, and that this "lordly worship shall continue until the Day of Judgment."[34] Usama's wish was much more than a command for Younis. "I am a spear at your disposal," Younis volunteered, "throw me wherever and whenever you see fit." Usama saw in Younis not just a committed jihadi, but also a strategic and critical thinker. Younis shared with Usama the view that religious extremism among jihadis was a liability to jihadism, and urged al-Qaeda's senior leaders to warn against it in their public statements. Usama was impressed, so much so that he forwarded an excerpt of Younis's letter to Atiya and Abu Yahya so that they might follow through on his suggestions concerning the threat from religious extremism.

In 2010, Usama was convinced that maritime attacks whose effects "would far exceed 9/11" could deliver a "decisive blow" that would ultimately force the United States to withdraw its military forces from the Muslim-majority states. Younis praised Usama's idea, observing that "maritime jihad," i.e., expeditions by sea, "had ceased with the fall of the Ottoman Empire" in 1923, and "renewing this type of jihad is one of the best deeds to get closer to God."[35] He was cerebral in his fervor. He did not want to rush into the maritime domain unprepared. Instead, he wanted to study the sea, this "mighty creation," for as long as was needed, and recruit the right individuals for the task.[36]

Al-Qaeda had been in hibernation mode for nine years, and Younis's enthusiasm to reactivate the "work" was just the kind of rebooting that Usama had been waiting for. After sharing with Younis his "balance of terror" strategy with the United States, Usama explained:

One of the most important works that our organization could achieve would be to carry out operations that would directly affect the security and economy of the American people as a whole. That is why terrorist operations inside America as well as those targeting oil-exporting countries would be the swiftest way to affect the American people directly and would cause them to put pressure on their politicians.

The plan that I am about to propose to you is of the utmost importance, and I hope that it would play a critical role in putting an end to the war that America has launched on the Muslim world.[37]

In 2010, when Usama was writing, the United States' import of crude oil was on the rise and critical to its economy.[38] Explaining to Younis his plans first through analogies, Usama proceeded:

It does not escape you that the importance of oil for the industrialized countries of the world today is analogous to the importance of blood for a human being. Excessive bleeding causes a person's death, short of that it would weaken him. . . .

If we assume that oil reaches the West, including America, through three pipelines, and suppose that we target and partially destroy one of them, it would be easy to fix it within twenty-four hours. . . . But if we destroy it completely, the effects of such an attack would lead to damaging around 30 percent of the Americans' economy, because to rebuild the pipeline would take several years. . . . With God's help, thrusting America into a severe economic crisis is within our reach.

The operational details had to be kept from everyone except Younis. We learn from other letters that "keeping secrets" was of the utmost importance for al-Qaeda's international terrorism. To avoid security breaches, even Usama was not privy to the specifics of the operational planning of al-Qaeda's terrorist operations, with one exception (most likely the 9/11 attacks). "Only the head of the external work and those tasked with carrying out the operation were privy to the operational details," Usama wrote in one letter. (In the case of the 9/11 attacks, only two of the hijackers, Muhammad Atta and Ziyad al-Jirahi, were privy to the operational planning; the others only learned of the details within a "very short period" prior to the attacks.)[39] That's why Usama's letter was "top secret" and not to be shared with anyone else in al-Qaeda. He had envisaged an elaborate plan that went beyond analogies to destroy the equivalent of a pipeline.

Anticipating that communication about operational details would cease once Younis departed *en mission*, Usama's letter was replete with practical ideas:

> Our plan is to sink a large number of crude oil tankers, prioritizing the largest vessels. We want to do so in several simultaneous attacks. . . . The number of these large vessels is limited in the world. Unlike cars, they cannot be manufactured that easily. . . . It is important to target as many vessels as possible, regardless of whether they are carrying crude oil or not. The main goal is to sink them, because that would cause the enemy huge losses, leading to a global economic crisis.

When assessing Usama's idea, Lieutenant Commander Kurt Albaugh remarked that Usama had done his research. Albaugh's exceptional career in the U.S. Navy has included serving as the captain of the USS *Devastator* (minesweeper), a warship designed to counter the threat of naval mines. When Usama was writing his letters, Albaugh was sailing the Gulf of Aden, deterring attacks on merchant vessels by Somali pirates. Oil tankers, he explained, range in sizes, and the large ones Usama was eyeing to blow up are called Very Large Crude Carriers (VLCCs). There are about 730 VLCCs in the world, and each one can carry 1.9–2.2 million barrels of crude oil.[40]

Usama considered the likelihood of the United States swiftly responding to the sinking of VLCCs, and wanted Younis and his team to be absolutely ready for the series of simultaneous attacks that would take place in different oceans to take advantage of "surprising the enemy." As Admiral William McRaven put it in his study of special operations missions, the element of surprise is critical "to achieve relative superiority."[41] The same is true for terrorists who seek to maximize the impact of an attack. Usama was mindful that unless the element of surprise is carefully planned, subsequent or delayed attacks risk failure, because "the enemy has the advantage of time" to respond or preempt the attacks. That is why he alerted Younis that

> we must not initiate anything unless we have put in place all the steps needed to carry out simultaneous attacks that would target oil tankers

along several shipping routes—starting from the Gulf, passing through Oman, Yemen, Somalia, all the way to the Cape of Good Hope in South Africa. Simultaneously, we would attack oil tankers departing from the ports of countries that export oil to America in North and West Africa, such as Algeria, Libya, Nigeria, and Ghana. We would also target oil tankers departing from Venezuela. We must carefully look into America's crude oil imports and target countries that export oil the most to America.

Given the geographical scope, the types of attacks could not be uniform across all shipping routes. For instance, Usama drew Younis's attention to the point that the attacks close to land where there was a jihadi presence, such as Yemen and Somalia, should be different from those in the Gulf where there was a U.S. military presence. In the former case, "the brothers could retreat after carrying out the operation," but in the Gulf, they would need to carry out suicide operations, lest they were captured.

As to the specifics, Usama's plans covered the entire spectrum, starting with the planning and acquisition phase:

It is important to conduct extensive and precise surveillance. This starts with purchasing or renting a small boat, if possible. It should be of high quality and should operate under the commercial cover of transporting goods. Some wooden boats can carry anywhere between 50 and 100 tons. They are common in that area, many merchants use such boats to transport goods from Dubai to Djibouti, Eritrea, or Somalia. We used to have one that we purchased in Dubai. . . .

Make sure that the surveillance boat is made out of wood or rubber to avoid being detected by the radars of vessels nearby. Avoid fiberglass boats, the preference is for a wooden boat. They are available for sale in Somalia. Their sale is illegal in some places, because they can be used to smuggle goods. . . .

The wooden boat should be purchased using the names of either Yemeni or Somali brothers. . . . It is important that everyone on the boat is from the same nationality, otherwise it would raise suspicion.

Albaugh noted that Usama's preference for a wooden boat suggests that "he was thinking of what is referred to as radar cross-section (RCS)." Thus, to avoid being detected by RCS, Usama advised:

It would be very important to cover all metals on the boat, such as weapons and the engine of the boat, because metals could be detected by the enemy's radar. The brothers should put a rubber cover on the engine when the boat stops. They could make one by purchasing a rubber tube for a truck wheel, cut it, and cover the engine like a cloth.

The operatives, Usama advised, should integrate themselves into the maritime universe that he wanted them to blow up:

We would place groups along the coastlines to conduct surveillance under cover of fishing. They would need to do fishing for real, i.e., purchase fishing boats, and sell fish to neighboring areas so that they could do the necessary reconnaissance to collect the exact times and dates of the vessels in relation to their shipping routes. . . .

The brothers need to conduct surveillance in the form of collecting data points of the marine traffic of oil tankers. For example, every time an oil tanker passes through the Strait of Hormuz, it would be necessary for the brothers to track its route on a maritime map, such as the time of its position in relation to the targeted shipping route. They could do so by adding the information [as dots] on the maritime map, showing the precise location of oil tankers at specific times (or thereabouts). Maritime traffic maps could be purchased from bookshops. We purchased one in Dubai in the past, I suppose that they are available for sale in Karachi since it is a coastal city. They should also be available on the internet.

According to Albaugh, "This information comes from a system installed on these ships called the Automated Identification System (AIS)." It is available to anyone, and "no registration or payment is required to access these trackers." In theory, Albaugh expounded, "it would give an attacker near real-time information that would greatly help with targeting."[42]

Covering even the most basic details, Usama also advised that the operatives needed to acquire other relevant knowledge:

> They need to be trained to differentiate between oil tankers and commercial vessels, and could do so by studying maritime encyclopedias or researching the subject on the internet. This is easy to learn: Crude oil tankers are very large, they do not carry containers on top like commercial vessels, because the oil is stored inside the vessel. It is also possible to differentiate between empty oil tankers and those that are full. This is important because it affects the volume of explosives we need to prepare to sink them successfully. Empty vessels are usually those returning to the Gulf. The color of the vessel's bottom hull is visible from the outside, whereas the bottom hull of the full vessel is mostly in the water.

Usama was referring to the way that vessels are painted. There is typically a division in the painting around a ship's draft marks. Thus, if the color of the hull below the draft marks—usually, but not always, red—is visible, one might infer that the vessel is only lightly loaded with cargo.[43]

Once the surveillance is done, the operatives can move on to the implementation stage of their mission, namely seizing, then exploding the vessels. Usama enumerated several possibilities as to how to seize vessels:

> —Placing the boat within a small distance of the front of the vessel, then holding a projector until the captain realizes that it is being seized;
> —Firing at the vessel; or

—Call the ship using an emitter (*jihaz masih*) to notify the captain that his vessel is seized, and unless he and his crew surrender, you will fire on the part of the vessel that stores the engine's fuel.

In general, captains are advised to surrender to [pirates/hostage-takers], and to avoid getting into arguments with them.

The seizing aspect of the plan was not carefully conceived. Albaugh observed that Usama's suggestions indicate that he was not well versed in the security measures that were in common use in the maritime industry at the time of his writing and that made it harder for pirates or other attackers to seize vessels.

After seizing the oil tanker, Usama instructed that the operatives should "release the Muslims on board the vessel using the rescue boats," and added that "releasing non-Muslims should also be considered." Then the vessel "should be blown up from the inside by lining up one boat behind another filled with explosives":

> The oil tankers could be exploded using boats, like [we did] with the USS *Cole*. The boats need to carry a large volume of explosives, preferably placed in an arch position, facing the vessel. If that is not possible, then the volume of explosives should be very large, measuring no less than 1 meter in diameter so that the lid cannot close.

Usama understood the mechanics of the plan's execution. According to Albaugh, the "arch position" is a "shaped charge" designed to focus and concentrate the explosive energy to penetrate deep into a target. Unless the explosives are shaped accordingly, Albaugh explained, the energy would spread, diminishing the force of the explosion at any single point and, thus, the extent of the penetration. Usama also displayed an intimate understanding of the environmental safety standards that are in operation to minimize risks to vessels when he wrote:

> The brothers should know that the fuel storage in the oil tanker is not attached to the external body of the tanker. This means that penetrating the

tanker from the outside does not necessarily mean penetrating the fuel storage inside the tanker, because there is space between them. The goal is to sink the oil tanker, and a single boat is unlikely to sink it. It is necessary to blow up two boats. The first should target the frontal tier of the vessel, while the second should target its middle. That is because oil tankers are divided into tightly sealed sections. Penetrating one of the sections will cause the oil tanker to drift sideways, but does not necessarily sink it, which is what happened with the USS *Cole*. . . .

At any rate, we should blow up the tank that stores the vessel's fuel even if it is empty to ensure that it is sunk. If it remains intact, it would be possible to prevent the vessel from sinking.[44]

Usama imagined that Younis and his team would sink enough VLCCs to cut off 30 percent of the U.S.'s crude oil supply. He envisaged seven simultaneous attacks on the following shipping routes:

1. The Gulf, from Iraq to the Strait of Hormuz;

2. Pakistan to the shores of Oman, noting that the British have a military presence in the Strait of Hormuz on the Omani side;

3. Yemen [Gulf of Aden];

4. Somalia to South Africa, this is the most important to target;

5. Nigeria and Ghana;

6. Libya and Algeria;

7. Venezuela.

The operation should take place anytime between August 25 and the middle of April. Outside these months, sea conditions are harsh. Choppy waters would make the use of small boats impossible.

Albaugh observed that Usama's choice of shipping routes is "logical," while also being "bold in scope and scale." Though it would be "extremely difficult to pull off," he opined, "it would not be impossible." Over 90 percent of international trade is by sea, and an attack on this scale would have widespread effects in the shipping industry. Albaugh warned that, if successful, such an attack would "undermine the security behind the free and open system for the exchange of goods," which is a key strategic goal of the U.S. Navy. To be sure, he added, "maritime security is always vulnerable, but that vulnerability is not at the forefront of public consciousness." Such an attack would adversely affect consumer confidence and the economy in general. On the military front, at least four out of the six U.S. geographic combatant commands would likely respond if attacks were mounted in all of the areas Usama envisaged, namely, CENTCOM, SOUTHCOM, AFRICOM, and EUCOM.[45]

Usama wrote most of his directives in late March 2010. Not long after, he authorized a budget of 200,000 euros to fund Younis's mission, hoping that the money would be made available by the "brothers in the Maghreb."[46] The timing for the attacks was not set. Usama and Younis were in agreement that they should proceed "slowly but surely." But Usama did not want Younis to be distracted by other projects. "We must proceed with the project of sinking the oil tankers as if we had nothing else to do," he urged Younis.[47]

In June 2010, we learn from Atiya that Younis was preparing to head to Iran if he could evade capture by the Iranian authorities. He would take six to eight "brothers" with him, and give them a three-month training course before sending them out into the field to begin planning their missions.[48] In September 2010, Younis wanted to discuss combining attacks inside America with the ones targeting oil tankers, but Usama thought "that the two must remain separate."[49] Either Usama prioritized the maritime attacks over others inside the United States, or he thought that it would overstretch Younis and his team's capabilities to concern themselves with both simultaneously. In December 2010, Usama learned from Atiya that Younis did not think that it was safe to head to Iran and had elected instead to take his team to a safe location inside Pakistan.[50]

Around the time Younis and his team were getting ready to depart North Waziristan on their mission, the Arab Spring broke out: Peaceful protests erupted, successfully bringing down the autocratic regimes in Tunisia, Egypt, and Libya. In his last letter, dated April 26, 2011, Usama recommended that if Younis and his team were in a relatively safe place, they should stay there until the regimes in Yemen and Syria fell. Presumably, he believed that they would have greater freedom of movement during such transitional periods.[51] Five days after, the SEALs raided Usama's compound. Most likely thanks to the recovery of Usama's letters, Younis was arrested in September 2011 by Pakistan's ISI.[52]

It was reported that in June 2013 the United States flew Younis from Bagram Air Base in Afghanistan and handed him over to the authorities in Mauritania. In April 2015, Younis was sentenced to twenty years in prison for "terrorist" activities.[53] "The Americans" would undoubtedly be relieved that Younis's "state of worship" is taking place in a prison cell and not as he pilots wooden boats to generate economic havoc of tsunamic proportions.

What If?

"There is many a slip between cup and lip," the ancient proverb goes. Usama's fate was SEAL-ed, and for years to come, Younis will have to continue his jihad in a prison cell in Mauritania. But what if al-Qaeda had succeeded in delivering Usama's plans?

Joseph Votel, former Commanding General of CENTCOM (2016–19), shared several observations about Usama's strategy.[54] "The scope of Usama's plans," he remarked, "is consistent with his focus on big events to move his strategy forward"; he surmised that "Usama was trying to regain some initiative." As to the feasibility of al-Qaeda executing Usama's planned operations, Votel noted that "it is exceedingly challenging to operate in the maritime domain," but "the science of it could be figured out," and al-Qaeda has a track record of being "patient." Should such attacks succeed, he postulated, the implications for the U.S. military would be significant. "Even if only one of the targeted oil tankers were to be sunk by al-Qaeda," it would engender a series of "near-term reactions on the part of the Department of Defense [DoD]." This would likely lead to pressure on the DoD "to shift resources to

the Gulf region," doubtless at the expense of those allocated to other areas—
such as the Indo-Pacific region, "where greater U.S. military presence is seen as
a hedge against China." Such attacks, he added, would also have an impact on
U.S. maritime security strategy, putting more focus on securing shipping lanes,
and in all likelihood placing more pressure on the Gulf nations to increase
their capabilities.

But Votel's assessment of Usama's overall strategy is certain to disappoint
al-Qaeda and any other groups harboring ambitions to change U.S. foreign
policy through terrorism. While he credited Usama with having correctly
identified the American people as the key to achieving his goal, Votel believed
that there was a "disconnect" with regard to the potential outcome of the
planned attacks: "Usama overestimated the impact that the terrorist attacks of
al-Qaeda, or any terrorist group, would have on the resilience of the U.S.
economy." When Votel shared his reaction in June 2020, it was via video call,
as COVID-19 had by then unleashed its offensive on the world. With the
latest news on his mind, he pointed out that, "despite the tragically high
number of American human losses and confirmed COVID cases" and
"notwithstanding the unprecedented economic downturn, the United States
continues to be the world's most powerful economy." In other words, sinking
oil tankers would be just as unsuccessful in undermining the U.S. economy as
the 9/11 attacks were in forcing the United States to withdraw its military
forces from Muslim-majority states.

General Votel shared other observations about the findings advanced in this
book. If it is true that international terrorist attacks after 2002 were inspired,
but not planned and executed, by Usama and his al-Qaeda and this had been
known, "our involvement in Afghanistan and Pakistan might have been
different," he pondered. Given that "our policy objective in that region is to
deter al-Qaeda from attacking the homeland and our interests abroad," he
explained, "this would suggest that we might have overestimated our foe."

If true, the inability of al-Qaeda to plan and carry out international
terrorism since 2002, and its tenuous relationship with the groups that did, has

additional implications for how the United States might deter terrorism. In the wake of the 9/11 attacks, the United States Congress passed the Authorization for the Use of Military Force (AUMF), a joint resolution authorizing the President "to use all necessary and appropriate force" against any person or entity that "he determines planned, authorized, committed, or aided the terrorist attacks that occurred on September 11, 2001."[55] Since then, military force has been used against groups that supported the 9/11 attacks *post factum* and in spirit, but that may not have been formally affiliated with al-Qaeda.[56]

Prior to serving as CENTCOM Commander, General Votel served as the Commanding General of U.S. Special Operations Command (SOCOM), and as such is well versed in the AUMF's legal intricacies. "The AUMF," he reflected, "gave us the legal framework to pursue terrorists, and we even leveraged it against ISIS," even though the group was fighting against al-Qaeda. "What did not take place, however," Votel lamented, "was revisiting and updating the AUMF." This, he went on, "would not simply have strengthened the legal basis but, equally importantly, the moral basis of our use of force." It is imperative, he thought, that "it should be self-evident for the American people, whose power Usama evidently understood, that our use of force always rests on lawful and moral grounds."

PART II
THE RISE OF THE "BROTHERS"
(2004–2011)

SOME "BROTHERS" ARE MORE BROTHERLY THAN OTHERS

*God showed mercy on al-Qaeda with the merger of Abu Musab al-Zarqawi,
whose group accomplished amazing victories for jihadis. This raised the value
of al-Qaeda's stocks. It was God's way of repaying the people of jihad for their
sacrifices in His path.*

Letter from Saudi scholar (Bishr al-Bishr) to Atiya, February 19, 2007

The merger between al-Qaeda and Abu Musab al-Zarqawi's group in Iraq in
December 2004, which we touched upon in Chapter Three, spurred other
jihadi groups in North Africa (2006–07), Yemen (2009), and—almost—in
Somalia (2012) to follow suit. These groups were not directly spawned by
al-Qaeda, but their leaders saw numerous benefits in joining the internationally feared al-Qaeda brand. They saw an opportunity to improve their standing
in the eyes of their followers and to gain international media attention, which
they hoped would help them to raise money and recruit new adherents.

In view of the numerous differences that we shall discover between al-Qaeda
and the groups it inspired, one might be tempted to wonder whether this part
of the book is a digression. But there are several reasons why al-Qaeda's mergers
with these groups should command attention.

The most obvious one concerns al-Qaeda's operational impotence after
9/11, which we now understand thanks to the Bin Laden Papers. Though
al-Qaeda was shattered, its brand lived on through the deeds of the groups that
acted in its name.[1]

Another reason concerns the value of the al-Qaeda brand to these groups. By virtue of purchasing "stocks" in al-Qaeda, as one letter put it, regional jihadi groups acquired shares in a brand with an international standing, and with that came global media attention. To paraphrase Brian Jenkins, terrorists want a lot of people watching, not just a lot of people dead.[2] Therefore, we should not dismiss al-Qaeda's non-kinetic contribution to these groups' operations.

The more important reason we must consider these groups has to do with al-Qaeda's ideological and strategic worldview. The mergers with regional jihadi groups represent spatial crossroads where religion and geography meet to unite the global community of Muslims. Al-Qaeda hoped that, with the rise of jihadi groups in different regions, jihadism would acquire the strength to re-create the historical *umma*.

But as we shall discover, the decision to bestow the al-Qaeda imprimatur on groups that al-Qaeda did not control or even influence turned out to be a miscalculation.[3]

Outsiders might be forgiven for thinking that Usama's commands were heard and obeyed by all in the jihadi landscape. The Bin Laden Papers, however, reveal that the reality was far more complicated and challenging for al-Qaeda. After 9/11, the al-Qaeda brand inhabited the minds of jihadis as well as those of their foes. Jihadi groups did not imagine that they could ever mount attacks matching the scale and symbolism of 9/11, so they rushed to give their allegiance to Usama to become part of al-Qaeda. Others even skipped the formalities altogether and unilaterally assumed the al-Qaeda brand as their own.

The jihadis' foes were also fixated on the brand, with the counterterrorism community often subsuming all jihadis under the umbrella of al-Qaeda. This was partly due to a lack of understanding of the ideological orientations and agendas of different jihadi groups, and partly out of convenience. The latter motive is especially important. As discussed in the last chapter, in the wake of the 9/11 attacks, the United States Congress passed the Authorization for the Use of Military Force (AUMF), a joint resolution granting the President authority to use force against persons or entities associated with the 9/11 attacks.[4] This meant that the AUMF could be applied to operations against jihadi entities that were connected to the group responsible for the attacks, i.e., al-Qaeda. Since the approval of Congress was not required, it sped things up considerably.

Was al-Qaeda behind the proliferation of jihadi groups around the world and their actions? We have discovered that al-Qaeda was "afflicted" after the fall of the Taliban. How then, one might ask, was al-Qaeda involved in the rise of regional jihadi groups? And what was the nature of al-Qaeda's relationship with them?

Before we explore these questions, it is helpful to understand the different "brotherly" dimensions that al-Qaeda assigns to Muslims in general and to jihadi groups in particular. In Qur'anic parlance, all believers are "brothers" and "sisters" in religion. Hence, the term "brother" is used before the names of virtually all jihadis mentioned in the letters. This, however, does not mean that all "brothers" are equal in organizational terms. For instance, al-Qaeda's own "brothers" are part of the group's inner circle, while members of other jihadi groups are "brothers" through religion only.[5] It is notable that Usama assigns the honorific "Sheikh" to his al-Qaeda associates (the brotherhood of religion that binds them is assumed), but does not apply the same title to the leaders of regional jihadi groups. Here, we will use "Brothers" with a capital "B" to refer to members of jihadi groups that merged with al-Qaeda.

By the time Usama was killed, al-Qaeda was in contact with groups from far and wide. They included those operating in the Af-Pak region, most notably the Afghan Taliban and the Pakistani Taliban, or TTP. There are also marginal references in the letters to Tajiks, Turks, Uzbeks, Bulgarians, Azerbaijanis, Dagestanis, and East Turkmens (from Xinjiang, China) operating there. Outside the Af-Pak region, al-Qaeda had contact with several Sunni militant groups in Iraq, Iran, North Africa (Algeria, Libya, and Egypt), West Africa (Mauritania and Nigeria), the Arabian Peninsula (Yemen and Saudi Arabia), East Africa (Somalia), Lebanon, and Gaza.

The most meaningful contacts outside the Af-Pak region were those that resulted in public mergers. The mechanics of the mergers consisted of an allegiance given by groups (and individuals in two cases) to Usama, recognizing his authority and undertaking "to hear and obey" his commands. This was followed by either Usama or Ayman admitting the individuals and/or groups into al-Qaeda. In some cases, the two acts were combined in a single public announcement. Usama hoped that such mergers would "raise the morale of Muslims who would in turn become more engaged and supportive of jihadis."

Contact between al-Qaeda and regional jihadi groups took different forms. In the case of Iraq, the initial contact between Abu Musab al-Zarqawi and al-Qaeda in early 2004 was through an envoy, Jaafar. Al-Qaeda also received voice messages from Abu Musab early on, and these were transcribed in the letters.

Beginning in 2004, the jihadi media were working on encryption and, by 2007, a software program called "Secrets of Jihadis" (*asrar al-mujahidin*) had been developed and was in use by al-Qaeda. Usama cautioned against adopting it, but Atiya, who was al-Qaeda's point of contact with the "Brothers,"[6] ignored his warnings and used the encryption software, though with reinforcement, "meaning encryption within encryption."[7] The letters also suggest that emails with large attachments were exchanged via "brothers" overseeing jihadi websites,[8] because the internet connection was not strong enough on al-Qaeda's end. Shorter emails were shared without actually being sent, so that they could not be intercepted: The login details of the same email address were shared between two parties who could then compose and save their emails in the drafts box. All the other party then had to do was to login to the shared email address and access the messages as drafts. For reasons that remain unclear, on at least two occasions, emails from al-Qaeda to Yemen had to go through Somalia.

In what follows, we will trail each group separately to assess the kind of relationship that al-Qaeda forged with each of them prior to Usama's death. It is important that we proceed with caution. Notwithstanding the uniqueness of the information revealed in the letters, we are only reading what the "Brothers" wanted al-Qaeda to know about them.

Iraq and the Birth of the Islamic State

The first and arguably most consequential merger that al-Qaeda forged after 9/11 was with Abu Musab al-Zarqawi's group, al-Tawhid wa-al-Jihad, in Iraq. The astute jihadi cleric Bishr al-Bishr observed that al-Qaeda would have come to an end, had it not been for "the amazing jihadi victories in Iraq, which raised the value of al-Qaeda's stocks."[9]

The world was first introduced to Abu Musab by the late Secretary of State Colin Powell, when he addressed the United Nations on February 5, 2003 to make a case for the U.S. invasion of Iraq. Powell claimed that Iraq's President, Saddam Hussein, was "harboring" Abu Musab and his group, building "on decades long experience with respect to ties between Iraq and Al Qaida."[10] In light of what we now know, Powell was unwittingly acting as a matchmaker. In 2003, Abu Musab and al-Qaeda were far from being an item, and it was the invasion of Iraq that brought them together. Also, when Abu Musab arrived in Iraq in 2002 after his release from Iran, he was not a guest of Saddam. He was likely helped by Sunnis in Kurdistan who opposed the Saddam regime.

After the Iraq War, our knowledge of Abu Musab's early history with al-Qaeda was slanted by a 2004 essay that was supposedly authored by Saif al-Adl, the leader of al-Qaeda's military committee before 9/11. This remarked on Abu Musab's commitment to jihad, but stressed his ideological rigidity and his impatience to establish an Islamic state, qualities that were apparent to both Usama and Ayman when they first met him in 1999. Saif purportedly saw Abu Musab's potential and valued his contacts and network in the Levant, but it took some convincing for Usama and Ayman to allow him to set up a training camp in Afghanistan.

We now know that when the essay was published in 2004,[11] Saif was imprisoned in Iran. As discussed in Chapter Two, Iran used al-Qaeda detainees to pressure Usama to stop Abu Musab's attacks on the Shia in Iraq, and we will learn much more about this in Chapter Nine. With this in mind, we can infer that if Saif had anything to do with the essay, it would have been heavily edited to suit Iran's objectives.[12] It wasn't until 2010 that the essay came to Usama's attention, and its false content upset him. Usama wanted Atiya to refute it publicly:

> After I read it, it became clear to me that it was falsely attributed to our brother Saif al-Adl. It is offensive to our brother Abu Musab, to our brother Saif, and to the organization as a whole. It is severe in its criticism of the brothers in Iraq for wanting to establish a state when the means of its success were not available.

For those of us who used Saif's essay to assess his group's relationship with al-Qaeda, we should have noticed something suspect about it. There was a clue that was immediately apparent to Usama:

> What makes it clear that the author is not our brother Saif is his claim that he received my authorization and that of Sheikh Ayman to deal with brother Abu Musab. At that time [i.e., in 1999], Sheikh Ayman's group and al-Qaeda had not merged. Therefore, anyone who knew us then would have surely said that the authorization had come from me and from Sheikh Abu Hafs al-Misri.[13]

During the 1999 events that Saif supposedly narrated, Abu Hafs was Usama's deputy. We should therefore trust Usama on this, and disregard the litany of media reports and academic writings that relied on Saif's essay to construct the early history between Abu Musab and Usama. And as we shall discover, the Bin Laden Papers do not point to any prior ideological tension between the two. On the contrary, Usama was enthusiastic about the merger with Abu Musab's group.

What was in it for Abu Musab?

We don't know if Abu Musab knew the extent to which al-Qaeda had been shattered when he sought a merger, but his enthusiasm to be part of the brand is palpable in the voice messages that reached Usama in transcribed format.[14] He wanted the world to know that his group is "a branch of the original" al-Qaeda and to be seen to be following in the footsteps of the "Father," i.e., Usama. Abu Musab was passionate, and in a universe in which he might have been afforded different kinds of opportunities, we could imagine him designing cards for Hallmark. His artistic leaning is apparent in an emotional booklet that he composed and designed for his family. It is made from papers torn from a spiral notebook, and features his creative drawings in the margins while his affectionate handwritten notes, including bits of poetry, occupy the middle of the pages.[15]

But there was more to Abu Musab's eagerness to merge with al-Qaeda than mere passion. When he reached out either in late 2003 or early 2004, a myriad of groups had been active in Iraq. By all available accounts, Abu Musab's group was the most powerful. But while Abu Musab's career included operations (and prison time) in Jordan and training in Afghanistan, he was Jordanian and his group's presence in Iraq was still only nascent. It dated back to just 2002, after Abu Musab's release from Iran.[16] Though many Iraqi individuals and small groups rushed to join him, and a flood of foreign fighters traveled to Iraq to wage jihad alongside him, Abu Musab struggled to forge solid relationships with established Iraqi groups.

Of particular importance were two other groups then operating in Iraq. The first was Ansar al-Islam, also known as Ansar al-Sunna, based in Kurdistan. It was Iraq's most established jihadi group, with roots going back to 1980, and it counted Kurds and Arabs among its members.[17] The second was a well-resourced, Iraqi-led jihadi group called the Islamic Army of Iraq which emerged soon after the war in 2003.

Abu Musab needed to persuade Iraqi militants to join a group led by himself, a Jordanian. In theory, there is no place for nationalism in jihadism, for "all believers are brothers in religion," as we noted earlier. Still, sensitivities over nationalities, ethnicities, and race can be detected among jihadis, and Abu

Musab faced this with Ansar al-Sunna. Abu Musab must have realized that if he became Usama's appointee in Iraq, it would increase his chances of convincing Iraqi groups to join him and fight under his command. To his credit, Abu Musab did not seek to merge with al-Qaeda under false pretenses. He insisted that the two Sheikhs, Usama and Ayman, should understand beforehand that "our strategy in Iraq differs from that anywhere else." To avoid any misgivings, sometime in 2004, he sent an envoy, Jaafar, "to explain to you our situation."[18]

Wakil Khan (most likely an alias of Tawfiq or Atiya) met with Jaafar. Based on the account the latter gave, Wakil related that "about 90 percent of jihadi operations in Iraq are orchestrated by brother Abu Musab and the groups that had joined him. . . . All the large operations, and most of the small ones, including the attacks against the UN office, in Hilla (Italians) and those in Basra, etc."

The "UN office" to which Jaafar was referring was the terrorist attack that killed Sérgio Vieira de Mello, the UN Special Representative for Iraq on August 19, 2003. "Hilla (Italians)" was most likely a reference to the November 2003 attack in Nasiriya outside an international military police base which killed twenty-six people, including twelve Italians.

Abu Musab's group was also attracting foreign fighters from neighboring countries. We learn that "the borders with Syria, Saudi Arabia, Kuwait, and Jordan are all accessible" and "the number of incoming brothers is large." Two days before Jaafar departed to meet with Wakil, "a hundred brothers from Saudi Arabia had arrived in Iraq." Nothing in the letters suggests that the governments of neighboring states were conspiring to support Abu Musab, but they clearly did not or could not control their borders with Iraq. However, it is noteworthy that Colin Powell accused only Syria of providing "direct support for terrorist groups" in Iraq through its borders.[19] The other states bordering Iraq, namely Saudi Arabia, Kuwait, and Jordan, were all U.S. allies, which might explain why they were spared similar accusations, at least in public.

Jaafar reported to Wakil that they had "no shortage of weapons" and that "more than 80 percent of the Iraqi army's weaponry" had fallen into their hands. He boasted that Abu Musab's group was "in competition with the

Americans to buy the remaining explosives and weapons" on the black market. They were "getting by" financially thanks to weapons and ammunition they amassed through the "spoils" of their military operations. Jaafar bragged that they had not needed to use hostages to fund their operations:

> For instance, when the CIA officer of Jewish origin was captured [i.e., Nicholas Berg],[20] the Americans offered a blank check in exchange for his return, but the brothers insisted on exchanging him for Iraqi jihadi detainees. When the Americans refused, Abu Musab beheaded him. . . . Still, jihad expenses are considerable, as you know. . . . Jaafar asked Abu Musab once, "How long does US$100,000 last?" He told him, "We're lucky if it covers expenses for three days."[21]

When Wakil enquired about attacks against the Shia, Jaafar acknowledged that "except for the killing of Baqir al-Hakim," all other attacks against the Shia were orchestrated by Abu Musab's group. Ayatollah Mohammed Baqir al-Hakim was the head of the Supreme Council of the Revolution in Iraq (SCIRI) and had returned to Iraq in May 2003 after two decades of exile in Iran. He was expected to exert considerable influence following the fall of Saddam.[22] Four months after his return, and after he delivered a Friday sermon calling for Iraqi unity, a car bomb detonated in a crowd of worshippers, killing the Ayatollah and eighty-five others. We can take Jaafar at his word and accept that Abu Musab's group was not behind the assassination, seeing that Jaafar was more than happy to take credit for all other attacks against the Shia.

Wakil was concerned about the indiscriminate targeting of the Shia. Though al-Qaeda rejects many of the Shia's theological premises, its priority was to "attack the Americans and their allies." Jaafar explained that the attacks "stem from the Shia's exploitation of the political vacuum" after the fall of Saddam. They were necessary, he added, because the Shia Badr Brigade "descended on Baghdad, taking over Sunni mosques, capturing Sunni Sheikhs and scholars, and assaulting women." Jaafar likely showed Wakil a note that Shia militants distributed in Basra to evict the Sunnis from the city. This warned "the Sunnis, the terrorists," that unless they "leave Basra and never return . . . bullets would be fired into their heads" to hasten "their transfer to hell."[23] A copy of the note was recovered from Usama's compound.

Jaafar gave Wakil the impression that Abu Musab had what it took to rally other jihadi groups in Iraq behind him. He indicated that "the number of groups joining Abu Musab was on the rise," and those that had already joined him did so "through a legal allegiance with an undertaking to wage jihad." By his count, "the number of individuals who joined Abu Musab's group were in the thousands, not to mention those from different countries." These groups, Wakil's letter related, "have complete control over Fallujah, Samarra, Buhriz, Baaquba, and large parts of Ramadi. So much so that police and army officers in Fallujah were appointed by jihadis."

Wakil, however, warned Jaafar that Abu Musab's group could be accused by the locals of being "foreigners serving outside actors," remarking on the absence of Iraqi leaders in its ranks. Jaafar explained that the latter was due "to the absence of experienced and veteran Iraqi jihadis," but assured Wakil that "Abu Musab has already put together an Iraqi leadership team that is now in charge of nearly everything on the level of the general leadership as well as the provinces." At that time, in 2004, according to Jaafar, Abu Musab had good relations with Ansar al-Sunna, the oldest militant group we mentioned earlier. Apparently, "many of Ansar al-Sunna's members had joined Abu Musab out of eagerness to wage jihad, because the group was not active in its own area, Kurdistan." As to the other group, the Islamic Army of Iraq, Jaafar noted that it was made up of "unknown Iraqis, but they seem to be good brothers and Abu Musab was on good terms with them."[24]

For the most part, Jaafar's account corroborates documented attacks, but we don't know if he was exaggerating the financial situation of Abu Musab's group. However, an outside observer might question Jaafar's response concerning the absence of Iraqis in leadership positions. His claim that there was an "absence of experienced" Iraqis is not consistent with his other claim, that Iraqis are "in charge of nearly everything."

Usama was not involved when Wakil was having his talks with Jaafar, but the "doctor," i.e., Ayman, had been briefed and approved the merger.[25] Ayman encouraged Abu Musab to proceed with making a "public announcement" in which he gave his allegiance to Usama.[26] The exchanges between Abu Musab and Wakil were concluded "forty-eight hours" before Abu Musab publicly pledged allegiance to Usama on October 17, 2004. On December 4, 2004, Usama publicly admitted Abu Musab's group, and conferred on him the title of "leader of al-Qaeda in Mesopotamia."

How did Usama envisage managing the "Brothers"?

We know from Usama's letters that he was mindful of the "shortcomings of managing from a distance." He also relied on couriers for all his communications with his "brothers" in al-Qaeda because he was wary of using emails and any means of transmission that could be intercepted by modern technology.[27] Though Usama's associates communicated with the "Brothers" using doubly encrypted software, everything that required Usama's approval had to wait for his letters to be hand-delivered by trusted couriers to and from his associates in North Waziristan.

In any case, Usama did not envisage hands-on management of the "Brothers." In this, as in most matters, Usama and his associates were guided by the Prophet Muhammad's example. They were inclined to "think well" (*husn al-zann*) of fellow Muslims—those committed to jihadism, in their case—and to accept that those who witness events as they unfold are better placed to make decisions than those who are absent.[28] In other words, Usama and his associates set al-Qaeda's broad strategy and Abu Musab was authorized to use his discretion as to how best to implement it. In principle, this was the template for all the "Brothers" who later joined al-Qaeda.

Was this a sensible approach? Theoretically speaking, it was not. But al-Qaeda's leaders were all "hiding" and lacked the ability to manage the "Brothers" directly. Usama was mindful of potential jihadi rivalries in Iraq and sought to prevent them. When he admitted Abu Musab's group into al-Qaeda, he advised that other jihadi groups in Iraq, "no matter how small in size," should "separately give allegiance to al-Qaeda in the media." Most likely, Usama reasoned that proceeding separately would mark and recognize the distinctness of each group, while the allegiance would display their union with al-Qaeda.

Also, it must have comforted Usama to learn that Abu Musab had forged solid ties with other Iraqi militant groups and he probably inferred that jihadi unity was forthcoming in Iraq. Abu Musab's outreach also gave Usama reasons to hope that jihadi groups outside Iraq might follow suit. In fact, and on his own initiative, Abu Musab proposed to send a letter to encourage his contacts in the "Algerian Salafi Group to follow the big brother," i.e., to give their allegiance to Usama.[29] We shall see later in this chapter that this eventually materialized. Usama was excited by the prospect of media processions of this sort, convinced that they would "raise the morale of Muslims, who would, in turn, become more engaged and supportive of jihadis."[30]

During Abu Musab's tenure (December 4, 2004—June 7, 2006), al-Qaeda faced two major problems in Iraq. First, contrary to Usama's hopes, Abu Musab's failure to unite Iraqi groups behind him resulted in jihadi infighting. Ansar al-Sunna refused to join Abu Musab even after he was publicly appointed by Usama as the leader of "al-Qaeda in Mesopotamia." Usama and his associates were receiving tabloid-like letters filled with inter-jihadi wrangling. Ansar al-Sunna claimed that Abu Musab was faking his popularity by "forming small fictitious groups with different names," and then "these groups went on to proclaim allegiance to al-Qaeda." This, it was claimed, was all about "publicity," giving the false impression that "groups and platoons were rushing to join al-Qaeda."[31]

The second major problem al-Qaeda faced was Abu Musab's indiscriminate attacks, which resulted in massive Iraqi casualties, particularly Shia. This was disturbing for the leaders of al-Qaeda. Usama and his associates wanted to be in the news not for killing Iraqis—regardless of their sectarian affiliations—but for inflicting injuries on American forces. While we cannot be sure about the claim that Abu Musab was faking his popularity in Iraq, his ruthless attacks were widely reported. Atiya assessed that "we cannot leave the brother to act on the basis of his judgement alone," and a December 2005 letter intercepted by U.S.

intelligence showed Atiya pressing Abu Musab to change his strategy. He urged him "to lessen the number of attacks, even to cut the current daily attacks in half, even less," pointing out that "the most important thing is for jihad to continue, and a protracted war is to our advantage." He instructed Abu Musab to seek the approval of al-Qaeda on consequential matters and also to consult regularly with Ansar al-Sunna for the sake of unity.[32]

With al-Qaeda pressuring him to unite with Ansar al-Sunna, Abu Musab changed the name of his group to the Jihadis' Advisory Council in Iraq in January 2006. He probably did so to project a more consultative leadership. But this didn't help him either, and he subsequently reported to al-Qaeda: "God is my witness, I first reached out to Ansar al-Sunna, but by God, the problem with these people has to do with their leaders who refuse to be led by others, even though 80 percent of their cadres and members have joined us."[33]

Abu Musab was also upset about rumors that he believed were maliciously spread by Ansar al-Sunna, and he complained in the voice messages he sent to al-Qaeda:

> They have been spreading lies about me. They say that I don't listen to suggestions; that I have caused them to despair, and they are fatigued by this.
>
> They say that I have become like the zealot Antar al-Zawabiri [leader of a notoriously extremist Algerian group killed in 2002]. Can you imagine?! Is that right?! Is that what it means to think well of your fellow Muslims? If it were up to me, I would strive to apply what I believe to be right. If the decision is up to you, you shall bear responsibility before God, for I am but a soldier, and know that I shall never disobey you (God forbid).[34]

Outsiders might be forgiven for failing to fathom how Abu Musab could consider himself mainstream, taking offense at being described as an extremist like Antar. But it is easy to imagine al-Qaeda's leaders, all socially distant in their respective hideouts, telling themselves: *That's not what we signed up for!* They found it all the more necessary to unite the two groups in Iraq. On

January 26, 2006, Ayman put on his matchmaker's hat and penned a letter to the leader of Ansar al-Sunna:

> My dear brother, I write to you this brief letter, but know that it is swelling with feelings. . . . Sheikh Usama instructed me to follow up with you on the issue of unity out of his desire to see Islam victorious in Iraq. . . . Do the brothers in Ansar al-Islam agree in principle to unite with al-Qaeda? If so, kindly send us a detailed proposal as to how you would like to proceed to achieve this unity.[35]

A meeting between al-Qaeda and two representatives from Ansar al-Sunna took place just before Ayman was about to send this letter. So a note from "al-Qaeda's special committee assigned to Iraq's affairs" was included in an addendum. It read: "We understood from brothers Abu al-Dardara' and Abu Muhammad in your group that, in principle, you support unity, but first, you wish to correct the ways of al-Qaeda in Mesopotamia so that unity is achieved on sound principles."[36] Al-Qaeda surmised from this meeting that, though there was a touch of exaggeration in Ansar al-Sunna's account, "there was a serious problem" that needed to be addressed with Abu Musab.

Public complaints about Abu Musab were also raised by the Islamic Army of Iraq. But when al-Qaeda investigated this further, it learned that the well-financed group was funded by Saudi Arabia. If this was accurate, Saudi Arabia may have wanted to undermine Abu Musab's group at whatever cost.

Al-Qaeda determined that a more hands-on approach was necessary to forge unity in Iraq and discussed sending Atiya there to keep a close watch on Abu Musab.[37] But before al-Qaeda could conclude its matchmaking, Abu Musab was killed in a U.S. airstrike on June 7, 2006. Days later, on June 13, his successor, Abu Hamza al-Muhajir, released a public statement giving the impression that he was following in Abu Musab's footsteps. In it, Abu Hamza appealed to his supporters: "do not to lay down your arms, do not rest, until each of you has killed at least one American." He also assured Mullah Omar, Usama, and Ayman that "we are as we have always been, marching on the path of jihad. . . . We are but a spear at your disposal, throw us wherever you like, and you shall find that we are but your obedient soldiers."

We don't know the intricate dynamics of the Iraqi militant landscape, but what transpired was highly irregular in the jihadi universe. In November 2006, Abu Hamza dissolved al-Qaeda in Mesopotamia (which had acquired different names by then), and gave his allegiance to Abu Omar al-Baghdadi, leader of the newly formed Islamic State of Iraq (ISI—not to be confused with Pakistan's intelligence agency). Abu Omar—an obscure Iraqi figure whose public statements were all audio-delivered to ensure his identity remained hidden—was designated the Commander of the Faithful (*amir al-mu'minin*) and Abu Hamza became his "Minister of Defense" and second-in-command.

The use of the word "State" in the name the Islamic State of Iraq and Abu Omar's title were odd, to say the least. In Islamic legal parlance, the "State" is the bureaucratic arm of the *umma*—the global community of Muslims—and the "Commander of the Faithful" is its leader. In a pre-modern nation-state setting, Muslims were urged to live in the abode of the Islamic state and give their allegiance to its leader. What were Abu Omar and Abu Hamza thinking? Was this an innocent attempt to unite jihadi groups in Iraq? Had they somehow lost their copy of al-Mawardi's *Ordinances of Government*, the textbook on Islamic public law? Was Abu Omar ousting Mullah Omar, the other Commander of the Faithful, and seeking to eclipse al-Qaeda? Was Usama expected to give his allegiance to Abu Omar?

Atiya was probably the only al-Qaeda leader to recognize immediately that the new semantics were dangerously irregular. On December 13, 2006, soon after the proclamation of the ISI, Atiya released a public statement that seemed to be highly supportive. But in between his cheers, Atiya was cutting Abu Musab's successors down to size:

> I should like to alert my brethren that this name, the "Islamic State of Iraq,"
> is just a descriptor of a social and political entity for jihadis and Sunnis. It
> is limited to this specific land of Islam. We should not forget that. . . .

Why did they not call it "Emirate" and chose to use the word "state" instead? This is a good question, but we should know that our brothers exercised their individual judgement and, after consulting with one another, they chose what they believed to be appropriate. . . .

As to the title "Commander of the Faithful," this designates the leader of the "state" that we just described. . . . Perhaps our brothers elected to use this title for reasons that are unknown to those of us who are afar.[38]

When Atiya released this statement, he was not yet a renowned al-Qaeda public figure.[39] As astute as his response was, it did not put an end to the criticisms that were being raised in jihadi circles. From al-Qaeda's perspective, the most concerning criticism of ISI came from the Kuwaiti scholar Hamid al-Ali. When he was asked online whether the proclamation of the ISI obligated Muslims to give their allegiance to its leader, Hamid unleashed a torrent of criticism. Citing a library's worth of Islamic legal texts, Hamid discredited the legitimacy of the ISI: "We advise that they should retract the proclamation of what has been called the Islamic State and return to their *status quo ante*, meaning a jihadi group that stands alongside other groups under the banner of jihad. . . . This so-called Islamic State of Iraq has no legal basis." Remarking on Abu Omar's obscure identity, Hamid went on to say that "there is nothing in Islam obligating Muslims to give their allegiance to a Sultan whose identity is unknown, who is hidden, and has no power and territorial strength."[40]

Hamid was a supporter of jihadism and his opinions mattered to Usama, not least because of his extensive knowledge of the classical Islamic corpus. But unlike Hamid, Usama's disposition was to "think well" of fellow Muslims, and he had a different take on the matter. He asked Ayman to launch a defensive campaign of the ISI and to make it known that this was not the time to quibble about semantics. Usama wanted Ayman to highlight that the real struggle was between "belief" and "unbelief," that is, "between those who want to make God's Word supreme"—represented by the leaders of the ISI—and "those who make kings and leaders supreme on earth"—represented by the United States and its local supporters.

But it is clear from Usama's letter that Hamid's response's troubled him. It was too powerfully scripted and legally supported to ignore. "I am not objecting to what the people of knowledge have said and that Hamid cited," Usama confessed to Ayman. "But I object to the fact that Hamid is ignoring the reality under which we live." Usama could relate to Abu Omar staying out of the public eye. "Who among us," he wrote, "is able to appear in public and consult with his brothers?" He asked Ayman to respond "calmly" to Hamid's criticisms by highlighting the jihadis' extenuating circumstances.[41]

What about unity with Ansar al-Sunna? We do not know first-hand their inner workings, but we can watch the show that both groups put on for al-Qaeda.

Abu Hamza sent a handwritten letter to the leader of Ansar al-Sunna in pursuit of unity, a copy of which was recovered in Usama's compound. It was filled with (insincere?) superlatives, and an undertaking "to be your obedient servant, your bodyguard if you so desire . . . all I ask is that you join hands with my Amir/leader and your brothers in the Islamic State and commit to fighting the people of unbelief." Abu Hamza went on to offer Ansar al-Sunna the ministries of their choosing "so that you may correct anything that you deem to be unlawful or corrupt." There was just "one condition: Do not touch the entity that is the Islamic State or its *amir*."[42]

Did Abu Hamza genuinely think that his letter would cause Ansar al-Sunna to unite with the ISI? Or did he know in advance that the outcome would be negative, and so wrote a letter that he wanted al-Qaeda's leaders to read and conclude: *How nice of the ISI to be so generous, and how unfortunate that Ansar al-Sunna is being difficult.* Probably the latter.

We learn from the response of the leader of Ansar al-Sunna, Abu Abdallah al-Shafii, that he believed that there was a great deal that needed correcting in the statehood project. He accused the ISI of extremism, including shedding the blood of Ansar al-Sunna fighters and other Sunnis. He equivocated on the question of unity, and insisted that the priority was for the ISI to change and moderate its beliefs.[43] Separately, Ansar al-Sunna alerted al-Qaeda that the ISI had been "confiscating the possessions of Sunnis who were not fighting the jihad"; "kidnapping and torturing people for minor suspicion"; and carrying out "martyrdom operations" where their Sunni foes were based, including in mosques.[44] Other complaints were raised about the ISI by its former chief judge, Abu Sulaiman al-Utaibi, who paid a visit to al-Qaeda in North Waziristan, but did not seem to be interested in giving allegiance to Usama or in being a team player.[45]

Al-Qaeda determined that Ansar al-Sunna was exaggerating and continued to think well of the ISI. One of Atiya's contacts in the jihadi media told him that Ansar al-Sunna was spreading malicious rumors, such as that "Abu Omar was just an illusion and does not exist. It was all Abu Hamza's 'game!'"[46] According to Ansar al-Sunna, it was the Egyptian Abu Hamza, and not the Iraqi Abu Omar, who was running the ISI. In other words, Abu Hamza simply needed to have an Iraqi leader as his front man. Atiya's contact also shared that Ansar al-Sunna "were so attached to their historical credentials" and felt entitled to take the lead. Apparently, "they do not profess such things, but everyone who knows them and mixes with them knows this."[47]

While we cannot be sure about the veracity of all the complaints about the ISI, it is clear that Abu Omar saw himself, in Islamic legal terms, as the legitimate leader of an Islamic state, thereby outranking the leaders of all jihadi groups. From our present vantage point, we may conclude that he was the founding leader of the global Islamic State that his successors proclaimed, again, in 2014.

The ISI's delusions of grandeur were apparent back in 2006. Its Ministry of Legal Affairs took much offense when Ansar al-Sunna continued to refer to Abu Hamza as the "leader of al-Qaeda" instead of recognizing that he had become a state "Minister."[48] The ISI's publications were at pains to stress that its leader was a Qurayshi, a descendant of the Prophet Muhammad's tribe— one of seven conditions for the office of the caliph.[49] It is noteworthy that Abu Omar did not correspond with al-Qaeda or meet with the leader of Ansar al-Sunna. In all likelihood, he thought that he outranked them, and delegated such matters to his "Minister," Abu Hamza.

By 2007–08, U.S. forces in Iraq had successfully, if temporarily, weakened the ISI. The policy that came to be known as the "Sunni Awakening" saw U.S.

forces forging ties with Sunni tribal sheikhs and led to a "tribal rebellion" against the ISI.[50]

We don't have letters from the ISI after late 2007. However, communications about the group reveal that there was much concern about its agenda and the religious rigidity that was increasingly apparent in the public statements of its leader.[51] A March 2008 letter from Ayman to Abu Omar went unanswered. Perhaps Abu Omar took offense that Ayman's letter did not address him in a sufficiently respectful manner. Ayman had written "Dear Brother/Commander of the Faithful . . .", which is the equivalent of addressing a CEO with "Dear Secretary/CEO."

But there were other factors at play that may explain the cessation of communications between al-Qaeda and the ISI. The leaders of al-Qaeda learned that "the situation of the Brothers is very bad and they have to keep moving their locations."[52] So bad that Atiya was preparing to eulogize the ISI. "God forbid," he wrote to Usama, "should the ISI collapse, we must be ready to support Islam and jihad there."[53] Clearly, the Sunni Awakening was having an impact, and subsequent letters that reached Usama had little to say other than "we have not heard from the Brothers in Iraq."[54]

In April 2010, Abu Omar and Abu Hamza were killed, and they must have turned in their graves when they were reported by the world's media as the "leaders of al-Qaeda in Iraq." By then, Usama had come to realize that the "Islamic State of Iraq" was not a suitable name after all, and determined that "we should come up with a plan to change it quietly." Al-Qaeda, he thought, should take advantage of the killing of the group's leaders to effect mergers between the ISI and Ansar al-Sunna and "as many other factions as possible." These mergers, he reasoned, should serve as an opportunity to change the name:

It would be agreed that a new entity with a new name would follow such a merger, and the new leader would be called the *amir* [i.e., leader] of this group and not by the title *amir al-mu'minin* [i.e., Commander of the Faithful]. It would be inappropriate to use a name that projects a greater entity than the actual reality of the group. In my view, it should be called at most "the Islamic Emirate of Iraq."[55]

But before Usama could act on this, within a month of Abu Omar and Abu Hamza's killing, the Shura Council of the ISI publicly announced its new leaders, Abu Bakr al-Baghdadi al-Husayni and Abu Abdallah al-Hasani. The statement claimed that both leaders were Qurayshis in order to establish their Islamic legal credentials to assume the office of the caliph; a copy of the announcement was recovered in Abbottabad.[56] It doesn't look like the group had performed the courtesy of informing al-Qaeda of its decision in advance. Most likely, al-Qaeda learned about the new leaders from the mainstream media and downloaded a full copy of the statement from a jihadi website.

The fortunes of the ISI changed under its new leadership. The group benefited from the United States' policy focusing on withdrawing its military forces (by 2011) and also exploited the sectarianism of Nouri al-Maliki's Iraqi government, which alienated Sunnis and undermined the gains that had been achieved under the Sunni Awakening policy. A noticeable increase in attacks against Christian neighborhoods, including churches, followed.[57]

Ayman disapproved of the group's new direction. On January 13, 2011, he had clearly reached the end of his tether when he wrote to Usama, urging him to take a more hands-on approach. Ayman believed that the ISI had not just targeted churches in Iraq, but was also behind the bombing of a Coptic church in Alexandria, Egypt, on January 1, 2011. He was very troubled, and his fury was palpable. "I do not understand," he wrote, "are the Brothers not content with the number of their current enemies, being so eager to add new ones to their list?"[58]

Ayman suggested to Usama that he should confirm Abu Bakr's appointment, but "make it known that this was a temporary appointment until further consultation." Ayman also thought that Usama should instruct them "to end their attacks against Christians in Iraq and Egypt," to stop "targeting the Shia indiscriminately," and to focus instead on the "threat emanating from America and Iran." Rather unusually, Ayman also took it upon himself to tell Usama what not to do:

> I hope that you do not conclude your letter by using expressions such as "you are better placed to judge what your situation requires" or "those who witness events are better placed to make decisions than those who are absent." Such expressions could be understood to annul all the guidance that preceded them. Instead, they should be told that "we await your views, and should you have any amendments to what we propose, be sure to send them to us before you act on your own, unless it is absolutely necessary."[59]

Clearly Ayman no longer believed that thinking well of fellow Muslims was working in the case of his "Brothers" in Iraq.

We do not know if Abu Bakr knew of Ayman's feelings, but we can be sure that he sensed them and waited for the right moment to let his spokesman respond. After Usama was killed, and three years into Ayman's leadership, Abu Bakr's group eclipsed al-Qaeda. When Ayman protested that Abu Bakr's group was not authorized to operate in Syria and was acting unilaterally, the group's spokesman, Abu Muhammad al-Adnani, emphatically stated that "the Islamic State is not a branch of al-Qaeda and it never was one." Addressing Ayman directly in his statement, he added, "should God allow that you set foot on its soil, you shall have no choice but to give allegiance to its *amir* and serve as a soldier in his army."[60] This was an unmistakable reference to the 2006 proclamation of "the Islamic State of Iraq" that saw Abu Hamza dissolve al-Qaeda and give allegiance to Abu Omar, the "Commander of the Faithful." In this case, Usama had been wrong to think well of his fellow jihadis, seeing that the name and the title were not matters of mere semantics.

North Africa

During 2006–07, al-Qaeda added North Africa to its global map when Ayman oversaw three mergers on behalf of Usama. These began with Egypt's Islamic

Group, followed by the most important—with the Algerian Salafist Group for Preaching and Combat (GSPC), then the Libyan Islamic Fighting Group (LIFG).

Islamic Group

In August 2006, Ayman announced al-Qaeda's merger with "an important branch of the Islamic Group," and indicated that the jihadi media outlet al-Sahab would "gradually produce and release this glad tiding as conditions permitted."[61] This turned out to be just a one-man show, with Muhammad Khalil al-Hakayma, a founding member of the Islamic Group, announcing that he had joined al-Qaeda.

The Islamic Group had been behind the 1981 assassination of Egypt's President, Anwar al-Sadat, and most of the group's leaders were subsequently executed or imprisoned. In 1997, a number of them renounced violence in a series of books they published under the title "The Initiative for Halting Violence." Ayman was of course critical of the "Initiative,"[62] and probably hoped that the merger with one of the group's founders might incite the "steadfast" among the rest to join al-Qaeda, even if their membership was *in absentia*. This did not happen.

Muhammad al-Hakayma had escaped to Iran after the fall of the Taliban, and when the authorities launched their campaign of arrests in late 2002, he "disappeared, cutting off all lines of communications" to evade capture.[63] Sometime in 2004, Muhammad sent a letter to Ayman, which we do not have. But the Bin Laden Papers do include a detailed letter that Muhammad sent to Ayman in 2008. This letter discussed at length how the Egyptian authorities orchestrated the release of a 2007 treatise by Ayman's one-time mentor, Dr. Fadl. In the treatise, which he wrote from his prison cell in Egypt, Dr. Fadl denounced the 9/11 attacks and blamed his former protégé and Usama for "causing the death of thousands of Muslims" by giving the United States an excuse to invade Afghanistan and Iraq.[64]

Muhammad's letter has more to add about this episode. Though it was widely reported that Dr. Fadl's treatise had been endorsed by other jihadi leaders in prison, Muhammad relates that most of them had not even read it. They were apparently furious and refused to talk to Dr. Fadl afterwards, treating him "like a dog." To be clear, Dr. Fadl's own writings are marked by religious extremism, yet he had the chutzpah to accuse Ayman and Usama of misinterpreting them.[65]

Ayman wrote a lengthy treatise, *al-Tabri'a*, that was also widely publicized, in response to Dr. Fadl's recantation. One of Usama's letters reveals that he would have preferred it if Ayman hadn't. "Overall, it was good," Usama wrote to Ayman, but he strongly disagreed with some of Ayman's interpretations of events during the early history of Islam. Usama was also troubled by Ayman publicly airing Dr. Fadl's dirty laundry: "Such responses would lead people to ask, '[If Dr. Fadl was that bad,] how could you accept having him as your leader.'" It would have been better, Usama thought, if al-Qaeda's Legal Committee had put out a response instead.[66]

Beyond relating the news of Egyptian jihadis, it does not appear that the addition of Muhammad to al-Qaeda had any operational value—unless we count the "knee brace and a packet of painkillers" that he sent to Ayman.[67]

Al-Qaeda in the Islamic Maghreb (AQIM)—née Salafist Group for Preaching and Combat (GSPC)

During an interview with the jihadi media outlet al-Sahab in August 2006, Ayman announced a "great tiding"—a merger with the "Salafist Group for Preaching and Combat (GSPC)," thereafter called "al-Qaeda in the Islamic Maghreb (AQIM)." He prayed that this "blessed merger" would serve as "a pin in the throats of the Crusaders . . . and bleed sorrow in the hearts of the apostates."

The GSPC rose from the ruins of Algeria's civil war (1991–2002), which saw anti-government forces splinter and turn against each other. So much blood was spilled that even Abu Musab al-Zarqawi found it repulsive. But the leaders of the GSPC that we meet in the letters are full-fledged jihadis who prioritized strategic and pragmatic considerations in their politics over the fanaticism of their predecessors.

As noted in the previous section, it was Abu Musab al-Zarqawi who set the merger in motion. A letter dated February 2004 and signed by one of the GSPC's leaders, Abu Haidara Abd al-Razzaq, a.k.a. "El Para," was recovered from Usama's compound. In it, El Para explains the politics of his group, seeks Usama's "counsel," and makes a proposal—"if possible, we wish to join hands to fight together the enemies of God."[68] In October the same year, El Para was arrested.[69] The letters don't reveal how contact was re-established, but in August 2006, Abu Musab Abd al-Wadud forged the merger with al-Qaeda.

Al-Qaeda knew little about the GSPC. Following their merger, it enquired about the group's capabilities and it wasn't until early 2009 that the leaders of what was now AQIM were able to share specifics about their group. We learn from AQIM's leader that his group used to operate in nine geographical zones, but in 2006, these had to be reduced to four "due to the decreasing number of jihadis." The group counted mostly Algerians among its members, plus an assortment of Libyans, Mauritanians, Tunisians, Nigeriens, and Malians. AQIM struggled to recruit people because most of its members had to flee the cities to the mountains, where they were "severely isolated." AQIM also suffered from "a large shortage" of qualified cadres and heavy weaponry.[70] The number of AQIM fighters was left blank for security reasons, and was likely included in a letter that was not recovered.[71]

On the financial front, the leader of AQIM happily remarked that his group was "for the first time in our history almost self-sufficient." Its funding had previously relied on the unpopular method of extorting taxes from the middle class, which made its tax collectors vulnerable to being arrested by the government. AQIM then adopted "hostage-taking" as its *métier*. It did this "for ransom" and/or for the freeing of imprisoned jihadis in the West and elsewhere. This had "numerous benefits," according to its leader:

> It is the best method to preach the goals of our jihad to a large segment of the society, many of whom respond surprisingly positively. When we take hostages, we treat the public exceptionally well, so well that they cannot believe it. We have so many amusing stories to share on that front.

Initially, al-Wadud relates, the group targeted locals, "the wealthy, of course." Fearing for their lives, he went on, these individuals pressured the government and, as a result, "severe legal measures" were introduced to punish the kidnappers. AQIM then shifted to kidnapping Westerners, prioritizing "Americans, English, Jews, and all European nationals." Al-Qaeda requested that Iranians be added to the list, and while al-Wadud promised that "we shall not forget your request should an opportunity arise," he explained that Iranians don't have much presence in Algeria, except in neighborhoods adjacent to their embassy.[72]

When al-Wadud was writing his letter in early 2009, his group had just concluded elaborate negotiations that saw the release of two Austrian hostages. "The brothers did their best to exchange the two hostages in return for the release of imprisoned jihadis," he reported, but Austria refused to meet their demands. Though a spokesman for Austria's Foreign Ministry asserted that "a ransom payment definitely did not come from Austria,"[73] we learn from al-Wadud that Austria had in fact paid "2 million euros" in return for the two hostages, "and it was agreed that this would be kept secret."

What was the value of this merger?

AQIM needed al-Qaeda's help on two major fronts, namely recruitment and (pragmatic) Islamic legal cover for its decisions. As noted earlier, AQIM was suffering from a shortage of manpower and hoped that if it merged with al-Qaeda, more foreign fighters would be inclined to join its ranks. Al-Wadud was impressed with how the leaders of al-Qaeda had championed Abu Musab al-Zarqawi in Iraq and wanted the same support for his group. But when al-Qaeda's public statements prioritized jihad in countries occupied by Americans, al-Wadud was peeved and bluntly asked for greater attention: "We have noticed that your political support of jihad in the Islamic Maghreb is minimal, noticeably less than what you did in support of Sheikh Abu Musab al-Zarqawi. We hoped that our virtuous Sheikhs would lend us more support on that front."

The response of the head of al-Qaeda's Legal Committee, Abu Yahya al-Libi, was swift. In June 2009, he released a public statement entitled "Algeria:

Between the Sacrifices of the Fathers and the Loyalty of Their Progenies."[74] On display was the importance of Algeria and North Africa to al-Qaeda's jihad. Abu Yahya's expression of solidarity was, of course, consistent with his jihadi worldview, but the letters reveal that he also needed a favor. It was rumored that his wife, who was in Libya, had remarried. A sympathetic Atiya asked AQIM to verify the story, and if she hadn't remarried, he enquired if the group might consider dropping the demand for ransom for one of its Western hostages in return for facilitating her travel to Iran. There, Abu Yahya's wife would stay with al-Qaeda's Sunni contacts until arrangements were made for her safe travel to North Waziristan.[75] We will return to this story.

AQIM also needed al-Qaeda to lend its legal and scholarly arm in support of pragmatic decisions tailored to its challenging circumstances. AQIM was guided by Islamic teachings, but it lacked scholars—learned in the Qur'an and Sunna and devoted to the study of jurisprudence—to steer its decisions. For instance, the group received constructive edits on its charter from Ayman.[76] But more than that, and to ensure the survival of his group, al-Wadud was desperate for the support of scholars who could justify taking advantage of political openings that some rigid jihadis in his group might consider unlawful.

AQIM's partnership with al-Qaeda paid off when al-Wadud faced a major dilemma in 2010. The government of Mauritania had reached out "through some channels," proposing to free members of AQIM and refrain from attacking the group, if, in return, the group abstained from attacking Mauritania. Al-Wadud jumped at the opportunity, but most of his men— particularly Mauritanians who "were wrathful" against the Mauritanian government—rejected the proposal outright. They argued that such a truce with the apostates (*muhadanat al-murtaddin*) was unlawful. Al-Wadud agreed with this legal premise, but believed that "their position did not take into consideration the extenuating circumstances under which they lived." In what sounded more like a personal plea than a formal legal query, he wanted al-Qaeda to look into this matter.[77]

Al-Wadud was asking for something that was virtually impossible. As he himself pointed out, according to the law of war in Islam, Muslims can enter into a truce with unbelievers,[78] but it is understood that apostates should be fought until they return to Islam.[79] Abu Yahya (who missed his wife) rose to the challenge. He opined that this matter was not settled in Islamic law, which meant that it was "open to interpretation." He found in the classical Islamic corpus a few instances on which he could build just the interpretation that al-Wadud needed. One of the historical examples he cited made it permissible for Muslims to correspond with apostates who had the military upper hand (*shawka*), and Abu Yahya deduced by analogy that this effectively amounted to a truce and the postponement of hostilities.[80] It is evident from the letters that al-Qaeda was quite preoccupied with researching the legality of such a truce and even consulted religious scholars in Saudi Arabia. Some of them saw its "benefits" while others wanted to think about it some more, but were nevertheless impressed with Abu Yahya's interpretation.[81]

Abu Yahya went even further, sympathizing with al-Wadud's position:

> Of course, we do not have the capability to confront the unbelieving states all at once, so what is the harm if we take a neutral stance regarding some of them . . .? What is important is that we consider these issues accurately, away from terrorizing and narrow-minded slogans.[82]

We don't know if Ayman was consulted. A younger and more rigid Ayman (in 1989) had argued the opposite. He had written a treatise on the same subject, using the very slogans that infuriated Abu Yahya.[83] Some jihadi scholars continued to cite Ayman's treatise to reject outright making a truce with apostates.[84]

Another legal matter that was subjected to noteworthy deliberations concerned "a veritable jihadi drama," namely the sexual deprivations of AQIM men due to their isolation in the mountains. We learn from the letters that about 90 percent of the fighters were unmarried, and most of those who were married led a near-celibate life, because they had been instructed to move their wives to the cities. The very few whose wives dwelled in the mountains were a liability to

AQIM: The bulk of the group's energy was devoted to meeting the women and children's needs, which were very challenging. The letters explain that this was "painful," particularly because "jihad suffered." On occasion, the fighters should have retreated, but chose instead to enter into unwinnable military confrontations out of fear that one of the "sisters" might fall captive if they did.[85]

AQIM shared details of its "drama" in response to a query from al-Qaeda. Intriguingly, though AQIM had not asked for a solution, al-Qaeda provided one anyway. Atiya's letter was "highly confidential" and to be shared only with AQIM's top three leaders. We could picture him dithering and blushing as he was composing the following passage:

> It concerns the problem of the poor celibate brothers and their overbearing situation. . . . I wrote to Sheikh Ayman about this and consulted with Sheikh Abu Yahya. Dr. Ayman wrote to us with his opinion. We all concluded—and on an exploratory basis that is far from being settled— that in view of the brothers' extenuating circumstances, we do not object to letting them know that it would be permissible for them to masturbate.

Of course, Atiya had done some homework on the subject and found that in the early history of Islam, "permission to masturbate had been granted by some of the righteous predecessors during conquest."[86] Still, he was at pains to qualify the proposal:

> This practice is not customary and it is rather embarrassing. The brothers in the Islamic and jihadi movements are not accustomed to broaching this issue. It could be misunderstood. It may have negative implications to which we have not been attentive. . . . What do you think? Should we avoid proposing it altogether and prescribe continuing exhaustive patience and fasting instead?[87]

The celibacy "drama" was specific to the men isolated in the mountains in North Africa, but something related was clearly happening at al-Qaeda's end. We learn from other letters that al-Qaeda's finances were tight in North Waziristan, and the group was having to deny its members their marriage requests. Most likely, al-Qaeda was testing whether making masturbation "permissible" would receive wider support from fellow "Brothers."

Unlike other "Brothers," it does not appear that AQIM became a liability to al-Qaeda. We get the sense that the leaders of the groups were like-minded, particularly on matters that required a pragmatic political approach. We also glean that AQIM wanted to serve as the conduit through which other groups in the Maghreb could join al-Qaeda, but without the competitiveness that we observed among Iraqi groups. For instance, in 2007, al-Murabitun, a group from Mauritania, sent a promising young man, Younis al-Mauritani—whom we met in Chapter Six—to North Waziristan to pursue a merger with al-Qaeda. When Ayman consulted AQIM about this, al-Wadud, who knew little about al-Murabitun at the time, noted:

> The group appears to be on the right path . . . but most of them lack experi-
> ence. As far as I am aware, only one of them has been to Afghanistan [i.e., the
> leader of al-Murabitun, Belmokhtar]. . . . In general, we advise that you
> direct such brothers to join us as a first step. We would provide them with
> training, support, and battlefield experience. . . . Then we would be in a posi-
> tion to endorse those who are suited. On another level, however, opening the
> door to little-known and small groups to join the original al-Qaeda might
> lead to negative consequences in the future, particularly because you have
> chosen for us the name al-Qaeda in the Islamic Maghreb. God knows best.[88]

AQIM was obviously protecting its North African turf, and al-Qaeda seems to have accepted al-Wadud's counsel as it did not follow up with al-Murabitun. However, as we discovered previously, the group's envoy, Younis al-Mauritani, impressed the leaders of al-Qaeda and stayed in North Waziristan.[89]

Sometime in 2009, AQIM shielded al-Qaeda from a group based in Nigeria known by the name Boko Haram.[90] Its leader, Abu Bakr Shekau, sent a letter saying he wanted a merger, but it is not evident from the files recovered by the SEALs whether the letter was addressed to AQIM or to al-Qaeda. At any rate, Shekau had not heard of al-Wadud and, more surprisingly, he knew very little about al-Qaeda or even its 9/11 attacks. Usama and Ayman could not have been flattered when they read his letter. "We have heard your leaders' speeches on cassettes," Shekau wrote, but went on to add that it was necessary "to learn more about al-Qaeda as an organization."[91] Al-Wadud offered Shekau training and financial support, but advised him not to declare jihad in Nigeria until his group was sufficiently prepared.[92] The relationship between Shekau and AQIM did not end well, and al-Qaeda was spared the drama. Shekau's group went on to suffer from internal splits, and AQIM subsequently made public its correspondence with the various warring factions.[93] (In 2015, the same Shekau gave his allegiance to the Islamic State, and this episode also ended in internal splits.[94] In June 2021, Shekau was reported to have died by detonating explosives on himself after fighting a rival jihadi group.)[95]

The relationship between AQIM and al-Qaeda seems to have been comparatively uncomplicated as long as the groups did not step on each other's turf. When they eventually did, the relationship experienced turbulence. In September 2010, AQIM kidnapped several French hostages (four men and a woman) and Usama rushed to take the lead in the negotiations before clearing it with AQIM. He instructed Atiya:

> I should like for you to send a letter to our brothers in the Islamic Maghreb immediately to let them know that they should not accept ransom from the French government. Instead, negotiations should be on the basis of political grievances only. The withdrawal of French forces from Afghanistan should be at the top of the list of grievances. They should also demand that the French government stop interfering in the affairs of the Islamic Maghreb.[96]

Usama added that "kidnapping women is delicate" and wanted AQIM to release the woman quickly and for ransom. He instructed that the hostages should be well treated and, most importantly, they should be apprised of their government's role in Muslims' grievances. He hoped that, upon her release, the woman "would mount a campaign against her French government."[97] But rather than waiting for the letter to reach AQIM, Usama took his grievances directly to the French people, releasing a public statement in November 2010 in which he demanded the withdrawal of French troops from Afghanistan. Otherwise, he threatened to have the hostages killed: "you shall be killed just as you have been killing [us]."[98]

Usama's statement was poorly timed, as AQIM's negotiations with the French government were already under way. In fact, the group only learned of Usama's demands through the media, and its leaders clearly thought that he was asking for the impossible, because the "brothers here had agreed to make reasonable demands."

One of AQIM's top leaders, Salah, informed Atiya that his group's demands, which included ransom, had been agreed to by the French. According to his letter, AQIM had also investigated the personal status of Abu Yahya's wife and had ascertained that she was still married to him, and the French had even agreed to facilitate her travel to Iran. But Salah lamented that after Usama publicly intervened with a different list of demands, the negotiations were "disrupted." Concerned that Usama focused exclusively on political demands in his public statement, Salah underlined "the extreme importance of the financial dimension of hostage-taking" for the survival of the group, but of course "we hear and obey our leader Sheikh Usama."[99]

It was reported that the female hostage was freed in February 2011, but the terms of her release do not come up in the letters, nor does it appear that Abu Yahya was reunited with his wife. Five days before he was killed, Usama privately reneged on his threat to kill the French hostages. By then, the French had intervened in Libya under NATO's command as part of a UN Resolution (1973) that authorized "all necessary measures to protect civilians." In the last batch of letters that he wrote in Abbottabad, Usama included the following passage:

> I should like to point out that in view of France's position in support of the Libyan people, it is no longer appropriate to kill the French hostages. This

would have negative effects, not least because the majority of the [Muslim] public is supportive of [French President] Sarkozy. If we need to kill them, we will do so once the events in Libya are over.[100]

Usama's intrusion was clearly a burden on AQIM and certainly on the French hostages, who had to endure three additional years in captivity, until they were freed in 2013.[101] The French government eventually killed al-Wadud in June 2020. Judging by the letters, the AQIM leader was missed by his confrères in al-Qaeda.

The Libyan Islamic Fighting Group (LIFG)

In November 2007, Ayman publicized that al-Qaeda was to add a third merger in North Africa, this time with a "distinguished group" (*kawkaba*) from the Libyan Islamic Fighting Group (LIFG). The LIFG was founded in 1995 by a group of Libyans who had fought in Afghanistan and, upon their return to Libya, sought to overthrow the President, Colonel Muammar al-Qadhafi. The group had been suppressed by the late 1990s, and many of its members took up jihad elsewhere, including in Afghanistan.

The "distinguished group" turned out to be Abu al-Laith al-Libi and Abu Yahya al-Libi, and possibly a few other Libyans. Abu al-Laith had been a field commander with an extensive network in Afghanistan.[102] He had given his partial allegiance to Usama in 2004, but it wasn't publicized. According to a 2004 letter, Abu al-Laith's allegiance to Usama was limited to Afghanistan and Pakistan, and he wanted to consult with the LIFG before giving his full allegiance.[103] He was a promising acquisition, but inattentive to operational security measures. Abu al-Laith was killed in early 2008, within months of his publicized merger with al-Qaeda. According to one letter, he was killed after "he visited a house that was already known to [the CIA] and while the drones were roaming above it."[104] The letters suggest that this was a great loss for al-Qaeda.

The second person was none other than the talented Abu Yahya, whom we have already met. Abu Yahya went on to become the head al-Qaeda's Legal

Committee, and incited Muslims to take up jihad in his passionate public statements. When the leaders of jihad were "martyred," Abu Yahya's fiery eulogies were especially consoling to the jihadi community. When Usama wanted to appoint him as Atiya's deputy in 2010, Atiya thought it would be more advantageous if "Abu Yahya continued to climb the ladder of knowledge," and "devoted his time to learning the Qur'an and the Sunna, to the study of jurisprudence, and to issuing authoritative legal opinions."[105] There is no hint of jealousy in Atiya's response, and he harbored no doubts about Abu Yahya's potential as his deputy. Rather, his response was a tribute to Abu Yahya's legal knowledge and research skills which were invaluable to al-Qaeda's political needs.

We learn from the letters that Abu al-Laith and Abu Yahya did not fully merge with al-Qaeda even after their union was publicized. Usama had appealed to both of them to merge fully with al-Qaeda just as Abu Musab in Iraq and AQIM had done.[106] The two must have hesitated and proposed to merge with AQIM instead. Ayman wrote to AQIM about this,[107] but by the time al-Wadud responded in March 2008, the merger had already been announced and Abu al-Laith had been killed.

According to the letters, Abu Yahya and his Libyan brethren had attached a "condition" to their merger, which was "to maintain their financial independence." This entailed "keeping their funding to themselves and investing it." Presumably, the Libyans had been receiving either separate donations or personal/family money. We learn from one of the letters that it was only in late 2010 that "an agreement was reached with our brother Abu Yahya to merge fully with al-Qaeda." Abu Yahya's decision coincided with AQIM's negotiations over the French hostages. He must have appreciated that al-Qaeda had interceded with AQIM to prioritize reuniting him with his wife over receiving a ransom. His decision to merge his finances fully with al-Qaeda brought "great joy" to everyone.[108]

Abu Yahya was killed in June 2012, just after honoring Usama with one of his most incendiary eulogies. The mighty United States "that spreads its military bases across the world and whose intelligence agencies infiltrate the hearts of all other states," he ridiculed, "celebrated the killing of one man as if it was a victory celebration over a massive warring army after a fierce and crushing battle."[109]

Al-Qaeda in the Arabian Peninsula (Yemen)

Of all the Brothers, al-Qaeda in the Arabian Peninsula (AQAP) is the only group that skipped the courtesies and formalities that went into the mergers—i.e., giving public allegiance to Usama before being officially admitted into the group. Instead, the group unilaterally assumed the al-Qaeda brand as its own. This was a sign of worse things to come.

The group had been operational in Yemen before it settled on its AQAP name in January 2009. Initially, it consisted of jihadis who escaped from Sanaa prison in 2006–07. Some of the escapees first headed to Somalia to fight against Ethiopian occupying forces.[110] They then returned to Yemen to continue their jihad against the government there, and jihadis from Saudi Arabia eventually flocked to join them.[111] In late 2007, news of their arrival in Yemen must have reached Usama, prompting him to remark in passing that "Abu Basir" was better qualified than someone he referred to as "the other undisciplined man."[112] In May or June 2008, Atiya sought Usama's guidance concerning "the brothers who expressed an interest in opening an al-Qaeda branch in Yemen." It didn't look like they were asking for permission, and Atiya awkwardly added that "they already had and had publicly announced their branch."[113] The group had indeed described itself as "al-Qaeda in the Arabian Peninsula in the Land of Yemen" in the inaugural issue of its Arabic magazine, *Sada al-Malahim* (January 2008).[114]

What did AQAP want from al-Qaeda?

Judging by the letters of its leaders, the group's rise was poorly planned. It was probably in 2009 that Abu Hurayra al-Sanaani, the group's second-in-command, sent an urgent letter to the leaders of al-Qaeda. He needed to brief them on a matter that he would have much preferred "to keep concealed":

With God's help, jihad has advanced in Yemen, the *muhajirun* [i.e., foreign fighters] and *ansar* [local jihadis] are multiplying, and our presence is visible in some places. . . . But the situation is far from easy. What I wish to say is that this expansion of jihad has highlighted our deficiencies concerning leadership and administration. It is clear to us that on that front, our abilities are nonexistent. . . . This threatens the total destruction of jihad in Yemen, God forbid (but I won't hide this from you). What we desperately need is a mature and well-grounded leader with foresight and knowledge in matters related to acquiring territorial strength . . . (you are better placed to know the needs of a nascent group).

Abu Hurayra was clearly desperate to introduce some order into the chaotic jihad in Yemen, and hinted that Abu Muhammad al-Misri would be the ideal candidate to lead them. "He is an example of the kind of leader that we need," he remarked, and "we know him and he knows us and our situation." He was clearly unaware that Abu Muhammad was detained in Iran; in any case, al-Qaeda was not in the habit of loaning out one of its own to lead regional groups.

At that time, it looked like the choices were limited to Abu Hurayra himself and Abu Basir. Abu Hurayra determined that it was his religious obligation to share with al-Qaeda his own shortcomings, however embarrassed that made him feel:

I regret that I do not have what it takes to fulfill this leadership role. Your brother [meaning himself] only completed elementary school and a few other courses,[115] and more importantly, he has neither experience that allows him to assess events wisely nor is he equipped to judge when, how, and where he should strike. His complete ignorance also extends to matters of basic governance. . . . By God, if I thought that I was up to the task, I would not have asked you to designate someone other than me to take on that role. . . . We are now supporting our brother Abu Basir and his brethren, but he is in desperate need of having statesmen by his side.[116]

Ultimately, Abu Basir became the leader of the group. But Abu Hurayra's letter must have unsettled al-Qaeda's leaders, not least because AQAP was escalating its attacks in Yemen and plotting international terrorism. The U.S. embassy attack in Yemen (2008) which killed ten policemen and civilians, the killing of four South Korean tourists there (2009), and the plot to explode a passenger jet over Detroit (2009) were just a few of the attacks that were reportedly carried out or attempted by AQAP.[117]

What was in the merger for al-Qaeda?

Al-Qaeda did not have a say in the matter. As noted earlier, the launch of AQAP was a unilateral decision that was practically imposed on al-Qaeda. As far as Usama was concerned, the "Brothers" in Yemen believed themselves to be in the midst of jihad, when, in reality, they were merely reacting to being chased by the authorities after their prison escape. Usama drafted several letters about Yemen that were recovered during the raid, but it is not clear if he ended up sending any, perhaps because Abu Basir is depicted as sophomoric at best. In his lengthiest draft letter (thirty-one pages), Usama asked Abu Basir:

> Did you actually plan and prepare for jihad at this specific time, taking into consideration the disproportion in power between you and the local, regional, and international enemies? Or is your presence a result of a few government attacks to which the brothers responded; and in the midst of this reactive battle, it occurred to you that you should persist, taking into consideration only the weak battalion against which you were fighting, i.e., the government of Yemen?[118]

"There were many powerful reasons," Usama thought, why the jihadis in Yemen should refrain from "getting into a military confrontation." It was not the government forces that he feared, but rather the presence of U.S. forces in neighboring Gulf states, ready to defend their allies against a jihadi entity that threatened their security.

The incoherent strategy of the Yemeni "Brothers" was clearly a challenge for the leaders of al-Qaeda. AQAP was led by two men, neither of whom believed he was fit for the job. Abu Hurayra professed his ineptitude, while Abu Basir chose to nominate Anwar al-Awlaqi, a Yemeni-American, to take his place. Anwar's English writings had incited many in the West who could not read Arabic to take up jihad. Usama refused to endorse him, not least because of his lack of battlefield experience. Anwar was most likely "the other undisciplined man" to whom Usama referred in his 2007 letter.

The lack of a suitable leader did not deter AQAP's ambitions. Abu Basir advised al-Qaeda that "if ever you wanted to seize Sanaa, now is the time." He explained that the deteriorating political situation created a window of opportunity to establish a jihadi state in Yemen. Otherwise, he feared being "outrivaled by the Muslim Brotherhood and the communists." According to Abu Basir, AQAP was so popular that "there is not a single area in Yemen where we lack supporters or sympathizers." He also boasted that his group enjoyed the support of "many of the tribes" and "tribal Sheikhs have given us their allegiance."[119]

In January 2010, after receiving Abu Basir's boastful assessment, the associates in Waziristan proposed to Usama:

The brothers believe that the war against the government is pretty much forced upon them. . . . Our view is that Yemen has numerous advantages, not least its proximity to Somalia. It is in our interest to expand the battle against the Americans to exhaust them and deplete their resources. But there has to be a plan . . . and the brothers must be up to the challenge. They should be cognizant of their size and abilities. They must not deceive themselves by the occasional win or by what people in the media say about them, otherwise they will delude themselves about a reality that does not exist! We must fully support them politically, morally, steer them in matters of law and jurisprudence, and share our expertise and experiences with them. We propose that you support them explicitly by mentioning their names and the names of their tribes. . . . We need to find ways and channels to communicate with them on a weekly basis, and daily if possible! We should steer the brothers to focus their attacks on two fronts: (1) targeting the Crusaders inside Yemen and conducting special operations against security forces, such as the intelligence agencies; (2) external work (which relates to our war against the spearhead, America). . . . It is necessary that we issue frank and stringent guidelines to the brothers there, stipulating that they must consult and check with us on all important matters; that they must not act on their own concerning matters that are remotely serious or might appear to be weird or a departure from our strategy. . . . Relations between Yemen and Somalia must be arranged, guided, and precisely ordered, so that both may form a united front. . . . As to the Houthis [i.e., an offshoot of the Shia in Yemen], we don't propose fighting them. We believe that it would be best to let the Houthis and the Yemeni and Saudi regimes all fight each other. May they do so, and when they do, we should not interfere. Instead, we should take advantage of the weaknesses of all to pursue our noble project.[120]

Usama was less hopeful than his associates about the abilities of the Brothers in Yemen. He ridiculed Abu Basir's proposal to establish an Islamic state in Yemen given that the basic components of statehood were nonexistent. He was also suspicious of Abu Basir's account of AQAP's popularity. Mindful that it takes considerable effort to gain tribal support, Usama asked Abu Basir to be more specific:

Kindly tell us more about the tribes that gave allegiance to the group, those that support it and those that do not. You don't need to mention their names to protect their security. But, for instance, you can indicate that "half of Shabwa's tribes gave their allegiance," or "a third of Hadramawt's tribes are supportive," etc.[121]

Usama drew Abu Basir's attention to the mistakes that jihadis in Iraq had committed when they alienated the tribes (a reference to the earlier Sunni Awakening in Iraq). He warned Abu Basir about the "danger of starting a war to establish a state on the basis that you hope that the people will fight alongside you . . . and before securing the loyalty of the tribes."[122]

Usama took it upon himself to educate Abu Basir not just about the basics of politics and strategy, but also about why "al-Qaeda prioritizes attacking the external ahead of the internal enemy." Though "the unbelief of the internal enemy is more repulsive," Usama explained, "the unbelief of the external enemy, America, is clearer and more harmful." As if he were giving a one-on-one tutorial, Usama asked Abu Basir: "Did you stop to look far enough to see the crouching armies behind the hills, i.e., the regional and international powers of unbelief? We must take all these powers into our practical, not just theoretical consideration."[123] To be clear, Usama's advice is not an indication that his terrorist aspirations diminished with age. Far from it. But by 2009, he was beginning to experience what we might describe as Brothers-fatigue. We shall find out later that he came up with a "new vision" for al-Qaeda to curtail the activities of the "Brothers" altogether.

It is likely that Usama decided not to send his lengthy letter to Abu Basir and refrained from disclosing to Abu Basir how he truly felt about AQAP. Instead, he shared his draft letter with Atiya and asked him to communicate al-Qaeda's opposition to any confrontation with Yemeni forces. Atiya complied, and stressed in his letter to Abu Basir that Usama had determined that war "against the apostate regime was not suitable at this point in time." The priority, he informed him, "was to invest all our resources to strike the head—America—and we do that by focusing on external work [i.e., international terrorism]."[124]

This did not please Abu Basir, who made it known that AQAP had "external work" of its own. We find Atiya in July 2010 griping that al-Qaeda was being left completely out of the loop:

With respect to the external operations that you mentioned in your letter, it would be good if you ran them by me first. If I then follow up asking for more details, it's because I have been authorized by the leadership (Sheikh Usama) to oversee external operations in all the regions. In other words, I should be informed about such operations so that I may liaise and organize such work. I have already notified you about this, and I hope that you let

THE BIN LADEN PAPERS

Sheikh Anwar know as well. Such matters should be highly secretive (limited to the leaders). Besides, we also have organizational protocols, experiences, and expertise in external work (especially that which targets the spearhead, America).[125]

It does not appear that Atiya was able to exercise much influence over Abu Basir. In his follow-up letter, Abu Basir merely informed Atiya that "we have an operation involving toxin (*sumum*) coming up, I am prepared to share the information if you like, but they say that the encryption software, Asrar al-Mujahidin, is infiltrated."[126]

Had Usama not been killed, it is unlikely that he would have succeeded in curtailing the terrorism of AQAP. Abu Basir's last letter to Atiya (February 2011) was assertive, dismissing outright al-Qaeda's proposal to put an end to AQAP's attacks against the government. "The men here would not understand it," he insisted, for "they would see this as a rapprochement with the regime that collaborates with the infidels." Abu Basir also wanted to incorporate the sectarian card into his jihad, knowing that this was against al-Qaeda's instructions:

The Sunni tribes, especially in the Houthi areas, are counting on us after some of the operations we carried out against the Houthis. I know that you have a different view on this issue. But the reality of war forces this upon us, and it is a military necessity. All the tribes are with us [against the Houthis] and they support us.[127]

Abu Basir ended his letter on a personal note, gleefully sharing that he had recently married the daughter of his deputy, Abu Hurayra. "She's twelve," he added. Marrying girls at a very young age is considered normal in the jihadi world, but Abu Basir sounded as if he was boasting on this occasion. Atiya's response did not include good wishes to the groom, and focused instead on urging moderation in his operations. He exhorted Abu Basir to adopt a policy of "leniency" and to take advantage of the political vacuum created by the Arab

Spring. If Abu Basir could demonstrate "good management (*husn idara*)" and "avoid getting into peripheral conflicts," Atiya advised, AQAP could "build a true Islamic jihadi authority in Yemen."[128] Doubtless, Atiya knew that this was wishful thinking on his part.

Abu Basir was killed in a drone strike in 2015 and was succeeded by the professedly "ignorant" Abu Hurayra, until he too was killed in a drone strike five years later. Neither was able to take advantage of Yemen's deteriorating political situation. Instead, it was the Houthis who seized the capital, Sanaa, and provoked a Saudi-led coalition to launch Operation Decisive Storm in 2015, aggravating the Yemenis' ongoing devastations.

Somalia

In February 2012, Ayman announced al-Qaeda's merger with the Somali militant group al-Shabaab. Of course, the Bin Laden Papers do not take us beyond May 1, 2011, but some letters allow us to reconstruct the context of this merger. Before we do, it is helpful to provide some historical context for al-Qaeda's involvement in East Africa, including Somalia's complicated political landscape.

In 1993, al-Qaeda sent its top leaders to Somalia to train clans fighting in the Ogaden region,[129] where Somalia and Ethiopia were embroiled in a conflict.[130] In 1998, al-Qaeda carried out simultaneous attacks that targeted U.S. embassies in Nairobi, Kenya and Dar es Salaam, Tanzania. In 2002, al-Qaeda operatives attempted simultaneous attacks in Mombasa: The first was a missile that narrowly missed hitting an Israeli El Al plane, while the other targeted an Israeli-owned hotel, killing thirteen people. As previously discussed, the operatives who carried out the Mombasa attacks were dispatched to East Africa before the 9/11 attacks, and stayed on. In 2002, the United States established a counterterrorism taskforce in Djibouti to track down al-Qaeda militants in the Horn of Africa.

In 2006, the Islamic Courts Union (ICU) took control of Somalia's capital, Mogadishu.[131] Their response to lawlessness was guided by their implementation of Islamic law. Their success in establishing order emboldened them to reject the national reconciliation process that was launched as part of a 2004 transitional government under the presidency of Abdullahi Yusuf, a long-time ally of Ethiopia, and backed by the UN and the African Union.[132]

On the sidelines, Islamist and jihadi groups were being formed independent of the ICU. On occasion, the jihadis liaised with elements within the ICU. To the outside world, particularly the U.S. counterterrorism taskforce in nearby Djibouti, this looked like *déjà vu*—i.e., a repeat of the Taliban harboring al-Qaeda and another 9/11 in the making. In July 2006, with the blessing of the United States, Ethiopian troops crossed the border into Somalia under the pretext that they were training the transitional government, prompting the ICU to declare a "holy war" against Ethiopia. When the Ethiopian parliament authorized "all necessary and legal steps to avert the danger arising from the repeated declaration of a 'holy war' against the country,"[133] it was in effect authorizing a retroactive measure, since Ethiopian forces had already unofficially invaded Somalia.

The ICU were forced to disband and withdraw from all cities in the face of Ethiopian ground- and air-force attacks. But political violence by Islamist and jihadi groups continued in Somalia. In response, the African Union deployed AMISOM (African Union Mission in Somalia) in March 2007 to carry out peace operations in support of the transitional government. In 2009, Ethiopia withdrew its forces from Somalia.

Outreach from Somalia

Fadil Harun—the al-Qaeda operative who planned the 1998 East Africa bombings and the 2002 Mombasa attacks—noted in his autobiography that he sent an email to al-Qaeda in late 2006 to brief "Sheikh Usama" about the situation in Somalia.[134] Though Usama refers to Harun in one of his 2004 letters, it does not appear from the Bin Laden Papers that contact was actually established between them, and it is unlikely that Harun's 2006 email ever reached al-Qaeda. The first Somali militants to initiate contact with al-Qaeda was the group Jaysh al-'Usra in 2007.[135] Contact was made through the Yemeni militants who fought in Somalia before returning to Yemen to form AQAP,[136] as mentioned previously.

According to Harun, Jaysh al-'Usra was formed in 2004 by the Kenyan Saleh al-Nabhan, who had been a member of an al-Qaeda cell in East Africa before parting ways with its leader "to pursue al-Qaeda's strategy in the region."[137] The group is named after the seventh-century "Raid of Hardship," which the Prophet Muhammad readied to defend his nascent Islamic state after hearing of a potential invasion by the Byzantines.[138] Echoing the seventh-century "Raid," Jaysh al-'Usra was "devoted to fighting the Crusader enemy and its subordinates, the apostates."[139] The Prophet Muhammad had averted the Byzantines' march on Medina, and Jaysh al-'Usra wanted to replicate the Prophet's raid and force back the Ethiopian forces that had invaded Somalia in July 2006.

As far as we can tell, the correspondence between Jaysh al-'Usra and Atiya was limited to legal queries related to the political situation in Somalia: A jurist had issued a legal opinion (*fatwa*) advocating that the (defeated) ICU should forge an alliance with the secularists who opposed the Ethiopian occupation of Somalia. Jaysh al-'Usra had counted the secularists among the "apostates" it was fighting, and wanted to consult al-Qaeda as to the legal merit of the *fatwa*. After carefully examining it, Atiya categorically determined that the *fatwa* was advocating an unlawful alliance, and was disappointed that a Muslim jurist would even entertain it. He lamented "[t]he huge difference between, on the one hand, the jihad of our brothers in al-Qaeda and those who follow their path . . . and, on the other hand, those who associate with jihad or resistance and follow the 'Muslim Brotherhood' and their like!"[140]

There is no mention of al-Shabaab in the letters signed by Jaysh al-'Usra. There was merely a generic reference to other jihadis working hard "to implement Sharia, which is not easy in this country."[141] Therefore, when Usama released a public statement cheering "the heroes of Somalia to keep up the fight" in March 2009,[142] he was responding to the concerns raised by Jaysh al-'Usra. He called on his "Muslim brothers in Somalia to be wary of initiatives that are dressed in the cloak of Islam when in reality they contradict Sharia."[143] A month earlier, Ayman had passionately argued for jihad in Somalia,[144] and we glean from one of Usama's letters that he had some quibbles about it. He wrote to Ayman:

> I was happy to postpone my statement about Somalia, otherwise it would have appeared that we differ on the subject. . . . It would be good if, when you call on Muslims to join jihad in Somalia in your future statements, you take into consideration skin color and encourage Muslims to coordinate with the local leaders before they head there.[145]

It seems that Usama wanted to avert any racial tensions that might result if Muslims from different races were to travel to fight in Somalia. He wanted local leaders to decide who should join them on the battlefield.

In early 2009, when all these exchanges about Somalia were taking place both in public and in private, Usama knew little about al-Shabaab and even confused it with the Islamic Party. Ayman had to explain to him that "Hasan Hersi was not the leader of al-Shabaab, he was in fact the leader of one of three [sic] factions that had merged to form the Islamic Party." Hasan was one of the Sheikhs that al-Qaeda's top leaders had met back in 1993 when they went to Somalia to train clans to fight in the Ogaden region.[146]

How did the contacts that began with Jaysh al-'Usra result in a merger between al-Shabaab and al-Qaeda in 2012? The leader of Jaysh al-'Usra, Saleh, was killed in September 2009. The leader of al-Shabaab, Mukhtar Abu al-Zubayr, then saw an opportunity. That same month, al-Shabaab released a video enti-tled "I Have Answered Your Call, Usama" (labbaika Usama), even though Usama had not been calling, not al-Shabaab anyway. Clearly, Mukhtar was hoping to merge his group with al-Qaeda.

Why was al-Shabaab so desperate to merge with al-Qaeda?

Mukhtar Abu al-Zubayr was likely inspired by the ICU and wanted to repli-cate what they had done on the governance front. When we first hear from him, we learn that his group was seeking to govern and was juggling several things at the same time: namely, "acquiring territorial strength and implementing Sharia as we fight the [foreign] aggressors and the apostates."[147]

Mukhtar was in desperate need of guidance. Unlike his strategically simplistic Yemeni peers, he was mindful of the regional (Kenya and Ethiopia) and international (AMISOM and the United States) challenges his group was facing. He was also eager to win Muslims' support while implementing Sharia. But Mukhtar was struggling to monopolize jihad in Somalia under his leadership. Though he claimed that his group had "succeeded in incorporating a large number of jihadi blocs," he wanted al-Qaeda's leaders to refer to al-Shabaab specifically in their public statements "for that would have a great effect on the morale of jihadis." It was not just the morale of his men that he wanted to heighten, Mukhtar also wanted to boost his own standing and encourage other groups to rally behind him.

Mukhtar was ambitious. He urged al-Qaeda to prepare "a coherent legal and political study to clarify the vision of the state which we aspire to establish."[148] In subsequent letters, he gladly welcomed al-Qaeda's advice on how to counter the drones, and also requested assistance connecting with an arms dealer, "because we have difficulties securing arms and explosive materials."[149]

Beyond this, Mukhtar was troubled by the al-Qaeda operative Fadil Harun. As mentioned earlier, Harun stayed in East Africa after the 2002 Mombasa attacks. What's more, he was critical of the formation of al-Shabaab in the autobiography that he posted online in early 2009. Atiya and Ayman had read Harun's text and were concerned about its content. Ayman wondered whether "the brother had fallen captive and that the book consisted of his detailed confessions [made under duress]."[150] We don't know what exactly Mukhtar was asking al-Qaeda to do about Harun. Atiya shared that Harun "was a source of pride for me and I considered him a treasure," but he was disappointed that "he volunteered information to the enemy for free" in his autobiography. If Mukhtar had hoped that Atiya would encourage him to eliminate Harun, he was disappointed. He assured Mukhtar that "we stopped the book's publication" on jihadi media, and hoped that Harun would "return to his good old self." [151]

Why did al-Qaeda hesitate?

By 2009, al-Qaeda had become wary of its name being associated with groups that thought they could punch above their weight. Almost a year after al-Shabaab released its "I Have Answered Your Call, Usama" video, we find Atiya trying to convince Mukhtar to keep the association between the two groups secret: "Is it wise that you keep your allegiance to Sheikh Usama secret? In my opinion, this is indeed possible and good. In fact, I recommend it. . . . In any case, the video cassette 'I Have Answered Your Call, Usama' was clear and its content pretty much amounts to an allegiance."[152]

Usama's position was even more minimalist. Not only did he advise Mukhtar to keep his allegiance secret, he suggested he should refrain from proclaiming a political entity at all:

> Our inclination is that your Emirate should be a reality to which the people grow attached without having to proclaim it. . . . It does not escape you that the international pressure that would follow proclaiming an Emirate in Somalia would be greater than that which followed the proclamation of the Islamic State of Iraq.[153]

By "should be a reality," Usama wanted al-Shabaab to win the people's support through good governance without formally governing them. We find both Usama and Atiya tutoring Mukhtar on how to be "lenient" with the people,[154] with Usama stressing that the attributes of a good leader include "forgiveness, justice, patience, and the kind treatment of his citizenry."[155] Usama specifically advised that Mukhtar should "do his utmost to remain neutral concerning the Sufi groups," who do not follow a rigid understanding of Islamic law, lest they "become a card in the hands of the enemy."[156]

Usama seems to have wanted more economic investment and less jihad for his Somali brethren. He was evidently concerned about "the severe poverty and malnutrition" in the country and feared that an association with al-Qaeda would make matters worse. He wanted to put together a plan to encourage the wealthy in the Gulf to invest in Somalia and alleviate their Muslim brethren's suffering.

He could not fly to the Gulf himself, so he suggested that a few "trusted Somali dignitaries" could go on such a trip to make a case for developmental and agricultural investment projects in Somalia. With such possibilities in mind, Usama reasoned that a public merger with al-Qaeda would thwart his plan.[157]

We gather from the letters that al-Qaeda had other concerns about al-Shabaab. We find Atiya disapproving of an attack that was attributed to al-Shabaab in the media. The attack in question targeted people watching the World Cup in Mogadishu in June 2010:

If this attack was carried out by our jihadi Brothers, this would be wrong, in my view. It must not be repeated. . . . The Sharia does not permit shedding the blood of those people for this sin, though watching football is more like a reprehensible act [*makruh*] rather than a sin [*ma'siya*]. . . . Politically, the harm of such attacks is obvious to an experienced observer. I would be surprised if the brothers [i.e., al-Shabaab] were behind this attack. It's highly unlikely.[158]

Atiya then commented on similar attacks in Kampala, Uganda, also targeting people watching the World Cup in July 2010. Though he saw that there was political merit to the attack, considering that it targeted a country of "unbelief," he urged restraint:

My inclination is that it would be best to avoid attacks of this nature. . . . [It is true] I heard that the BBC is reporting that some in the Ugandan opposition are using this attack to call on their government to withdraw its forces from Somalia. . . . This is good, and it is in our interest. But, as I said, this is enough for now.[159]

Usama also discouraged al-Shabaab from mounting attacks:

Regarding your attacks against AMISOM, it is important that you think long and hard on how best to minimize the tragic attacks against Muslims, such as those that targeted the Bakaara Market [killing forty-five people]. It is best that you avoid attacking AMISOM's bases, and consider targeting them at the airport upon their departure or arrival. Alternatively, you could attack them inside Somalia only if you could mount large special operations, such as digging tunnels that reach inside their barracks and simultaneously attack them from the outside. In any case, we hope that you look into this matter very carefully before you act on it.[160]

In his response, Mukhtar complied with Atiya's and Usama's wishes and sent his allegiance in writing. But we can sense that he was troubled by their insistence on keeping the merger secret, rightly pointing out that "we are already considered by both our enemies and our friends to be part of al-Qaeda."[161] In January 2011, Mukhtar sent al-Qaeda "1 million dollars" via someone who believed that "he was merely delivering a sum of money to complete a business transaction."[162] Mukhtar also asked Atiya to connect him with an arms dealer. As late as March 2011, Atiya found it challenging to collect the money, let alone arrange a shipment of weapons—the drones were overwhelming al-Qaeda in North Waziristan. Atiya couldn't bring himself to reveal his hopelessness, so he feigned enthusiasm. "Of course," he wrote. And just in case Mukhtar followed through, Atiya qualified his response by adding: "if you can secure shipping by sea." It is obvious from his letter that the shipment was not forthcoming anytime soon.

We also learn from Atiya that Usama remained reluctant to make the merger public, but that Ayman was supportive of an announcement.[163] In February 2012, ten months after Usama was killed, Ayman and Mukhtar made their wishes come true and proclaimed the merger between al-Shabaab and al-Qaeda. In 2014, Mukhtar was killed in a drone strike in Somalia, but he left behind a group that continues to make its mark not by winning the public's support, as Usama had advised, but through suicide attacks.

The "New Vision"

Confined to his Abbottabad compound and with no visitors or phone calls to distract him, Usama had ample time to meditate on the actions of the Brothers. We discovered in Chapter Six that Usama decided to change al-Qaeda's strategy in 2010. In the course of devising his new strategy, he thought long and hard about the Brothers who had lost sight of global jihad. He found himself comparing them to jihadi groups who were marked by their local jihad and had risen (and fallen) during the 1960s through the 1990s. He wrote to his associates:

> You are well aware that many of the groups that insisted on starting their jihad against the local enemy had their path obstructed and did not achieve their goals. For example, when the Muslim Brotherhood in Syria fought against the regime of Hafez al-Asad for nearly a decade, it led to a catastrophe when the regime eliminated thousands of them during the uprising in Hama [in 1982]. This caused a shock, and though it has been nearly three decades, its effects continue. The same is true about the Islamic Group and the Jihad Group in Egypt, and the brothers in Libya, Algeria, and the Arabian Peninsula.[164]

Usama feared that the "new generation" of jihadis operating under the umbrella of al-Qaeda were destined to suffer the same fate. Because they were preoccupied with fighting the "local enemy," i.e., the regimes of Muslim-majority states, Usama lamented that they had become a "liability" to global jihad.

What was Usama going to do about this?

Usama's new al-Qaeda strategy included a component to tame the Brothers, and the "errors" of AQAP were mostly on his mind. During his final year, Usama was working on a "new vision" for al-Qaeda that would see jihadism usher in a "new phase of reform and development."[165] His priority was to put a swift end to the Brothers' indiscriminate attacks in Muslim-majority states. "We shall only enter into a struggle with the local regimes," Usama determined, "when the leader of global *kufr* [i.e., America] is drained of its powers and is near collapse." Until then, the Brothers should only resort to violence if they are attacked by the regimes. "This way," he reasoned, and in the eyes of the world, "it would be obvious that we are oppressed and the rulers are the oppressors."[166]

In addition, Usama wanted to concentrate terrorism in the hands of al-Qaeda, and centralize all media releases by jihadi groups. To that end, he tasked Atiya with preparing "a memorandum of understanding," laying out al-Qaeda's guidelines and requiring the leaders of regional jihadi groups "to be most careful about curbing military attacks":

> Some of the attacks they carried out should have been halted, in view of the unnecessary civilian casualties that resulted. . . . It does not escape you that Muslims' blood is sacred, not to mention that the Muslim public was repulsed by such attacks. . . . It is necessary to reinforce to all the Brothers the importance of being transparent, sincere, and fulfilling their promises, and of being wary of betraying their oaths.[167]

Usama also wanted Atiya to include in his memorandum guidelines concerning the jihadis' media releases. On this front, he was disappointed with both the Brothers and the jihadi media:

> I request that you ask the Brothers to avoid giving interviews to the jihadi media. I previously indicated that such interviews are not suitably animated and lack the professionalism of those trained in journalism. This might give people the wrong impression, such as jihadis are backward and so on. Besides, the brother conducting the interview is often not qualified and struggles to choose the appropriate question.[168]

To address this problem, Usama proposed creating a new position for a general director who would oversee all media releases. The general director would be "authorized to stop any media release that's not in line with al-Qaeda's strategy" or "if it distracts attention away from the main goals of the jihadis, such as the Palestine cause." For instance, Usama could not believe that Abu Dujana al-Khurasani's operation that killed seven CIA officers was described "as a revenge for the killing of [Baitullah] Mehsud," the leader of the TTP. The jihadi media "should have spoken first about Palestine," Usama fumed.[169]

Usama planned to announce his "new vision" on the tenth anniversary of the 9/11 attacks. But he wanted to make sure first that the Brothers agreed to al-Qaeda's guidelines:

We want to hear the reactions of the Brothers to our proposal. Because I plan to release a statement to announce that we are starting a new phase to correct the mistakes we made, and reclaim, God willing, a large segment of those who lost their trust in the jihadis. We want to establish ongoing communications between the jihadis and their *umma* to reassure the public. This requires that our strategy is understood by all the Brothers and is translated into reality. We wouldn't want our actions to contradict our words.[170]

Usama was confident that various media outlets would compete to secure exclusive coverage of his tenth-anniversary statement. He showed no interest in collaborating with the jihadi media. Though he and his associates were disappointed by Al Jazeera's coverage of al-Qaeda, Usama still instructed Atiya to check if the news channel would be prepared to cover his tenth-anniversary event. He envisaged that al-Qaeda and Al Jazeera would agree on a set of questions, the responses to which Usama would audio-record to be aired in a Q&A format. He hoped that this could be arranged with Al Jazeera's correspondent in Pakistan at the time, Ahmed Zaidan.[171] The letters reveal that Zaidan was giving the leaders of al-Qaeda media advice that went beyond the call of his journalistic duties; but given al-Qaeda's disappointment with Al Jazeera's coverage, Zaidan likely did so independent of his bosses.

Usama floated the possibility of feeding Al Jazeera several statements, on the understanding that they would start their coverage earlier, on September 1, 2011.[172] Usama also considered reaching out to "an impartial and professional American TV channel such as CBS"; "we would send them the material that we want to reach the American public on this anniversary."[173]

The SEALs aborted Usama's big event and the "new vision" he was excited to announce. To be clear, even if he had not been killed, there was little chance that the Brothers would have agreed to Usama's "new vision." We discovered earlier that contact with the Islamic State of Iraq ceased in late 2007, and when its leaders were killed, the group unilaterally announced their replacements without consulting al-Qaeda. We also discovered that Yemen's Abu Basir rejected outright putting an end to political violence against the regime. On the other hand, AQIM might have complied with Usama's "new vision," provided that the group could maintain its hostage-taking to fund itself. Usama probably counted on this, and was hoping that AQIM would put up 200,000 euros to fund his maritime attacks which we discussed in the previous chapter.[174] Al-Shabaab would have likely signed up to Usama's "new vision," but one wonders if the group would have complied with al-Qaeda's guidelines.

Ayman, who succeeded Usama, had little chance of seeing through Usama's vision. The Bin Laden Papers likely gave the CIA much information to help them track down Usama's most trusted associate, Atiya (killed August 2011), and al-Qaeda's leading legal scholar, Abu Yahya (killed June 2012). Not only did Ayman lose his top associates, he also had to suffer watching the ascent of the Islamic State of Iraq which eclipsed al-Qaeda and whose leaders publicly humiliated him. Though the leaders of AQAP, AQIM, and al-Shabaab maintained their loyalty to al-Qaeda, at no point was there any suggestion that Usama's vision was being advanced.

In 2019, in the inaugural issue of the jihadi magazine *Umma Wahida*, Ayman cited the following lines from one of Usama's 2010 letters to Atiya: "I plan to release a statement to announce that we are starting a new phase to correct the mistakes we made, and reclaim, God willing, a large segment of those who lost their trust in the jihadis." But rather than signaling that he was moving forward with Usama's vision, we find Ayman pondering: "Do we have this kind of courage to enable us to be a role model for the *umma* so that we may gain its trust and support?"

PART III
THE FAMILY

8

THE "FIRST MARTYR"

Blood has been shed in our family
Now that Khadija is among the martyrs
Felicitation and tidings to her family
Praise and laud the Lord for this gift. . . .

Oh, the sorrow of losing my Khadija
If only I could give birth to my Khadija one more time[1]

Siham, Usama's third wife, to Daoud, her son-in-law, 2007[2]

Usama bin Laden had likely been living with his fourth wife, Amal, and their two children, Safiya and Asiya, since at least 2003. After resuming contact with his associates in 2004, Usama was joined by his third wife, Siham, their son Khaled (1989–2011) and their two daughters Mariam (b. 1990) and Sumayya (b. 1992) in late 2004.[3] Their eldest daughter, Khadija, her husband, and their three children were likely in North Waziristan at the time. The letters do not disclose where Siham and her children had been hiding before they reunited with Usama, but it is clear that they were not residing with Khadija and her family. When the SEALs raided the compound, the Bin Laden household comprised sixteen people, nine of whom were children between the ages of two and eleven. Five of the seven adults were women.

Women are not part of al-Qaeda's public image. Though the jihadi literature praises the role of the *mujahidat* or female jihadis, it confines their contributions to supportive roles as mothers, sisters, and daughters, and excludes them from taking part in fighting alongside men on the battlefield. Jihadi ideologues repeatedly stress that the *mujahidat* mothers' blessing is "the most powerful incentive" to spur their sons to long for martyrdom, and count on the jihadis' wives to support their husbands by bringing up their children to love jihad. And women in general are expected to incite their male relatives to join the jihad, and shame them if they cower in fear.[4]

Usama's wives and daughters were all this, and much more. We read in the letters that Siham was often "busy with [her husband] working on the public statements" that we heard Usama deliver over the years. Usama and Siham's daughters, Sumayya and Mariam, hardly had time to write letters, "busy" as they too were "working with their father on his public statements." Though away in North Waziristan, Khadija may have composed poetry that her father recited to enrich his public statements. On occasion, Siham's son Khaled was also occupied helping his father "with important matters."

Through Siham and her children's lenses, we follow Usama both as a family man and a leader, whose concern for fellow Muslims "weighs heavily on his mind." Siham saw a husband who raised his children "with kindness and warmth," while also striving to improve the plight of fellow Muslims. They all believed themselves to be treading God's path, and that those who chose the burden of this path were "destined for Paradise." In 2007, we find Siham sorrowfully celebrating her family's "first martyr," when Khadija, at the age of nineteen, died giving birth to her fourth child. In Siham's poetry, we hear an aching mother who made a Solomonic trade-off, praising her Lord for the "gift" that left her tormented by "the sorrow of losing my Khadija."

What kind of family life did the Bin Ladens have in Abbottabad? How did they maintain their security cover while raising nine children in the compound? And how did the nine children spend their days while confined to the compound? The more than 100 family letters that were recovered during the raid reveal that the Bin Ladens strove to provide the nine children in the compound with a normal domestic life in a highly abnormal setting.

THE "FIRST MARTYR"

The "Myrtle of Jihad"

In the Papers, we first meet the Bin Ladens in 1999, in Kandahar, Afghanistan, on the day of Khadija's engagement. On that day, we find Siham composing poetry, "when Khadija's fiancé came to see her and she was twelve years old."[5] Khadija's fiancé, Daoud, was born in Medina, Saudi Arabia.[6] He was almost thirty, with proven jihadi credentials that had qualified him to be in Usama's circle.

Siham's poems were handwritten on pieces of paper torn from a spiral note-book, and Khadija had guarded them dearly throughout her years of displace-ment. Despite her efforts, some of the lines were rendered illegible by spilled water, possibly during the family's rush to flee Afghanistan. One of the poems was initially entitled "The Jasmine at the Break of Dawn," but Siham must have thought that the title was too bland when she scratched it out and replaced it with "Myrtle of Jihad":[7]

My little girl . . .
My jasmine, how rapidly you've grown. . . .
Declare to the world that you are the best of daughters
Whose virtue is testament to the piety of her parents . . .
You are my healing balsam . . .
My little girl, this beauty of yours
Is but a great gift from God, the Lord of the Universe . . .
Your radiant smile, the allure of your eyes
Are the epic of my love for years to come
Rise and assume the exalted responsibilities
And let history record the kinship to which you belong
History is a witness that your father is the lion of the Arabian Peninsula
He dusted off servility and rose from the den
He reached glories, loftiness and virtues
He rode the saddle of dignity and [. . .] of Islam
He carried the banner of God's Judgment

Calling on Muslim young men to rise and take up jihad
Rise, O Muslims, and expel the People of the Cross.

Water erased much of the ink, making the last verse indecipherable.[8] But one surmises from the remaining legible words—"from the purest site"—that Siham's poem was reaching its crescendo, inciting Muslims to rise up and expel U.S. military forces from Saudi Arabia, home to Islam's two holiest places.

In Arab culture, when poetry is recited, it is often memorized by the listeners, who then verbally transmit it to others. In the letters, Siham often expressed her emotions in poetry, and we can assume that she elocuted her poem during Khadija's engagement, and her incitement to jihad was likely echoed beyond the female-only guests gathering. In another shorter poem, Siham announces "glad tidings" to her future son-in-law, Daoud, celebrating Khadija as the "pearl of her era." She honors the fiancé with the lofty designation of being the "lion" of his birth city, Medina—just short of the exalted lionhood of the Arabian Peninsula depiction that she ascribes to her husband. Siham praises the "critical mind" of her "pearl," describing Khadija as a "little flower who flourished from the same mold [that produced] the best of people," and whose beautiful "scent" fills the country. "Guard Khadija well," Siham charges Daoud, and in case he did not realize it, her poem spelled out that "the bliss of living with Khadija is a gift from the Lord."[9]

We can surmise from other recovered letters that Khadija was homeschooled by her mother, who completed her doctorate in Qur'anic grammar after her marriage. Siham reportedly accepted Usama's proposal on condition that she could continue her education.[10] Putting her studies to good use, she took the lead in schooling the Bin Laden children in a rigorous program of Islamic education. Among the recovered Bin Laden Papers is a 2001–02 curriculum she devised, comprising twenty-seven lessons.[11] The first began on February 3, 2001, consisting of an introduction to *Kitab al-Manasik*, a book devoted to the study of Islamic rites and ways of worship. The last lesson was set to take place on January 20, 2002. The course would certainly have been disrupted in

October 2001 by the U.S. invasion of Afghanistan. Like her siblings, Khadija would have followed this and other intensive curricula.

Combing through the family letters, it becomes clear that Daoud loved Khadija. For nearly six years, the two of them and their children "shared a single room, and on occasion two connected rooms."[12] Daoud could not imagine another married couple who were "more in love" than them. "I am the jealous type," Khadija warned her husband. "You made me change my feelings about having more wives," Daoud assured her, for "I no longer think about, nor will I ever think about, other women so long as I have you in my sight."[13] When they went out shopping, Khadija often searched for dressmaking fabric that pleased her husband. "Which fabric should I buy?" she would ask him, as she gazed at the different textures. "It is you who make everything beautiful," he often responded, and it made her laugh.

At Home with the Bin Ladens

According to U.S. officials, the Abbottabad compound was built in 2005,[14] and it is possible that the Bin Ladens had moved there by August that year. The letters do not discuss the move, but Usama describes his hideout as consisting of "two independent houses, including separate courtyards." In the other house lived two Pakistani brothers, "Abu Khaled and Abu Muhammad," who provided "security cover, and their visible presence gave the impression that locals were living in the house."[15] There are no references to the domestic lives of the Pakistani brothers in the letters. But in the aftermath of the raid, it transpired through media reports that the two brothers had been living with their wives and children next door, and had even kept Usama's identity hidden from their respective families.

In late 2004, Usama had his third child with Amal, a boy they named Ibrahim/Abraham. When they moved to Abbottabad in 2005, Usama's household comprised his two wives (Siham and Amal), his three children with Siham (Khaled, sixteen; Mariam, fifteen; and Sumayya, thirteen), and his three children with Amal (Safiya, four; Asiya, two; and the newborn Ibrahim).[16]

The Bin Ladens endeavored to be self-sufficient. They raised goats,[17] chickens,[18] a cow and its calf,[19] and relied sparingly on the security guards to purchase other basic needs. Usama explained:

> We bake our own bread, and purchase grains in bulk. Our regular shopping needs consist of fruit and vegetables.
>
> Concerning doctors, our medical needs are very limited. We adhere to the tried-and-true method that *prevention is better than cure*. We know which medications are required to treat children's common illnesses, such as colds, etc. We keep them at home for when the necessity arises. In general, the children do not need to see a doctor unless they suffer from a toothache or a broken bone. The same is true for the adults. Visits to the doctor are rare, once a year on average, as we keep medications for most illnesses at home.[20]

The Bin Ladens adhered to such extreme security measures that the children were "not allowed to play in the courtyard" without "an adult who can control their voices." Just before he was killed, Usama urged his associates, who were being watched by spies and hunted by the CIA drones in North Waziristan, to do the same, remarking that "we have successfully adopted these measures for nine years."[21]

Perhaps the strictest security measure of all was that the Bin Ladens did not have access to the internet or a phone. All communications were through electronic letters delivered by couriers at a location away from the compound. Khaled and Siham were learning Pashto and Urdu, and it is possible that the two of them left the compound only to attend to vital needs, such as taking the children to the doctor.[22]

Usama's youngest wife, Amal, hardly features in the Bin Laden Papers. Except for one short letter that Khadija addressed to her in 2005, no other writings by or about Amal were recovered.[23] She lacked the tertiary education of the other wives. While we cannot extrapolate much about the wives' interactions with one another, Amal's children appear to have been loved by all. Her eldest, Safiya, must have been highly regarded even at the age of eleven, since Usama used the patronymic "Umm Safiya" (i.e., the mother of Safiya) to refer to Amal,[24] instead of privileging his first-born son, Ibrahim, per Arab customs. It is likely that this was a sign of Usama's affection and esteem for Safiya, whom we shall meet later helping her step-nephew, probably her age, with his homework.

Away from the Family in Waziristan

The first letter we read by Khadija was composed in late August 2005, five years after she had last seen her family.[25] She was seventeen and already the mother of three—Abdallah, followed by his sister, Aisha, and his younger brother, Usama. "We all enjoy listening to your voice messages," she wrote to her father. She might have been referring to watching Usama on the news when she wrote that her eldest wanted to impress his grandfather: "Abdallah especially longs to see you, and is studying hard to send you a letter in his own handwriting."

Like Usama's associates, Khadija had not heard from her father since he "disappeared" into the mountains of Tora Bora in late 2001. Only in 2005 did she learn that "God had blessed us with a new sister and brother, Asiya and Ibrahim," referring to the two children Usama and Amal had during 2003–05. When Khadija wrote her letter, Ramadan—a month of fasting in the Islamic lunar calendar—was less than six weeks away. Yearning to observe the holy month in the company of her parents and siblings, she wrote: "Father, I have one request: Please do not miss taking advantage of any opportunity that would allow us to visit you. I hope that my request does not impose or infringe upon your security. Your safety is most important."[26]

Arrangements were discussed several times for Khadija and her family to join the others in Abbottabad, but "security conditions did not permit." Specifically, Usama's security guards did not want to be burdened with even more people. Instead, Khadija was showered with all the familial love and support that letters could convey, including her mother's poetic verses expressing her longing. Mariam, fifteen, wrote of her "strong longing" for news of her sister, optimistic that their hardship was "but a passing dark cloud," and prayed that they be "reunited soon." We find Mariam enquiring about the books that Khadija was using to homeschool her eldest, Abdallah, and promising to send her sister "other educational books."[27]

In 2005, Usama and Siham's thirteen-year-old daughter, Sumayya, used her advanced Islamic learning to toughen up Khadija, who was aching to be with her family. She drew parallels between today's jihadis and Muslim historical figures who refused to profess "falsehood" against Islam. "The followers of Muhammad today," Sumayya reminded her sister, "are fighting in God's path" and are "being similarly persecuted, enduring various forms of torture in the prisons of Arab and Western tyrants." Despite all this, "the jihadis," Sumayya remarked, "are patient, confident in the righteousness of their cause, and steadfast in their commitment to God's path." She wanted her sister to be inspired by the jihadis' fortitude and to recognize that the grief of their separation "pales in comparison with the jihadis' tribulations," and that "our problems, my sister, are but a trivial sacrifice in God's path." She prayed that Khadija's sons would grow to become jihadis, for there is "no better or more noble path than that trodden by Prophets and Messengers."[28]

It is not difficult to see the imprint of Sumayya's contributions to her father's statements, given her ability to interweave Islamic history with contemporary politics. In one document, it is recorded that "Sumayya co-authors" the statements, and one of Siham's poems reflects her esteem for her daughter: "God has gifted you the pride of being one of the grandchildren of he who restored the Two Sanctuaries."[29] Siham was stating that Sumayya was descended from the praiseworthy man, i.e., Usama's father, whose construction company restored the Islamic holy sites at Mecca and Medina.[30] The poem goes on to paint Sumayya's commitment to God's path as the equivalent of having "erected an edifice in Islam that would last until the End of Days."[31]

Siham's letters to Khadija were brimming with motherly affection. She was worried about the health of her daughter who had undergone "dilution and curettage" after a miscarriage and had also suffered from "typhoid and malaria."[32] She urged Khadija "to eat well, especially milk and meat." Siham appealed to Khadija not to spank her children to discipline them, but to raise them "with kindness and warmth, as your father says."[33] Apparently, the same man behind the 9/11 attacks disapproved of corporal punishment.

Siham did not always have the time to communicate at length with her daughter, and we find her writing "this letter in haste, for I am busy with your father working on the public statements." The Bin Ladens often learned at very short notice that the courier would be picking up the letters. When this happened, Usama's public statements and letters to his associates in Waziristan were given top priority. We read in the letters that Mariam and Sumayya were closely involved "in preparing research and topics with their father," and when Usama's public statements were reported by the world media, "their writings were broadcast on television."[34] Khaled made "some contributions," essentially helping to video and audio-record his father's public statements.[35] Siham too was involved in drafting her husband's statements, and the red edits discovered on the recovered documents were likely her polishing the final drafts.[36] Even remotely, Khadija probably contributed poetry to her father's public statements. "Your father thanks you for the contribution you sent him," Siham lauded her daughter in one letter. "It was appropriate and he included it in the statements he sent," she added, and "they will likely be released in the next few days."[37]

In Waziristan, Khadija was tasked with finding a suitable wife for her brother Khaled. Usama had not been successful in this endeavor, even though it was high on his to-do list after he resumed contact with his associates. In 2004, Usama had written to his deputy, Ayman al-Zawahiri, to enquire as to the suitability of Hajar, a girl for whom Ayman served as guardian.[38] We don't know why this arrangement did not work out. So, Siham and Usama gave Khadija "complete authority" to find a wife for her brother, taking into account that "religiosity, character, and beauty are important for Khaled."[39]

The same urgency was not extended to finding spouses for Mariam and Sumayya, who were also of marital age by their parents' standards. It is likely that the two girls found it easier to adjust to life in hiding than their brother. We glean from the letters that they had better research skills than Khaled, and likely found it rewarding that their research played a central role in their father's public statements. When they were not helping their father, the books that Siham's children read included an encyclopedic work (twelve volumes) on Islamic ethics and customs; Ibn Khaldun's *Muqaddima*, a magisterial introduction to history; and the collected works of the Egyptian poet Ahmed Shawqi.[40]

Khaled probably did not find his own contributions as rewarding. He recorded his father delivering his public statements, and one of his letters to the jihadi media outlet al-Sahab suggests that he was struggling and welcomed advice on how to improve his skills. He remarked on the "poor-quality video" he had produced,[41] perhaps referring to a 2007 video in which Usama's face appeared like a bad drawing,[42] prompting reports that the video was fabricated.[43] Beyond that, he regularly corresponded with al-Sahab to ask for the purchase of electronic equipment, such as cameras and USB devices, and to ask for materials to be downloaded from the internet for his father's perusal. When they settled in Abbottabad, Khaled raised goats and chickens.[44] Later, we learn that, "in addition to his interests in raising chickens, he also has a cow that has a one-month-old calf."[45] (A video of the calf suckling recorded by Khaled was recovered from the compound.)[46]

When Khadija took charge of finding Khaled a wife, his fortunes changed. The daughter of an Egyptian fighter in North Waziristan had been promised to another "brother,"[47] but her parents were prepared to change their minds when Khadija put Khaled's name forward. Usama was pleased. "If the girl is suitable," he wrote to Khadija, "propose [on our behalf] to her parents." He added that "if they accept, you would have our blessing, and if they decline, keep looking for more than one so that we may have a choice."[48] Umm Abd al-Rahman, the mother of the bride-to-be, agreed to the marriage proposal on condition that her daughter remain by her parents' side for the first four years of her marriage. We don't know whether she insisted on this because her daughter was still a child. She also assumed that Khaled would take up jihad, as one does in jihadi circles. Siham agreed, but politely suggested postponing the marriage until

Usama's security conditions improved. We shall see that the postponement of Khaled's marriage went on considerably longer than anyone anticipated.

After successfully arranging a wife for Khaled, Khadija had other good news to share with her mother. Siham's brother, Saad, had sent his sister money, and was visiting the "land of jihad," most likely North Waziristan. Siham was elated by the opportunity to write to her brother, who had, in fact, introduced her to Usama:

> I am living the bliss of *al-ribat* [i.e., being on the frontiers of jihad], I am wrapped with the cloth of patience. . . . This, my brother, is indeed a Grace from the Lord. My dearest brother, it was sufficient for me to hear of your letter, let alone read it.[49]

Siham, however, had a pressing request: "May God reward you for the sum of money you sent me. It was timely. Please send me as much as you can."[50] In case Saad did not appreciate the urgency of her request, Siham tasked Khadija with writing to her uncle "in your own handwriting" to let him know that "I am in urgent need of 100,000 euros of my own money that he is holding for me." (She advised Khadija "not to use the phone in general" and, if she had to use it, she "should not discuss money matters over the phone.")[51] It is reported that Siham had earmarked her dowry for the Afghan jihad,[52] and we gather from her letters that she wanted to finance al-Qaeda's jihad from Abbottabad.

In Mourning

On the second day of the 2005 Ramadan Eid (November 4), Siham had a "strange feeling." She told Mariam that she felt a "deep chagrin" as she thought of Khadija. "All I could do," she wrote to Khadija, was "pray that God may protect you."[53] Translating her feeling in verse, she wrote:

> Your image is constantly in my eyesight
> And I pray for my eyes to truly see you.

211

Siham may have experienced some sort of premonition. In 2007, letters from Waziristan brought news of Khadija's passing, leaving Siham devastated both at losing her daughter and at not being present at her funeral. Usama too was heartbroken. In one of his letters, Khaled describes that Usama was "very emotional" upon learning of Khadija's passing, and "his facial expressions changed dramatically."[54]

Umm Abd al-Rahman, Khaled's future mother-in-law, was by Khadija's side when she died and sent Siham a detailed letter about what had happened. We learn that Khadija had experienced several infections before and during pregnancy, and suffered a severe hemorrhage during labor. "I feel numbness in my entire body," she told Umm Abd al-Rahman within minutes of delivering her fourth child. Khadija's husband, Daoud, immediately arranged for "two brothers of the same blood type to be brought in to donate blood." But within minutes of their donation, Khadija "turned yellow." As she took her last breath, repeating the Shahada: "There is no god but God, and Muhammad is His messenger."[55]

Umm Abd al-Rahman sent the newborn girl to her own home and instructed that she "should be fed honey." She then accompanied her son and Daoud, who carried his wife's corpse to the car, and they headed together to "the house of the leader." This was probably Hajji Uthman, who was al-Qaeda's leader in Af-Pak and who was hiding in North Waziristan at the time. The following morning, Umm Abd al-Rahman found herself having to prepare a corpse for burial for the first time:

> This was very difficult for me. It was my first time having to wash and clothe somebody, so I took a book [on burial rites] with me to consult as I prepared the corpse. And whose corpse? None other than that of my dear Khadija. . . . If only you could see the amazing smile on Khadija's face. It was as if she was alive. After I washed her corpse, I saw a light shining on her face. By God, her index finger was raised as if she was uttering the Shahada.[56]

When it was time to bury Khadija, her widower "felt almost paralyzed, and could hardly walk."[57] Daoud later told some Pakistani "brothers" that "my love is buried in the land of Masoud," and they endearingly told him that he had become one of them, i.e., a member of Waziristan's "Masoud tribes."[58] He could not contain his grief. "The dearest was everything to me," he wrote to his mother-in-law.[59] In a rather unusual sorrowful expression, he wrote to Usama that "had it not been that my religion forbids it, I would have worn Khadija's clothes and jewelry, and told the world that I am wearing my beloved's clothing." Daoud consoled himself with signs that made him believe that Khadija was in Heaven:

> One of the *ansar* [i.e., Pakistani local supporters] saw a light shining out of the dearest's burial site. When he dug Khadija's grave in the direction of the Ka'ba [i.e., the direction of prayer toward Mecca], a beautiful cool air was released through an opening. It is customary for the *ansar* brothers to open the grave up to three times. The beautiful cool air that came out calmed my heart. She was smiling as if she was asleep. My aunt Siham, the dearest Khadija assuredly ascended to Heaven and is now in Paradise, God permitting.[60]

There exist in martyrological literature several examples of martyrs' "smiles" and "sweet smells" coming from their corpses.[61] In this instance, it is not clear from Daoud's letter whether he experienced these signs in a dream or in real life. In any case, Siham was emotionally moved by his account and wanted to know "the address of the cemetery." She also asked Daoud that if he visited his wife's grave on Eid al-Adha, he should "tell the dearest I shall not stop praying for her until I happily join her as a martyr, God willing."[62]

Notwithstanding his grief, Daoud felt an urgency in securing his four children's future well-being. Within days of Khadija's death, he proposed marriage to a widow who had three children of her own. "What forced me to do that," he wrote to his in-laws, "was the situation of my children, my most precious."[63] By then, the Bin Ladens probably felt that their hideout was secure, and we find a grieving Siham pleading with her son-in-law to send her grandchildren to Abbottabad. "God is my witness, it is not my intention to bar you from your children," she assured him, "and I pray from the bottom of my heart that God may fortify you with patience."[64] To console him, Siham shared a hint of her own sorrow:

Barred from eulogizing my Khadija by the Tragedy [of exile]
Do tell me, I beg you, who could substitute for me [i.e., mother's love]?
I compose some verses for history
To relate the story of my exile and grief.
Sixty months I have been chasing her image,
My tears whispered my longing,
My last memory of you, my daughter,
You bent to kiss my forehead, then my hand,
Fifty-five days Khadija has been in her grave
To the Lord, I pray, bring me to her,
It is in my Khadija that I confide,
With whom should I now share my pain and distress? . . .

Khadija is my sister, my friend, my companion.
She was the first to call me the dearest word [i.e., mother].
Oh the sorrow of losing my Khadija.
If only I could give birth to you, my Khadija, one more time.[65]

Siham had to reconcile her pain with the commitment to the cause of jihad that claimed her daughter. According to the Islamic tradition, women who die in childbirth count as martyrs,[66] and in the eyes of her family, Khadija was "the first martyr" in the Bin Laden family.[67] Martyrdom is the belief that those who struggle in God's path are on a fast track to Paradise—the rest have to wait in their graves till the Resurrection. In the same letter in which Siham poured out her grief, she told her son-in-law to write to her relatives in the Hijaz (Saudi Arabia) to inform them of Khadija's passing, and to "send them the following words from me":

Blood has been shed in our family.
Now that Khadija is among the martyrs,
Felicitation and tidings to her family,
Praise and laud the Lord for this gift.

The poem went on to shame the men in her family who did not take up jihad:

Our women and children are facing the upheaval [of the battlefield]
While some men are cowardly and servile.[68]

The widow to whom Daoud had proposed declined, and he resigned himself to the idea that his children would be better off with their grandparents in Abbottabad. It wasn't easy for Daoud to send his children to live with the world's most wanted man. But at that time, the drone campaign over North Waziristan was intensifying,[69] so much so that his children couldn't get the medical attention they needed.[70] Daoud's eldest, Abdallah, who was probably six or seven, "was traumatized by the loss of his mother and cried whenever her name was mentioned." He was also suffering from a chest pain for which he was being treated with honey and a herbal remedy.[71] Daoud's daughter Aisha, who was five or six, "often woke up crying during the night," and suffered from a pain in her ear which was treated with a few drops of warm olive oil. His son, Usama, who was four or five, was doing relatively well.[72]

Daoud, however, determined that the infant child, Fatima, was too young to travel with her siblings, and wanted her to be breastfed before sending her to Abbottabad. The Pakistani wife of a trusted Syrian "brother" offered to nurse her for the first eight days, then a friend of Siham suckled the little Fatima for several months.[73] The use of wet nurses is a custom that predates Islam. According to the historian Martin Lings, it was common for "all the great families of Arab towns to send their sons, soon after their birth, into the desert, to be suckled and weaned and spend part of their childhood amongst one of the Bedouin tribes."[74] This custom created a bond between the Bedouin of the desert and the towns. Some Muslims maintain this practice today. In the case of jihadis, it also engenders an enduring bond among families. When boys and girls are suckled by the same woman, they become like brothers and sisters, and attention must be paid to prevent them from getting married in the future. When little Fatima arrived in Abbottabad, the woman who had breastfed her sent a list of names of all the babies she had suckled so that Siham could keep track.

Daoud's children were transported from North Waziristan by a trusted intermediary and dropped off at an undisclosed location, where Khaled then picked them up. It was one of those rare occasions when Khaled left the compound, because "it was essential for the children to be met by a family member to collect them."

Before the children's move to Abbottabad, their homeschooling had consisted of rote learning the Qur'an with their father and basic writing and spelling lessons with their mother.[75] Abdallah had been struggling with his writing skills.[76] In Abbottabad, the schooling of the children was more rigorous. One of the documents recovered is entitled "Daily Schedule." The first morning lesson was at 6:15 a.m., the second at 7:00. They broke for breakfast at 7:30, then resumed their studies for a third lesson at 8:00. The fourth was at 10:00. They then broke for prayer at noon and likely had lunch. The fifth and likely last lesson of the day was at 2:30 p.m. and was devoted to mathematics.[77]

The children's education was shaped by the Saudi curriculum, but Siham urged her son-in-law to search for the curricula used in Yemen and Qatar—the latter, she thought, was better designed to engage and develop students' intellectual potential. Most likely, Usama's children with Amal followed the same "Daily Schedule" with Khadija's children. According to one letter, Khadija's eldest, Abdallah, enjoyed studying with "his aunt Safiya," Amal's eldest. Safiya, who was probably his age or a year older at most, was evidently affectionate toward her step-nephew. In October or November 2006, Usama and Amal had a fourth child, a girl they named Zainab, and, in the middle of 2008, they had their fifth, a boy they named Hussein.

Usama's grandchildren enjoyed their Abbottabad environment. They liked being around their uncle Khaled, in large part because they loved playing with the cat that was always loitering around him.[78] They listened to songs, which, in compliance with Islamic law, were chanted without instrumental accompaniment. Some of the songs were undoubtedly played to encourage the kids to eat healthy meals. One of them was about the joy of eating tomatoes, after which "my cheeks will turn red."[79] Another—"I Have Become Fat, Mama!"—was about eating "goats and rice" and "becom[ing] stronger and fit." The same song talks about "meeting my friends at a restaurant,"[80] something that the Bin Laden children could only dream about. They listened to and watched children's *anashid* (Islamic a cappella music) that chanted the alphabet,[81] and others that expressed the joy of Ramadan approaching.[82] They also watched pedagogical videos for children, one of them featuring two girls talking endearingly about their cats and remarking that the Prophet Muhammad's companion (Abu Hurayra) also had a cat.[83] Another featured an English song about the days of the week, suggesting that English was part of the children's schooling in Abbottabad.[84] Like Siham and Khaled, they also learned Urdu and Pashto, which would eventually allow them to blend in with the locals in the Af-Pak region.

Usama read stories to the children after dinner. In the morning, the children went to Khaled for more stories.[85] On the occasion of at least one Eid, marking the end of Ramadan, the children recited the Qur'an and poetry, after which Usama distributed prizes.[86] We get to hear their performance in the audio recordings recovered by the SEALs.[87] When it was the little Fatima's turn, we hear the adult women in the room giggling, as she confidently recited a few words of her poem—leaving out most of the syllables.[88]

In August 2010, we encounter three of Daoud's four children writing short letters to their father, who was still in Waziristan. Abdallah shared that in addition to having memorized suras (chapters) 17 and 18 of the Qur'an, he was "studying every day," and also "praying five times"—one of the Five Pillars of Islam. Aisha longed for "all of us to meet again," and was hoping to fast in Ramadan for the first time that year. She cheerfully shared that they had new clothes for Eid and that her baby sister, Fatima, "has grown, her hair is longer, and we play together." Daoud's son, Usama, wrote that he had memorized "up to Sura al-Qari'a" (chapter 101 of the Qur'an)." In about a month, he added, "I will start praying with my grandfather." He too longed to be reunited with his father, and "when the situation eases," he wrote, "we shall all pray together."[89]

Probably in 2008, Daoud was remarried *in absentia* to Khadija's sister Mariam, who raised the children as her own. He asked his mother-in-law if it was appropriate for him to write to Mariam,[90] as al-Qaeda observed a strict segregation of the sexes, which meant that women could mix and correspond only with their husbands and with men who are their *mahram* (a male blood relative whom it is unlawful to marry, such as a son, a father, or a brother).[91] We do not know if Siham granted permission, and it does not appear that Daoud and Mariam ever exchanged letters.

Daoud eventually took another wife, Sarah, who was fine with the polygamous arrangement, because "it was best for the children."[92] They had a son, Saad, and Sarah was pregnant when Daoud was killed in a drone strike in September 2010. Mariam became a widow before her marriage was consummated.[93]

Siham had lamented in her poetry that she could not give birth to her beloved Khadija "one more time." In December 2010, Sarah wrote to Siham that she was seven months pregnant, and if she gave birth to a girl, she was intent on naming her Khadija.[94]

9

THE ESCAPES

Six months ago, [while we were still in detention in Tehran,] I seriously began to look for a way to escape. . . . At midnight, I would jump out of the widow and make my way to the square-shaped fence to monitor the movement of the security guards, while my sister waited for me by the window.

Letter from Saad bin Laden to his father,
Usama bin Laden, August 5, 2008[1]

Usama bin Laden's second wife, Khairiah, their son, Hamza, and six of his children by his first wife, Najwa, had been among those who fled to Iran in early 2002. They had crossed the border illegally, and in December 2002, the Iranian authorities tracked them down. When he resumed contact with his associates in 2004, Usama learned of the detention of his family. Usama's associates knew little about their real conditions at the time, but they were given the impression that they were under "house arrest." Usama treated this matter as part of the broader issue of al-Qaeda detainees. The letters suggest that Iran sought to establish contact with him that year, but Usama insisted that any contact was "conditional" on the release of one of al-Qaeda's top leaders, "so that we may have some clarity about the situation and the people they are detaining."[2] In 2007, Usama's fatherly feelings took a front seat. Upon learning of his daughter Khadija's passing, the "very emotional" Usama changed course and began to think of the detention of his wife and children as a family ordeal.

In late 2007, as arrangements were under way to bring Daoud and Khadija's children to Abbottabad, Usama penned a letter to his oldest half-brother, Bakr, pleading for help to secure the release of his family in Iran. Bakr, who lived in Saudi Arabia and presided over the Bin Laden family business, had publicly condemned and denounced Usama's activities in 1994, and reportedly cut off all ties with him. However, this did not stop Usama from at least trying. Siham, whose children were not in Iran, marshaled her own family's network in Saudi Arabia "to work on releasing the children from Iran."

It wasn't until 2010 that al-Qaeda publicly admitted that Iran was detaining its leaders and Usama's family. Why, one might justifiably ask, didn't Usama and his associates speak publicly about the detainees much earlier? What did al-Qaeda do, if anything, to force Iran to begin releasing them in 2009? And why did Iran ultimately release most of Usama's family in 2010?

As we shall see, the Bin Laden Papers address all these questions.

Iran in Usama's Dreams

Usama paid considerable attention to the interpretation of dreams. In the Islamic tradition, dreams (*ru'ya*) can serve as a divine instrument for God to use to guide His believers.[3] Usama's 2007 letter to his brother Bakr reveals that he had been having recurring nightmare-like dreams about Iran, long before his family fled there. We learn that Usama had one such foreboding dream in 1987:

> I dreamed that I was in al-Burud, south of Jedda, peering to the east over-looking the valley of Wadi Fatima, when I saw a dusty cloud. It turned out to be a high wave, tsunami-like, surging from the east. Then I saw the destruction in the valley that the wave left behind, and noticed the wrecked car of the camel herders who were not mindful of what had befallen them. I said to myself while I was still dreaming: "Such are the Bedouin, they are inattentive."[4]

Usama recounted this in his 2007 letter to Bakr. Back in 1987, Usama interpreted the dream to mean "that the eastern origin of the wave indicated that the Rafida are the enemy."[5]

In 1990, Usama had another dream, so full of foreboding that it prompted him to warn publicly "of the threat of the Rafida Khomeini" and of Iraq's (secular) Saddam Hussein.[6] This was in the form of a lecture that was recorded on a cassette, a copy of which Usama gave to Bakr. Usama predicted that the Baathist "Saddam was about to invade the region," and Bakr retorted that "you just want to scare us." Usama probably thought that Bakr was just as "inattentive" as the Bedouin he had seen in his earlier dream. Six months later, Saddam invaded Kuwait, resulting in the Gulf War (1990–91). Usama had his *I told you so* moment. "Today," he said to Bakr in 1990, "the threat of Saddam and his party is minuscule compared to that of the Rafida."[7]

In addition to reminding Bakr of these dreams in his 2007 letter, Usama had actual afflictions to report that were closer—too close—to home. "Some of our father's grandsons and granddaughters are under house arrest in Iran," a sorrowful Usama wrote:

[My wife] Umm Hamza, my daughters Fatima and Iman,[8] and my sons too—Saad, Uthman, Muhammad, Hamza and Laden—all are detained in Iran. . . .

When America launched its unjust military campaign against Afghanistan, it repeatedly targeted the families of Arab jihadis, including their women and children. . . . Some of those who survived headed to Iran without coordination with the authorities in Tehran. . . . The authorities later arrested and imprisoned them. It has reached me that my family is under house arrest.

Usama shared that his family "had been detained for years now," and that "we have repeatedly requested their release in the direction of Pakistan, but Iran has not responded."

As mentioned before, Bakr had publicly denounced Usama's activities in 1994 after his brother refused "to make amends with the Saudi government, and abandon the path of political opposition and exile."[9] If Bakr had indeed cut off all ties with his younger brother, Usama ignored the fact. His 2007 letter was filled with warm greetings to "all the family," especially to "my dear mother . . . may she be pleased with me." But Usama was also critical of the Bin Ladens of Saudi Arabia for their "neglect to defend religion":

> It is a great sin to neglect supporting the jihadis in Iraq. If the jihadis did not defend Muslim men and women against the Christians and the Rafida's aggressions in Iraq, how else would the *hara'ir* [i.e., noble Muslim women who are not enslaved] in the Arabian Peninsula be protected from being defiled by the Rafida? Your tardiness in suppressing the Rafida's violent agitation, allowing their threat to grow and expand, is truly disgraceful.

But the ultimate purpose of the 2007 letter was to enlist Bakr's help. Usama believed that Bakr's brothers-in-law had the necessary contacts to secure the release of his family in Iran.[10] Bakr's wife, Haifa Nabulsi, is Syrian and of Palestinian origin,[11] and Usama might have reasoned that her brothers could use their contacts with the Syrian regime to intercede with Iran on behalf of his family since Syria and Iran maintained close ties. "Perhaps," Usama pleaded, "you could help secure their release to the Waziristan region in Pakistan." Once "I know that they are safe with the tribes," he added, "I would have peace of mind."[12] Anticipating Bakr's reluctance to be involved, Usama deliberately evoked the memory of their father: "You would be doing a pious deed as a homage to your father," he implored.

To ensure that her husband's letter was not swept under the carpet, Siham wrote a separate letter to Khadija's husband, Daoud, who seemed to have the ability to send letters to Saudi Arabia. In it, Siham included the phone number of Usama's mother, knowing that she would lobby Bakr to secure the release of her grandchildren.[13] Siham also instructed Daoud to write to her own family and ask them to marshal their own network to help "release the children from Iran."

The courier who was meant to deliver Usama and Daoud's letters to Saudi Arabia was captured in Pakistan, and we can assume that Bakr was spared having to choose between helping secure the release of his nieces and nephews and ignoring their plight.[14] And Usama's "Rafida" nightmares continued.

THE ESCAPES

Al-Qaeda's Iran Dilemma

As we discovered in Chapter Two, in December 2001, Mullah Omar ordered the Arabs to evacuate Afghanistan. Those who fled to Pakistan were arrested, and Arab jihadis and their families had nowhere else to go but west, to Iran. Usama himself had "disappeared" before Mullah Omar issued his order. According to a 2008 letter by Usama's son, Saad, it was Khaled Sheikh Muhammad (KSM) who ordered al-Qaeda's top leaders and members of Usama's family to flee to Iran "in view of how dangerous the situation was at the time."[15] As it turned out, they found themselves moving out of the frying pan into the fire.

Usama and his associates never missed an opportunity to highlight Muslims' grievances, yet they waited until 2010 to publicize that Iran was detaining al-Qaeda's leaders and their families. How can this uncharacteristic delay be explained?

This was clearly a problematic issue for the leaders of al-Qaeda, not least because many of their "enemies" continually accused them of conspiring with Iran. In May 2003, the Saudi-funded newspaper *al-Sharq al-Awsat* reported that Saad, Usama's son, and Saif al-Adl "left Iran following the Riyadh attacks in May 2003." The article alleged that the two had been given shelter in Iran by Muhammad al-Islambuli, who had "strong ties with Iran's Revolutionary Guard."[16] Muhammad is the brother of Khaled al-Islambuli, the man who assassinated the Egyptian President, Anwar al-Sadat, in 1981. Though impressive in its detail, the article was entirely inaccurate. The Bin Laden Papers reveal that, at the time of the Riyadh attacks, Saad was on hunger strike, protesting his unbearable conditions "in a secret prison underground near the airport of Tehran." Saif too may have been in the same prison at that time.

Despite the detainment of its top leaders, al-Qaeda restrained its public criticisms of Iran. When Usama's associate Atiya engaged with the jihadi community online in 2006, he put on a brave face: "We've talked a lot about Iran, but let me tell you this: God willing, if the jihadis—al-Qaeda and those who support it—took on Iran, they would spite Iran greatly and transform its peaceful existence through a torrent of terror."[17]

What was preventing al-Qaeda from delivering on its threat? Atiya did not share with his audience that Iran was holding al-Qaeda's leaders and Usama's family. Also, he could not disclose that al-Qaeda was "afflicted," that its members were instructed by Usama to "hide," and the group's "external work," i.e., international terrorism, was nonexistent. Instead, and pretending that al-Qaeda was in full command, Atiya presented a Realpolitik position: "Today, the jihadis are cautious. They have their own considerations, which are always changing, as is always the case. Don't think that you [i.e., the Iranians] are safe, and you know what these words mean!"[18]

Behind the scenes, Atiya was quite troubled. Not only was al-Qaeda unable to attack Iran, but, fearing for the safety of the detainees, he and other leaders had to mute their hostility toward Iran in their public statements. Atiya needed advice as to whether al-Qaeda should publicly reject the reports that accused it of conspiring with Iran, many of them originating in Saudi Arabia. Through an intermediary, he turned to the cleric Bishr al-Bishr in Saudi Arabia for advice. Bishr was under house arrest, but Atiya's "trusted intermediary" was able to visit him and discuss al-Qaeda's affairs at length with the cleric. Bishr advised al-Qaeda to ignore completely the rumors about its association with Iran:

> Responding to such lies would only serve to spread them. . . . Articles making such accusations belong to the dustbin of history, and do not worry about them. I am surprised how people do not see these articles' blatant falsehood. It's like mixing fire with water, how else would al-Qaeda and Iran work together!! . . . Do not concern yourself with clarifying what is already clear. . . . If someone were to claim that Sheikh Usama is an agent of Israel and America, should we dignify it with a response!?[19]

This reassured Atiya somewhat. But he continued to be perplexed by this issue, and we find him elaborating al-Qaeda's dilemma in a 2007 letter to Usama and Ayman: "Concerning how we treat Iran in our media statements, it is undoubtedly entwined with how we deal with it politically. I have thought long and hard about this, and I won't hide from you that I am in a bit of a quandary about this."

Atiya was mindful that al-Qaeda needed to take into consideration that "Iran is detaining our brothers." Iran was also a state that did not have diplomatic ties with the United States, which meant that the CIA presence there, if any, was far more limited than in Pakistan. This allowed al-Qaeda to use Iran as "a passageway . . . serving as a logistical outlet for our movements." Those entrusted to move money and smuggle people through Iran were instructed to prepare themselves to commit suicide if they were captured lest they disclosed al-Qaeda's secrets under duress.[20] Days before he wrote his letter, Atiya's own wife and children had joined him in North Waziristan, most likely smuggled there through Iran. However, in his internal communications, Atiya was far from muted:

> This evil and heretical state is undoubtedly our enemy and is a looming threat to the Islamic *umma*. This includes Iran's criminal and harmful policies, and the fact that it sides—sort of—with our enemies against us. I don't want to say that our silence is causing people to doubt our sincerity. That, I don't believe, because the good people in the *umma* . . . understand the reasons behind our silence. . . . But I must say that the prejudiced and biased enemies, those who are looking for anything to accuse us of, are exploiting it!! It is all the more vexing that our fellow countrymen (*min bani jildatina*) are undoubtedly promoting this view whenever they are given the opportunity by the media.[21]

Atiya did not believe that al-Qaeda, as he put it in a letter to Usama, "could afford to wait endlessly until the Iranians released our brothers." He was certain that the Iranians "would never release the detainees," and "are holding them to pressure us, for they know that they are hitting us where it hurts." He went as far as to pray for "an American strike against Iran" to provide al-Qaeda with the opportunity to destabilize Iran. But he reasoned that Iran and the United States would likely "end up resolving their problems through a compromise of sorts."

Atiya suggested launching a "political campaign" that involved "a change in our language about Iran, gradually uncovering its hypocrisy and enmity toward

Islam and Muslims." His plan required them to proceed "gradually." Otherwise, he feared that the "enemies" would think that al-Qaeda and Iran "used to love each other, just like butter and honey," and that "a recent brawl must have led to this reversal."

It was necessary, Atiya believed, that al-Qaeda be ready to time its political campaign with "an attack" inside Iran or "take serious measures to kidnap a few heavyweight Iranians." Perhaps then, Atiya calculated, "the criminals would be shocked, terrified, and would attempt to connect with us." If this happened, he added wishfully, "we would have an opportunity to negotiate with them" over the detainees. Atiya considered approaching "our Kurdish brothers" to plan an attack inside Iran. He was probably thinking of Arif Abu Shadia, who had reached out to al-Qaeda earlier that year to introduce his Kurdish group and give his allegiance to Usama. According to Arif's 2007 letter, his group was familiar with Iran's territories bordering Iraq. His men had "entered Iran secretly" after the group's bases "were attacked by the Americans in Iraq's Kurdistan." Though Iran captured many members of his group and sent them back to Iraq, Arif was happy to report that "some of them had managed to return to Iran through the mountains."[22]

Usama did not need much convincing, but he likely wanted to secure his family's release before launching a "political campaign" against Iran. His letter to his brother Bakr was composed a month after he received Atiya's proposal. In 2008, al-Qaeda began "to train Kurdish brothers" to send to Iran. We also learn that Abd al-Malik al-Balochi, the leader of Jundallah, an Iranian Sunni group "actively working against Iran," met with al-Qaeda's leaders in Waziristan and "discussed the issue of our detained brothers." Abd al-Malik told them that "the Iranian government was extremely weak" and would likely acquiesce if al-Qaeda "threatened to attack if Iran didn't release the brothers." Alternatively, he volunteered to share with al-Qaeda the "names of four Baluch who were spying for America in Iran," and suggested that al-Qaeda should send a letter to the Iranians, offering to give them their names in return for the release of the detainees.[23]

The letters do not reveal that al-Qaeda succeeded in attacking Iran and there is nothing to suggest that contact was made with Iran about the Baluch who were "spying for America." However, al-Qaeda's leaders went on to escalate their "political campaign," with Ayman publicly accusing "Iran of conspiring with America" against the jihadis. The media campaign was such a priority that, to coordinate it effectively, Ayman took unprecedented risks twice in 2008 (February and August) and met in person with Hajji Uthman and Atiya. The letters do not disclose the location of these meetings.[24] It is doubtful, however, that al-Qaeda's anti-Iran rhetoric made a dent in Iran's strategic decisions.

But then something unexpected happened.

The First Escape

While al-Qaeda was aimlessly trying to come up with an effective strategy against Iran, Saad—Usama's son by Najwa—was planning his escape from the detention center in Yazd, Iran. At that time, as we shall discover, some detainees were still in Tehran while others were moved to Yazd. We learn a lot from the long letter Saad penned to his father on August 5, 2008, shortly after his escape:

Six months ago, [while we were still in detention in Tehran,] I seriously began to look for a way to escape. . . . Then the Iranian authorities moved me, my brothers, our families, and Saif al-Adl's family to another detention compound in Yazd, a city in the middle of Iran. The place was surrounded by two fences, one was 3.5 meters high, while the other was much higher, but under construction. We had been in Yazd for two weeks when signs of my sister Iman's psychological distress were becoming visible. I promised her that I would find a solution.

At night, the security guards locked the door of our residence and surrounded the house with an additional square-shaped temporary fence. . . . I used screwdrivers to loosen the bolts of one of the windows. At midnight, I would jump out of the widow and make my way to the square-shaped fence to monitor the movement of the security guards, while my sister waited for me by the window.

Saad created a small opening in the fence to monitor the security gate and, after a while, he observed a pattern. At night, the security guards worked two-hour shifts: "during the first hour," Saad noticed, "the guard was usually alert and did not move, but during the second hour, he would get restless and was constantly moving," no doubt to keep himself from falling asleep.

On June 7, 2008, the night of his escape, Saad enlisted the help of his brothers Hamza and Laden.[25] Laden monitored the gate, and when he signaled to Hamza and Saad that the restless guard had moved, the two brothers ran to the gate. Next, Saad quickly stepped up onto Hamza's clasped hands, then onto his shoulders. Hamza then lifted his brother high enough to jump over the gate (most likely the gate that was 3.5 meters high). Saad had to clamber without his brother's assistance over a second gate that was monitored "by Iranian intelligence," but "with God's grace, the guards were asleep."

As a child, Saad always ran "far ahead of everyone," his brother Omar recalled.[26] The same habit saw him pull a Forrest Gump on that fateful night when he escaped from Iran: After breaking out from the detention center, he ran as far away as he could, eventually finding himself at a bus stop. He "purchased a bus ticket to the city of Kerman." In case he was being pursued, he took precautions: "On the way, I got off the bus in the city of Rafsanjan, then I caught a private car to Kerman. There I changed cars to the city of Bam, then another car to the city of Zahedan."[27]

Zahedan is one of the cities where Arab jihadis had first settled after they fled Afghanistan in 2001–02. Saad was therefore able to connect with a network of Sunni Iranian supporters:

> I headed to the house of one of the Baluch brothers. I told him the story and that it was imperative that I leave Iran at the earliest possible opportunity before Iranian intelligence found out. The following day, the Baluch brother arranged a meeting with one of the Arab brothers on your side [i.e., a supporter or member of al-Qaeda], who immediately arranged my travel. I spent fifteen days traveling, and I am now among the brothers in Waziristan.[28]

Upon his arrival in North Waziristan, Saad wrote a detailed letter to his father, chronicling the dire conditions of the detainees in Iran. As noted before,

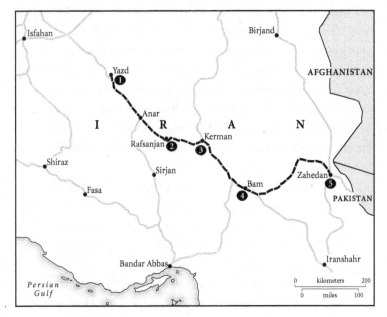

Saad bin Laden's escape route.

up until then Usama had been under the impression that members of al-Qaeda and his family were "under house arrest" in Iran. After reading Saad's letter, he learned for the first time what his family and other detainees had been subjected to in Iran.

We learn from Saad that it was in December 2002 that the Iranian authorities tracked down members of al-Qaeda and their families. Initially they imprisoned only the men, and the women and children were allowed occasional visits. This went on for about eighteen months before the men were moved to "bastioned detention centers" in Tehran, guarded by Iranian intelligence, to live together with their women and children. They were not treated like ordinary prisoners.[29] The authorities may have hoped that this would appease the men, who had been on hunger strike to protest their prison conditions. In the detention centers, the men could marry, have (more) children, socialize, and study with al-Qaeda's senior leaders. The prison authorities were also spared from having to organize conjugal visits, which are granted to ordinary prisoners under the law. From an Iranian security perspective, those visits were challenging, particularly because segregation of the sexes had to be observed. Some detainees had managed to escape during the commotions when male security guards were replaced by female guards, and women often smuggled in mobile phones and laptops to their husbands.[30] Thus, by keeping them under the one roof, the authorities lessened the likelihood of al-Qaeda's presence becoming publicly known.

These "detention privileges" notwithstanding, Saad related that the prison authorities treated the detainees inhumanely. It took four years and "persistent requests" before they agreed to provide educational materials so that the children could be schooled. The most "tragic" kind of mistreatment, according to Saad, was the medical neglect of the detainees. Whenever they fell sick, they were taken to a hospital with a "bad reputation" where "everyone suffered great afflictions." All ailments, regardless of their severity, were treated with "painkillers." The wife of Muhammad al-Islambuli, Umm Jaafar, fell ill and was twice taken to this "bad" hospital. Both times, the doctors insisted that "there was nothing wrong" with her, only for her to die within days of her second visit.

Saad reported that after a few years in detention, "the calamities piled up, and the psychological problems increased." We learn that Usama's two daughters, Iman and Fatima, were psychologically distressed. Iman's condition manifested itself as skin problems. Fatima suffered from severe psychological problems.[31] Saad disclosed that she completely isolated herself from the rest. In 2006 or 2007, after Iman and Fatima's conditions worsened, the prison authorities allowed them to call their mother, Najwa—who had left Afghanistan for Syria days before the 9/11 attacks. Lest their presence in Iran became known to the CIA if telephone signals were being monitored, they were taken to the Afghan border to place the call. Usama's second wife, Khairiah, asked to call her family in Saudi Arabia, but the Iranian authorities denied her request. When in 2009 Najwa co-authored a book with her son Omar, she omitted any reference to the fate of her six children, no doubt fearing for their safety.[32]

Fatima's condition continued to deteriorate. Saad revealed that "she became like the dead among the living." Sulaiman Abu Ghaith, who had served as an al-Qaeda spokesman on one occasion after 9/11 and was also detained in Iran, proposed to marry Fatima. Saad and his brothers "hesitated a lot," but eventually agreed to Sulaiman's proposal, hoping that this would improve Fatima's condition. They got married in late 2007.

It is difficult to imagine how Sulaiman could have cheered Fatima given the litany of his own problems. We discover that when he was first detained, the Iranian authorities repeatedly denied him permission to contact his wife in Kuwait. In Iran, Sulaiman took a second wife, the widow of Abu Hafs al-Misri, and they had twins—a boy and a girl. The boy fell ill and the prison authorities did not take him to hospital until it was too late, and Sulaiman "watched his son die before his eyes."

After four years of being denied contact with his first wife, Sulaiman went on hunger strike. After twenty-one days, the prison authorities finally took him to the Afghan border to call his wife. Sulaiman probably wished that he had never made that call: He learned that his wife had remarried after being told that he was dead. This news led to "the deterioration of his physical and psychological health," and he began to suffer from a severe headache that lasted for months. In view of Sulaiman's distress, it is curious that Saad and his brothers agreed to let him marry their sister.

According to Saad, "prison had its benefits," for it was "a school of life where manliness is born." Among the benefits he recounted was the men's ability to study with the leaders of al-Qaeda. Abu Hafs al-Mauritani, the leader of al-Qaeda's Legal Committee before 9/11, schooled Usama's sons in jurisprudence, while Sulaiman taught them the art of oratory. They seem to have been diligent in their studies, so much so that Sulaiman, Saad, Uthman, and Muhammad took turns delivering the Friday sermon. Eventually, Saad relates, "all educational activities ceased due to the deteriorating psychological conditions" of the detainees. He narrates some of the negotiations the detainees had with Iranian intelligence:

We often told them: "We want to know the response of the Iranian National Intelligence Council to our demand to leave Iran." They told us: "It is impossible for you to leave, but we will give you more privileges in detention." Then their leader, whose real name I know [i.e., most likely a public figure], said: "You shall only be allowed to leave Iran in one of two scenarios, namely, if America bombs Iran, or when America is wiped off the map." He then added: "The Sheikh [i.e., Usama] asked us to protect you and we promised him that." Of course, none of the brothers believed him. I responded scornfully: "How nice of you to protect us by brutally breaking into our homes while our women were asleep; by imprisoning us; and by afflicting us with all sorts of new ailments."

When it became clear that the negotiations were futile, "we could not take it any longer, and lost our patience." Around March or April 2008, Saad narrated,

[m]ost of the brothers, women, and children stormed out of their rooms, boldly overtaking the guards and crossing two of the three gates surrounding the compound. They crossed two of the three gates. They sat there for a day, while some of us began negotiations with Iranian intelligence through a judicial representative.

Probably because Saad was the most vocal, the judicial representative offered to release him and a few others, but Saad rejected "the double standard" outright. Saad witnessed the authorities "unleash the special forces on us," and a bloody confrontation—which the detainees later referred to as "Bloody Sunday"—ensued:

Fifty members of the security forces—wearing bulletproof vests and helmets, and armed with canes, tear gas, and pepper spray—stormed into the detention center. The brothers initially told them in Persian: "*Aram bash*" [i.e., calm down], but the special forces launched into beating us.

Those whom I saw being beaten included Abu al-Khair, who got angry and took a pipe that was by his side and smashed the head of the officer who was beating him. Several members of the special forces turned on him, beating him mercilessly, and used pepper spray on his face. When one of them attacked me, I hit him with a hammer. Then I saw Sheikh Sulaiman [Abu Ghaith] take a piece of iron and start fighting like someone who does not fear death. . . . He broke the hands of some and injured others, but they outnumbered him and hit him hard on his head until he fell. They sprayed pepper in his face and continued to beat him until he lost consciousness. Then he awoke, muttering indistinct words, before he lost consciousness again.

Fatima, who witnessed the fighting from a distance, rushed to tend to her husband. When the Iranian female squad team failed to stop her, the male squad intervened and hit her with a cane across her shoulders. The men were then rounded up, handcuffed, and put on a bus. Saad recounted:

Most of the brothers had been injured. Abu Jaafar [i.e., Muhammad Islambuli] was loudly repeating *hasbuna Allah wa-ni'ma al-wakil* [i.e., roughly: we trust in God, He will see to it that our affairs are justly arranged], and this angered one member of the special forces who hit him with a cane on his head and face many times. After that, they took Sheikhs Sulaiman and Abu Hafs to hospital, and forcibly took Hamza and me off the bus.

The Iranian authorities imprisoned the men who took part in the fighting. This did not deter the rest of the "men and women who went on an indefinite hunger strike." For his part, Saad "pretended to the Iranians that I repented, because I wanted them to feel reassured [by my compliance] to pursue my escape plan, and they did." The prison authorities decided to take measures to prevent another "Bloody Sunday." One of the officials came to Saad and told him:

"We shall separate you all for four months, after which we will move you all together again to a better housing compound. If you refuse, we won't release the prisoners." I agreed because of my sister Fatima [whose husband had been taken away and imprisoned separately], but I insisted that they promise, through an agreement ('ahd), that they would release the prisoners immediately after they moved us to the city of Yazd. They kept their promise.

Except for Fatima, Usama's family and that of Saif al-Adl were thus moved to another detention center in the city of Yazd. Following "Bloody Sunday," the prison authorities "began to change our living conditions somewhat." They gave each detainee a monthly stipend, which was usually granted to ordinary Iranian prisoners with financial needs.[33] The new living conditions in both Tehran and Yazd included "some outings, such as shopping and some excursions to public gardens," supervised by security guards, and an "improved response" to the detainees' medical needs. Despite these upgrades, Saad was determined that he must escape and find a solution. Not long after "Bloody Sunday," and two weeks after the move to Yazd, he successfully broke free.

Saad's detailed letter was likely the catalyst that led al-Qaeda to take an aggressive measure against Iran. In November 2008, within a few months of Saad's escape, al-Qaeda kidnapped a "heavyweight"—Hesmatollah Atharzadeh, the commercial counselor at the Iranian consulate in Peshawar.[34] By then, al-Qaeda had learned a thing or two about hostage-taking from the letters of the North African group AQIM. In late 2009, Iran began the gradual release of the detainees. According to Atiya:

We believe that it is our efforts—the escalation of our political and media campaign, the threat that we sent [to Iran], the kidnapping of their commercial counselor in the Peshawar consulate, and the other things that they saw and feared—which may have contributed to speeding up the release of the detainees.[35]

Atiya's assessment is far from accurate, not least because Iran began to release the detainees before the diplomat was freed in March 2010. In all likelihood, Atiya did not believe it himself when he wrote that Iran "saw and feared" their efforts, since he went on to admit that "the criminals [i.e., the Iranians] did not even send us a letter, nor did they communicate anything to the brothers they released . . .!" Instead, he admitted that the Iranians sent the detainees to Zahedan to a "Baluch brother who then transferred them to us."[36] Judging by the letters of those who were released following Saad's escape, it was the detainees' actions rather than al-Qaeda's "efforts" that likely caused Iran to change its policy.

The Second Escape

We learn from Ayman's brother-in-law, Abu Sahl al-Misri, who was released from Iran in early 2010, that Usama's family was subjected to stringent security measures to prevent a repeat escape. The authorities eventually allowed the Bin Ladens, escorted by security guards, occasional visits to see Fatima, who remained with her husband in detention in Tehran. According to Abu Sahl, early in 2009, the Iranians promised to release Usama's wife Khairiah and Saad's wife, but they kept "putting it off for months." Sometime in June or July 2009, he continues, "the Iranians even set the date and time of travel" of Khairiah, Laden, Iman, and Saad's wife and her children to Waziristan. The detainees were convinced that the Iranians would follow through this time. As Khairiah was getting ready, her only child, Hamza, composed his first and only letter to his father from Iran to send with his mother. Hamza was thirteen when he had last seen his father, and

had not imagined that our separation would be as long and as bitter since my brothers Khaled, Bakr [i.e., Laden], and I said our farewell to you at the olive grove near the foot of the mountain. It's been eight years, and I continue to remember how I gazed at you while you stood under the olive tree, handing each one of us a prayer bead (*subha*) so that we could remind ourselves of the Lord.[37] Then you said goodbye, and it's as if we took our last breath when we parted ways.[38]

Hamza went on to share with his father that "God has bestowed upon me a good wife and blessed me with two children, a son that I named after you, and a daughter that I named after my mother." He also touched on the "distressful situations that I went through, and would have loved to see you, even if for a minute, to consult with you on how best to handle them," but he comforted his father that the same tribulations had taught him "to be a man."[39] To please his father, Hamza enumerated the large number of classical Islamic texts that he had studied in prison under the guidance of al-Qaeda's Sheikhs.

Hamza expressed his strong desire to "serve religion" and worried that he would die in detention before he had the opportunity to join the jihadis on the battlefield. Beneath Hamza's eagerness to be a mujahid and his professed manliness, his fear was palpable. Not knowing when, if ever, he would be released, he beseeched his father: "I have one request: Try all appropriate means to secure our safe release from the Iranians' grip."[40]

Hours before Khairiah and the others were due to be released, the Iranians "suddenly postponed their travel indefinitely." We don't know why the Iranians repeatedly made promises that they did not keep, and we cannot be sure whether, as Saad wrote, these "masters at making us lose our nerve . . . took pleasure in torturing us psychologically." At any rate, Khairiah did not get to deliver Hamza's letter to his father in 2009.

When their hopes of being released were dashed, Iman decided that she too was going to escape. About a week before Eid al-Adha in November 2009, Iman, Khairiah, Laden, and Saad's wife were allowed to go out shopping, accompanied by three security guards. The prison authorities assigned two men to guard Laden, but underestimated the women, only assigning one female security officer to guard all three. Abu Sahl related:

Iman managed to escape from the female guard. She ran to a store adjacent to the Saudi embassy, and from there she entered the embassy. . . . Iman expected that Laden would follow her, but he was unable to escape because the security around him was tight. . . . The Saudi embassy gave Iman a mobile phone, which she used to contact her mother in Syria. She told her that she was trying, through her brother Abdallah [who lived in Saudi Arabia], to travel first to Saudi Arabia, and then to Syria.[41]

It is possible that Abu Sahl was not entirely forthcoming in his letter to Usama about Iman's escape. He probably couldn't bring himself to write to Usama that his daughter, who was not supposed to mix with men without a *mahram*, took it upon herself to escape on her own. According to Jean Sasson, who was in contact with Iman's mother, Najwa, the plan was for Iman to escape on her own all along, seeing that she "was a young girl who might receive more assistance." When she escaped her security guard, Sasson reported:

Iman ran as fast as she could . . . through the streets of Tehran until she saw a man she felt had a kindly demeanor. She approached the man and told him that she was a Saudi and she had to get to the Saudi embassy. This man took her home to his wife and children and there they heard the story before Iman was driven to the Saudi embassy.[42]

At any rate, following Iman's escape to the Saudi embassy, the Iranians could no longer deny that they were detaining Usama's family. Her brother Abdallah, who lived in Saudi Arabia and who appears to have been distant from his family's politics, did not hesitate to help his sister. The Saudi embassy submitted Iman's papers to facilitate her travel out of the country to Saudi Arabia, but the Iranian authorities refused. They clearly preferred sending Iman to her mother in Syria, whose regime was close to Iran.

Iman's travel plans stalled, and she was kept at the Saudi embassy for several months. In early 2010, her brother Abd al-Rahman—who left Afghanistan with his mother days before 9/11 and was "known for his distance from the media"—gave an interview to Al Jazeera, publicizing his sister's ordeal and the detention of his father's family in Iran. Iman's brother Omar, who lived in Qatar, also called for her release.[43]

Usama was fretting in Abbottabad, and no longer wanted to keep a lid on his family's detention. He considered allowing Saad's letter to be posted online to expose Iran's mistreatment of the detainees, but did not go through with it. He probably did not want to divulge private information about his daughters. Instead, he enlisted his daughter Mariam to draft a letter addressed to Ayatollah Khamenei, Iran's Supreme Leader:

> This letter is to call on you to release my detained family in Iran.
>
> It should have come to your knowledge that my brothers Abd al-Rahman and Omar spoke out about the detention of my aunt, my two sisters, and four of my brothers with their wives and children in Iran, and they called on you to release them. I hereby reinforce their call and confirm that my family unofficially entered Iran after the [2001] Crusader air campaign targeted especially Arab families in Afghanistan.
>
> After a year of their presence in Iran, security forces arrested them. When this reached us, we wrote many times to the government of Tehran and called on officials to release them, promising that they would never return to Iran, but to no avail.
>
> We repeated our request after my brother Saad escaped. He told us about the tragedies that they endured inside Iranian prisons, leading to multiple deaths and the spread of skin and psychological diseases among the women and children. . . . For six years [before Saad's escape], the government kept putting off their release, using the detainees to pressure my father to stop the attacks of al-Qaeda in Iraq against political forces and militias loyal to Tehran. My father's response in one of his public statements addressed to the people of Iraq made it clear that everyone who stands in America's trench is a lawful target for us, regardless of his race or creed.
>
> Sagacious and level-headed people reject and are indeed repulsed and disgusted when imprisoned daughters and children are threatened to coerce

a man into doing something. . . . Why should the oppressed women and children be used as cards in disagreements among men. If my father is forced to choose between sacrificing his six children and his eleven [*sic*] grandchildren in Iran[44]—even if he had to watch them being beheaded one by one—and supporting or helping Arab or non-Arab leaders against Muslims, be certain that he would choose his religion and sacrifice himself and his children to avoid hurting Muslims.

The letter was originally signed by Mariam, but before it was released on a jihadi website,[45] Usama decided to have it signed by his son Khaled instead.[46] Even if Khaled's letter reached Khamenei, it is doubtful that it led to Iman's release from Iran.

But in March 2010, Iran likely "promised" to release Iman and the rest of Usama's family in return for the Iranian diplomat that al-Qaeda had kidnapped.[47] We don't know if, on this occasion, Iran negotiated directly with al-Qaeda, and we also don't know why Iran did not threaten worse treatment of the detainees to secure the release of its diplomat. The letters reveal that Iran had wanted to keep its detention of al-Qaeda's leaders secret, presumably believing that this forced al-Qaeda to refrain from attacking it. But Iman's escape to the Saudi embassy and the publicity that followed forced a change of policy. An Iranian intelligence official told Usama's sons that, with Iman's escape being publicized, "their value was no longer important," and Iran was going to "start processing their travel out of Iran." What's more, the Iranian authorities told the detainees that they had to be moved elsewhere, "because Iman knows the detention compound's exact location." Because of all this, one intelligence official told the "brothers" in prison, "the al-Qaeda file must now be closed."[48]

By then, the detainees had had enough. In late June or early July 2010, soon after being moved to a new compound, a "huge riot broke out." The prison authorities had clearly had enough too. They sent in "special forces dressed in black and masked" and "arrested the men." The detainees understood that they were facing a "make-or-break" scenario with their captors and, of course, "God humiliated them and strengthened our [i.e., the detainees'] resolve." The arrested men were kept for "101 days" away from their families.[49]

Thanks to Iman's escape, which publicized Iran's detention of members of al-Qaeda and their families, Iran hastened the release of most of the detainees, except the top leaders. Soon after Iman was allowed to leave the Saudi embassy and travel to Syria, Iran released her brother Laden, also to Syria. In August 2010, it released her brothers Muhammad and Uthman, as well as Usama's wife Khairiah and their son, Hamza. For reasons unknown to Usama, only Khairiah and Hamza were allowed to go to Waziristan, while Najwa's sons were sent to Syria. Fatima and her husband, Sulaiman, were freed in 2013. Sulaiman was captured again the same year in Jordan and brought to the United States.[50] In 2014, he was sentenced to life in prison.[51]

A Note about Saad

Saad had been a member of al-Qaeda before the 9/11 attacks and, in his 2008 letter, he reaffirmed his allegiance "one more time" to his father. Following his escape to North Waziristan in 2008, he learned of his half-sister Khadija's passing, and prayed that they would meet again "in Paradise." He also wrote to his father of his longing to "kiss your head and kneel down to kiss your hands."

Saad had leadership ambitions and displayed an aura of command unmatched by his brothers Khaled and Hamza. Though he was ready to serve Islam in whatever capacity his father decided, he suggested that he should help with al-Qaeda's efforts to release the detainees still in Iran. He told his father that he had been "aching" to address the *umma* publicly and felt that he had the capacity to do so in an original manner. But he feared that speaking publicly would prevent him "from working with the brothers," because very few people in North Waziristan knew his true identity for security reasons. Within about a year of his escape, Saad was killed in a CIA drone strike.[52] He may have been lax about operational-security measures, as suggested by his request to withdraw up to 5,000 euros from his father's account to buy a car. It is doubtful that his father granted him permission.

Saad left two handwritten wills, one for his wife, the other for his father. The first, addressed to "my dearest and most loyal wife," read like an amorous letter. In it, he recognized that his wife had suffered much "psychological distress," and expressed gratitude for "all that you put up with in detention."[53] He assured her that "you fill my heart with love and beautiful memories," and "I shall not take another wife, because I will never find a woman like you."[54] He hoped to stay alive "in the land of jihad until God reunites us in this world and my eyes get to relish the sight of you and my children."[55] But if "God wills it that I should die," Saad noted, "I have no objections if you wish to remarry." He amatively added, "but I strongly desire that you choose to be my wife in Paradise." According to Islamic belief, women who marry more than one man during their lifetime get to choose the one they want to be married to in the hereafter. Saad urged his wife to strive to marry their daughters, Asma and Duha, to jihadis when they came of age,[56] and to send their son, Usama, to the battlefield to fight with his grandfather in God's path.[57]

Saad's other will was brimming with gratitude to his father, not least for "instilling the importance of jihad in our hearts." It also contained a tally of his financial obligations in this world so that he might secure his eternal life: Saad informed his father that Abu Burhan al-Suri, who had been in Usama's circle since the 1980s, had loaned him money to cover his marriage expenses.[58] Saad wanted to make sure that if this money had not been from his father's account, "please pay it off so that my soul is not locked in my grave." According to Islamic belief, the souls of Muslims who die in debt are locked in the grave and cannot reach Paradise until the debt is paid off.[59] Saad also asked his father to look after his wife and children and to establish charitable trusts (*sadaqat jariya*) in his name,[60] "for I am in utmost need of spiritual sustenance if I am to reach the eternal abode."

The Real Relationship Between al-Qaeda and Iran

On February 16, 2012, U.S. Director of National Intelligence James R. Clapper Jr. testified before the Committee on Armed Services that Iran and al-Qaeda have "a kind of shotgun marriage or a marriage of convenience." He spoke of a "standoff arrangement" that al-Qaeda had with Iran, "allowing them to exist there but not to foment any operations directly from Iran because they are very sensitive about, hey, we might come after them there as well."[61] By then, the U.S. intelligence community had had over ten months to explore the documents covered in this book, and they should have deduced that al-Qaeda had not consummated any relationship with Iran, let alone a "marriage of convenience." Six years later, on May 8, 2018, President Trump announced that the Joint Comprehensive Plan of Action (JCPOA), or the Iran deal that the Obama administration had reached, "must either be renegotiated or terminated." Iran, he stated, "supports terrorist proxies and militias such as . . . al Qaeda."[62] Days before he left office as Secretary of State, Mike Pompeo asserted that Iran had become a "new base" for al-Qaeda, a relationship that the group had had with Tehran "for nearly three decades."[63]

Are such statements a reflection of bad intelligence, anti-Iran lobbying, incompetence, or a misreading of the Bin Laden Papers? The jihadi cleric Bishr al-Bishr had advised Atiya to ignore such "blatant falsehoods," for they belong to the "dustbin of history." But clearly, the "dustbin" is resistant to being emptied.

Perhaps the false rumors did not just originate from the U.S. government and anti-Iran lobbying groups. The letters suggest that Iran may have spread rumors of its own, perhaps to sow division among jihadi groups. We learn from Usama's son Hamza that the Iranian government was spreading "rumors that the brothers in Iran are content with their situation there, or that they do not desire to leave Iran, or that they are concerned about the [dangerous] situation in Waziristan." He assured his father "that these rumors have nothing to do with the [harsh] reality inside the prison." In fact, nine days before he and his mother were released, al-Qaeda's top Sheikhs met in detention. Among those present at the meeting were Muhammad al-Islambuli, Ahmad Hasan Abu al-Khair, Abu Muhammad al-Misri al-Zayyat, Saif al-Adl, Sulaiman Abu Ghaith, and Abu Hafs al-Mauritani. They instructed Hamza to pass on the following message to Usama:

From your brothers in the oppressive Iranian intelligence prison to our brothers in Khurasan. . . . For years we have been waiting for God to free us, through you, the soldiers of God, the guardians of the creed. Based on our seven and a half years of experience with those people, we propose the following: Those people, "the Iranians," do not respond except through force. God knows that we shall not be freed unless the jihadis resort to force. What we want you to do is to kidnap Iranian officials, then negotiate with their government without publicizing it.

One of the "Sheikhs" even asked Hamza to tell Usama that "if Waziristan is dangerous and under excessive bombing, we [prefer] to go there to achieve martyrdom; as for this life in detention, it is a life of servility, only God knows its bitter taste."[64]

If Clapper is taken at his word, this had to be the most inconvenient "marriage of convenience" ever.

Iran may also have spread rumors that al-Qaeda was collaborating with the United States. We already met Abu al-Walid al-Misri (Mustafa Hamid) briefly in Chapter One. He had been a close advisor to Usama before 9/11 and had regularly lectured on politics in al-Qaeda's training camps in Afghanistan during the 1980s and 1990s.

We learn from the letters that Abu al-Walid was among those who had escaped to Iran after the fall of the Taliban, but that he was not detained with the rest. During his years in Iran, Abu al-Walid wrote many books about the history of jihad in Afghanistan. Al-Qaeda was convinced that he was spreading "falsehoods" to please the Iranian regime. As early as 2002, Usama's private notes reveal that Abu al-Walid, using a pseudonym, had said "some very harsh words" about him to the media, "giving the impression that we [i.e., al-Qaeda] are America's collaborators."[65]

In 2009, the prison authorities must have shared some of Abu al-Walid's writings with the al-Qaeda detainees to infuriate them. Subsequently, the highly trusted Abu al-Khair, mentioned earlier, wrote a lengthy letter to Abu al-Walid. In it, he accused him of writing about "matters that have nothing to do with reality or truth!!" He wrote furiously:

> I discussed your writings with the brothers [who are detained] with me. You know too well that most of them are members of al-Qaeda's Shura Council and all of them lived through the events that you describe in the book. What is even more astonishing is that you lived through these events with us!! The brothers could not believe that you would go so far as to fabricate falsehood and twist the truth for the sake of adopting the Iranian narrative.[66]

We don't know whether the prison authorities transmitted Abu al-Khair's letter to Abu al-Walid, and there is nothing to suggest that Abu al-Walid responded if they did. Abu al-Khair must have given a copy of his letter to Hamza before he was released from Iran.

In 2011, Abu al-Walid returned to Egypt and, in 2015, his views gained a wider platform when he co-authored a book with Leah Farrall, *The Arabs at War in Afghanistan*, exculpating himself from Usama's tragic decisions.[67] Abu al-Walid, who chided Usama in his book for all things terrorism, including issuing the 1996 "Declaration of Jihad," did not anticipate that his old friend had affectionately lauded him for his own role in global jihad.[68] In Usama's 2002 private notes, Abu al-Walid features as "our Sheikh in politics, and we learned so much from him."[69] Usama's notes go on to credit Abu al-Walid for having drafted the 1996 *Declaration of Jihad* and "for insisting on releasing it publicly."[70]

On his website, Abu al-Walid notes that he "left Egypt in 2016, first to Qatar, then Iran," and that "he and his family currently reside in Iran for medical treatments."[71]

It is reported that, in 2015, Iran agreed to release six al-Qaeda detainees, including its top leaders, in exchange for an Iranian diplomat who had been captured by AQAP. Four of the detainees were allowed to head to Syria, but al-Qaeda's top two leaders were confined to Iran under the deal.[72] They were

Saif al-Adl—the leader of al-Qaeda's military committee until his detention and the father-in-law of Usama's son Uthman—and Abu Muhammad al-Misri—the leader of al-Qaeda's "external work" before 9/11 and father-in-law of Usama's son Hamza. Though they could not leave the country, they seem to have been allowed freedom of movement within Iran. In 2020, it was reported that Abu Muhammad al-Misri had been killed by an Israeli operation in Iran.[73]

For obvious reasons, the Bin Laden Papers do not provide us with insights as to how U.S. and Iranian officials were gathering good and bad intelligence. Nevertheless, they reveal at least three relevant facts: (1) Al-Qaeda was able to maintain a clandestine presence in Iran, through Jundallah or the "Baluch brothers"—Sunni militants opposed to the Iranian regime. This allowed al-Qaeda to use Iran, as one letter put it, as a "passageway . . . serving as a logistical outlet for our movements." (2) Notwithstanding their dismal conditions, the detainees' abilities to force Iran to change its policy were greater than all of al-Qaeda's "efforts" put together. (3) Iran is no more capable than the United States of policing its borders and of tracking down "illegals" within its territory.

10

THE FINAL CHAPTER

I have exhausted all my efforts, God alone knows how hard I tried to convince [my security guards] to allow you to join us [in Abbottabad]. Despite all this, I sorrowfully regret that it has become clear to me that due to their soaring fatigue, they are completely shut off to any discussion. They even threatened to abandon all of us completely.

Usama bin Laden to his wife Khairiah, January 3, 2011[1]

When Usama ordered the release of the Iranian diplomat in March 2010, he had been promised that his entire family would be freed in exchange. He was hopeful that his family's release from Iran was therefore within sight. To that end, Usama prepared different scenarios and security measures that should be followed once they had been ushered into Pakistan.

One might assume that once Usama's wife and children were released, they would all reunite in Abbottabad provided that their safe passage could be arranged. However, such a homecoming was inconceivable. Besides the dangers from CIA drones and Pakistani intelligence, Usama's own security guards vetoed the reunion. The leader of al-Qaeda whose public statements could terrorize the world was himself living in fear. Usama's security guards were "worn out" by the security measures they had to follow, and had threatened to leave if additional members of Usama's family arrived at the compound.

We've already discovered that Usama's hopes and plans rarely, if ever, materialized. On this occasion, however, a partial and short-lived reunion with

Khairiah did eventually take place. How did Usama envisage his family's transfer out of Iran? How did he engineer his reunion with Khairiah? And how did Usama spend the final chapter of his life? The answers can be discovered within the Bin Laden Papers.

Hopes and Anticipations

Following her escape, Usama's daughter Iman was stuck in the Saudi embassy in Tehran for several months. But after al-Qaeda released the Iranian diplomat in March 2010, Iran allowed Iman to travel to Syria. Soon after, her brother Laden was released, also to Syria. Usama understood that this was part of Iran's "promise," intended to show the rest of the detainees that their captors were serious about "releasing them next." If Iran had indeed made this "promise," we don't know if it was communicated directly to al-Qaeda or through the "Baluch brothers." At the height of his wishful thinking in the middle of 2010, Usama expected that "all members of my family" would be released. Had that been true, twenty-one family members would be set free, counting his grandchildren and daughters- and sons-in-law.[2]

Usama wanted additional security measures in place to safeguard his family upon their release. He assumed that his already freed son, Laden, had telephoned "the family" in Syria and/or Saudi Arabia to let them know that he was out and that the others would soon follow. To that end, Usama wrote to Atiya: "It does not escape you that phone calls are monitored, and the enemy will learn about my family's release from Iran. If the intelligence official is very vigilant, he will realize that members of my family will be joining me, and will track their movements to find me."[3] In this instance, Usama was most likely thinking about a CIA or Pakistani intelligence official. In other letters, it crossed his mind that Iran might very well be coordinating with the United States through Pakistan's intelligence agency, the ISI.[4] Though Atiya's predecessor had assured Usama that Iran was releasing the detainees "without the knowledge of the Pakistanis,"[5] Atiya and Usama both noticed a worrying pattern.[6] Several of those who had been freed from Iran were subsequently captured by the ISI.[7]

247

Anticipating that his family's movements would be monitored, Usama sketched out an elaborate series of maneuvers to throw the authorities off the trail. He suggested that the "brothers" entrusted with picking up his family should change cars "in the tunnel between Kohat and Peshawar." The family should then be driven to "one of the covered markets in Peshawar and change cars again," before being taken to a secure location.[8]

Not leaving anything to chance, Usama penned letters that would be waiting for his family upon their arrival in Waziristan, instructing them to leave behind everything that they had brought with them from Iran. "The Iranians," he warned, "could not be trusted," and it is "possible that they have planted tracking devices in the items that you brought along with you."[9]

As was often the case, not everything went according to Usama's plans. Most of his family was released in August 2010, and though Usama expected them all to be ushered into Waziristan, Iran only allowed Khairiah and Hamza's family to travel there.[10] It insisted on sending Usama's sons Uthman and Muhammad, and their respective families, to Syria.[11] Usama's daughter Fatima was the last family member to be released. Iran insisted that al-Qaeda's senior leaders would be released last,[12] and Fatima was married to one of them. She and her husband, Sulaiman, would not be freed until 2013.[13]

Usama was pleased by the prospect of reuniting with his wife Khairiah and their son, Hamza, and his family. Besides the joy of this homecoming, Usama was looking forward to having his wife's input into his public statements. He was also counting on having Hamza by his side and able to relieve Khaled, who was desperate to go to Waziristan to marry the girl that his sister Khadija had arranged for him.

Khaled could not contain his excitement. When it appeared that things were finally moving in the nuptial direction, he rushed to make travel arrangements. In October 2010, his enthusiasm saw him write a letter containing TMI—too much information—to two individuals, one of whom Atiya believed should not be privy to sensitive issues. Khaled asked them for a fake ID, and informed them that he would be calling them from Peshawar when he arrived there.[14] The vigilant Atiya, who likely inspected all communications, amended Khaled's letter, addressing it only to the "trusted intermediary."[15]

The "Security Guards"

Khairiah had probably been in North Waziristan for a couple of months when her passage to Abbottabad was arranged in early December 2010.[16] Atiya determined that it was not safe for Hamza and his family to accompany her.[17] Usama and Atiya did not take Khairiah's travel to Abbottabad lightly. Usama had of course feared that Iran might track his wife to get to his hideout, and had instructed that she "should replace everything, including items the size of which could fit in the eye of a needle since tiny tracking devices have been developed and could be injected into even a pill."[18] Also, after learning that his wife had had a dental filling in Iran, he asked Atiya to investigate the matter lest the Iranians had inserted a tracking device in the filling. Khairiah's clandestine passage from North Waziristan to Abbottabad involved a stopover, staying with the family of Muhammad Aslam, a trusted "intermediary." Aslam's location is undisclosed; he probably resided in Peshawar.[19]

Despite Atiya's efforts to arrange a safe passage for her, Usama's "security guards" refused to allow Khairiah to make her way to Abbottabad. As stated above, they were "exhausted" by the stringent measures that they had been following for years, and did not want additional members of Usama's family to add to their burden. They made their position clear to Usama. Soon after Khairiah's arrival at the Aslam family residence, Usama had the unenviable task of penning a letter to his wife, who had "patiently endured years of detention in Iran," to let her know that their reunion was not feasible:

> I have been trying to arrange your move [to Abbottabad] since the moment I heard that you arrived [in North Waziristan], but this matter is complicated. For many years now, I have been living in the company of some local brothers who are worn out by my presence due to the security measures that they must follow. They also have difficulty attending to some of my requests, particularly when I ask to have members of my family visit.[20]

We learn from other letters that the "local brothers" were Usama's "security guards," Abu Khaled and Abu Muhammad. Their job description was atypical. The VIP they were in charge of protecting did not require vehicle escort services or crowd-control monitoring. Instead, for over eight years, they had been providing Usama and his family with "security cover," creating the impression that Pakistanis lived in the compound. Given that Usama was the world's most wanted man, it is not surprising that they were "exhausted" and wanted to separate from him. They had to forgo leading normal lives and comply with constant stringent security measures to evade the Pakistani authorities and the CIA.

It was difficult for Usama to tell Khairiah that she couldn't join him, and wanted his wife to know that

I have exhausted all my efforts, God alone knows how hard I tried to convince them to allow you to join us. Despite all this, I sorrowfully regret that it has become clear to me that due to their soaring fatigue, they are completely shut off to any discussion. They even threatened to abandon all of us completely.[21]

When he wrote this letter, which is dated January 3, 2011, it appeared that their reunion would have to wait until Usama found new security guards and/ or moved away from Abbottabad. All he could do was "pray" that his wife's sacrifices "count toward your good deeds in the hereafter."[22] In the meantime, there was much that Khairiah could do to help, despite the distance between them. In another draft of the same letter, we find Usama soliciting his wife's input to his public statements:

I should like to involve you in some of my affairs during this period. We are nine months away from the tenth anniversary of the blessed attacks on New York and Washington, and it is critical that we exploit their media value to recall the victories that Muslims accomplished and communicate our views to the general public. . . . Accordingly, I have sent you everything

I have on my computer so that you may contribute to the public statements that we are preparing to release on this very important anniversary.[23]

To that end, and until "God the Almighty brings joy to our hearts when we have you among us and benefit from your support and input in person to our public statements," Usama ensured that his wife had access to everything she needed. He sent "money to the brother at your end to buy you a laptop, its accessories, and USBs," and urged his wife to "send me your letters, including other writings and suggestions that you have for me, such as ideas that I should include in the public statements."[24]

Usama's letter displayed his care for Khairiah's well-being. He wanted to know if her accommodation was comfortable and well heated, and "enclosed small modest gifts to keep you warm." He also assured his wife that the rest of the family in Abbottabad, "including the kids," were eager to see her. Lest she doubted her husband's commitment to their marriage, Usama vowed that "I am eagerly desirous to be settled with you as my wife," and "in the event that it is not feasible to finalize your trip in the next few weeks, I shall visit you myself—by God's Grace."[25] Usama had not left the compound since his arrival in Abbottabad, but he was clearly intent on visiting Khairiah.[26] Probably that same day, he wrote to one of his contacts to enquire about the best time and route to travel to avoid checkpoints. He was going to take his youngest wife, Amal, and their children along, most likely in order to assume the appearance of an ordinary family.[27]

The security guards' intransigence also meant that Khaled's replacement, Hamza, had to remain in North Waziristan for the time being. Khaled was devastated that his wedding had to be postponed yet again. A couple of months earlier, his mother, Siham, had written to his future mother-in-law, Umm Abd al-Rahman, to postpone Khaled's travel, requesting "four more months," no more. Siham was "embarrassed" for repeatedly postponing her son's marriage, and she was mindful that she had exhausted the patience of Khaled's future in-laws. Khaled painfully concluded that his arranged marriage was no longer possible, and decided to initiate his own search for a different wife. He sent a letter to a member of al-Qaeda, enquiring about "a good wife, who is a virgin, with good character, religious, compliant, and around twenty years old."[28]

It was necessary for Usama to have one of his sons by his side in the compound. In early January 2011, it became clear that Hamza was not coming, and Khaled despaired. Like the security guards, he had become psychologically drained by the living conditions in Abbottabad. It was probably on January 6, 2011 that Khaled went to bed "extremely sad." He woke up during the night, and couldn't get back to sleep. He decided to formalize his membership of al-Qaeda in writing. After typing "allegiance" as the heading, Khaled found himself venting his despair on the computer screen:

I am terribly exhausted by our existing situation. I feel like I am failing to act according to what is required of me, as if I am frozen. I also feel that my capabilities have regressed by more than 50 percent due to the constant pressure of your [i.e., Usama's] security situation, which looms over our lives. I believe that I can do much more, but nobody will allow me to leave, fearing this and that. And so, we're stuck.

We cannot stop worrying, not even for a single minute, day and night. Ninety percent of our thoughts are preoccupied with security measures, and the rest of our thoughts concern separating [from the security guards] and about my marriage.

We are in a true prison, denied the most basic rights intrinsic to humans. . . .

You [i.e., my father] have aged, may God prolong your life. I cannot see you in this extremely difficult situation and sit idle. I cannot stand it, and this is not my character.

It is imperative that I leave alone to find a more comfortable setting for you. I must find a way, soon.[29]

After typing these notes, Khaled prayed intensely for their security conditions to change and beseeched God to facilitate his marriage. And when he fell asleep, the Prophet Muhammad knocked on the door . . . in his dream.

THE FINAL CHAPTER

A Dream

We learn from one of Siham's letters that Khaled dreamed:

> I was in a house like the one we are living in, and as I was praying to God
> to ease our conditions and facilitate my marriage, I heard a knock on the
> door. When I went to answer it, I found the Messenger of God, Muhammad,
> at the door. He smiled as he entered the house. Then he asked me: "Why
> did you rush and send the letter [i.e., in reference to postponing his marriage
> for four months]? Be patient, all the issues shall be resolved, one by one." He
> then patted me on the shoulder and said: "Do not be upset," and he left.[30]

When he awoke the following morning, on January 7, 2011, Khaled was
elated. He rushed to consult a large dictionary about the interpretation of dreams,
Tafsir al-Ahlam. He discovered there that when "any of God's prophets appears in
a dream," relief from one's distress will follow and/or victory will supersede defeat.[31]

Naturally, Khaled shared his dream with the family. We discovered in the
previous chapter the importance of dreams for Usama, and how they helped
him interpret international affairs. The same was true for the rest of his family
in Abbottabad. Everyone interpreted Khaled's dream as a divine sign that
Khaled's marriage to Umm Abd al-Rahman's daughter was back on track,
which also meant that a reunion with Khairiah and Hamza was imminent.
Siham promptly composed a letter to Umm Abd al-Rahman to relate the
breaking news, asking her to ignore her previous request to postpone the
marriage for four months. She confidently recounted Khaled's dream, which
was sufficient to make her case, and went on to add: "Khaled always tells me:
'I am very ambitious, and I thank the Lord who helped me find a good, patient
and pious wife, who will support me to pursue jihad until we have reclaimed
all of Palestine, from the Jordan River to the Mediterranean Sea.'"[32]

We can't be sure whether Khaled had indeed communicated these ambitions to his mother, or whether Siham was improvising. The latter was clearly
in a good and hopeful mood when she composed the letter. She even went on

to strike an amorous note on her son's behalf, citing a couplet from a romantic poem that tells the story of God reuniting two people long after they had given up on ever meeting again, because they were destined to be together. The poem is attributed to a seventh-century poet known as "Majnun Layla," a man who was madly—literally—in love with a certain Layla.[33]

On January 7, 2011, Khaled took pleasure in writing a joyful letter to his "dear aunt Khairiah." Much as meteorologists use atmospheric physics to forecast the weather, Khaled relayed his dream to assure his aunt that their reunion was imminent.[34]

Then a "Written Agreement"

Usama, who had notified his wife days earlier that their reunion was not feasible, now set out to translate Khaled's dream into reality. Though the security guards had made it clear to Usama that Khairiah and Hamza could not join him in Abbottabad, he met with them to broach the subject yet again. And yet again, they were unyielding. Usama's persistence led to two consecutive quarrels, on January 12 and 13. The security guards must have shouted at him. On the 14th, Usama decided to pursue his negotiations in writing:

> I write this letter as a continuation of the conversation that we had last night and the night before, and in the interests of resolving our differences calmly, as we agreed. The conversation last night led to a visible nervous tension, and the health of everyone requires a calm dialogue about the problem we seek to resolve. . . .
>
> We have been treading together this great path [i.e., in God's path] for longer than eight years. I ask God that our march together counts toward our deeds in the hereafter. We shall never forget what you have done for us.
>
> I had in the past requested that you facilitate Khairiah's arrival, but you declined on account that our number is already too large, and the burden is much too heavy on you. We indeed appreciate the enormous burden of our presence on you and the importance of easing the pressure.[35]

Usama proposed two solutions. He was prepared either (1) to send members of his family to another location if the security guards allowed him to bring Khairiah to Abbottabad, or (2) to relieve his security guards of their obligations to him "in nine months, meaning after the tenth anniversary of the 9/11 events," if they allowed him to bring Khairiah, then Hamza and his family.

Usama was aware that the security guards had nothing to fear from him, but hoped that they would fear God. His letter stressed that the brotherhood in Islam that binds them is much greater than the angry words that were exchanged and reminded them of the Qur'anic verse that exhorts Muslims to assist one another. The same verse warns Muslims that if they do not, God is severe in His punishment.[36] He concluded his letter with: "Your brother, who is grateful to you for your kindness, who cannot find the right words to thank you, who prays that God has in store the greatest rewards for you."[37] In Arabic, pleading and gratitude are sometimes interchangeable.

Usama's letter was not well received. One of the security guards, Abu Khaled, was in poor health and inconsolable. Usama had to compose a follow-up letter:

It has reached me from brother Amer that you misunderstood some of the words I said during our recent meetings. God knows that they were not intended the way you appear to have understood them, and I shall make it known to you at the earliest possible opportunity, when your health improves—by God's Grace. If there are other issues that [I said and annoyed you], and brother Amer did not let me know about them, I implore you to let me know. If I was in the wrong, I will apologize, and if you misunderstood my intention, I will clarify it.[38]

We don't have the security guards' account of what they had been enduring and the kind of considerations they had to weigh. For a few years, Usama had been trying to find at least one "trusted brother" to replace them, and we get a glimpse of the brothers' lives through the job description that Usama had outlined in one of the letters. The qualities such a "brother" must show include:

—He must be committed to our cause, leaving absolutely no room to doubt his loyalty.

—He mustn't be on a wanted list, and his security record must be clear. He should also have an official ID. If it is old, he should renew it.

—He should have the purchasing power to rent houses and other purchases.

—He must be able to keep secrets, even from his family and those closest to him.

—He must have a good character and be calm, patient, forbearing, quick-witted, and well versed in the enemies' machinations.

—He must be disciplined, willing to refrain from visiting his family if this poses a threat.[39]

We can be confident that the two brothers had been committed to the cause. They may well have been patient and calm when they first accompanied Usama in late 2001, when he "disappeared into the mountains of Tora Bora." But it is not surprising that by 2010, they had reached the end of their tethers. Keeping secrets from everyone and refraining from visiting their families would have been stressful under any circumstances. To do so knowing that the world's most powerful country was hunting them must have been nerve-racking.

At any rate, we learn from the letters that after "an exhausting month of discussions" with the security guards, it appeared to the Bin Ladens that Khaled's dream was about to come true. On February 3, 2011, Usama concluded a "written agreement" with the security guards. He undertook to find alternative security arrangements by the tenth anniversary of 9/11 or soon thereafter. In return, the security guards agreed to let Khairiah, then Hamza and his family, come and stay in Abbottabad.[40] Muslims are religiously instructed to deliver on their promises, and the guards knew that Usama would make good on his word.[41]

Meanwhile, Khairiah, who was still living with the Aslam family, was suffering from "extreme dizziness."[42] She was likely stressed out at the thought of being indefinitely separated from her son and prevented from being with her husband. On February 3, 2011, the day the "obstacles were resolved" with the security guards, Usama wrote to his wife to announce the "glad tidings." But the news of Khairiah's dizziness had made him anxious, and in the same letter Usama nervously enquired: "When did your dizziness start? How long did it go on for? Please provide more details as to its symptoms. Also include the date when it was diagnosed and treated."[43] He went beyond the routine caring questions: "It does not escape you the importance of dates when it comes to many medical issues." Realizing that he was pushing for more information that might offend his wife, he added: "Please pardon my insistence, perhaps I am exhausting you with my request for more details."

What sort of concerns did Usama have? We can safely assume that he was not accusing his wife of infidelity. What did he mean by "the importance of dates" to "medical issues"? Did his imagination run wild, causing him to fear that his sixty-year-old wife had been artificially impregnated by a medical practitioner in Iran to achieve some nefarious objective? Usama urged his wife to see a doctor before she left for Abbottabad. Specifically, he wanted her to do an X-ray or ultrasound, and "if no alien body is found, we would have certainty [and peace of mind] to overcome our doubts."[44] Whatever alien body Usama was referring to—be it a fetus, a tumor, or a microchip—he clearly concerned.

Siham also rushed to write to Umm Abd al-Rahman on the day when the "written agreement" was concluded. She related the details of the arrangement, which "pleased us very much," because they could now proceed to set a wedding date. Siham was confident that "we shall be able to meet with you after the tenth anniversary of the 9/11 attacks and the American withdrawal from Afghanistan."[45] Little did Siham know that her son's chances of being met by seventy-two damsels in the afterlife (one of several blisses awaiting the martyr in Paradise) were greater than marrying one in this world.

The Arab Spring

While Khairiah was stuck at her undisclosed location, the Arab Spring—a whirlwind of political change—was sweeping through the Arab world. Peaceful protest erupted in Tunisia on December 18, 2010, toppling President Zain al-Din bin Ali, before spreading to Egypt, then Yemen, Libya, Bahrain, and Syria. Khairiah made the final leg of her journey, arriving in Abbottabad on February 11, 2011, on the day "when the worst dictator, Husni Mubarak [of Egypt], was toppled," as she put it in a letter to Hamza, who was still in North Waziristan. "May the rest of the dictators follow," she added.[46]

Like the rest of the world, al-Qaeda had not expected or prepared for the Arab Spring. The Bin Ladens were thrilled, but the "revolutions" (*thawrat*) were a political event like no other, and Usama was challenged to respond given the rapid and unpredictable changes that were unfolding each day. The Abbottabad family followed the events on the news, and they met each day "upstairs" to discuss them as they prepared Usama's public response.

We know about these brainstorming sessions thanks to a 220-page hand-written notebook that the SEALs recovered. Fearing the possibility of an imminent attack and that the notebook might contain "clues that would reveal ongoing al-Qa'ida plots," the SEALs took photographs of the pages "in the urgent hours after the raid" and sent them for immediate review by CIA analysts.[47] The CIA inaccurately described the notebook as "Bin Ladin's journal" when they declassified it.[48] It turned out to be a transcription of the family discussions that took place "upstairs" during the last two months of Usama's life. The entries are arranged by date (March 6–May 1, 2011).[49]

We can reconstruct the story of this notebook from its cover page, contents, and a few other letters. Sometime in 2010, Abd al-Rahman al-Maghrebi, who oversaw al-Qaeda's media output, was preparing to produce a biography of Usama in Q&A format.[50] It was intended to serve as an authoritative account of the life and jihadi career of the leader of al-Qaeda. To that end, Abd al-Rahman sent Usama a long list of questions that filled forty-five pages. In early February 2011, Usama and one of his daughters, possibly Mariam, started responding to Abd al-Rahman's questions. In the middle of the notebook's cover, using a red pen, Mariam wrote: "Abu Abdallah's [i.e., Usama's] Memoirs." But the two of them were much too preoccupied with the events of the Arab Spring at that time to expend much effort on the Q&A.

They spent just one sitting working on the memoirs, filling less than four pages of the notebook.

In the meantime, and starting in either December 2010 or January 2011, most of the adults in Abbottabad had been gathering on one of the top floors of the compound each day, sometimes twice a day, to discuss the events of the Arab Spring. Their strategizing included preparing Usama's public statement in response to the "revolutions," as they described the events. Those early family discussions had been transcribed in a different notebook that was not recovered by the SEALs (or that has not been declassified). By March 5, 2021, the first family notebook was full, and Mariam decided to transcribe subsequent family discussions in the notebook that was meant to record her father's Q&A responses, most of which was blank. To avoid confusion, Mariam added a new title on the cover, this time in a blue pen: "Latest developments—Continuation of volume (1)—About the revolutions in the Arab world, beginning of March 2011." Someone else later added in black: "Historical events and the points of views of Sheikh Abdallah [i.e., Usama]."

Notwithstanding the uniqueness of the recovered notebook, it is near-impossible to understand everything in it. To start with, it is not always easy to decipher, because the transcriber had to write fast to keep up with what was being said and, on occasion, sentences were left incomplete. Most likely, the transcriber was very familiar with the information that she left out and was confident that she would be able to recall it easily later. Sometimes, the notebook was used to transcribe Arab Spring news that they watched on television. And, on a few occasions, the same notebook was used to record the thoughts of the transcriber, and to draft Usama's letters to his associates.

In the pages of the notebook, we discover the extent to which Usama counted and, indeed, depended on the help of his family, particularly his daughters Mariam and Sumayya. On one page, we find him soliciting their input, asking them to "start thinking about the public statement" and "to put together the ideas" that should be included. We also observe Usama's understandable confusion, given how rapidly the events of the Arab Spring were unfolding

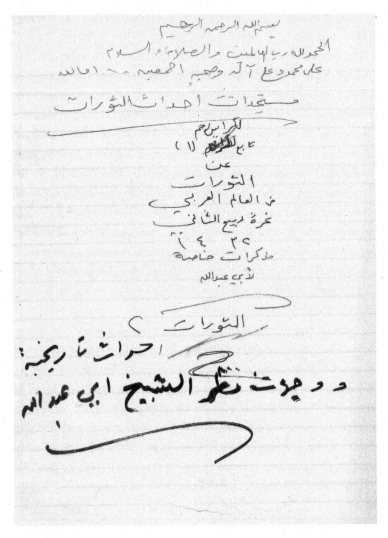

simultaneously in multiple countries. One day, we hear Usama utter that "our speech must be flexible, because when the Libyan regime falls, fear will ensue among the rest of the regimes in the region." A couple of days later, we find him resigned to the prospect that "we cannot do anything except to intensify our prayers."

As the Arab Spring progressed, Usama was concerned about the "young revolutionaries who need time to organize themselves." At one point, he was no longer sure that the "revolutions" were a positive development at all. "These revolutions, it is said, were born prematurely," he lamented, and "that is why they were marred with confusion and chaos." Eventually, Usama determined that "we want to protect these revolutions so that they can proceed along the right path." He didn't want revenge:

> It is important that the revolutionaries do not call for revenge, for this would engender an ocean of problems. . . . We shall settle for the slogan "Leave" [i.e., addressed to the dictators]. The Consultative Council would see to it that the revolutionaries are persuaded not to seek revenge. Sagacious people understand that revolutions include those who want revenge. They would remind them of the lessons learned of the Prophet's *idhhabu fa-antum al-tulaqa'*.

The last line, which roughly means "go, I am setting you free," is ascribed to the Prophet Muhammad when he triumphantly entered Mecca. It is cited as a reflection of Muhammad's political leniency toward the Meccans whom he chose not to enslave, even though they were his lawful booty.[51]

Usama's public response to the Arab Spring went through at least sixteen different drafts.[52] To judge by the names of the files on which they were saved, Sumayya and Mariam did much of the heavy lifting in drafting their father's public response.

The dynamics between Usama and his daughters are on display in the notebook. Sumayya, by then aged nineteen, comes across as strong-spirited. She pushed her tentative father to take a stand. "People await your position about the West's intervention in Libya," she pressed. Usama was unsure about this, bemoaning that "the Libyans are sensitive to criticism." Usama had learned from an associate's letter that a few Libyan Islamic Fighting Group members were impatient to leave North Waziristan to fight in Libya. Their leader, Uns al-Libi, had complained that Atiya was not "up to the responsibility" because he had withheld permission for them to leave. They decided to go without his consent, and held him "responsible before God" should anything bad happen to them.[53] Atiya explained to Usama that Uns, who "always had a difficult temper" and who had been detained in Iran, "was in a bad way and his mental state had severely regressed during his detention."[54] Usama might have been thinking about the defiance of Uns and his "brothers" when he told Sumayya that the Libyans' "partisanship is akin to that between tribes—the eastern Libyans are one thing, while the western Libyans are something else." Usama went on to stress that "I have not seen anything like it and we should be careful in our discussions with the Libyan brothers."

It was clear to Sumayya that the "revolutions" were presenting a broader challenge for jihadism. "What are the negative and positive effects on the jihadis as a result of these revolutions?" she probed. "It is possible," she warned, "that some among the new generation will believe that political change could occur without jihad." Sumayya was identifying a profound challenge that the Arab Spring posed to jihadism. Jihadi leaders had consistently pointed to the West's support of Muslim dictators against their people, and the truth of this bolstered the jihadi cause. Yet in Libya, the West intervened in support of the people against the dictator, Muammar al-Qadhafi. The Bin Ladens were watching the news when the UN passed Resolution 1973, authorizing "all necessary measures to protect civilians."[55] The French President, Nicolas Sarkozy, was successful in securing a military operation under NATO command which was launched on March 31, 2011. Sumayya realized that the West's intervention conflicted with the jihadis' message and insisted that "some points needed to be addressed" in her father's response.

Usama concurred. "This is a very difficult position," he admitted to Sumayya, conceding that the "people rejoiced" at the West's intervention. Jihadis, he agonized, "have no option but to remain silent." Separately, Usama wrote a letter to the leader of the jihadi group in North Africa, AQIM, that had kidnapped French hostages. It was "no longer appropriate to kill the French hostages," Usama advised, because the "majority of the [Muslim] public is supportive of Sarkozy."[56] At this point, we hear Usama dwell on the political and operational impotence that prevented al-Qaeda from engaging. "We are now somewhat hampered from acting," he lamented, "our capacities are limited, and we have problems with the rank and file, and the multitude of deaths among the brothers."

Mariam was twenty-one and, in contrast to her sister, she probably preferred getting things done quietly. In the previous chapter, we encountered her commitment to jihadism through the letter she addressed to Iran's Supreme Leader, berating him for detaining the jihadis' women and children. Most likely, it was Mariam who transcribed the family conversations, because we do not hear from her often in the material. In the early pages of the notebook, we meet Mariam gently urging the rest of the family to "think calmly." During one of the family conversations, Usama suggested making a causal link between a public statement he had released in January 2004 and the Arab Spring. In the 2004 statement, Usama had asserted that "rulers should be made accountable," that the *umma* "has the right to choose its ruler," and a council of independent scholars and clerics should be set up "to fill the vacuum caused by these religiously invalid regimes."[57] Khairiah liked the idea, and someone drafted a paragraph that established this link. The idea did not sit well with Mariam and the paragraph was not included in the (near) final draft. Mariam likely removed it, probably fearing that the protesters who toppled dictators in Tunisia, Egypt, and Yemen would deride her father for taking the credit for their actions. In a separate "to-do list" document, Mariam noted that a council of independent scholars should be formed behind the scenes in the wake of the Arab Spring. To that end, she suggested sending instructions to the "brothers" in al-Qaeda to liaise on this matter with the Kuwaiti scholar Hamid al-Ali through his webpage, but "without explicitly stating that the letter is from my father."[58]

As they were making the final edits, Sumayya stressed that the tone of her father's statement should have both style and substance, "for people delight in good words combined with a strong, accentuated voice."[59] Usama's statement was audio-recorded in the early hours of April 27, just a few days before the

May 1 raid. After listening to the tape, they decided that it would benefit from more "solidarity with the *umma*" and needed to be more explicit about "al-Qaeda's politics concerning the revolutions." One of them thought that it was best to avoid recording late at night, "because the fatigue is transparent in the voice."

The SEALs raided the compound before the Bin Laden family had a chance to amend it. Not long after, the U.S. government released Usama's audio statement, as recorded on April 27. It probably did so to prove that the SEALs' raid had been successfully carried out, undermining the claims of conspiracy theorists to the contrary.

On Sons and Daughters

It is common for the ruling families of the Gulf, where Usama came from, to designate a "favorite" son as "heir" and other sons as back-ups. By contrast, the Bin Laden Papers reveal that Usama embraced meritocracy within al-Qaeda and insisted on examining members' bios before he approved their promotion. Thus, the numerous reports claiming that Usama was grooming his son Hamza as his heir to al-Qaeda find no basis in the Bin Laden Papers.

The letters, in fact, shed a completely different light on Usama's opinion of Hamza's potential or lack thereof. When Hamza was about to be released from Iran, his father proposed sending him and "other incoming brothers" to Qatar to pursue religious studies, and eventually to incite Muslims to join the jihad. There was no favoritism involved. Atiya had remarked that it was safer for the "brothers" to remain in detention in Iran, fearing that they would perish if they came to North Waziristan, where the CIA drone campaign was successfully eliminating militants.[60] Usama couldn't wait for the detainees to be released from Iran, and opted to send Hamza to Qatar, if North Waziristan proved difficult. He reasoned that Hamza was "a child when he was imprisoned and could not be indicted" on terrorism charges in Qatar.[61] At any rate, Usama had no say in the matter, and Iran ultimately decided to send Hamza and his mother to Waziristan.

The last discussion recorded in the 220-page notebook took place hours before the raid on the compound at 1:00 a.m. local time on May 1, 2011. During that session, Usama said to his family: "I told Khaled, and I shall say the same to Hamza, that it is not appropriate to make a public appearance unless it is carefully executed." If his sons were to assume a public role, their statements needed to be "precise and significant" and should "serve as a sign-post for the future they are seeking to establish." He was firm that "we shall not release public statements for Hamza or Khaled unless we are fully prepared to be in a position that would allow us to sustain it on a regular basis and be prepared to have a high standard." Usama was fond of making his points through analogies, so he explained that just as a new television station should not be launched unless it has enough material "to broadcast for an entire year as well as a crew that supports its daily production," the same should be applied to any public role that his sons Hamza and Khaled might assume.

Usama's wives and daughters had served as his reliable "crew" for years, and one might assume that they could do the same for Khaled and Hamza. Could it be that Usama was discouraging his sons from assuming a public role?

On May 1, 2011, Hamza was not ready for primetime, and this was even obvious to his mother. After she arrived in Abbottabad and observed first-hand the advanced writing abilities of Hamza's half-sisters, it was immediately apparent to Khairiah that her son had some catching-up to do. It is "heart-ening," she wrote to him, that Mariam and Sumayya "participate in preparing research and topics with their father" and "their writings are broadcast on tele-vision."[62] She instructed her son that "the issue to which you need to devote your attention the most is to read and listen to all your father's public state-ments. This way, when God facilitates our reunion, you will be on the same page as the group here."

Usama, too, might have sensed that Hamza was far from ready. Not only did his son lack battlefield experience, but his letters contained passages that were painfully long on sentimental expressions and short on vision and strategy. Usama probably took his cue from Atiya, who described Hamza as "good and decent, but, of course, he is a young man who spent many years in prison."

Atiya noted that, due to the CIA drone surveillance over Waziristan, "the poor lad is now living in prison-like conditions." Though Hamza was eager "to receive training in one of the military camps" and did not want "to receive any special treatment," Atiya easily tempered his enthusiasm because "he was less insistent than his brother Saad."[63] Usama's son Saad, who dramatically escaped from Iran and was later killed by a drone in 2009, had displayed in his letters not just loyalty to al-Qaeda, but also confidence, independent thinking, and leadership potential. In the same letter, Atiya included the names of "brothers" in al-Qaeda who should be promoted to positions of responsibility, and neither Hamza nor Khaled had made the cut. To be sure, they were not in contention. Atiya still sought Usama's permission to allow Hamza "some limited movement" to attend a special training course on preparing explosives. Usama was hesitant, and advised that Hamza's training should be limited.

Years after the raid, Hamza made his public début as a voice of global jihad in 2015. Usama's successor, Ayman al-Zawahiri, introduced his inaugural statement with much fanfare. "I present to you," he excitedly proclaimed, "the lion, son of the lion; the jihadi, son of the jihadi." Ayman did not suggest that Hamza was destined to take on his father's role, but he prayed that his appearance in the jihadi landscape would serve as a "lump that would cause God's enemies to choke."

Al-Qaeda may well have reasoned that the son of Usama bin Laden was their best chance against the Islamic State, the group that had eclipsed al-Qaeda by then. Most likely, they hoped that, like his father, Hamza would incite Muslims to act and inspire jihadi attacks with his use of the signature "We are at your beck and call, Hamza." He called on jihadis to act on their own, emulating Nidal Hasan, a U.S. Army Major who carried out the Fort Hood shooting in 2009, and the Tsarnev brothers, who carried out the Boston Marathon bombing in 2013. Hamza's series of speeches made no visible impact, however.

Hamza's voice sounds a lot like his father's. But his public statements are more reminiscent stylistically of Ayman than of his father. They are like stilted undergraduate lectures and would have benefited from the input of his aunt Siham and his half-sisters Mariam and Sumayya. Hamza was reported killed in July 2019, and President Trump confirmed the fact two months later.[64]

Contrary to what was reported by some, Hamza did not make it to Abbottabad. On May 1, 2011, he was either preparing to head to Abbottabad or already *en route* there, because Atiya had by then arranged his and his family's safe passage. Khaled was the only adult son by Usama's side when the SOF raided the compound. According to the SEAL who shot Usama, the CIA analyst who worked on Usama's file for years had told them before the raid that they should expect his son Khaled to be "armed and ready, his father's last line of defense."[65] She was partially correct. Khaled was in the compound, but he was unarmed and clearly not ready. It was not difficult for the SEALs to locate him. One of them simply whispered his name, and Khaled responded: "What?" He was shot before the SEALs got to Usama.[66]

After the raid, Saudi Arabia allowed the survivors from the compound to return there, and it is reported that Usama's wives Siham, Khairiah, and Amal settled in Jeddah. Presumably, Mariam and Sumayya, his children by Amal, and his grandchildren are there as well. Their movements are probably closely monitored by the government, and to borrow a line from one of Khairiah's letters, Mariam and Sumayya's writings are now unlikely to be "broadcast on television."

11

THE REAL COURIER

Most disasters are caused by unreliable couriers.

Ahmad al-Naysaburi, late tenth-century Ismaili author[1]

"Tonight, I can report to the American people and to the world that the United States has conducted an operation that killed Osama bin Laden, the leader of al Qaeda," Barrack Obama announced on May 2, 2011.[2] The President's announcement came within hours of the Abbottabad raid and after Admiral William H. McRaven conducted a "PID" (positive identification) on Usama's body.[3]

During the government briefings that followed the Abbottabad raid, U.S. intelligence officials noted the importance of Usama's "courier"—whose name was left out—to the success of the mission. The "courier" referred to turned out to be none other than Abu Ahmed al-Kuwaiti, one of the security guards whom we have already met in previous chapters and who lived in an adjacent house in the Abbottabad compound. It was therefore plausible that Abu Ahmed should have acted as Usama's courier, leaving little necessity for further speculation.

When I embarked on writing this book, it did not cross my mind that I would find clues within the Bin Laden Papers themselves that would shed light on how the CIA discovered Usama's hideout. But during the course of reading the letters, two aspects made me ponder the CIA's "courier" narrative. First, Usama wrote in great detail about the extent to which he and his family relied on Abu Ahmed and his brother. Of all the tasks that Usama enumerated, serving as his courier was not part of either of the brothers' job descriptions. Second, and what really piqued my attention, were references in the letters to a "closed circle" consisting of two intermediaries and a courier in between. The longer I meditated on those suggestive references, it became clear to me that it was this clandestine trio that served as a conduit between Usama in Abbottabad and his associates in North Waziristan.

Of course, the hunt for Usama is a chapter that ended with the Abbottabad raid. But why did U.S. intelligence keep out of their briefings the actual story about Usama's "closed circle"? By the end of this chapter, we will have discovered many of the missing parts in the "courier" narrative and pieced them together. The courier was indeed central to the story, but Abu Ahmed was merely tangential. We shall also find out why the identity of the real courier was kept out of the intelligence briefings that followed Usama's killing. To be clear, we don't know first-hand what went right for the CIA, but we can reconstruct from the letters what went wrong for Usama.

So, if it wasn't Abu Ahmed, who then was the real courier? First, let's chart the official narrative.

The "Courier" Narrative

The official who recounted the "intelligence trail" that led to the Abbottabad hideout stressed the importance of Usama's courier: "One courier in particular had our constant attention. . . . Detainees also identified this man as one of the few al Qaeda couriers trusted by bin Laden. They indicated he might be living with and protecting bin Laden."[4] He was referring to Abu Ahmed al-Kuwaiti, whose name had been mentioned by some of the post-9/11 detainees who were subjected to the CIA's "enhanced interrogation techniques,"[5] a euphemism for the Agency's "Torture Program."[6] But for years after 9/11, the official admitted, the CIA hadn't been able to identify the true name or location of this courier.

After he fled Afghanistan in late 2001, Usama had been presumed to be hiding in the tribal regions of Pakistan or Afghanistan, and we can assume that the CIA was searching for him there. But in August 2010, the CIA identified the residence of Abu Ahmed and his brother in "a compound in Abbottabad, Pakistan, a town about 35 miles north of Islamabad."[7] According to a declassified CIA memo, an intercepted phone call allowed intelligence agencies to locate Abu Ahmed in Peshawar, Pakistan. They then tracked him "to his white jeep, with a distinctive rhinoceros image on the spare tire mounted on the rear of the vehicle. Unwittingly, al-Kuwaiti led them to a compound in Abbottabad, Pakistan."[8]

The CIA had noticed that the two brothers had been observing "extensive operational security" and "were being so careful." This reinforced their belief that they were tracking the right people.[9] By March 2011, the CIA were closing in on Usama, and President Obama "chaired no fewer than five National Security Council meetings on the topic." On April 29, the President gave the SEALs their marching order to carry out the Abbottabad raid.

The Alternative Narrative

The CIA's narrative was contested by the distinguished journalist Seymour M. Hersh in his 2015 *London Review of Books* article "The Killing of Osama bin Laden." One of Hersh's key contentions was that Pakistan's ISI had located Usama and had been holding him "hostage" in Abbottabad as leverage against al-Qaeda since 2006. In August 2010, according to Hersh, a former senior ISI officer betrayed Pakistan's secret to the CIA's station chief in Islamabad. This rogue officer wanted to claim the $25 million bounty the United States had offered under its Rewards for Justice program for information leading to Usama. Hersh's contention that Usama had been a "hostage" is false.

Even a casual reading of the Bin Laden Papers makes it abundantly clear that Usama and his associates went to great lengths to hide from the Pakistani authorities. And it is inconceivable that Usama himself was unaware that he was being held hostage.[10]

On the face of it, the CIA's "courier" narrative appeared convincing, particularly because Abu Ahmed and his brother lived next door to Usama. But the

Bin Laden Papers reveal that a far more complex operation was in play in the hunt for Usama.

The "Closed Circle"

To appreciate the missing pieces in the CIA's narrative, it would help to understand the different roles the "security guards," "courier," and "intermediaries" played in Usama's "closed circle." Before we examine these questions, however, it bears repeating that the letters were saved on "SIM cards" that seem to have been placed in an "envelope" and needed to be "extracted." So, none of the people involved in this secret operation carried an actual stack of letters.

Security Guards

As previously discussed, we know from the letters that the Bin Ladens lived next door to two brothers Usama referred to by the names of "Abu Muhammad and Abu Khaled" and whom he described as his "security guards." The Bin Ladens and their guards lived "in two independent houses with separate courtyards in the same compound."[11] Their most important contribution to the Bin Ladens was to provide "security cover" by giving the impression that locals lived in the compound. They also did "grocery shopping, mostly fruit and vegetables," on a regular basis for the Bin Ladens.[12] To minimize the burden on the two brothers, the Bin Ladens tried to be as self-sufficient as possible. "We bake our own bread," Usama wrote in one letter, and "purchase grains/legumes in bulk." Though nine of the sixteen people who lived in the compound were children, the Bin Ladens' visits to the doctors were "rare, once a year on average." Usama explained that "we adhere to the tried-and-true method that *prevention is better than cure*" and "we keep medications for most illnesses at home."[13]

Understandably, providing security cover for the world's most wanted man took its toll on Abu Ahmed and his brother—they had been with Usama for nearly nine years by the time the SEALs raided the compound. After their move to Abbottabad in 2005, the security guards dictated who got to stay in the compound. When Usama requested that additional family members be allowed to live with him, they often declined, and when he persisted, they threatened to abandon him.[14] Since at least 2009, they had made it clear to Usama that they wanted out. They were "exhausted" and could no longer suffer the stringent security measures they had to follow.

In 2009, Hajji Uthman proposed two Pakistani brothers who were members of al-Qaeda to replace Abu Ahmed and his brother, but the candidates didn't meet Usama's inflexible security requirements. It wasn't enough to be loyal to al-Qaeda, Usama needed people whose finances allowed them to purchase a compound the size of his own and whose "security record must be clear." Naturally, it was unreasonable to expect that anyone in al-Qaeda would be able to meet such criteria.[15]

In late 2010, Atiya was looking into the suitability of another Pakistani "brother," whose traits appeared to fit the job description that Usama had in mind. This "brother owns one or several grocery stores in Lahore; he is knowledgeable, trustworthy, understands real estate, and knows all about leading a civilian life." Atiya was also going to enlist the trusted Pakistani operative Ilyas Kashmiri to search for a suitable security guard for Usama.[16]

While the CIA was closing in on Usama, the search for new security guards was gaining momentum. It was a question of time. Meanwhile, Usama managed to convince his security guards to stay with him for a bit longer. On February 3, 2011, he concluded a "written agreement" with the two brothers, promising to relieve them of their obligations to him "by the tenth anniversary of the 9/11 attacks or shortly thereafter." So, at the time of the raid, the two brothers were still on duty.

Courier and Two Intermediaries

When Usama re-established contact with his associates in 2004, he instructed them that correspondence "shall follow the closed-circle model."[17] Over subsequent years, references to the couriers in the letters are vague. The Bin Ladens often remarked that their letters were written in haste because they had been notified, at very short notice, that the courier was about to pick them up. Clearly, the courier could not have been the man living next door.

But thanks to a few precious letters composed in 2010–11, we can reconstruct some of the missing pieces in the CIA narrative. In 2010, most likely in July, Usama wanted to enhance the security measures that he and his associates had in place, and wrote in a long draft letter that was intended for Atiya's attention:

—The two brothers—the intermediary on your side and the other on mine—should change their routine. They should meet to exchange the letters only in one of the closed markets, like business centers/malls.

—The brother who picks up the letters from Waziristan should prepare a report after each trip to apprise you of the security situation. He should let you know whether the security situation seemed normal to him, or if recent developments had occurred, such as: additional control procedures; interrogations; photographing commuters. If there were noticeable changes, he should assess whether everyone was targeted or select groups. Or perhaps the changes he observed were the result of replacing inspection personnel with others who were more vigilant and attentive.[18]

Usama's notes reveal that the "closed circle" that facilitated his correspondence consists of one courier, i.e., "the brother who picks up the letters from Waziristan," and two "intermediaries" (*wasit*): one from Atiya's side and another from Usama's.

'*Intermediary*' on Atiya's side

'the brother who picks up the letters' (the **COURIER**)

'*Intermediary*' on Usama's side

In 2010, Usama enquired about sending his public statements directly to the jihadi media outlet *al-Sahab* for faster releases. Fortunately for us, out of an abundance of caution, Atiya rejected the idea in a letter brimming with revelations about the "closed circle":

> I thought long and hard about this, and I concluded that this is not advisable. There is no added value. In fact, doing so would entail more movement on the part of the intermediary and unnecessarily expose our communications to more people.
>
> Currently, our communications with you are through one of our most trusted *ansar* brothers [i.e., local Pakistani supporters]. Indeed, he is one of the most ardent supporters of al-Qaeda. We strongly believe him to be so. At this point, only Abu Yahya [i.e., Atiya's deputy] and myself know about this intermediary. It was recently, and only as a precautionary measure, that I shared this with Abu Yahya, after Sheikh Saeed [i.e., Hajji Uthman, Atiya's predecessor] was killed.
>
> The courier is the brother-in-law of this trusted *ansar*/local Pakistani brother. Thus, when the courier collects the letters, he hands them over to his brother-in-law, the trusted brother [local Pakistani] I just mentioned, and he, in turn, passes them onto me at his earliest convenience. (He has no idea about the origin of the letters and who is behind them, but he knows that they are important.) It is possible that he senses that they are from of our two Sheikhs [i.e., Usama or Ayman], because he has been doing this for a long time. He is currently dealing with me, he did the same with Sheikh Saeed before me, and with Khaled al-Habib before him. He is clever, we consider him to be trustworthy, and he has given his allegiance to you. Sheikh Saeed accepted/performed the *ansari*'s allegiance in my presence about a year ago. Sheikh Saeed had consulted me about this. It was important to establish a firm bond with the trusted *ansari*, because giving allegiance (*bay'a*) is very important for the Pashtun. He himself wanted to be bound to us through a *bay'a*.
>
> In short, it is best that all letters are delivered only to one person (and this person is me), and I would then send them forth to their destinations,

e.g., to Abu Yahya, the media, and so on. That would be best and most secure. Otherwise, the *ansari* brother would have to deliver the letters to various destinations himself. Meaning, he would open up the envelope to extract the SIM cards and so on.[19] Whereas now I do this myself. . . . One of our greatest problems at the moment is movement!! . . . The trusted *ansari* is aware that if anything should happen to me, he would deliver the letters to Abu Yahya.[20]

Since Usama was not privy to all the identities of those who made up the "closed circle," we can safely assume that he did not know, let alone meet, the actual courier. At any rate, Atiya's detailed explanation, combined with Usama's earlier notes, chart the movement between the actual courier and the intermediaries who made up the "closed circle." The intermediary in North Waziristan met with Atiya and, at most, suspected that the letters that his brother-in-law delivered to him might have been from one of the two Sheikhs.

Of course, the vigilant Atiya did not include the names of the trusted intermediary and the courier in the same letter. But thanks to a lapse in security in one of the letters by Usama's son Khaled, we learn more about them. We have already discovered that Khaled was impatient to get married and Atiya intercepted/edited one of his letters, which included "too much information." Khaled had addressed his letter to "Abdallah al-Sindi and Abu al-Harith al-Sindi," requesting a fake ID to facilitate his travels. The names of these two individuals come up in the letters as trusted individuals who run occasional errands for Atiya and other jihadis. But when Khaled sought to write directly

Atiya's
Intermediary
is a trusted
Pakistani and is
*brother-in-law
of the courier*

Courier
*brother-in-law
of the
intermediary
on Atiya's
side*

Intermediary
on Usama's
side
?

to Abu al-Harith, the attentive Atiya removed the name and later justified his intervention to Usama:

> I apologize for interfering in the letters for the first time, but I deemed it necessary. It was a security intervention on my part. I reviewed Khaled's letter and amended its content. . . .
>
> The amendment concerns the following: the need to keep Abu al-Harith away from all sensitive matters, and to address the letter only to Abdallah. I also deleted the paragraph about Khaled's ID because I already asked Abdallah to send it directly to me.
>
> The reason for keeping the virtuous brother Abu al-Harith out of this has to do with the nature of his work. He has administrative responsibilities, including raising funds and looking after some families in Karachi. He also oversees a team of several brothers who work closely with him, and has an extensive network of connections and relationships. It is not suitable to correspond with him or to involve him in sensitive matters such as this.[21]

Clearly, Abdallah and Abu al-Harith are running some sensitive errands for al-Qaeda, and one of Atiya's letters to Usama explicitly designates "Abu al-Harith al-Sindi [as] the brother-in-law of Abdallah al-Sindi." Since Abdallah interacts "directly" with Atiya, he is obviously the "trusted *ansari*," i.e., the intermediary on Atiya's side, and Abu al-Harith is his brother-in-law, and none other than the actual courier who likely led the CIA to Usama's hideout.

The role of the intermediary on Usama's side is not spelled out, but letters addressed to Muhammad Aslam were filed under the name "*wasit*," i.e., intermediary, which suggests that he was the intermediary on Usama's side. It is not surprising that Aslam was trusted enough to play such a sensitive role given that he and his family hosted Usama's second wife, Khairiah, for several months before she arrived in Abbottabad.[22] What's more, Usama trusted Aslam to find replacements for his security guards,[23] and wanted him to safeguard 100,000 euros of al-Qaeda's budget.[24]

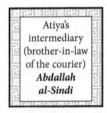

Atiya's
intermediary
(brother-in-law
of the courier)
*Abdallah
al-Sindi*

Courier
(brother-in-law
of Atiya's
intermediary)
*Abu al-Harith
al-Sindi*

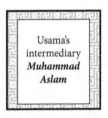

Usama's
intermediary
*Muhammad
Aslam*

We do not glean from the letters that Aslam personally delivered or picked up letters to and from Abbottabad. Most likely, the courier, Abu al-Harith, delivered the letters to Aslam, who then handed them over to Usama's security guards (Abu Ahmed or his brother) in a public place. The exchanges might have taken place in Peshawar, where the CIA located Abu Ahmed al-Kuwaiti in 2010. Either way, Usama's security guards never went back and forth between Abbottabad and North Waziristan to deliver and pick up the letters. They were merely the last leg of a highly complex operation for letters coming in, and played an equally minor role for outgoing communications.

The courier, Abu al-Harith, had no way of knowing that he was the conduit for the world's most wanted people. Judging by Atiya's letters, Abu al-Harith was a businessman. He was financially comfortable, though not wealthy.[25] His "network of connections" included jihadi families, whose needs he served, no doubt for a fee,[26] in a business-like capacity (e.g., providing a fake ID for Khaled). For all he knew, the deliveries he made to Aslam were no different from the mundane ones he handled for other jihadi families. So, from Atiya's perspective, the less Abu al-Harith knew about his clients the better, which is why he didn't want Khaled to be in direct contact with him.

How Did Usama's "Closed Circle" Fail?

The Bin Laden Papers point to two scenarios that may or may not have been connected.

First Scenario

In August 2010, when the CIA's search for Usama was finally moving in the right direction, Iran released Usama's wife Khairiah, their son, Hamza, and his family, and they were all ushered to North Waziristan. Usama wanted al-Qaeda to take additional security measures because Iran realized "that members of my family would join me and it would track their movements to find me."[27] Khairiah had expected that Iran would release her and Hamza in the direction of Syria, as it did with the rest of Usama's family. She was surprised when she and her son were ushered to North Waziristan instead. When she shared this with Usama, alarm bells sounded. "Did you hear anything after your release," Usama enquired, that might have "caused or forced Iran to release you in the first place, and in the direction of Waziristan in particular?"[28]

In November 2010, Usama and Atiya were ever more concerned that Iran and Pakistan's intelligence agency, the ISI, were conspiring against al-Qaeda, specifically regarding the detainees in Iran. We learn from Atiya: "So far, Iran hasn't released any of the senior important al-Qaeda leaders. But a tragic incident occurred for the first time: Three brothers and their families were detained by the Pakistanis near Quetta immediately upon their release from Iran."[29] We don't know if Iran was coordinating with the ISI. We also don't know about the kind of relationship the CIA had with the ISI. But if the CIA had learned of Khairiah's release in August, whether through shared intelligence with the ISI or relying on its own means, this would have been a gift with much more to give. The CIA would have expected that Khairiah would eventually join her husband.

But we discovered in the previous chapter that Usama's security guards vetoed Khairiah's stay in Abbottabad. For all its promise, by early February 2011, the intelligence value of tracking Khairiah's movements would have appeared to have reached a dead end. For several months, Khairiah stayed with the family of Aslam, the intermediary on Usama's side. Still, though Khairiah didn't lead the CIA to her husband's doorstep, the Agency was still moving in the right direction. It would have uncovered one segment of the "closed circle," namely, Usama's intermediary, Muhammad Aslam.

Second Scenario

One of Usama's notes reveals that he had learned that the intermediary on Atiya's side, Abdallah al-Sindi, was detained for a brief period by the ISI. We don't know the exact date of his capture, though it might have preceded August 2010, when the CIA claimed to have picked up a hot lead. Although Abdallah had "no idea about the origin of the letters," he knew that they were "important" and might have volunteered the information for a handsome bounty. It is also possible that the ISI official who interrogated him suspected a nefarious connection and tailed him upon his release. Surprisingly, it does not appear that the brief detention of Abdallah weighed heavily on the mind of Atiya. He saw him as the "trusted *ansari*" who was "one of the most ardent supporters of al-Qaeda," so there was nothing to worry about.

Another turning point occurred in January 2011, when the actual courier was captured by the ISI and the CIA's search for Usama likely gained momentum. In a letter dated April 5, 2011, Atiya lamented: "I regret to inform you that the brother Abu al-Harith al-Sindi (the brother-in-law of Abdallah al-Sindi) has been detained by Pakistani intelligence in Karachi. This happened over two months ago. . . . We pray for his release." We don't know how the letters from North Waziristan were delivered subsequent to Abu al-Harith's capture. Perhaps Atiya took additional risks to ensure that Usama was aware of this significant development.

How could Usama have missed this? He didn't. But in 2010–11, he had a lot on his plate. He was putting together a "new vision" for al-Qaeda to announce on the tenth anniversary of the 9/11 attacks, and it required taming the unruly "Brothers" in Yemen, Iraq, Somalia, and North Africa. He was also planning attacks "the effects of which would far exceed 9/11." The events of the Arab Spring not only consumed much of his time, but also undermined some of the core principles of his jihadi worldview. If all this were not enough, Usama was at the mercy of his security guards and "God alone knows how hard" he had to plead to be reunited with his wife Khairiah. Also, Khaled's arranged marriage had been hovering for several years, and it depended on planning Hamza's safe passage to Abbottabad. We can be thankful that Usama was a family man, which was likely the cause of his ultimate downfall.

After Khairiah finally made it to Abbottabad, Usama wanted to speed up Hamza's safe passage. Atiya had refused to comply with Usama's directions to send Hamza earlier and insisted on being extra-vigilant. It wasn't just Hamza, but the security of the intermediary too that was at stake, he cautioned Usama.[30] Atiya also made it clear to Usama that "keeping Hamza with us here [i.e., in North Waziristan] despite the threat of being killed in God's path is better than risking his capture, which would be a calamity for all of us!!"[31] By April, however, Atiya was prepared to send Hamza and proposed three different options, the most viable being to send him to Sind via Baluchistan.

On April 20, Usama sat with one of his daughters to prepare a letter to Atiya, and the notes for that letter were recorded in the 220-page handwritten notebook discussed in the previous chapter. Usama's daughter jotted down several bullet points, one of which read as follows:

The need to look into the impact of Abu al-Harith's capture and its repercussions on the brothers in Sind's tribal area, especially as it relates to sending Hamza there. Also, beware of reaching out to Abdallah al-Sindi independently. He may be under surveillance, for he was captured before and is related to Abu al-Harith.[32]

As they wrote the letter dated April 26, 2011, they checked off all the bullet points in the notebook except for the one concerning Abu al-Harith's capture. Though this clearly weighed on Usama's mind, one would think he should have started packing. Instead, there was so much else going on he likely chose to downplay it to hasten Hamza's journey to Abbottabad. On April 29, President Obama authorized the mission, and the SEALs descended on Usama's compound two days later.

Of course, the Bin Laden Papers cannot reveal what the courier, Abu al-Harith, shared with the ISI. We also don't know whether he and his brother-in-law,

Abdallah, had both conspired against al-Qaeda. While we can be confident that Abdallah was the conduit between Atiya and the real courier, Abu al-Harith, it bears repeating that neither of them knew who was behind the letters. The CIA also could not be sure that the man in the compound was Usama bin Laden, and President Obama authorized the Abbottabad raid on a probability basis.

All the same, the information revealed in the letters about Abdallah and Abu al-Harith is too important to ignore. Could it possibly be unrelated, a mere coincidence? Or did Abdallah, who suspected that the letters were "from one of our two Sheikhs," willingly go to the ISI when he was supposed to have been briefly "detained"? If so, did the ISI share with the CIA the intelligence it gathered from the two men? Or was the CIA spying on the ISI?

The "courier" narrative, starring Abu Ahmed al-Kuwaiti, was convenient. If the CIA tracked the location of Usama through the "closed circle," the Agency had good reasons not to disclose the names of the trio involved during the intelligence briefings that followed the raid. True, Usama was dead, but the CIA still had a smaller but sizable fish to fry. The Agency would have wanted to keep a lid on the identity of the courier as it was tracking down Atiya. On August 22, 2011, within four months of Usama's killing, Atiya was reported killed by a drone strike. This may not have been possible if Abu al-Harith's name had been publicized.

To date, unlike Abu Ahmed al-Kuwaiti, Abu al-Harith al-Sindi remains an obscure name.

EPILOGUE

Hell is full of good meanings, but Heaven is full of good works.

Proverb

"Your father, may God protect him, has reached a towering level of knowledge about the affairs of the *umma*," noted Usama bin Laden's third wife, Siham, in a 2011 letter. She was writing to Hamza, Usama's son by his second wife, Khairiah. Siham took it upon herself to provide Hamza, who had just been released from Iran after nearly nine years of detention there, with a snapshot of his father. "The leader of the *umma*"—meaning her husband—

> always says that the *umma*'s crisis is not due to a shortage of religious scholars who memorize the Qur'an. Rather, it suffers from a deficit of experts in both religion and contemporary affairs. . . . What preoccupies your father the most is finding ways to spread knowledge and learning among Muslims, and to transmit the knowledge of the few men of understanding by creating centers of research and strategic studies. He is also preoccupied with finding ways to extricate the *umma* from poverty, hunger, and illness. . . . He always says that Muslims need to have healthy bodies and minds, because malnutrition breeds generations of individuals who are intellectually inferior.[1]

While Siham was writing her letter in the wake of the Arab Spring, in conversations with his family, Usama was admiring the "more than 10,000 centers for research in America" and lamenting the dearth of such centers in the Arab world.[2] Yet, it is ironic that the man who cared so much about advancing knowledge among his fellow Muslims founded no schools or research centers of his own.

In 2010, Usama estimated his fortune—to which he had either limited or no access—to be at least $49 million, but the thought of bequeathing a sum to found a school did not even cross his mind when he composed his handwritten will (*wasiyya*). Usama requested that most of the one-third of his estate distributed there be "spent on fighting in God's path." (According to Sunni Islamic law, bequests should not exceed more than one-third of the estate's total value.)[3] Usama chose his words carefully: He wanted his money to be spent on "fighting" (*qital*) and not on "jihad" (struggle), lest his executors decided to use the money toward a center for spiritual striving—one of the meanings of "jihad."

Time and again, the reader of the Bin Laden Papers hits upon disconnects between Usama's goals and his deeds. The most striking concerns the vast chasm between his global vision and the absence of the means by which to realize it.

To be clear, Usama did not see himself as a mere disrupter. He believed that the terrorist attacks his organization carried out would achieve concrete political goals. First and foremost, Usama sought to transcend national borders and unite the global community of Muslims, re-creating the historical *umma* that was once held together by a common political authority. In late 2000, after al-Qaeda's USS *Cole* attack, he believed that his goal was within reach. Usama told journalists that the attacks represented a "critical turning point in the history of the *umma*'s ascent toward greater eminence." In an ostentatious tone, he went on to say that the United States knew only too well who "struck its destroyer, but because of its weakness, it avoids admitting it directly."[4] According to Usama's logic, the 9/11 attacks should have handed al-Qaeda the keys to the *umma*'s gates. They were supposed to deliver the "decisive blow" that would force the United States to withdraw its military forces from Muslim-majority states, allowing the jihadis to fight the "apostate regimes," i.e., autocratic rulers, on a level playing field.

Usama miscalculated. Though he had no regrets, in 2010, he admitted to his associates that his "victorious" 9/11 attacks did not produce the "decisive blow" he had expected, and spent that year charting a new strategy that would achieve a "balance of terror" with the United States. His plans included a detailed study of how to blow up and sink "a large number of crude oil tankers," thereby destroying "30 percent of the American economy" and adversely affecting "the income of every American." Such attacks, Usama envisaged, would cause the "original source of power"—Americans—"to feel the suffering of our people." He assumed that Americans would, in turn, take to the streets as they had during the Vietnam War, calling on their government to change its foreign policy.[5]

Usama's earnest determination to pursue his transnational goals when he himself could not even step safely through the gate of his own compound is confounding, to say the least. It's not as if his associates in North Waziristan were agile either, and after the fall of the Taliban regime, "hiding" (*kumun*) had become their *modus operandi*. While Usama was developing his "balance of terror" strategy, his associates' letters reveal that their main objective was simply to survive. The CIA drone campaign is contested under international law,[6] but it was having devastating effects on militants in the FATA, and Usama's top associate predicted that "it is inevitable that we shall endure great suffering and many of us will be killed."

Was Usama counting on his "Brothers"—i.e., regional jihadi groups acting in al-Qaeda's name in Iraq, Yemen, North Africa, and Somalia—perhaps? Quite the contrary. His letters reveal that he did not believe them to be reliable partners. We find him lamenting that they had become a "liability" to global jihad. Usama had good reason to complain. Their own letters expose the fact that, beneath their vows of allegiance, the "Brothers" had no desire to act in unison toward a common goal. The parent group of the Islamic State that Usama had welcomed into al-Qaeda in 2004 declared itself a state in Iraq in 2006, without consultation, or territory for that matter, and, after 2007, stopped responding to al-Qaeda's letters altogether. The Yemen-based group al-Qaeda in the Arabian Peninsula (AQAP) unilaterally assumed the al-Qaeda brand as its own in 2009 and went on to reject al-Qaeda's instructions to put an end to its sectarianism and attacks against the local government. And the Somalia-based group al-Shabaab was too ambitious for Usama's liking. Its leader, Mukhtar al-Zubayr, wanted a public merger with al-Qaeda which Usama did not want to grant, and wished to declare a state of which Usama did not approve.

On whom, then, was Usama counting to gather Muslims into the promised *umma*?

In the modern bordered world, terrorism has destabilized states and, in some cases, even led to decolonization. But it has never come close to giving birth to an empire-like *umma*. Thus, for Usama to entertain the possibility—nay, the certainty—that by terrorizing the "enemy," the jihadis could somehow create and build the *umma* required much imagination. Factor in that the jihadis were variously hiding, incompetent, unruly, extremists, and disunited, and Usama's optimism borders on delirium.

For a man who wanted to change the world, Usama was not worldly. The man who methodically charted near-faultless plans to blow up oil tankers and derail locomotives in the United States had only a perfunctory understanding of international relations.

Usama's letters reveal that he was well versed in accounts of early Islam. We often find him strategizing by citing the Prophet Muhammad's triumphs and learning from the challenges he faced as he transformed his followers into a community (*jama'a*) that eventually grew into an *umma*.

But Usama was not well read outside Islamic history. He appreciated and described as "sagacious" (*'uqala*) Western non-Muslim thinkers who were critical of their governments' foreign policies. However, Usama's knowledge of such thinkers was superficial at best, most likely based on Arabic media reports. A copy of Noam Chomsky's *Hegemony or Survival: America's Quest for Global Dominance* was recovered from the compound, along with other English-language books on international relations, but nowhere do the letters suggest that Usama had actually bothered to read them. It is unlikely that he was fluent in English. Though his letters stressed the importance of learning about the "enemy," his knowledge of American history did not go beyond browsing mediocre articles on the subject. In some of his letters, Usama displayed a sound assessment of the impact of the anti-war protests during the Vietnam War on U.S. foreign policy, but his descriptions of American presidents and their policies suffered from numerous inaccuracies.

For someone who wanted to take on the world's greatest power, Usama's ignorance of American politics might invite ridicule. And in view of al-Qaeda's operational impotence and its inability to control jihadi groups acting in its name, Usama's political goals were alarmingly sophomoric. In the end, his repeated miscalculations meant that his leonine post-9/11 goals did not go beyond empty threats, unexecuted plans, and more than a little wishful thinking.

But if al-Qaeda supporters were to search through the Bin Laden Papers, they would most likely dwell on the proofs they provide that Usama was sincere and incorruptible. The letters never suggest, or even hint, that Usama sought to advance his personal interests at the expense of al-Qaeda or that he ever entertained political deals that would have compromised his jihadi principles. Usama's supporters would thus recognize that their leader was as consistent about his ideals in his private communications as he was in his public statements.

In the non-jihadi world, any ovation for Usama's incorruptibility is unlikely to eclipse his terrorism credentials. But political establishments would do well to take seriously the political grievances that Usama voiced. Most Muslims do not long to be suicide bombers, as Usama would have liked, but they also don't want to suffer the whims of the autocratic rulers whom Usama sought and failed to overthrow. That is why Usama's enmity toward Western democracies that support Muslim dictators will continue to resonate with some long after his demise.

It would be remiss of the reader of the Bin Laden Papers not to observe the disconnect between the real, diminutive Usama and al-Qaeda and the behemoth shadows they cast over the corridors of power in the decade following 9/11. To be sure, the letters reveal that some counterterrorism efforts, particularly the CIA drone campaign over the FATA, played a key role in suppressing jihadism. But the letters equally reveal that other intelligence assessments that focused excessively on al-Qaeda diverted valuable resources away from other, more threatening jihadi groups. The obsession with the al-Qaeda brand distracted the counterterrorism community from discerning the divisions within jihadism. Despite clear signs that the jihadi landscape was divided, counterterrorism authorities fixated on Usama's questionable command of global jihad. In 2014, their misassessment allowed the Islamic State to eclipse al-Qaeda.

These faulty intelligence conclusions are comparable to those drawn and acted upon during the Cold War. Though the differences between the Cold War's two hegemons and global terrorism's non-state actors are self-evident, some similarities are worth noting. During the Cold War, as Greg Thielman put it, the United States was preoccupied with closing the "strategic gaps that the Soviet Union was perceived to be opening." Much later, archival materials revealed that "Moscow had been struggling mightily merely to catch up with the technological advances and superior resources of the United States."[7] Similarly, the global "war on terror" saw al-Qaeda growing stronger by the day following the Taliban's fall. And yet, as we have discovered, far from being a growing threat, al-Qaeda was crippled within a couple of months of the launching of Operation Enduring Freedom on October 7, 2001, and it never recovered its operational arm during Usama's lifetime.

The continuing threat of terrorism should by no means be taken lightly, and it bears repeating that the 9/11 attacks represent the deadliest foreign assault on U.S. soil to date. The challenge is how governments should respond to and prevent terrorism without augmenting the stature of terrorists and enhancing their base of followers. Though the 9/11 attacks turned out to be a Pyrrhic victory for al-Qaeda, Usama still changed the world and continued to influence global politics for nearly a decade after. We now know from the Bin Laden Papers that the man whose post-9/11 public statements were brimming with threats was in actuality powerless and confined to his compound, overseeing an "afflicted" al-Qaeda.

APPENDIX 1
USAMA BIN LADEN'S WILL

The Bin Ladens are a wealthy family in Saudi Arabia, largely due to the fortune amassed by Usama's father, Muhammad bin Laden.[1] But as of 1996 (or earlier), when Usama was forced to leave Sudan, it became difficult for him to access his inheritance, the bulk of which was in shares in the family business—the Saudi Bin Laden Group.[2] The entire family business came under close scrutiny after al-Qaeda carried out the 1998 East Africa bombings.

In his detailed study *The Bin Ladens: An Arabian Family in the American Century*, Steve Coll reports that the Saudi Bin Laden Group continued to transfer money to Usama's Swiss bank account after he left Saudi Arabia for Sudan in 1991.[3] Coll further reports that in a letter written in 2000 in response to a U.S. Treasury request, the Saudi Bin Laden Group disclosed that over his lifetime, Usama "had received a total of about $27 million, but never all at once." He "had received regular dividends and salaries, beginning in the early 1970s and ending in the early 1990s," averaging "slightly more than $1 million per year." Usama was likely the recipient of an additional $8 million from another distribution of family wealth, and he either took it out in cash or reinvested it.[4]

The Bin Laden Papers reveal that Usama continued to receive funds earmarked for him after the letter was written in 2000.[5] It is not clear whether they originated from his shares in the family business or from donations in his name to finance the jihad.[6] But Usama was not flush with cash. In late 2004, he sought to borrow 1 million euros, and by 2010, his personal account was virtually empty. This was the account that Usama used to cover his family expenses, and on occasion to finance al-Qaeda. After al-Qaeda received $5 million in exchange for an Afghan diplomat it had kidnapped in 2008, Atiya deposited a "small gift" in Usama's account.[7] Usama accepted the sum, but insisted that he considered it as a "loan."[8] In January 2011, a few months before he was killed, Usama owed al-Qaeda 30,000 euros.[9]

Usama's handwritten will (*wasiyya*), which he likely penned in late 2010, sheds light on his finances. We learn from it that:

> The money in Sudan amounts to nearly $29 million, of which I received $1.2 million in Sudan; $800,000 in Jalalabad; $1.25 million is in Qandahar—according to the intermediary; and $12 million from the side of my brother, Bakr bin Muhammad bin Laden, is invested in Sudan on behalf of the Bin Laden Group.[10]

Though $29 million is an impressive sum, there's reason to believe that Usama's fortune was far greater than that.

According to Islamic law, inheritances are to be divided among the nearest relatives following a systematized order of succession, privileging male relatives.[11] Bequests in the form of a *wasiyya* are subject to restrictions, and the scholar of Islam, Rudolph Peters, explains that they "may not exceed one-third of the value of the estate," and are "null unless they are ratified (*idjaza*) by the heirs."[12] We can therefore infer that the sums designated in Usama's *wasiyya* were at most only one-third of his fortune, and it is possible that they were less than that.

Mindful that his *wasiyya* would be null unless his relatives agreed, Usama requested that "my brothers, sisters, aunts, and offspring ratify (*an yujayyizu*) my *wasiyya*, so that all my liquid assets [i.e., cash] in Sudan are spent on fighting in God's path."[13] Usama's *wasiyya* reveals that he had entered into agreements to recover the remainder of his liquid assets from Sudan, and had promised Abu Hafs al-Mauritani and Abu Ibrahim al-Iraqi 1 percent each of the amount they manage "to extricate from the government of Sudan." In compliance with Islamic law, Usama asked that 2 percent be deducted from his liquid assets in Sudan toward paying off any possible debts.

Usama likely wanted to bequeath money to those in his family who might not receive a share under Islamic law. He wanted a total of 600,000 Saudi riyals ($160,000) of the cash in Sudan to be invested equally on behalf of his sisters, Mariam, Iman, and I'tidal. Of his estate outside Sudan, Usama wanted some cash—300,000 Saudi riyals ($80,000)—and gold to be divided among his aunts, uncles, and cousins.[14]

At the time when Usama wrote his *wasiyya*, his daughter Khadija had died (2007) and so had her husband (2010), leaving behind four children. Usama's son Saad was also dead (2009), leaving behind a wife and three children. Usama wanted Saad's wife and her children to receive half the share that would typically be allotted to a son according to Islamic law, and Khadija's children to receive half the share allotted to a daughter. It is possible that Usama's orphaned grandchildren may have otherwise missed out under the Sunni inheritance system.

Since Usama's bequest could not exceed more than one-third of the total value of his estate, he likely estimated that his fortune was at least $49 million in 2010–11.[15]

APPENDIX 2
DRAMATIS PERSONAE

The names of the main *dramatis personae* are truncated for readability in this book. Often (but not always), they are referred to using their first name (e.g., "Usama" for "Usama Bin Laden"; "Ayman" for "Ayman al-Zawahiri") or the first part of their aliases (e.g., "Atiya" for "Atiyatullah al-Libi") or the first part of their *kunya*—i.e., the honorific name they adopted—e.g., "Abu Musab" for "Abu Musab al-Zarqawi"). Accordingly, the list below is in alphabetical order based on the name by which they are referred to in the book. It should be noted that, in keeping with strict security measures, most of the people cited in this book penned their letters using aliases that they changed periodically. Sometimes they did not even sign their letters and assumed that the addressee would easily guess their identity from the content.

Abdallah Khan

Took charge of al-Qaeda until 2004 following the fall of the Taliban regime and Usama bin Laden's disappearance. One of the letters reveals that "the Taliban are the ones who appointed Abdallah Khan as military commander." The Afghan by that name features in the "Guantanamo files" as the "former Taliban Commander of Kandahar Airfield." According to the WikiLeaks files, one of the Guantanamo detainees was mistaken for Abdallah and was captured after he "left Chawchak village for Khandahar [*sic*] to sell goods at a bazaar" on January 29, 2003. The other, more likely possibility is that Abdallah Khan is the alias for Abd al-Hadi, the Arab leader of the foreign fighters' brigade (*liwa' al-ansar*), a unit that Mullah Omar set up in June 2001. When Usama resumed contact with his organization, he removed Abdallah Khan from his position.

Abd al-Malik al-Baluchi

Leader of Jundallah, a Sunni militant group operating in Iran. He features in a 2008 letter, after having met the leaders of al-Qaeda in North Waziristan.

Abdallah al-Sindi

Part of a "closed circle" consisting of two intermediaries and a courier. This clandestine trio served as a conduit between Usama bin Laden in Abbottabad and his associates in North Waziristan. Abdallah was the intermediary on Atiya's side in North Waziristan. See also **Abu al-Harith al-Sindi** and **Muhammad Aslam**.

Abu Ahmed al-Kuwaiti

The alias of Ibrahim Saeed Ahmed. He was a Pakistani national and not, as his alias suggests, of Kuwaiti origin. He and his brother lived in the same compound as Usama bin Laden. Their primary role was to provide "security cover," i.e., giving the appearance that locals lived in the compound. They also attended to the Bin Laden family's basic needs (e.g., grocery shopping) and escorted them to the doctor on rare occasions. In the letters, Bin Laden refers to Abu Ahmed and his brother as "Abu Khaled and Abu Muhammad." In the aftermath of the raid, it transpired in media reports that the two brothers had been living with their wives and children next door, and had even kept Bin Laden's identity hidden from their respective families.

Abu Bakr al-Baghdadi

The alias of Ibrahim Awad Ibrahim al-Badri al-Samarrai. In 2010, he succeeded Abu Umar al-Baghdadi as the leader of the Islamic State of Iraq. Under his leadership, the group changed its name to the Islamic State of Iraq and the

Levant/Syria (ISIL/ISIS) in 2013 and proclaimed itself as the Islamic State in 2014. He was killed in 2019.

Abu Basir

The alias of Nasir Abd al-Karim Abdallah al-Wuhayshi, the leader of the Yemen-based group al-Qaeda in the Arabian Peninsula (AQAP). He was killed in 2015.

Abu Hafs al-Mauritani

The alias of Mahfouz Ould al-Walid. He was one of the al-Qaeda leaders who crossed illegally into Iran and was detained there until 2012. Prior to his detention, he headed al-Qaeda's Legal Committee.

Abu Hafs al-Misri

An alias of Subhi Muhammad Abu Sitta al-Jawhari (as was Muhammad Atef also). In 1996, he became Usama bin Laden's deputy and thereby al-Qaeda's second-in-command. His role included overseeing al-Qaeda's military committee. He was killed in November 2001. His daughter Fatima is married to Usama bin Laden's son Muhammad.

Abu Hurayra al-Sanaani

An alias of Qasim Yahya Mahdi al-Raymi. He was the deputy of Abu Basir, the leader of al-Qaeda in the Arabian Peninsula (AQAP), and succeeded him in 2015. He was killed in 2020.

Abu al-Harith al-Sindi

The actual courier who facilitated communications between Usama bin Laden and his associates in North Waziristan. He was the conduit between the intermediary on Bin Laden's side and the intermediary on the North Waziristan side. He was captured by Pakistan's security agency, the ISI, in early 2011. See also **Abdallah al-Sindi** and **Muhammad Aslam**.

Abu al-Khair

Ahmad Hasan Abu al-Khair al-Misri was the alias of Abdallah Muhammad Rajab Abd al-Rahman. He was part of Usama bin Laden's inner circle. In 2002, he was among those who fled Afghanistan and crossed illegally into Iran. He was released in 2015 and was killed in Syria in 2017.

Abu al-Laith al-Libi

A member of the Libyan Islamic Fighting Group (LIFG) and a field commander based in the Af-Pak region. In 2004, he gave a "partial" allegiance to Usama bin Laden, agreeing to fight under al-Qaeda's banner in Afghanistan and Pakistan. This remained unpublicized. Though he and Abu Yahya al-Libi publicly merged with al-Qaeda in 2007, the letters reveal that they did so still only on the basis of a partial allegiance and they kept their finances separate. Abu al-Laith was killed in 2008.

Abu al-Tayyib

An al-Qaeda supporter and informer based in Saudi Arabia. His real identity is unknown.

Abu Muhammad al-Adnani

An alias of Taha Subhi Falaha, who was the official spokesman of the Islamic State. He was renowned for his ardent defense of the divine legitimacy of the Islamic State and his vociferous criticisms of jihadi groups, including al-Qaeda, that did not give their allegiance to the caliph, Abu Bakr al-Baghdadi. He was killed in 2016.

DRAMATIS PERSONAE

Abu Muhammad al-Misri

An alias of Abdallah Ahmad Abdallah, one of al-Qaeda's top military leaders. In early 2002, he was among those who crossed illegally into Iran; he was detained there in December that year. He was reportedly released in 2015 but prevented from leaving Iran. In 2020, it was reported that he had been assassinated in Tehran.

Abu Musab al-Suri

An alias of Mustafa Sit-Mariam Nassar, a renowned and prolific jihadi strategist. In 2000, he founded the group Majmu'at Mu'askar al-Ghuraba' in Afghanistan and, on April 9, 2001, he gave his allegiance to Mullah Omar. He was reportedly captured in 2005.

Abu Musab al-Zarqawi

An alias of Ahmad Fadil al-Nazzal. He was the leader of the group al-Tawhid wa-al-Jihad, which was operational in Iraq following the 2003 U.S. invasion. In December 2004, Usama bin Laden publicly admitted him into the al-Qaeda fold and appointed him "the leader of al-Qaeda in Mesopotamia." He was killed in June 2006. In the letters, he is also referred to as "al-Azraq."

Abu Talha al-Almani

A German convert who joined al-Qaeda in 2006 or 2007 on condition that he be assigned to carry out a "martyrdom operation." In 2010, he was killed during the operation led by Sirajuddin Haqqani of the Taliban on the U.S. Bagram Air Base.

Abu Talha al-Sudani

An alias of Tariq Abdallah. He was an al-Qaeda operative who eventually formed his own group in East Africa. His terrorist activities included the planning of the 2002 Mombasa attacks. In the letters, he is referred to as al-Dawsari.

Abu Omar al-Baghdadi

An alias of Hamid Daoud Muhmmad Khalil al-Zawi. He was the leader of the Islamic State of Iraq (2006–10) and gave himself the title of *Amir al-Mu'minin* (Commander of the Faithful). Those who proclaimed the Islamic State in 2014 consider him to be the founder of their state/caliphate.

Abu Yahya al-Libi

An alias of Muhammad Hasan Qa'id. He was a member of the Libyan Islamic Fighting Group (LIFG) and, in 2007, he and Abu al-Laith al-Libi joined al-Qaeda on a partial allegiance basis. Abu Yahya became the head of al-Qaeda's Legal Committee and, arguably, its most passionate spokesman. He was killed in 2012.

Adam (Yahya) Gadhan

A.k.a. Azzam al-Amriki or The American Azzam. An American national who converted to Islam and joined al-Qaeda. His fluency in Arabic saw him give public statements with near-native pronunciation. He was consulted on media matters, and the Bin Laden Papers include a lengthy letter he authored on al-Qaeda's media strategy for the tenth anniversary of the 9/11 attacks. On occasion, he translated English passages for Bin Laden's perusal. In the letters, he is referred to as Azzam and Abu al-Nur.

Ahmed Shah Masoud

Leader of the Northern Alliance, a coalition of militant groups opposed to the Taliban. He was killed on September 9, 2001. His assassination is attributed to al-Qaeda.

Arif Abu Shadia

Leader of a jihadi Kurdish Iraqi group. In 2007, he was in communication with al-Qaeda, but little else is reported about him.

DRAMATIS PERSONAE

Muhammad Aslam

Part of a "closed circle" consisting of two intermediaries and a courier. This clandestine trio served as a conduit between Usama bin Laden in Abbottabad and his associates in North Waziristan. Aslam was the intermediary on Bin Laden's side. He was highly trusted by Bin Laden, so much so that he hosted his second wife, Khairiah, for a couple of months after her release from Iran. See also **Abdallah al-Sindi** and **Abu al-Harith al-Sindi**.

Atiya

Short for Atiyatullah. This was an alias of Jamal Ibrahim Ishtiwi al-Misrati. He was arguably one of al-Qaeda's most important leaders. His responsibilities included overseeing al-Qaeda's external relations—i.e., serving as the point of contact with jihadi groups and associates outside Afghanistan and Pakistan. He began releasing public statements in 2005. In December 2007, Usama bin Laden tasked him with being one of the official spokesmen of al-Qaeda. In 2010, Atiya succeeded Hajji Uthman/Mustafa Abu al-Yazid (killed in May 2010) as the leader of al-Qaeda in Afghanistan and Pakistan. He was killed in August 2011. In the letters, Atiya is also referred to as Atiyatullah and Mahmoud. It is possible that he was the same person as Raja' and Wakil Khan.

Ayman al-Zawahiri

Usama bin Laden's successor. In 2000, his group, the Jihad Group (Jama'at al-Jihad), and al-Qaeda merged. He gained prominence after 9/11, becoming al-Qaeda's public face through his many public statements and voluminous writings. He became Usama bin Laden's deputy, probably after Abu Hafs al-Misri was killed in November 2001, but it was only in a 2004 letter that Usama formally designated him as such. In 2011, Ayman succeeded Bin Laden as the leader of al-Qaeda. In the letters, Ayman is referred to as the doctor/Abu Fatima/Abu Muhammad/one of the two Sheikhs/Kalim.

THE BIN LADEN PAPERS

Baitullah Mehsud

Leader of the Pakistani Taliban (TTP). He was killed in 2009.

Belmokhtar

An alias of Khaled Abu al-Abbas, leader of the North African jihadi group al-Murabitun. Around 2007, he sought to merge his group with al-Qaeda and, to that end, he sent an envoy, Younis al-Mauritani, to North Waziristan to meet with al-Qaeda's leaders. The merger did not eventuate.

Bishr al-Bishr

Saudi cleric sympathetic with al-Qaeda and jihadism generally. In early 2007, he was under house arrest when he corresponded—through an anonymous intermediary—with Atiya.

Daoud

One the aliases of Abdallah who married Usama bin Laden's daughter Khadija in 1999. Bin Laden entrusted him with overseeing his finances and other al-Qaeda matters. His other aliases include Abd al-Latif and Abu Abdallah al-Halabi. He was killed in 2010.

El Para

An alias of Abu Haidara Abd al-Razzaq, one of the leaders of the Salafist Group for Preaching and Combat (GSPC). In 2004, he sent a letter to Usama bin Laden seeking a merger with al-Qaeda. He was reportedly captured in 2005.

Fadil Harun

An al-Qaeda operative who acted as the lead planner for the 1998 East Africa bombings. In 2000, he was dispatched from Afghanistan to East Africa to plan the 2002 Mombasa attacks. He was killed in 2011. In the letters, he is referred to as al-Zawl/Yusuf al-Qumari/Yaaqub/Abu al-Fadl.

DRAMATIS PERSONAE

Hafiz

See **Hajji Uthman**.

Hajji Uthman

One of the aliases of Mustafa Abu al-Yazid, who became the leader of al-Qaeda in Afghanistan and Pakistan in 2006. His chief responsibilities included overseeing al-Qaeda's finances. He was also referred to in the letters by the aliases Sheikh Saeed and Hafiz Sultan. He was killed in May 2010.

Hakimullah Mehsud

Succeeded Baitullah Mehsud as the leader of the Pakistani Taliban (TTP) in 2009. He was killed in 2013.

Hamza Bin Laden

Usama bin Laden's son by Khairiah. He was among those who fled to Iran in early 2002 and was subsequently detained there. He was released with his mother in 2010 and ushered to North Waziristan. He is also referred to as Abu Mu'adh in the letters.

Hamza al-Rabia

Appointed the leader of al-Qaeda's "external work," i.e., international terrorism, by Usama bin Laden in 2004. He was reported killed in 2005.

Ilyas Kashmiri

His full name is Muhammad Ilyas Kashmiri. The leader of a Pakistani jihadi group that worked closely with al-Qaeda.

Jaafar

Envoy of Abu Musab al-Zarqawi who met with al-Qaeda's leaders in late 2003 or 2004.

Khadija

Usama bin Laden's daughter by Siham. In 2007, she died at the age of nineteen while giving birth to her fourth child. In the letters, Khadija is described as the "first martyr" in the Bin Laden family.

Khairiah

Usama bin Laden married Khairiah Sabar, his second wife, in 1985. She was seven years his elder. In 1989, she gave birth to their only child, a son they named Hamza. In early 2002, she, Hamza, and six of Usama's children by Najwa crossed the border illegally into Iran. About a year later, they were arrested and detained there. In August 2010, Khairiah and Hamza were released and ushered to Waziristan. Khairiah reunited with her husband in February 2011. The Bin Laden Papers include letters about and by Khairiah and Hamza.

Khaled al-Habib

Appointed military commander of al-Qaeda by Usama bin Laden in 2004, reporting directly to Tawfiq, leader of al-Qaeda in Afghanistan and Pakistan. Khaled may have acted as the leader of al-Qaeda in Afghanistan and Pakistan in 2005–06. He was killed in 2009.

Khaled Bin Laden

Usama bin Laden's son. In late 2004, he was reunited with his father and was killed during the Abbottabad raid. In the letters, he is also referred to as Abu Sulaiman.

Khaled al-Mihdar

One of the 9/11 hijackers.

DRAMATIS PERSONAE

Mariam

Usama bin Laden's daughter by Siham. In late 2004, she was reunited with her father and worked closely with him on drafting his letters and public statements.

Mukhtar Abu al-Zubayr

An alias of Ahmed Abdi Godane, leader of al-Shabaab. In 2009, he sought to merge with al-Qaeda, but this did not materialize under Usama bin Laden's leadership. Al-Shabaab finally merged with al-Qaeda in 2012, and Mukhtar was killed in 2014.

Mullah Dadullah

A Taliban military commander who was assassinated in 2007. His supporters, including leaders of al-Qaeda, believe that Taliban leaders (who were seeking peaceful negotiations with the United States) were behind his assassination.

Mullah Mansur Dadullah

The younger half-brother of Mullah Dadullah, and his successor. He firmly believed that the "insincere" Taliban were behind his half-brother's assassination. He was reported killed in 2015.

Mullah Omar

Leader of the Islamic Emirate of Afghanistan (1996–2001). In the jihadi world, he was recognized as the Commander of the Faithful (*amir al-mu'minin*)—i.e., the leader of the global Muslim community. He died in 2013, but the Taliban did not publicize the fact until 2015. In the letters, Mullah Omar is also referred to as our friend/Hajji Salim Khan/Amir al-Mu'minin.

Najwa Ghanem

Usama bin Laden's maternal cousin, whom he married in 1974. They had eleven children. Cousin marriage is common in the Middle East. Days before the 9/11 attacks, Najwa left Afghanistan to go to Syria, taking her son Abd al-Rahman and her youngest daughters, Ruqayya and Nour. In 2009, she co-authored a book with her son Omar, who left Afghanistan for the last time in April 2001. Omar wished "for the bin Laden name to become linked with peace rather than with terrorism," and is reported to suffer from mental illness. In the book, Najwa narrated her life with "my cousin," "my groom," and "the father of my children," Usama bin Laden, and noted that when she left Afghanistan, she "was not seeking a divorce."[1] Nevertheless, she was pleased that she "saved" the children she took with her, but her "heart broke into little pieces" for leaving behind six other children, who fled to Iran and were subsequently detained (Fatima, Laden, Saad, Uthman, Muhammad, and Iman/Asma'). Her eldest, Abdallah, lived in Saudi Arabia at the time.

Rabia Nawwaf al-Hazmi

One of the 9/11 hijackers.

Saad Bin Laden

Usama bin Laden's son by his wife Najwa. In early 2002, he was among those who crossed illegally into Iran and was detained there. In 2008, Saad escaped from detention and made his way to North Waziristan. He was killed in 2009.

Saif al-Adl

One of al-Qaeda's top military leaders. In early 2002, he was among those who crossed illegally into Iran. He was detained in December that year and was reportedly released in 2015 but prevented from leaving Iran.

Saleh Al-Nabhan

An al-Qaeda operative based in East Africa. Also known as Yousef al-Tanzani, he was killed in 2009.

Siham

Siham bint Abdallah bin Hussein, Usama bin Laden's third wife. It is reported that she accepted his marriage proposal on condition that she could continue her education. Bin Laden accepted this, and she completed a Ph.D. in Qur'anic grammar after their marriage. They had three daughters and one son: Khadija (1988–2007), Khaled (1989–2011), Mariam (b. 1990), and Sumayya (b. 1992). Khadija and her family hid in North Waziristan. Siham and her three other children reunited with Bin Laden in late 2004. The letters do not reveal why Siham and the other three children did not flee to Iran, nor do they disclose their place of shelter prior to rejoining Bin Laden. According to U.S. officials, the Abbottabad compound was built in 2005, and it is likely that Bin Laden and his two families moved there that year. Arrangements for Khadija and her family to join them were discussed, but Bin Laden's security guards would not allow it. After Khadija's death in 2007, his guards allowed her children to live in Abbottabad with their grandparents. The Bin Laden Papers reveal that Siham, Mariam, and Sumayya contributed to the public statements that Bin Laden released, while Khaled recorded them.

Al-Subay'i

One of the jihadis—he was a member of the Libyan Islamic Fighting Group (LIFG)—who were detained in Iran. Abu Abd al-Rahman Uns al-Subay'i was released in 2010 and was ushered to North Waziristan. In 2011, he and a few others left to fight in Libya without al-Qaeda's authorization. In the letters, he is also referred to as Abu Uns and Abd al-Qayyum.

Sulaiman Abu Ghaith

A senior al-Qaeda leader who was among those who crossed illegally into Iran in 2002. He was detained there until his release in 2013, when he was subsequently captured in Jordan and brought to the United States. In 2014, he was sentenced to life in prison. In 2007, while in detention in Iran, he married Usama bin Laden's daughter Fatima.

Sumayya

One of Usama bin Laden's daughters by Siham. In late 2004, she was reunited with her father and worked closely with him on his letters and public statements.

Tawfiq

In 2004, Usama bin Laden appointed Tawfiq the "general leader of al-Qaeda" in Afghanistan and Pakistan. This was a new senior position, and Tawfiq reported directly to Usama. When it was not possible to consult with Usama in a timely fashion, Tawfiq was authorized to make decisions, after consulting with his trusted associates and subordinates. In the letters, he is also referred to as Jargh al-Din. Tawfiq was likely the same person known as Abu Hasan al-Sa'idi/Abu Ubaida al-Misri/Abd al-Hamid. He might have possibly been Wakil Khan. If so, he died in 2007.

Al-Wadud

Abu Musab Abd al-Wadud was the leader of the Salafist Group for Preaching and Combat (GSPC) in North Africa. In 2006, the GSPC merged with al-Qaeda and became known as al-Qaeda in the Islamic Maghreb (AQIM). He was killed in 2020.

Wakil Khan

In charge of al-Qaeda's external relations in 2004. It is likely that Wakil Khan is one of Atiya or Tawfiq's aliases.

DRAMATIS PERSONAE

Younis al-Mauritani

Belmokhtar's envoy to al-Qaeda, probably in 2007. Though a merger between Belmokhtar's group and al-Qaeda did not eventuate, Younis made an impression on al-Qaeda's leaders and stayed in North Waziristan. He became Abu Yahya's deputy on al-Qaeda's Legal Committee. In 2010, Bin Laden entrusted him with planning large-scale terrorist operations (blowing up oil tankers). In September 2011, he was arrested by Pakistan's ISI and was subsequently handed over by the United States to Mauritania. In 2015, it was reported that he had been sentenced to twenty years in prison for terrorist activities. In the letters, he is referred to as Sheikh Younis/Younis al-Mauritani/(Abu) Saleh al-Mauritani.

Usama Bin Laden

The leader of al-Qaeda. In the letters, he is referred to as Abu Abdallah/Azmarai/ Mawlawi Zamarai/Chief/Teacher/Father/The Sheikh.

Sheikh Azzam

Abdallah Azzam was Usama bin Laden's mentor. In 1984, he established the Services Bureau which hosted Arabs who wanted to support the Afghan cause. He was killed in 1989.

Abd al-Rahman al-Maghrebi

Oversaw jihadi media, a role that he occupied from at least 2004. On occasion, he translated relevant English literature for Usama bin Laden's perusal. By early 2011, he was consulted on most major matters. Atiya counted on Abu Yahya al-Libi and al-Maghrebi. In the letters, he is also referred to as Munir.

ENDNOTES

Prologue

1. Admiral McRaven (Ret.) related this in his presentation at the Special Operations Policy Forum, New America, September 2019. He did so in response to a question that can be accessed at around 07:54:00 on the following link: https://www.newamerica.org/conference/special-ops-2019/.
2. Admiral William H. McRaven, *Sea Stories: My Life in Special Operations*, New York/Boston: Grand Central Publishing, 2019, p. 310.
3. William H. McRaven, *Spec Ops: Case Studies in Special Operations Warfare: Theory and Practice*, New York: Presidio Press, 1996, p. 20.
4. Ibid., p. 4.
5. Ibid., p. 19.
6. https://www.navy.com/seals.
7. McRaven, *Sea Stories*, p. 296.
8. Ibid., pp. 296, 315.
9. Ibid., p. 313.
10. McRaven, *Spec Ops*, p. 20.
11. McRaven, *Sea Stories*, p. 321.
12. Ibid., pp. 320–1.
13. Ibid., p. 321.
14. Conversation with Colonel (Ret.) Liam Collins, Special Forces.
15. McRaven, *Sea Stories*, p. 321.
16. Email correspondence with Admiral McRaven. See also McRaven, *Sea Stories*, p. 321.

Introduction

1. McRaven, *Sea Stories*, p. 321.
2. Nelly Lahoud, Stuart Caudill, Liam Collins, Gabriel Koehler-Derrick, Don Rassler, and Muhammad al-'Ubadydi, "Letters from Abbottabad: Bin Laden Sidelined," CTC, May 3, 2012, https://ctc.usma.edu/letters-from-abbottabad-bin-ladin-sidelined/. See in particular Section I, "From Abbottabad to the CTC: The 17 Declassified Documents."
3. https://valor.militarytimes.com/hero/5554.
4. See more about the blood chit at https://www.airforcemag.com/article/1098chit/.
5. https://www.911memorial.org/visit/museum/exhibitions/in-memoriam.
6. This definition of philology is attributed to the Russian-American linguist and literary theorist Roman Jakobson (1896–1982). See Helge Jordheim, "Philology and the Problem of Culture," in Harry Lonnroth (ed.), *Philology Matters!: Essays on the Art of Reading Slowly*, Leiden: Brill, 2017, p. 15.
7. For consistency, each author is referenced using just one of his aliases. The "*Dramatis Personae*" at the end of the book should be consulted for more details about their identity.
8. https://www.ctc.usma.edu/letters-from-abbottabad-bin-ladin-sidelined/. References to this set of documents follow those on the CTC website, and each starts with "SOCOM-2012."

9. ODNI, "Bin Laden's Bookshelf," https://www.dni.gov/index.php/features/bin-laden-s-book-shelf. References to these sets of documents follow ODNI's: The document cited is referenced by using the English title of the document as given on the ODNI website, but analysis and translation of the content rely on the original Arabic.
10. https://www.cia.gov/library/abbottabad-compound/index.html.
11. https://www.cia.gov/library/abbottabad-compound/index_audio.html.
12. https://www.cia.gov/library/abbottabad-compound/index_converted_documents.html.
13. https://www.cia.gov/library/abbottabad-compound/index_images.html.
14. https://www.cia.gov/library/abbottabad-compound/index_video.html.
15. References to these documents follow those on the CIA's website, comprising the file type (i.e., PDF, IMG, VID, AUD) and the corresponding number.
16. CIA, "Bin Ladin's Journal," https://www.cia.gov/library/abbottabad-compound/index.html.
17. https://www.cia.gov/library/abbottabad-compound/index.html.
18. See, for instance, Douglas Frantz, "U.S.-Based Charity Is Under Scrutiny," *The New York Times*, June 14, 2002.
19. "CIA Releases Nearly 470,000 Additional Files Recovered in May 2011 Raid on Usama Bin Ladin's Compound," CIA, November 1, 2017, https://www.cia.gov/stories/story/cia-releases-nearly-470000-additional-files-recovered-in-may-2011-raid-on-usama-bin-ladins-compound/.

Chapter 1: "The Birth of the Idea"

1. IMG-030337, Tawfiq/Abu al-Hasan al-Saidi, September 8, 2004.
2. IMG-058732 (1), Khaled al-Habib to Usama bin Laden, 2004.
3. IMG-040538, Usama bin Laden's notes, September 2002.
4. Eric Malnic, William C. Rempel, and Ricardo Alonso-Zaldivar, "EgyptAir Co-Pilot Caused '99 Jet Crash, NTSB to Say," *Los Angeles Times*, March 15, 2002, https://web.archive.org/web/20160404110130/http://articles.latimes.com/2002/mar/15/news/mn-32955.
5. The "idea of using planes" as inspired by al-Batouti was also mentioned by the jihadi leader in Yemen, Abu Basir al-Wuhayshi, in the jihadi magazine *al-Masra*; part 1 in issue 3, January 30, 2016, and part 2 in issue 4, February 9, 2016, can be accessed at https://jihadology.net/wp-content/uploads/_pda/2016/01/al-masracc84-newspaper-3.pdf (login required). According to the *9/11 Commission Report*, Khaled Sheikh Muhammad (KSM) first suggested the idea to Usama in 1996, https://www.govinfo.gov/content/pkg/GPO-911REPORT/pdf/GPO-911REPORT-23.pdf, pp. 147–9. It is noteworthy that KSM mentioned this after his capture in 2003 and did not share it with the journalist Yosri Fouda who interviewed him in Pakistan in April 2002. See Yosri Fouda, *Fi Tariq al-Adha: Min Ma'aqil al-Qa 'ida ila Hawadini Da'ish*, Cairo: Dar al-Shuruq, 2015, pp. 67–8.
6. Abu Hafs was killed in November 2001 during the U.S.-led war on Afghanistan, and Abu al-Khair escaped to Iran in 2002 and was detained.
7. In 2010, Usama wrote asking "for all the last testaments of the nineteen brothers," PDF-002730, October 11, 2010.
8. Usama bin Laden, "Among a Band of Knights," trans. James Howarth, in Bruce Lawrence (ed.), *Messages to the World: The Statements of Osama bin Laden,* New York: Verso, 2005, pp. 194–5.
9. PDF-004225, Usama bin Laden draft letter to Hajji Uthman and Atiya, early 2010.
10. The fifth page is missing, and it is clear that he dictated those pages: IMG-052993; IMG-046353; IMG-007097; IMG-038618; IMG-025138; IMG-053149.
11. On Usama's political life prior to 1996, see Steve Coll, *The Bin Ladens: An Arabian Family in the American Century*, New York: The Penguin Press, 2008, especially Part III.
12. On the pressure to leave Sudan for Afghanistan, see Fadil Harun, *al-Harb 'ala al-Islam*, vol. 1, p. 250. See also Peter Bergen, *The Osama bin Laden I Know: An Oral History*, New York: Free Press, 2008, p. 158.
13. Anne Stenersen, *Al-Qaida in Afghanistan*, Cambridge: Cambridge University Press, 2017, pp. 56–62. For the phase that preceded the Taliban, see Thomas J. Barfield, "Problems in Establishing Legitimacy in Afghanistan," *Iranian Studies*, vol. 37, no. 2, June 2004, pp. 263–93.
14. Thomas Barfield, *Afghanistan: A Cultural and Political History*, Princeton: Princeton University Press, 2012, p. 260.
15. Usama compliments Younis Khalis, who had helped him to move from Sudan to Afghanistan, and Jalal al-Din al-Haqqani.

16. PDF-003928, Usama bin Laden notes.
17. See "Declaration of Jihad" (1996), in Lawrence, *Messages to the World*.
18. John Miller, "Greetings, America. My Name Is Osama Bin Laden . . .," *Esquire*, February 1, 1999, accessed on https://www.pbs.org/wgbh/pages/frontline/shows/binladen/who/miller.html.
19. https://www.fbi.gov/history/famous-cases/east-african-embassy-bombings.
20. Fadil Harun, *al-Harb 'ala al-Islam*, vol. 1, p. 378. The autobiography was posted online in early 2009.
21. Steven Strasser (ed.), *The 9/11 Investigations*, New York: Public Affairs, 2004, p. 156.
22. See, for instance, the former commander in the Libyan Islamic Fighting Group (LIFG), Noman Benotman, "An Open Letter to Osama bin Laden," *Foreign Policy*, September 10, 2010; his views are also reported by Peter Bergen and Paul Cruickshank, "The Unraveling," *The New Republic*, June 11, 2008. See also Ayman al-Zawahiri's one-time mentor Dr. Fadl, *al-Ta'riya* (part 1), *al-Masri al-Yawm*, November 18, 2008, https://www.almasryalyoum.com/news/details/1930360.
23. Mustafa Hamid and Leah Farrall, *The Arabs at War in Afghanistan*, London: Hurst, 2015, pp. 238–9.
24. Cited in Cathy Scott-Clark and Adrian Levy, *The Exile: The Stunning Inside Story of Osama bin Laden and Al Qaeda in Flight*, New York: Bloomsbury, 2017, p. 47.
25. Ibid., p. 48.
26. "Letter to Shaykh Abu Muhammad 17 August 2007," ODNI, 2016.
27. PDF-004225, Usama bin Laden draft letter to Hajji Uthman and Atiya, early 2010. The letter suggests that Usama was aware of the operational details of only one attack, most likely the 9/11 attacks.
28. I am thankful to Michael Cook, who read several internal documents and relevant texts on this issue and helped me understand that this is a neologism.
29. Abu Musab al-Suri, *Da'wat al-Muqawama al-Islamiyya*, p. 727. Abu Musab al-Suri is a renowned jihadi strategist and a prolific writer. He founded the group Majmu'at Mu'askar al-Ghuraba', which had an association with the Taliban, in 2000, and on April 9, 2001, he pledged allegiance to Mullah Omar: see ibid., pp. 729, 734. He completed his 1,600-page book in September 2004. See also Brynjar Lia, *The Architect of Global Jihad*, London/New York: Hurst/Columbia University Press, 2008.
30. PDF-023945, Ayman al-Zawahiri to Usama bin Laden, January 2011.
31. IMG-052993, Usama bin Laden's notes, September 2002 (he most likely dictated them).
32. See "Muslim Bomb," interview with Al Jazeera in 1998, in Lawrence, *Messages to the World*.
33. It was the second caliph in Islam, another Umar (644–56), who first gave himself that title, which has become synonymous with the title of the caliph. See Patricia Crone, *God's Rule: Government and Islam*, Columbia: Columbia University Press, 2004, p. 18.
34. https://www.dia.mil/News/Articles/Article-View/article/567026/attacks-on-uss-cole-spurred-dias-counterterrorism-mission/.
35. He faced opposition from everyone except Ayman al-Zawahiri, Usama's successor as the leader of al-Qaeda. At that time, Ayman was the leader of the Egyptian Jihad Group.
36. IMG-052993, Usama bin Laden's notes, September 2002.
37. Al-Sahab, *Qanadil min Nur* (8), includes the Usama bin Laden press conference in early 2001. This must have occurred in late February 2001 or thereabouts, because Usama's responses referenced the February 17, 2001 airstrikes carried out by the United States and Britain in Iraq. The video of this gathering was released in May 2021, using previously unavailable footage: https://archive.gnews.bz/index.php/s/kg2NbAXaf6kGSbx.
38. IMG-025138, Usama bin Laden's notes, September 2002.
39. IMG-052993.
40. IMG-007097, Usama bin Laden's notes, September 2002.
41. Paul L. Heck, "Jihad Revisited," *Journal of Religious Ethics*, vol. 32, no. 1, 2004, pp. 95–128; on how the classical formulation was adopted by jihadis, see Nelly Lahoud, "The Evolution of Modern Jihadism," *Oxford Research Encyclopedia, Religion*, August 2016.
42. IMG-007097.
43. IMG-038618.
44. According to UNESCO, the two Buddhas are part of a cultural and archaeological landscape that was developed between the first and thirteenth centuries in the Bamiyan Valley: https://whc.unesco.org/en/list/208/.
45. My thanks to Michael Cook for this pointed observation.

46. PDF-023388. This is the "nineteen-page letter" that came to prominence after the CIA declassified the Abbottabad files on November 1, 2017. It is from Atiya to his intermediary in Saudi Arabia and was to be shared with the jihadi cleric Bishr al-Bishr, who was under house arrest at the time.

47. The "decisive blow" comes up in Usama's letters in various forms. For instance, in PDF-003181, it is *hasm al-harb*, in PDF-004225, it is *ijbar al-'aduw 'ala inha'i i'tida'ihi . . . bi-quwwa wa-sur'a* (forcing the enemy to end their aggression forcefully and swiftly).

48. IMG-038618.

49. Ibid.

50. This is the equivalent of telling someone who states the obvious: "No shit, Sherlock!"

51. IMG-053149, Usama bin Laden's notes, September 2002.

52. Ibid.

53. Stenersen, *Al-Qaida in Afghanistan*, p. 92; Bergen, *The Osama bin Laden I know*, pp. 296–7.

54. Details of anguish and heroism are recorded in the 9/11; Commission Report, pp. 11–13, https://govinfo.library.unt.edu/911/report/911Report.pdf; On targeting the White House or the U.S. Capitol, p. 155 and according to KSM's interview with Yosri Fouda, *Fi Tariq al-Adha*, pp. 67–8.

55. The 9/11 Memorial & Museum, https://www.911memorial.org/911.

56. See interview with Pervez Musharraf, "Frontline," *PBS*, https://www.pbs.org/wgbh/pages/frontline/shows/campaign/interviews/musharraf.html.

57. Abdul Salam Zaeef, *My Life with the Taliban*, ed. Alex Strick van Linschoten and Felix Kuehn, London: Hurst & Company, 2010, pp. 135–7.

58. Pervez Musharraf, "Frontline," *PBS*.

59. "Presidential Address to the Nation," The White House, October 7, 2001, https://georgewbush-whitehouse.archives.gov/news/releases/2001/10/20011007-8.html.

60. PDF-023388, Atiya to a "trusted intermediary" in Saudi Arabia.

61. Ibid.

62. IMG-030337, Tawfiq/Abu al-Hasan al-Saidi, September 8, 2004.

63. Abu Musab al-Suri, *Da'wat al-Muqawama*, p. 729.

64. IMG-030337.

65. PDF-023388.

66. PDF-010240, Abu 'Abd al-Rahman Uns al-Subay'i, October 13, 2010.

67. IMG-030337 (1/4), September 8, 20044.

68. PDF-023388.

69. Ibid.

70. Ibid.

71. PDF-003594, Usama bin Laden to Abu Muhammad and Abu Khaled, January 14, 2011.

72. The interview was with the journalist Rahimullah Yusufzai on October 7, 2001, the day Operation Enduring Freedom was launched. Cited in Peter Bergen, "The Man Who Wouldn't Hand Over Bin Laden to the U.S.," *CNN*, July 29. 2015, https://peterbergen.com/the-man-who-wouldnt-hand-over-bin-laden-to-the-u-s-cnn-com/.

73. Ibid.

74. Qur'an 49:10.

75. Abu Musab al-Suri, *Afghanistan wa-al-Taliban wa-Ma 'rakatu al-Islami al-Yawm*, 1998, p. 36.

76. Michael Cook, *Muhammad*, Oxford: Oxford University Press, 1983, pp. 18–19.

77. See, for instance, the discussion about Liwa' al-Ansar set up by Mullah Omar in June 2001, in Abu Musab al-Suri, *Da'wat al-Muqawama al-Islamiyya*, pp. 787–8.

78. PDF-003213, Atiya and Abu Yahya al-Libi to Hakimullah Mahsud, December 3, 2010.

79. United Nations Security Council, Resolution 1267 (1999). See also Resolutions 1189 (1998), 1193 (1998), and 1333 (2000), https://www.un.org/securitycouncil/sanctions/1267/resolutions.

80. Security Council—3—Press Release SC/6567 392, 1st Meeting (AM), August 28, 1998.

81. "U.S. Tells Taliban to Close New York Office," *The New York Times*, February 10, 2001,

82. Gilles Dorronsoro, "The World Isolates the Taliban," *Le Monde Diplomatique*, June 2001, https://www.globalpolicy.org/the-dark-side-of-natural-resources-st/water-in-conflict/41438.html.

83. AFGP-2002-600321, "Letter to Mullah Muhammed 'Umar from Bin Laden," CTC, https://ctc.usma.edu/harmony-program/letter-to-mullah-muhammed-umar-from-bin-laden-original-language-2/.

84. Abu Musab al-Suri, *Afghanistan wa-al-Taliban wa-Ma 'rakatu al-Islami al-Yawm*, p. 36.

85. Yusuf al-Shawli, interview with Abu Hafs al-Mauritani, "Mahfouz wuld al-Walid. al-Qaeda wa-harakat Taliban," *Al Jazeera*, November 30, 2001.

86. PDF-023405, Hajji Uthman to Usama bin Laden, October 2007; see also PDF-023447, Atiya to Usama bin Laden, May–June 2008.

87. PDF-017045, Usama bin Laden to Hajji Uthman, December 17, 2007. "AQ Accounting Ledger," ODNI, 2017 suggests that al-Qaeda financed/subsidised "the budget of Dadullah."

88. PDF-023405, see "US-Taliban Talks: Who Is Mullah Baradar?" *Al Jazeera*, May 1, 2019, https://www.aljazeera.com/news/2019/05/us-taliban-talks-mullah-baradar-190501184035063.html.

89. "Senior Afghan Taliban Leader, Mullah Obaidullah, Is Dead," *BBC*, February 13, 2012, https://www.bbc.com/news/world-asia-17011844.

90. "Taliban Leader Mullah Akhtar Mansour Killed, Afghans Confirm," *BBC*, May 22, 2016, https://www.bbc.com/news/world-asia-36352559.

91. PDF-023900, Ayman al-Zawahiri to Usama bin Laden, May 16, 2010.

92. Qur'an 16:91.

93. A range of similar issues that come up include treaties, oaths, and allegiances.

94. The Taliban announced his death in 2015. See Bergen, "The Man Who Wouldn't Hand Over Bin Laden to the U.S."

95. "Agreement for Bringing Peace to Afghanistan between the Islamic Emirate of Afghanistan which is not recognized by the United States as a state and is known as the Taliban and the United States of America," February 29, 2020. It can be accessed on https://www.state.gov/wp-content/uploads/2020/02/Agreement-For-Bringing-Peace-to-Afghanistan-02.29.20.pdf.

96. Ibid.

Chapter 2: Jihadis Between Borders

1. PDF-023388, Atiya to Bishr al-Bishr through a "trusted intermediary."

2. Usama mentions in passing that he had gone into the "mountains of Tora Bora and elsewhere" in a draft letter he composed in late 2009: PDF-00387.

3. The vanguards are of course the non-Afghans, including Arabs who had fought against the Soviet Union's occupation of Afghanistan during the 1980s.

4. Abu Musab al-Suri, *Da'wat al-Muqawama*, pp. 724–5.

5. Ibid.

6. PDF023388, Atiya to a "trusted intermediary" in Saudi Arabia.

7. PDF-023388.

8. Anne Stenersen, *Al-Qaida in Afghanistan*, Cambridge: Cambridge University Press, 2017, pp. 134–41.

9. Abu Musab al-Suri, *Da'wat al-Muqawama*, p. 787.

10. Abu Saad, "To Abu al-Faraj and 'Abd al-Hadi," November 19, 2002, ODNI, 2016.

11. PDF-003732, Ayman al-Zawahiri to Usama bin Laden, October 20, 2004.

12. Fadil Harun, *al-Harb 'ala al-Islam*, vol. 1, pp. 56–7.

13. As translated by James Howarth: Usama bin Laden, "A Muslim Bomb," in Lawrence (ed.), *Messages to the World*, pp. 71–2.

14. Ibid., p. 72. It is reported that General Hamid Gul of the ISI (Pakistan's intelligence agency) warned Usama of an imminent U.S. attack against him in retaliation for the 1998 East Africa bombings. If true, this was a reference to Operation Infinite Reach, which involved military strikes against Sudan and Afghanistan in late August 1998. See Lutfi Flissi, "al-Wasit al-Tijari li-Bin Ladin fi Qabdat al-Amn al-Jaza'iri," October 16, 2007; see also Declan Walsh, "Pakistan's Spymaster Hamid Gul: Angel of Jihad or Windbag Provocateur," *Guardian*, May 31, 2011.

15. Steve Coll, "The Unblinking Stare: The Drone War in Pakistan," *The New Yorker*, November 17, 2014, https://www.newyorker.com/magazine/2014/11/24/unblinking-stare.

16. PDF-010240, Abu Abd al-Rahman al-Subay'i to Usama bin Laden, October 13, 2010.

17. IMG-058732 (1/5), IMG-065081 (2/5), Khaled al-Habib, 2004.

18. "Guantanamo Inmates Say They Were 'Sold,'" *Associated Press*, May 31, 2005, http://www.nbcnews.com/id/8049868/ns/world_news/t/guantanamo-inmates-say-they-were-sold/.

19. This was the first interview that Ayman al-Zawahiri conducted with the jihadi media arm *al-Sahab*, transcribed by Jihadi media on October 11, 2002.

20. PDF-003604, Wakil Khan, October 18, 2004.

21. 113th Congress, 2nd Session, Senate Report 113-288, Report of the Senate Select Committee on Intelligence Committee Study of the Central Intelligence Agency's Detention and Interrogation Program, December 9, 2014, https://www.intelligence.senate.gov/sites/default/files/publica tions/CRPT-113srpt288.pdf.

22. For background on the conflict, see A.N. Yamskov, "Ethnic Conflict in the Transcaucasus: The Case of Nagorno-Karabakh," *Theory and Society*, vol. 20, no. 5, October 1991, pp. 631–60.

23. Fadil Harun, *al-Harb 'ala al-Islam*, vol. 1, p. 116. We learn from Harun's autobiography that jihadis initially considered Turkmenistan because it would have been the closest for them to pass through, then cross the Caspian Sea to get to Azerbaijan to support the Azeris. See also Abu Musab al-Suri, *Da'wat al-Muqawama*, p. 501. He notes that the President in Turkmenistan forbade the building of new mosques and the printing of additional copies of the Qur'an.

24. Fadil Harun, *al-Harb 'ala al-Islam*, vol. 1, p. 116. At the time, jihadis fighting in Afghanistan learned about the Iranian landscape through Iraqi Kurds, who had fled Saddam's regime and were trained in Iranian camps. Ironically, Sunni militants emerged from these camps opposed to the Shia regime. They went on to develop jihadi tendencies after the news of jihadis fighting the Soviets in Afghanistan reached them. About this specific point, see Hani al-Siba'i, "al-Harakat al-Islamiyya al-Jihadiyya," http://www.albasrah.net/moqawama/maqalat/sba3iansar_140304.htm.

25. My thanks to Anne Likuski (Stenersen) for pointing out that the Northern Alliance controlled the border to the north.

26. PDF-000770, PDF-000852, PDF-017029 (most likely the last one was the final letter he sent), Usama bin Laden to his brother Bakr bin Laden, December 2007. In sectarian parlance, the "Rafida" is a reference to those who rejected the legitimacy of the first three caliphs who succeeded the Prophet Muhammad, the founder of Islam, and whom Sunnis consider to be among the four "rightly guided caliphs." For the origin and usage of the term, see E. Kohlberg, "al-Rafida," *Encyclopaedia of Islam* (2). On how the first four caliphs became considered as the rightly guided caliphs in the ninth century, see Patricia Crone, *God's Rule: Government and Islam*, New York: Columbia University Press, 2004, pp. 27–8.

27. PDF-023388.

28. Ibid.

29. Ibid. PDF-010240.

30. Hamid Dabashi, "Who Is the 'Great Satan'?", *Al Jazeera*, September 20, 2015, https://www.aljazeera.com/indepth/opinion/2015/09/great-satan-150920072643884.html.

31. "President Delivers State of the Union Address," January 29, 2002, https://georgewbush-whitehouse.archives.gov/news/releases/2002/01/20020129-11.html.

32. IMG-063213, IMG-020402, Abu Hammam al-Gharib to Usama bin Laden, undated, most likely around 2009.

33. PDF-010240.

34. PDF-023388.

35. PDF-010240.

36. PDF-023388.

37. Ibid.

38. Ibid.

39. PDF-010240.

40. According to media reports, Jundallah was founded in 2002. So, it is possible that the "Baluch brothers" who supported al-Qaeda were already active in some capacity before they formed their group.

41. PDF-023513.

42. PDF-023388.

43. PDF-010240. This letter might have been an exchange with leaders of al-Qaeda in Iran before their detention: "Letter to Mawlawi 'Abd al-'Aziz," ODNI, 2016.

44. PDF-004992, Saad Bin Laden, August 5, 2008. In the same prison were Muhammad Shawqi al-Islambuli and the son of Abu Jihad.

45. PDF-004992, Saad bin Laden, August 5, 2008.

46. PDF-010240.

47. Ibid.

48. As translated in Michael Cook, *The Koran: A Very Short Introduction*, Oxford: Oxford University Press, 2000, p. 14. Those categories are best read in the broader context of chapter 2 of Cook's book.

49. PDF-010240.
50. Ibid.
51. PDF-023388.
52. Ibid.
53. "Deadly Attacks Rock Baghdad, Karbala," *CNN*, March 2, 2004, http://edition.cnn.com/2004/WORLD/meast/03/02/sprj.nirq.main/.
54. On how I dated and connected the coded words in the letter, see my study *Al-Qaʿida's Contested Relationship with Iran: The View from Abbottabad*, New America, September 2018.
55. This single two-page document can be accessed as two separate documents: "My Generous Brother Tawfiq," declassified March 1, 2016, https://www.dni.gov/files/documents/ubl2016/arabic/Arabic%20My%20Generous%20Brother%20Tawfiq.pdf; and "Letter from Hafiz," declassified May 20, 2015, https://www.dni.gov/files/documents/ubl/arabic2/Letter%20from%20Hafiz%20-%20Arabic.pdf.
56. Ibid.
57. Ibid.
58. PDF-003874, Usama bin Laden, 2004.
59. The treatise mentioned is by ʿAbd al-ʿAziz al-Jarbuʿ, and it is roughly rendered as "Select Legal Studies on the Permissibility of Committing Suicide for Fear of Disclosing Secrets."

Chapter 3: Global Jihad on Autopilot

1. PDF-023392, "trusted intermediary" from Saudi Arabia to Atiya, February 19, 2007.
2. PDF-001673, Khairiah to Hamza, 2011. Khairiah, Usama's second wife, wrote in 2011 that Asiya was then eight.
3. See A.J. Wensinck, "Asiya," *Encyclopaedia of Islam* (2). According to the biblical story (Exodus 2:5–10), the daughter of Pharaoh adopted Moses.
4. See the introductions to Usama bin Laden's public statements in Lawrence, *Messages to the World*.
5. PDF-003874, Usama bin Laden's notes.
6. Usama bin Laden, "To the Allies of America," in Lawrence, *Messages to the World*. Some in al-Qaeda were not pleased with such boasting and a 2002 letter urged the Sheikhs to admit that "we are weak" and oppressed. "To our respected Shaykhs," ODNI, 2016.
7. See above, Chapter One. He may have initially "disappeared" together with Ayman, and the two spent time "in the mountains of Tora Bora" (as Usama implies in a 2009 draft letter—PDF-003871). But when they resumed correspondence in 2004, their letters suggest that they hadn't seen each other since 2002. In February 2008, Ayman managed to meet in person with Hajji Uthman, Atiya, and Habib (PDF-023454). In August 2008, he met with Hajji Uthman and Atiya, "Letter to Shaykh Azmarai," ODNI, 2016. On Usama's attitude towards Iran in 2009, see "Letter to Haj ʿUthman," ODNI, 2017.
8. PDF-003874, Usama bin Laden's notes, late 2004. My thanks to Thomas Hegghammer for the helpful conversation we had about the events.
9. IMG-030337, Tawfiq to Usama bin Laden and Ayman al-Zawahiri, September 8, 2004.
10. IMG-058732, Khaled al-Habib to Usama bin Laden, 2004.
11. PDF-003732, Ayman al-Zawahiri to Usama bin Laden, October 20, 2004. Given that the 2004 letters suggest that Usama had been incommunicado, the 2002 letter ("Dear Brother Abu-al-Faraj and ʿAbd-al-Hadi," ODNI, 2016) is unlikely to be by him. It deals with distributing money, and my hunch is that it was by Hajji Uthman, who oversaw the financial side of al-Qaeda.
12. PDF-003967, Usama bin Laden to his sons Uthman and Muhammad, January 7, 2011.
13. Hamza al-Rabia was reported killed in 2005: *CNN*, December 4, 2005, http://www.cnn.com/2005/WORLD/asiapcf/12/03/pakistan.rabia/.
14. PDF-004000, Usama bin Laden to Hamza al-Rabia; see also PDF-003874, draft letter to Tawfiq.
15. PDF-004000.
16. Ibid.
17. PDF-023883, Atiya to Mukhtar Abu al-Zubayr, July 15, 2010.
18. We know that that the two aliases refer to Harun and Talha thanks to two references in Fadil Harun, *al-Harb ʿala al-Islam*, vol. 1, pp. 402, 474. For a study of the autobiography, see Nelly Lahoud, "Beware of Imitators: Al-Qaʿida Through the Lens of Its Confidential Secretary," CTC, 2012.

19. Fadil Harun, *al-Harb 'ala al-Islam*, vol. 1, pp. 422–3.
20. PDF-004000, Usama bin Laden to Hamza al-Rabia, 2004.
21. My thanks to Anne Likuski (Stenersen), who explained that Zikuyak "(зикояк in Russian) is an Afghan nickname for a Soviet-made anti-aircraft gun (ZGU-1), which becomes 'Ziku-yak' in Dari."
22. PDF-004000.
23. Ibid.
24. Ibid.
25. Ibid.
26. Ibid.
27. PDF-003592, Usama bin Laden to Tawfiq, late 2004.
28. "The Guantanamo Files—Abdullah Khan," *WikiLeaks*, https://wikileaks.org/gitmo/prisoner/950.html.
29. This is thoroughly covered in Anne Stenersen, *Al-Qaida in Afghanistan*, Cambridge: Cambridge University Press, 2017, pp. 134–41. To be clear, Tawfiq's letter complaining about Abdallah Khan does not mention the brigade (*liwa*) and refers to the actual al-Qaeda organization (*Tanzim*).
30. PDF-003592, Usama bin Laden, late 2004. This is explicitly stated in this letter.
31. The literal translation is "independent judgement," but in this case, it is used in a negative sense to imply unilateral decisions.
32. IMG-058732 (1/5), Khaled al-Habib to Usama bin Laden, 2004.
33. IMG-065081 (2/5), Khaled al-Habib to Usama bin Laden, 2004.
34. PDF-003604, Wakil Khan, October 18, 2004.
35. At the time of writing, Zia-ur-Rahman Madani was on the UN's Sanctions List, which stated that he "has facilitated fund raising in the gulf on behalf of the Taliban since 2003": https://www.un.org/securitycouncil/sanctions/1988/materials/summaries/individual/zia-ur-rahman-madani.
36. It is possible that Wakil Khan is the same as or the same person who later assumed the aliases Atiya and Mahmoud.
37. PDF-003732, Ayman al-Zawahiri to Usama bin Laden, October 20, 2004.
38. See above, Chapter One, specifically Usama's 2002 notes.
39. See the BBC timeline of the Madrid attacks: http://news.bbc.co.uk/2/shared/spl/hi/guides/457000/457031/html/.
40. IMG-000667 (3/5), Khaled al-Habib, 2004.
41. The missives exchanged were likely audio-recorded before being transcribed in the letters. The chronology that I propose is as follows: 1. Abu Musab sends Jaafar to meet with al-Qaeda; 2. Jaafar brings back PDF-004648 (al-Qaeda's response); 3. Abu Musab responds: PDF-003600; 4. al-Qaeda responds: PDF-004505; 5. Abu Musab responds: PDF-004325. If my chronology is correct, Abu Musab initiated the contact with al-Qaeda. This is not conclusive.
42. In April 2004, a statement signed by Abu Musab al-Zarqawi was released, as well as a video titled "Riyah al-Nasr" featuring Abu Anas al-Shami.
43. PDF-004325, Abu Musab al-Zarqawi, 2004.
44. PDF-003600, Abu Musab al-Zarqawi, 2004.
45. Ibid.
46. PDF-003592, Usama bin Laden (to Tawfiq most likely), late 2004.
47. PDF-002879, Usama bin Laden to Abu Fatima/Ayman al-Zawahiri and Tawfiq, December 9, 2004.
48. PDF-003874, Usama bin Laden's notes, late 2004. On the kaldar, see https://www.reuters.com/article/us-afghanistan-currency/afghans-slow-to-warm-to-their-stable-currency-idUSBRE85J0BZ20120620.
49. PDF-002879.
50. Ibid.
51. PDF-002653, Usama bin Laden, addendum, December 2004.
52. Usama bin Laden, "The Towers of Lebanon," trans. James Howarth, in Lawrence, *Messages to the World*, p. 244.
53. PDF-002879, Usama bin Laden to Tawfiq, December 9, 2004.
54. PDF-003128, Atiya to Usama bin Laden, June 19, 2010.
55. See, for instance, Philip Smucker, "How Bin Laden Got Away," *Christian Science Monitor*, March 4, 2002; "Tora Bora Revisited: How We Failed to Get Bin Laden," A Report to Members of the

Committee of Foreign Relations, United States Senate, November 30, 2009, https://www.govinfo.gov/content/pkg/CPRT-111SPRT53709/html/CPRT-111SPRT53709.htm.

56. Muhamad al-Shafi'i, "Muhamad Shawqi al-Islambuli (Abu Khaled) shaqiq qatil al-Sadat waffara li-A'da' "al-Qaeda" maladhan aminan fi janubi Iran," *al-Sharq al-Awsat*, issue 8942 May 23, 2003, https://archive.aawsat.com/details.asp?article=172395&issueno=8942#.X-DKUeTsEIQ.

57. AFGP-2002-003251, Abu Hudhayfa to Abu 'Abdallah (i.e., Usama bin Laden), June 21, 2000, CTC, https://ctc.usma.edu/wp-content/uploads/2013/09/A-Memo-to-Sheikh-Abu-Abdullah-Original1.pdf.

58. PDF-023388, Atiya to Bishr al-Bishr through a "trusted intermediary."

59. Muhammad al-'Ubaydi, *Khattab* (Jihadi Bios Project, ed. Nelly Lahoud), CTC, March 2015.

60. Ministry of Interior statements accessed through archive.org.

61. "Timeline: Saudi Attacks," *BBC News*, http://news.bbc.co.uk/2/hi/middle_east/3760099.stm.

62. PDF-023392, February 2007. A biography of Bishr al-Bishr can be accessed on http://www.tarhuni.org/i3teqal/olama/beshr.htm, and some of his writings may be accessed on http://www.ilmway.com/site/maqdis/MS_5647.html.

63. PDF-023514, Abu al-Tayyib from the Arabian Peninsula/Saudi Arabia to Usama bin Laden, February 25, 2008.

64. PDF-023392, "trusted intermediary" from Saudi Arabia.

65. PDF-023514, Abu al-Tayyib, February 28, 2008.

66. Robert W. Jordan with Steve Fiffer, *Desert Diplomat: Inside Saudi Arabia Following 9/11*, Sterling, VA: Potomac Books, 2015, p. 40.

67. See Report of the Senate Select Committee on Intelligence Committee Study of the Central Intelligence Agency's Detention and Interrogation Program, p. 193, ft. 1136; and also p. 205, ft. 118.

68. On the FBI's response to the presence of the Bin Ladens in the United States following 9/11, see Steve Coll, *The Bin Ladens*, in particular chs. 36–7.

69. On how "preconditions" and "precipitants" lead to terrorism, see Martha Crenshaw's superb article "The Causes of Terrorism," *Comparative Politics*, vol. 13, no. 4, July, 1981, pp. 379–99.

70. Usama bin Laden, "Depose the Tyrants," in Lawrence, *Messages to the World*.

71. PDF-002879, Usama bin Laden to Abu Fatima and Tawfiq, December 9, 2004.

72. As translated and cited in Martin Lings, *Muhammad: His Life Based on the Earliest Sources*, p. 171. With thanks to Michael Cook for stressing the importance of the name.

73. SOCOM-2012-0000016, Usama bin Laden notes.

74. "US Judge: Saudi Royals Must Answer Question in 9/11 Lawsuit," *Associated Press*, September 11, 2020, https://apnews.com/article/lawsuits-archive-courts-ac77fbfb343c5133019153eb864a820d.

75. PDF-023392, "trusted intermediary."

76. PDF-023514, Abu al-Tayyib from the Arabian Peninsula.

77. PDF-023392, "trusted intermediary."

78. Ibid. I am reading the Arabic word *abdannahum* as the plural of verbal form IV "Abdana," which means "to offer a fattened cow or she-camel as a sacrifice." See almaany.com.

79. PDF-023514, Abu al-Tayyib from the Arabian Peninsula.

Chapter 4: Al-Qaeda "Hides"

1. PDF-003874, Usama bin Laden notes, late 2004.

2. Ibid.

3. PDF-003592, Usama bin Laden, draft letter intended for Tawfiq, late 2004.

4. PDF-003874, Usama bin Laden, draft letter, late 2004.

5. PDF-002879, Usama bin Laden to Abu Fatima and Tawfiq, December 4, 2004.

6. Ibid.

7. PDF-003592, Usama bin Laden, draft letter intended for Tawfiq, late 2004.

8. AFGP-2002-000112: see article 6, the Arabic version, CTC.

9. PDF-003592.

10. Ibid.

11. Ibid. See "Firasa," *Encyclopaedia of Islam* (2), "a technique of inductive divination which permits the foretelling of moral conditions and psychological behavior from external indications and physical states." I don't have the sense that Usama meant it to that extent.

12. PDF-003592, Usama bin Laden, draft letter intended for Tawfiq, late 2004.

13. Ibid.

14. On the competing views as to who thought of founding the Services Bureau, see Thomas Hegghammer, *The Caravan: Abdallah Azzam and the Rise of Global Jihad*, Cambridge: Cambridge University Press, 2020, esp. pp. 206–13.

15. Ibid., p. 341.

16. *Tarikh al-Ma'sada*, CTC. On the various interpretations of these documents, see the summary in Hegghammer, *The Caravan*, pp. 352–6. See also Mustafa Hamid and Leah Farrall, *The Arabs at War in Afghanistan*, London: Hurst, 2015, pp. 107–12.

17. *Tarikh al-Ma'sada*, CTC.

18. It is somewhat puzzling that it was also called Ma'sadat al-Ansar instead of Ma'sadat al-Muhajirun (see above, Chapter One). Perhaps the name was out of deference to the Afghans, or most likely it was used in a literal sense to signify "helpers" without the *ansar/muhajirun* connotation?

19. *Tarikh al-Ma'sada*, CTC.

20. PDF-003592, Usama bin Laden's draft letter intended for Tawfiq, late 2004.

21. I benefited from much consultation/*shura* with Michael Cook about this issue.

22. We glean this from PDF-023945, Ayman al-Zawahiri's January 2011 letter to Usama bin Laden.

23. About the case against the BIF, see https://www.treasury.gov/resource-center/terrorist-illicit-finance/Pages/protecting-charities_execorder_13224-b.aspx.

24. PDF-003592, Usama bin Laden's draft letter to Tawfiq, late 2004.

25. PDF-023950, Abu Yahya al-Libi, most likely to the North African group, 2009.

26. PDF-003592, Usama bin Laden's draft letter for Tawfiq, late 2004.

27. PDF-003874, Usama's notes, 2004.

28. PDF-004119, Jargh al-Din to Abd al-Rahman al-Maghrebi, most likely early 2005.

29. Ibid.

30. A 2010 letter by Atiya alludes to this, but we cannot be sure.

31. PDF-023429, Abu Abdallah al-Halabi/Daoud to Abu Sulaiman/Khaled (Usama's son), *c.* December 18, 2007. Tawfiq is here referred to as Abu Ubaida al-Misri.

32. Craig Whitlock and Karen DeYoung, "Senior Al-Qaeda Commander Believed to Be Dead," *Washington Post*, April 10, 2008, https://www.washingtonpost.com/wp-dyn/content/article/2008/04/09/AR2008040901793.html?hpid=moreheadlines.

33. PDF-017949, most likely Atiya to Usama bin Laden and Hajji Uthman. Hajji Uthman is Mustafa Abu al-Yazid, and he also goes by several aliases, including Sheikh Saeed and Hafiz Sultan.

34. PDF-023566, Internal Report, around July–August 2008.

35. IMG-031090 (1/5).

36. Brian Glyn Williams, *Predators: The CIA's Drone War on al Qaeda*, Washington, D.C.: Potomac Books, 2013, p. 12.

37. Ibid., pp. 11–12.

38. Abubakar Siddique, cited in Coll, "The Unblinking Stare."

39. See Williams, *Predators*, p. 44.

40. Coll, "The Unblinking Stare.".

41. Craig Whitlock and Kamran Khan, "Blast in Pakistan Kills Al Qaeda Commander: Figure Reportedly Hit by U.S. Missile Strike," *Washington Post*, December 4, 2005, https://www.washingtonpost.com/wp-dyn/content/article/2005/12/03/AR2005120301473_pf.html.

42. Al-Sahab Video, September 2005. In his *The Al Qaeda Factor: Plots Against the West*, University of Pennsylvania Press, 2012, Mitchell D. Silber notes that "an official inquiry by the British government reported that the tape claiming responsibility had been edited after the attacks and that the bombers had no direct support from al-Qaeda," p. 124.

43. PDF-018260, Hajji Uthman to Usama bin Laden, March 1, 2006.

44. http://news.bbc.co.uk/2/hi/uk_news/8243799.stm.

45. PDF-017949, most likely Atiya to Usama bin Laden and Hajji Uthman.

46. Atiya to Usama bin Laden, 22 August 2009, ODNI, March 2016.

47. PDF-004588, PDF-003627, PDF-023584, Usama bin Laden to Atiya and Abu Yahya al-Libi, December 5, 2010. Consulting with Michael Cook about these letters was most helpful.

48. PDF-023945, Ayman al-Zawahiri to Usama bin Laden, January 2011.

49. PDF-023405, Hajji Uthman to Usama bin Laden, October 2007; see also PDF-023447, Atiya to Usama bin Laden, March–June 2008.

50. PDF-023405.

NOTES to pp. 95–103

51. PDF-017045, Usama bin Laden to Hajji Uthman, December 17, 2007.
52. PDF-023447, Atiya to Usama bin Laden, March–June 2008.
53. PDF-003774, Usama bin Laden to Ayman al-Zawahiri, May 7, 2008. Ayman wanted Usama's advice on whether to send a detailed letter to Mullah Omar, knowing that it was going to be read by those who disliked al-Qaeda; see PDF-023454, Ayman al-Zawahiri to Usama bin Laden, March 5, 2008.
54. Ibid.
55. PDF-023900, Ayman al-Zawahiri to Usama bin Laden, May 16, 2010. Different kinds of divisions within the Afghan Taliban over money are reported in a March 2011 letter: "Please Give Me Your News," ODNI, 2016.
56. PDF-004029, Atiya to Usama bin Laden, July 8, 2010.
57. PDF-004835, Usama bin Laden to Mullah Omar, September 24, 2010.
58. It can be accessed on https://www.state.gov/wp-content/uploads/2020/02/Agreement-For-Bringing-Peace-to-Afghanistan-02.29.20.pdf.
59. Eleventh Report of the Analytical Support and Sanctions Monitoring Team, United Nations Security Council, May 27, 2020.
60. "Tahni'at al-Umma al-Islamiyya 'ala Nasri Allah fi Afghanistan al-Abiyya," *al-Sahab*, August 2021.
61. Ayman al-Zawahiri, "Nasihat al-Umma al-Muwahhida bi-Haqiqat al-Umam al-Muttahida," November 23, 2021; Michelle Nichols, "Taliban names Afghan U.N. envoy, asks to speak to world leaders," Reuters, September 21, 2021, https://www.reuters.com/world/asia-pacific/exclusive-taliban-names-afghan-un-envoy-asks-speak-world-leaders-2021-09-21/

Chapter 5: The "Calamity"

1. PDF-004402, Security Committee Report, May 17, 2010.
2. Peter Bergen, David Sterman, and Melissa Salyk-Virk, "America's Counterterrorism Wars: Tracking the United States' Drone Strikes and Other Operations in Pakistan, Yemen, Somalia, and Libya," *New America*, https://www.newamerica.org/international-security/reports/americas-counterterrorism-wars/.
3. Bob Woodward, *Obama's Wars*, New York: Simon & Schuster, 2010, p. 5.
4. PDF-003128, Atiya to Usama bin Laden, June 19, 2010. See also PDF-023767, Hajji Uthman to Usama bin Laden, March 8, 2010.
5. "Some Reactions to the Speech of al-Hafiz Abu Talhah al-Almani," ODNI, 2016.
6. PDF-003128, Atiya to Usama bin Laden, June 19, 2010.
7. PDF-023844, Elisabeth Anna Windischmann to Usama bin Laden.
8. Williams, *Predators*, p. 12.
9. PDF-003128.
10. PDF-010898, Daoud to Usama bin Laden, middle of 2010. When news of Usama's family being released from Iran was confirmed, Daoud asked Usama whether he should "arrange housing for them in Karachi or Baluchistan."
11. PDF-003874, Usama's notes, 2004.
12. Syed Shoaib Hasan, "Islamabad's Red Mosque," *BBC News*, July 27, 2007.
13. Usama bin Laden, "Hayya 'ala al-Jihad—Kalima ila Ahli Pakistan," August 2007.
14. PDF-023447, Atiya to Usama bin Laden, May–June 2008.
15. Ibid.
16. PDF-023513, Hajji Uthman to Usama bin Laden, April 16, 2008.
17. Ibid.
18. Bruce Riedel, "Al Qaeda's Latest Loss," *Brookings*, June 4, 2011, https://www.brookings.edu/opinions/al-qaedas-latest-loss/
19. Ibid. On the Mumbai attacks, see Soutik Biswas, "Mumbai 26/11 Attacks: Six Corpses, a Mobile Phone Call and One Survivor," *BBC*, November 26, 2018, https://www.bbc.com/news/world-asia-india-46314555.
20. PDF-003776, Muhammad Ilyas Kashmiri to Usama bin Laden, May 31, 2010.
21. PDF-023513, Hajji Uthman to Usama bin Laden, April 16, 2008.
22. "Jihad in Pakistan," ODNI, 2016.
23. "Key Afghanistan Taliban Commander Killed in US Air Strike," *BBC*, December 2, 2018, https://www.bbc.com/news/world-asia-46418776.

316

24. PDF-023566, Internal Report, June 2008.
25. PDF-023568, list of names to be read alongside PDF-023566.
26. "Obituary: Hakimullah Mehsud," *BBC*, November 1, 2013, https://www.bbc.co.uk/news/world-asia-24464506.
27. PDF-023566.
28. Steve Coll, "The Unblinking Stare: The Drone War in Pakistan," *The New Yorker*, November 17, 2014, https://www.newyorker.com/magazine/2014/11/24/unblinking-stare.
29. Bergen, Sterman, and Salyk-Virk, "America's Counterterrorism Wars." CIA drone attacks were used as early as October 7, 2001 in Afghanistan, see Audrey Kurth Cronin, "The Future of America's Drone Campaign: Time for a Clean Break With a Failed Approach," *Foreign Affairs*, October 14, 2021, https://www.foreignaffairs.com/articles/afghanistan/2021-10-14/future-americas-drone-campaign
30. Zahid Ali Khan, "Military Operations in FATA and PATA: Implications for Pakistan," ISSI-Islamabad, 2014, http://www.issi.org.pk/wp-content/uploads/2014/06/1339999992_58398784.pdf.
31. Woodward, *Obama's Wars*, p. 5.
32. PDF-023750, Hajji Uthman to Usama bin Laden, October 18, 2009.
33. PDF-023767, Hajji Uthman to Usama bin Laden, March 8, 2010. Al-Maghrebi's name is included in SOCOM-2012-0000012, which contains the names of those released from Iran, https://ctc.usma.edu/app/uploads/2013/09/Letter-from-Atiyahtullah-Al-Libi-Original.pdf.
34. PDF-004402, Security Committee Report, May 17, 2010.
35. PDF-004413, Hajji Uthman to Usama bin Laden, April 14, 2010.
36. PDF-023765, Hajji Uthman to Usama bin Laden, March–April 2010.
37. Matthew Rosenberg, "C.I.A. Cash Ended Up in Coffers of Al Qaeda," *The New York Times*, March 14, 2015, https://www.nytimes.com/2015/03/15/world/asia/cia-funds-found-their-way-into-al-qaeda-coffers.html.
38. Usama bin Laden, "Risala ila Ikhwanina fi Pakistan—wa-Qatiluhum," May 2009. Note that he avoided saying "jihad in Pakistan," most likely heeding Atiya's advice.
39. Ayman al-Zawahiri, "Ikhwani wa-Akhawati al-Muslimin fi Pakistan," June 2009.
40. PDF-004555, Atiya to Usama bin Laden, October 6, 2010.
41. PDF-003128, Atiya to Usama bin Laden, June 19, 2010.
42. PDF-002659, Atiya to Usama bin Laden, July 17, 2010.
43. Ibid.
44. Lutfi Flissi, "al-Wasit al-Tijari li-Bin Ladin fi Qabdat al-Aman al-Jaza'iri," *al-Shuruq Online*, October 16, 2007; Declan Walsh, "Pakistan's Spymaster Hamid Gul: Angel of Jihad or Windbag Provocateur," *Guardian*, May 31, 2011.
45. PDF-002659, Atiya to Usama bin Laden, July 17, 2010.
46. Ibid.
47. Ibid.
48. SOCOM-2012-0000004, Adam Gadahn to al-Qaeda's leaders, January 2011.
49. SOCOM-2012-0000015, Usama bin Laden to Atiya, October 21, 2010. Two months later, Usama wrote to Mullah Omar, urging him to release public statements condemning indiscriminate attacks such as those carried out by the Pakistani Taliban. "To Emir Al-Mo'mineen," ODNI, 2016.
50. SOCOM-2012-0000007, Atiya and Abu Yahya to Hakimullah Mehsud, December 3, 2010.
51. PDF-003213, Atiya and Abu Yahya al-Libi to Hakimullah Mehsud, December 3, 2010.
52. Ibid.
53. PDF-004402, Security Committee Report.
54. For the timeline of drones in Yemen and Somalia, see Bergen, Sterman, and Salyk-Virk, "America's Counterterrorism Wars." Yemen: https://www.newamerica.org/in-depth/americas-counterterrorism-wars/us-targeted-killing-program-yemen/; Somalia: https://www.newamerica.org/in-depth/americas-counterterrorism-wars/somalia/.
55. PDF-004345, Atiya to jihadis in Yemen, Somalia, and beyond on how to evade drones, June–July 2010. I am grateful to Stuart Caudill, who served in the U.S. Army and read an earlier version of this chapter. Though he could not share classified information with me, it was most helpful discussing with him al-Qaeda's findings.

56. See Air Combat Command, "RQ-1/MQ-1 Predator Unmanned Aerial Vehicle," November 5, 2008, https://www.acc.af.mil/About-Us/Fact-Sheets/Display/Article/199130/rq-1mq-1-predator-unmanned-aerial-vehicle/; Air Force Technology, "Predator RQ-1/MQ-1/MQ-9 Reaper UAV," https://www.airforce-technology.com/projects/predator-uav/; U.S. Air Force, "MQ-1B Predator," September 23, 2015, https://www.af.mil/About-Us/Fact-Sheets/Display/Article/104469/mq-1b-predator/; Air Force Technology, "Predator RQ-1/MQ-1/MQ-9 Reaper UAV," https://www.airforce-technology.com/projects/predator-uav/; U.S. Air Force, "MQ-9 Reaper," https://www.af.mil/About-Us/Fact-Sheets/Display/Article/104470/mq-9-reaper/.
57. Coll, "The Unblinking Stare."
58. PDF-003157, Usama bin Laden to Ayman al-Zawahiri, October 16, 2010.
59. PDF-002730, Atiya to Usama bin Laden (with Atiya's responses in brackets), October 11, 2010.
60. The parts of Woodward's *Obama's Wars* in the document are largely based on pp. 1–8.
61. PDF-004946, notes about and excerpts from Woodward's book *Obama's Wars* shared with Usama bin Laden.
62. PDF-002746, Usama bin Laden to Atiya, January 6, 2011.
63. PDF-005032, Atiya to Usama bin Laden (with Atiya's responses in brackets), January 26, 2011.
64. Ibid.
65. PDF-004402, Security Committee Report.
66. See "Defending Privacy," in Michael Cook, *Commanding Right and Forbidding Wrong in Islamic Thought*, Cambridge: Cambridge University Press, 2000, pp. 80–2.
67. Abu Yahya al-Libi, *al-Mu'lim fi Hukm al-Jasus al-Muslim* (A Guide to the Legal Judgement Concerning a Muslim Spy), Markaz al-Fajr al-I'lami, 2009.
68. Mark Mazzetti, "Officer Failed to Warn C.I.A. Before Attack," *The New York Times*, October 19, 2010, https://www.nytimes.com/2010/10/20/world/asia/20intel.html.
69. PDF-004402, Security Committee Report.
70. Ibid.
71. As discussed in previous chapters, al-Qaeda's 2002 Mombasa attacks were planned in 2000 and the operatives who carried them out were dispatched to East Africa before 9/11.
72. PDF-003592, Usama bin Laden, late 2004.
73. Atiya to Usama bin Laden, August 22, 2009, ODNI, 2016. Atiya had received a report about the "external work" (PDF-023842) that details the difficulties in carrying out international terrorism. In 2008, Usama wanted al-Qaeda to attack Denmark in response to the publication of cartoons that featured a caricature of the Prophet Muhammad ("Dear honorable brother Shaykh Azmaray," ODNI, 2016). But we learn from a 2010 letter by Usama that al-Qaeda's "capabilities were not sufficient" to mount such an attack and could only "target the Danish embassy in Islamabad" (PDF-002772).
74. Ibid.
75. "New York Terror Case: Indictment Announced," The FBI, September, 24, 2009, https://archives.fbi.gov/archives/news/stories/2009/september/zazi_092409; Peter Bergen, *United States of Jihad: Who are America's Homegrown Terrorists, and How Do We Stop Them?*, New York: Crown Publishers, 2016, Chapter "Leader-Led Jihad"; Erica Orden, "Najibullah Zazi, who plotted to bomb the New York subway, gets a second chance," CNN, September 28, 2019, https://www.cnn.com/2019/05/01/us/najibullah-zazi-new-york-subway-bomb-plot-sentencing/index.html. My thanks to Peter Bergen for a very helpful conversation about these issues.
76. PDF-023772, Muhannad al-Abyani/Tufan, "Arhibuhum," February 13, 2010; subsequently, inspired by Tufan, Abu-Salih Al Somali wrote in 2010 about the use of hydrogen peroxide in bombs. His manual—PDF-010805 - "Terror Franchise: The Unstoppable Assassin Techs Vital role for its success"—describes "Arhibuhum" as "extremely important" and should be followed. It is reported that the 7/7 London bombings, the 2006 and 2009 failed plots were all orchestrated by the same person, Rashid Rauf, and a certain Salah al-Somali was involved. (See Raffaello Pantucci, "A Biography of Rashid Rauf: Al-Qa'ida's British Operative," *CTC Sentinel*, July 2012, Vol. 5, Issue 7.) Neither Tufan's treatise, which the leaders of al-Qaeda refused to publish, nor Abu-Salih's manual, suggest that the two men had any intimate knowledge of the 7/7 London bombings or the failed 2006 and 2009 plots. On the views of al-Qaeda's leaders about Tufan's plans, see PDF-023884, Atiya to Usama bin Laden, August 28, 2010; PDF-003133, Usama bin Laden to Atiya, September 25, 2010.
77. PDF-023935, Hajji Uthman to Usama bin Laden, January 25, 2010.
78. PDF-003128, Atiya to Usama bin Laden, June 19, 2010.
79. Atiya to bin Laden, November 2010, ODNI.

Chapter 6: The "Americans"

1. PDF-004225, Usama bin Laden draft letter to Hajji Uthman and Atiya, early 2010.
2. PDF-011006, Younis al-Mauritani to Usama bin Laden, March 18, 2010.
3. PDF-003702, Usama bin Laden to Younis al-Mauritani. Most likely, this was the first letter that Usama sent him.
4. This is a 220-page handwritten document (family document).
5. PDF-004384, Usama bin Laden to Atiya, July 5, 2010.
6. Al-Suri, *Da'wat al-Muqawama*, p. 726.
7. Ibid., pp. 54, 726.
8. PDF-004225, Usama bin Laden draft letter to Hajji Uthman and Atiya, early 2010.
9. As translated by James Howarth, in Lawrence, *Messages to the World*, p. 105. Usama was often poised when he delivered his public statements, but when he delivered his *qasam*, his tone was noticeably different. It can be accessed at https://archive.org/details/Qasam-Benladen.
10. Eric Tucker and Michael Balsamo, "US to Send Home Some Saudi Military Students After Shooting," *Associated Press*, January 12, 2020, https://apnews.com/726126ca1c1e0afb752b3323 4201137c.
11. Muhammad Saeed al-Shamrani, "Ayyuha al-Sha'b al-Amriki," December 6, 2019.
12. PDF-004225, Usama bin Laden draft letter to Hajji Uthman and Atiya, early 2010. See also PDF-003959 (similar draft).
13. PDF-004225.
14. PDF-004225, PDF-003959.
15. PDF-004225, PDF-003959.
16. As translated by James Howarth, in Lawrence, *Messages to the World*, p. 141.
17. PDF-004225, PDF-003959.
18. PDF-004225. The U.S. population was higher, see the table at https://www.multpl.com/united-states-population/table/by-year.
19. PDF-004225, PDF-003959.
20. For example, Usama did not seem to be aware that military conscription predates American independence and that several conscription laws had been enacted prior to the Vietnam War. It was Lyndon B. Johnson (and not Richard Nixon) who expanded the conscription law out of concern that minorities were bearing the brunt due to exemptions favoring white men. See Timothy J. Perri, "The Evolution of Military Conscription in the United States," *The Independent Review*, vol. 17, no. 3, Winter 2013, pp. 429–39; Michael Beschloss, *Presidents of War: The Epic Story, from 1807 to Modern Times*, New York: Broadway Books, 2019, p. 546; Max Hastings, *Vietnam: An Epic Tragedy, 1945–75*, New York: Harper Perennial, 2019, p. 161.
21. Hastings, *Vietnam*, pp. 384–6. Stanley Karnow, *Vietnam: A History*, 2nd edn., New York: Penguin Books, 1997, pp. 613, 625.
22. PDF-004225. See also "Letter to Shaykh Mahmud 2," ODNI, 2017.
23. PDF-003776, Muhammad Ilyas Kashmiri to Usama bin Laden, May 31, 2010.
24. PDF-023884, PDF-002746.
25. PDF-003871, Usama bin Laden to Ayman al-Zawahiri, 2009.
26. PDF-023888, Atiya to Abu Basir, July 18, 2010 (the letter includes excerpts of Usama's guidance).
27. "Letter Dtd 5 April 2011," ODNI, 2015.
28. PDF-023908, Ayman al-Zawahiri to Usama bin Laden, May 31, 2010.
29. PDF-023935, Hajji Uthman to Usama bin Laden, January 25, 2010.
30. PDF-004350, Younis al-Mauritani to Usama bin Laden, March 25, 2010. This is also reported in an interview with Belmokhtar himself. See the study by Andrew Wojtanik, "Mokhtar Belmokhtar: One-Eyed Firebrand of North Africa and the Sahel," ed. Nelly Lahoud, Jihadi Bios Project, CTC, February 2015. The original interview with Belmokhtar can be accessed at https://www.menadefense.net/algerie/les-clins-doeils-du-borgne-belaouar-sexprime-dans-un-entretien/.
31. PDF-004436, Report by Younis al-Mauritani, August 14, 2007.
32. PDF-004350, Younis al-Mauritani to Usama bin Laden, March 25, 2010.
33. PDF-023935, Hajji Uthman to Usama bin Laden, January 25, 2010.
34. This is from Usama's first interview after 9/11. As translated by James Howarth, in Lawrence, *Messages to the World*, p. 128.
35. PDF-004350, Younis al-Mauritani to Usama bin Laden, March 25, 2010.

36. Ibid.
37. PDF-003181, Usama bin Laden to Younis al-Mauritani, March 17, 2010.
38. See EIA—US Energy Information Administration, https://www.eia.gov/dnav/pet/hist/LeafHandler.ashx?n=PET&s=MCRIMUS1&f=M.
39. PDF-004225, Usama bin Laden draft letter to Hajji Uthman and Atiya, early 2010.
40. I am grateful to Kurt Albaugh (U.S. Navy) for the valuable discussion we had about this section on May 12, 2020.
41. McRaven, *Spec Ops*, p. 9.
42. Interview with Kurt Albaugh. He added that "AIS was definitely in use in 2010—I'm just not sure about the ability to access that information via the internet."
43. Interview with Kurt Albaugh. For more on this, see https://www.wartsila.com/encyclopedia/term/draught-marks.
44. PDF-003181.
45. Interview with Kurt Albaugh. About the U.S. geographic commands, see https://www.centcom.mil/ABOUT-US/COMPONENT-COMMANDS/.
46. PDF-011131, Usama bin Laden to Ayman al-Zawahiri, December 3, 2010.
47. PDF-002772, Usama bin Laden to Younis al-Mauritani, July 6, 2010.
48. PDF-003128, Atiya to Usama bin Laden, June 19, 2010.
49. PDF-003775, Usama bin Laden to Younis al-Mauritani, September 25, 2010.
50. PDF-004740, Usama bin Laden to Atiya, December 3, 2010.
51. PDF-000939, Usama bin Laden to Atiya, April 26, 2011.
52. "Al-Qaeda Chief Younis al-Mauritani Held, says Pakistan," *BBC* September 5, 2011.
53. Ahmed Mohamed, "Mauritania Sentences Alleged al-Qaida Leader to 20 years," *Associated Press*, April 21, 2015.
54. Interview with General (Ret.) Joseph L. Votel, June 16, 2020. General Votel's observations were made in response to my summary of Usama's plans and objectives. Details of his decorated U.S. military career can be accessed at https://www.defense.gov/Our-Story/Biographies/Biography/Article/602777/general-joseph-l-votel/.
55. For the full text, see Public Law 107-40-Sept. 18, 2001, https://www.congress.gov/107/plaws/publ40/PLAW-107publ40.pdf.
56. See Nelly Lahoud and Liam Collins, "How the CT Community Failed to Anticipate the Islamic State," *Democracy and Security*, August 2016.

Chapter 7: Some "Brothers" Are More Brotherly Than Others

1. The 2002 Mombasa attacks were able to be carried out owing to the fact al-Qaeda had dispatched its operatives to East Africa pre-9/11, in 2000.
2. Brian M. Jenkins, "The New Age of Terrorism, The RAND Corporation," p. 119, https://www.rand.org/content/dam/rand/pubs/reprints/2006/RAND_RP1215.pdf.
3. This chapter draws in part on Nelly Lahoud, "Bin Laden's Catastrophic Success: Al Qaeda Changed the World—But Not in the Way It Expected," *Foreign Affairs*, September–October 2021. https://www.foreignaffairs.com/articles/afghanistan/2021-08-13/osama-bin-ladens-911-catastrophic-success
4. For the full text, see Public Law 107-40-Sept. 18, 2001, https://www.congress.gov/107/plaws/publ40/PLAW-107publ40.pdf.
5. It should be noted that in the eyes of jihadis, Muslims who do not support jihadism do not qualify as "brothers." Instead, they are designated as "apostates," "hypocrites," "heretics," and the like.
6. PDF-002730, Atiya and Usama bin Laden, October 11, 2010.
7. PDF-023401, most likely Atiya, 2007.
8. PDF-023956, Atiya to Mukhtar Abu al-Zubayr, December 27, 2010.
9. PDF-023392, Bishr al-Bishr relayed this to Atiya's "trusted intermediary" in Saudi Arabia, February 19, 2007.
10. "U.S. Secretary of State Colin Powell Addresses the U.N. Security Council," February 5, 2003, https://georgewbush-whitehouse.archives.gov/news/releases/2003/02/20030205-1.html.
11. This first came to my attention in Fuad Hussein, *al-Zarqawi: al-Jil al-Thani li-al-Qa'ida*, Beirut: Dar al-Khayal, 2005. But the essay might have already been in circulation on jihadi websites. I

am one of those who had relied on this essay in my previous research to assess the early history between Abu Musab and Usama, which I now know to be false.

12. If the essay was not drafted by Saif and highly edited by Iranian authorities, it would not surprise me if elements within Ansar al-Sunna were behind it. They would have known about Abu Musab's background and his travel to Afghanistan. This will become clearer in the course of this chapter.

13. PDF-002730, Atiya and Usama bin Laden, November 10, 2010.

14. For superb background on Abu Musab al-Zarqawi, see Joby Warrick, *Black Flags: The Rise of ISIS*, New York: Doubleday, 2015, the first seven chapters.

15. On one of the papers, he notes that he wrote the introduction and conclusion in his own handwriting, but he asked a "brother" to help him write the rest because he was too busy. It is unlikely that the "brother" did the drawings.

16. See above, Chapter Two.

17. See "Ansar al-Islam," *Al Jazeera*, February 9, 2004, https://www.aljazeera.net/encyclopedia/movementsandparties/2014/2/9/%D8%A3%D9%86%D8%B5%D8%A7%D8%B1-%D8%A7%D9%84%D8%A5%D8%B3%D9%84%D8%A7%D9%85; and "Ansar al-Islam al-Kirdiyya. Min al-Ta'sis hatta 'Daesh,'" December 21, 2019, http://www.islamist-movements.com/32212.

18. PDF-003600, Abu Musab al-Zarqawi to al-Qaeda, early 2004.

19. Cited in "Syria Backs 'Iraqi People' in War," *CNN*, March 31, 2003, https://www.cnn.com/2003/WORLD/meast/03/31/sprj.irq.us.syria/.

20. See "Zarqawi Beheaded US Man in Iraq," *BBC*, May 13, 2004, http://news.bbc.co.uk/2/hi/middle_east/3712421.stm.

21. PDF-003604, Wakil Khan, October 18, 2004.

22. "Iraqis Welcome Exiled Cleric Home," *BBC*, May 12, 2003, http://news.bbc.co.uk/2/hi/middle_east/3019831.stm.

23. IMG-019664. The note is littered with sectarian language that draws on the civil wars in early Islam, e.g., "Basra belongs to those who follow *ahl al-Bayt*" and "bullets would be fired into the heads of Mu'awiya and Yazid's descendants."

24. PDF-003604, Wakil Khan, October 18, 2004.

25. The term "doctor" is used in Abu Musab's letter. Al-Qaeda's letter has "the companion of the Father."

26. PDF-004648, unknown, related to Abu Musab al-Zarqawi, 2004.

27. PDF-003223, Usama bin Laden to Atiya, 2010.

28. These are guided by two Hadiths (reported sayings and deeds of the Prophet Muhammad). The first suggests that Muslims should think well of fellow Muslims (*husn al-zann*)—Jami' al-Tirmidhi 3604f, Bk. 48, Hadith 240. The second (*yara al-shahid ma la yara al-gha'ib*) is in the spirit of Musnad Ahmad 628/Bk. 5, Hadith 65. The two Hadiths can be searched on Sunnah.com. Letters reflect that Usama and his associates were guided by these Hadiths—see, for instance, PDF-023513 and PDF-002879.

29. PDF-003600, Abu Musab al-Zarqawi to al-Qaeda leaders, 2004.

30. PDF-002879, Usama bin Laden to Abu Fatima/Ayman and Tawfiq, December 9, 2004.

31. PDF-023401, an exchange between Atiya and an intermediary with a senior position in the jihadi media outlet Markaz al-Fajr and who used to assist Ansar al-Sunna with their media.

32. Atiya to Abu Musab al-Zarqawi, December 12, 2005, https://ctc.usma.edu/wp-content/uploads/2013/10/Atiyahs-Letter-to-Zarqawi-Original.pdf.

33. PDF-017949, most likely Atiya to Usama bin Laden and Hajji Uthman, 2006. The letter transcribed a series of voice messages from Abu Musab al-Zarqawi.

34. Ibid.

35. PDF-017785, Ayman al-Zawahiri to Abu Abdallah al-Shafii, January 26, 2006.

36. Ibid.

37. PDF-018260, Hajji Uthman to Usama bin Laden, March 1, 2006.

38. Atiya, "Kalimat fi Nusrat Dawlat al-'Iraq al-Islamiyya," December 13, 2006.

39. Atiya began releasing public statements in 2005, and in early 2006, he took part in a lengthy Q&A online. It was in December 2007 that Usama tasked him with being one of the official spokesmen of al-Qaeda. See PDF-017045, Usama bin Laden to Hajji Uthman, December 17, 2007.

40. Hamid al-Ali, response to a question on his website, April 4, 2007.

41. PDF-004928, Usama bin Laden to Ayman al-Zawahiri, 2007.
42. IMG-067996, IMG-053227, IMG-051717, Abu Hamza al-Muhajir to Abu Abdallah al-Shafii, April 29, 2007.
43. PDF-003740, Abu Abdallah al-Shafii to Abu Hamza al-Muhajir, 2007
44. PDF-003596, two letters: the original text by Abu al-'Abbas, the deputy leader of Ansar al-Sunna; and in brackets, the responses from Raja from al-Qaeda.
45. PDF-023425, Ayman al-Zawahiri to Abu Omar al-Baghdadi, March 6, 2008.
46. PDF-023401, Atiya, June–July 2007.
47. Ibid.
48. PDF-123763, a detailed report prepared by "Your brothers in the Ministry of Legal Affairs, Islamic State of Iraq," 2007.
49. Al-Mawardi, *The Ordinances of Government*, trans. Wafaa H. Wahba, Reading, England: Center for Muslim Contribution to Civilization, 1996, p. 4.
50. David Petraeus, "How We Won in Iraq," *Foreign Policy*, October 29, 2013.
51. PDF-003212, letter addressed to Hafiz Sultan/Hajji Uthman; see also PDF-009341.
52. PDF-023513, Hajji Uthman to Usama bin Laden, April 16, 2018 (he indicates that they hadn't heard from them for about four months).
53. PDF-023447, Atiya to Usama bin Laden, March or April 2008.
54. PDF-004555, Atiya to Usama bin Laden, October 6, 2010.
55. PDF-002935, Usama Bin Laden notes, middle of 2010.
56. PDF-004433, Majlis Shura, Islamic State of Iraq, 2010. For background on Abu Bakr al-Baghdadi, see William McCants, "The Believer: How an Introvert with a Passion for Religion and Soccer Became the Leader of the Islamic State," *Brookings*, 2015, http://csweb.brookings.edu/content/research/essays/2015/thebeliever.html.
57. "Baghdad Church Hostage Drama Ends in Bloodbath," *BBC*, November 1, 2010.
58. PDF-023945, Ayman al-Zawahiri to Usama bin Laden, January 13, 2011.
59. PDF-002935, Usama bin Laden notes, middle of 2010.
60. Abu Muhammad al-Adnani, "Udhran Amir al-Qaeda," May 2014.
61. Ayman al-Zawahiri, "Qadaya Sakhina," interview with al-Sahab, August 2006.
62. Ayman discusses this "Initiative" in his *Fursan tahta Rayat al-Nabi* (Knights under the Banner of the Prophet), pp. 181–200.
63. PDF-004992, Saad bin Laden to Usama bin Laden, August 5, 2008.
64. Dr. Fadl, *al-Ta'riya* (1), *al-Masri al-Yawm*, November 18, 2008, https://www.almasryalyoum.com/news/details/1930360.
65. About Dr. Fadl's treatise, see Nelly Lahoud, *The Jihadis' Path to Self-Destruction*, London/New York: Hurst/Columbia University Press, 2010, pp. 232–39.
66. PDF-003871, Usama bin Laden to Ayman al-Zawahiri, 2009.
67. PDF-023532, Muhammad Khalil al-Hakayma/Abd al-Hakim al-Afghani/Harun to Ayman al-Zawahiri, February 11, 2008.
68. IMG-059923, Abu Haidara Abd al-Razzaq Amari al-Awrasi (?), leader of the 5th Region, to Usama bin Laden, February 12, 2004.
69. Salima Mellah and Jean-Baptiste Rivoire, "El Para, the Maghreb's Bin Laden," *Le Monde Diplomatique*, February 2005, https://mondediplo.com/2005/02/04algeria.
70. PDF-023749, a list of several letters from different leaders in AQIM addressed to Raja' (most likely another alias for Atiya). The letters were composed between January 20 and May 6, 2009. Note that the ODNI in 2017 declassified an "addendum" about AQIM by Saleh/Younis al-Mauritani, dated August 19, 2007 and its contents are inaccurate, because Saleh was not a member of AQIM, but from al-Murabitun. The document I am citing is by the leader of AQIM and those closest to him.
71. PDF-023749.
72. Ibid.
73. "Austria Denies Ransom in Qaeda Hostage Release," *France24*, November 2, 2008.
74. Abu Yahya al-Libi, "Al-Jaza'ir: Bayna Tadhiyat al-Aba', wa-Wafa' al-Abna'," June 2009.
75. PDF-023962, Atiya to Abu Muhammad Salah, December 11, 2010.
76. PDF-023376, Ayman al-Zawahiri to Abu Musab Abd al-Wadud, October 18, 2007.
77. PDF-003742, Abu Musab Abd al-Wadud to Usama bin Laden and Ayman al-Zawahiri, March 16, 2010.

78. See Ibn Rushd, *The Distinguished Jurist's Primer*, trans. Imran Ahsan Khan Nyazee and Mohammad Abdul Rauf, Reading: Garnet Publishing, 2000, The Book of Jihad, Section 6, The Permission for Truce, pp. 463. The focus is on the disbelievers (*kuffar*) and polytheists (*mushrikun*) and not the apostates.

79. *Shaybani's Siyar*, trans. Majid Khadduri, Islamic Law of Nations, Baltimore: The Johns Hopkins Press, 196, p. 223 (seems permitted?). Note that in 2007 Atiya had written to Jaysh al-'Usra (see below, section on Somalia), advising that "it is not permitted to have a truce with the apostates, except out of necessity (but it was open to interpretation)." See PDF-023404, Atiya to Jaysh al-'Usra, September 2007.

80. Abu Yahya found this view in Ibn Qayyim al-Jawziya's *Zad al-Ma'ad*.

81. PDF-023438, unknown (most likely Atiya who had contacts in the kingdom) to Abu Yahya al-Libi, 2010.

82. PDF-023579, Abu Yahya al-Libi to Abu Musab Abd al-Wadud, October 7, 2010. Abu Yayha also sought to moderate other "Libyan brothers" in 2009, but it's not clear if it was at the request of AQIM. See "Letter from Abu Yahya," ODNI, 2017.

83. Ayman al-Zawahiri, *al-Hiwar ma' al-Tawaghit: Maqbarat al-Da'wa wa-al-Du'at*, first published in 1989, http://www.ilmway.com/site/maqdis/MS_10841.html. Chapter 3 is devoted to this very issue.

84. See for instance, the chapter "Butlan Muhadanat al-Murtaddin," by Abu al-Hasan al-Rashid, http://www.ilmway.com/site/maqdis/MS_11240.html.

85. PDF-023821, Salah Abu Muhammad to Atiya, January 22, 2010.

86. Atiya did not specify his source, but it is included in Ibn al-Jawziyya, *Jami 'I al-Fiqh*, ed. Yusri al-Sayyid Muhammad, Dar al-Wafa' li-al-Tiba'a wa-al-Nashr, 2000, vol. 5, pp. 174–5.

87. PDF-023962, Atiya to Abu Muhammad Salah, December 11, 2010.

88. PDF-023485, Abu Musab Abd al-Wadud to Ayman al-Zawahiri, March 28, 2008 (note this document includes two letters).

89. PDF-011131, Usama bin Laden to Ayman al-Zawahiri, December 3, 2010.

90. At the time the official name of the group was Jama'at Ahl al-Sunna wal-al-Jama'a li-al-Da'wa wa-al-Jihad, before it merged with the Islamic State in 2005.

91. Abu Bakr Shekau, "Praise Be to God the Lord of All World," ODNI, 2016.

92. See PDF-023816 and PDF-023799.

93. *Nasa'ih wa-Tawjihat Shar'iyya min al-Sheikh Abi al-Hasan Rashid li-Mujahidi Nigeria*. The booklet was released by AQIM and it includes some of the letters that were recovered from Abbottabad. I had several helpful conversations about this with Jacob Zenn.

94. See Jacob Zenn, *Unmasking Boko Haram: Exploring Global Jihad in Nigeria*, Denver: Lynne Rienner Publishers, 2020, chs. 9–10.

95. "Abubakar Shekau: Nigeria's Boko Haram Leader Is dead, say Rival Militants," *BBC*, June 7, 2021, https://www.bbc.com/news/world-africa-57378493.

96. PDF-003133, Usama bin Laden to Atiya, September 26, 2010.

97. PDF-004740, Usama bin Laden to Atiya, December 3, 2010.

98. Usama bin Laden, "Min Usama bin Laden ila al-Sha'b al-Faransi," November 2010.

99. PDF-002655, Salah/possibly al-Wadud to Atiya, December 21, 2010.

100. PDF-000939, Usama bin Laden to Atiya, April 26, 2011.

101. "Freed French Hostages Return Amid Ransom Speculation," *BBC*, October 2013, https://www.bbc.com/news/world-europe-24739716.

102. See Kevin Jackson, *Abu al-Layth al-Libi*, in Nelly Lahoud (ed.), Jihadi Bios Project, February 15, CTC.

103. PDF-003732, Ayman al-Zawahiri to Usama bin Laden, October 20, 2004.

104. PDF-023513, Hajji Uthman to Usama bin Laden, April 16, 2008.

105. PDF-002659, Atiya to Usama bin Laden, July 17, 2010.

106. PDF-017164, Usama bin Laden to Abu al-Laith and Abu Yahya, 2007.

107. PDF-023376, Ayman al-Zawahiri to Abu Musab Abd al-Wadud, October 18, 2007.

108. PDF-010238, Atiya to Usama bin Laden, November 23, 2010.

109. Abu Yahya al-Libi, "Usama: Masiratu 'Izzin wa-Khatimatu Sharaf," 2011.

110. Fadil Harun, *al-Harb 'ala al-Islam*, vol. 2, pp. 57–120.

111. For the historical roots of the group and the timeline of its (early) operations in Yemen, see Gabriel Koehler-Derrick (ed.), *A False Foundation? AQAP, Tribes and Ungoverned Spaces in Yemen*, CTC, October 3, 2011.

NOTES to pp. 180–190

112. PDF-017143, Usama bin Laden to Ayman al-Zawahiri, December 17, 2007.
113. PDF-023447, Atiya to Usama bin Laden, May–June, 2008
114. *Sada al-Malahim*, issue 1, 2008.
115. It is not clear whether his qualifications (*al-ta'sisi wa-ba'd al-mulhaqat*) refer to elementary school followed by some middle-school classes, or high school and a few vocational courses. It is doubtful that it means first year of university and a few electives.
116. PDF-023740, Abu Hurayra/Qasem al-Raymi to the leaders of al-Qaeda, undated.
117. "Al Qaeda Blamed for U.S. Embassy Attack," *CNN*, September 17, 2008; "Al Qaeda Blamed for Yemen Attack," *CNN*, 2009; "Al Qaeda Leader Behind Northwest Flight 253 Terror Plot Was Released by U.S.," *ABC News*, December 28, 2009.
118. PDF-023642, Usama bin Laden to Abu Basir, most likely 2010.
119. PDF-023741, Abu Basir, letter in response to Hajji Uthman, most likely late 2009.
120. PDF-023935, Hajji Uthman and Atiya to Usama bin Laden, January 25, 2010.
121. PDF-023642, Usama bin Laden to Abu Basir, most likely 2010.
122. Ibid.
123. Ibid.
124. PDF-023888, Atiya to Abu Basir, July 18, 2010.
125. Ibid.
126. PDF-023625, Abu Basir to Atiya, February 10, 2011. It was indeed reported that AQAP had been procuring materials to produce the poison ricin. Annasofie Flaman, "Yemen's al-Qaeda Want Toxic Bombs," *PRI*, August 15, 2011.
127. PDF-023625, Abu Basir to Atiya, February 10, 2011.
128. PDF-001292, Atiya to Abu Basir, March 27, 2011.
129. Fadil Harun, *al-Harb 'ala al-Islam*, vol. 1, pp. 118–172.
130. Paul B. Henze, *Layers of Time: A History of Ethiopia*, New York: Palgrave, 2000, chs. 8–9.
131. The ICU's rise dates back to 1994 when Somalia had been without a government since 1991. This is a highly complicated episode and the nature of the ICU's ties with al-Shabaab should not be exaggerated. See Cedric Barnes and Harun Hassan, "The Rise and Fall of Mogadishu's Islamic Courts," *Journal of Eastern African Studies*, vol. 1, no. 2, July 2007, pp. 151–60; Ken Menkhaus, "Somalia: A Country in Peril, a Policy Nightmare," Enough Strategy Paper, September 2008.
132. Zeray W. Yihdego, "Ethiopia's Military Action Against the Union of Islamic Courts and Others in Somalia: Some Legal Implications," *The International and Comparative Law Quarterly*, vol. 56, no. 3, July 2007, pp. 666–76.
133. Cited in ibid., p. 670.
134. Fadil Harun, *al-Harb 'ala al-Islam*, vol. 2, p. 82. For a study of the autobiography, see Nelly Lahoud, *Beware of Imitators: Al-Qa'ida through the Lens of Its Confidential Secretary*, CTC, June 4, 2012.
135. PDF-023811, Jaysh al-'Usra. The letter's heading indicates that it had originally been sent to the Yemeni "Brothers."
136. On the AQAP connection: Fadil Harun recounts that those who escaped from prison in 2006–07 initially headed to Somalia and fought against the Ethiopian occupation. See Fadil Harun, *al-Harb 'ala al-Islam*, vol. 2, pp. 57–120.
137. Ibid., vol. 1, p. 310; see vol. 2, pp. 20–26. According to Harun, when planning for the 1998 East Africa bombings was under way, Abu Muhammad al-Misri sent a letter to Abu Hafs al-Misri with three young men who were traveling to Afghanistan. Saleh was one of the three and was seventeen years old at the time. Saleh had been part of Talha al-Sudani's group, but disagreed with him and they parted ways. Saleh al-Nabhan is the same as Yousef al-Tanzani.
138. Martin Lings, *Muhammad: His Life Based on the Earliest Sources*, Cambridge: The Islamic Texts Society, 2002, p. 319.
139. PDF-023811, letter from Jaysh al-'Usra.
140. PDF-023404, Atiya to Jaysh al-'Usra, September 2007.
141. PDF-023811, letter from Jaysh al-'Usra.
142. Usama bin Laden, "al-Nizal, al-Nizal, Ya Abtal al-Sumal," al-Sahab, March 2009.
143. Ibid.
144. Ayman al-Zawahiri, "Min Kabul ila Mugadishu," February 2009. This was a montage featuring other Somali figures in the same video.

324

145. PDF-017043, Usama bin Laden draft letter to Ayman al-Zawahiri.
146. PDF-023850, Ayman al-Zawahiri to Usama bin Laden, March 12, 2009.
147. PDF-023983, Mukhtar Abu al-Zubayr to the General Leadership and the Sheikhs in Khurasan, March 5, 2010.
148. Ibid.
149. PDF-000931, Mukhtar Abu al-Zubayr to Atiya, January 26, 2011.
150. PDF-023567, Ayman al-Zawahiri to unknown, June 20, 2009.
151. PDF-023883, Atiya to Mukhtar Abu al-Zubayr, July 15, 2010.
152. Ibid.
153. PDF-003223, Usama bin Laden to Mukhtar Abu al-Zubayr, notes, 2010.
154. Ibid.
155. PDF-005666, Usama bin Laden to Mukhtar Abu al-Zubayr, August 6, 2010.
156. PDF-003223, Usama bin Laden to Mukhtar Abu al-Zubayr, notes, 2010.
157. Ibid.
158. PDF-023883, Atiya to Mukhtar Abu al-Zubayr, July 15, 2010. I could not find this attack reported in the media.
159. Ibid.
160. PDF-005666, Usama bin Laden to Mukhtar Abu al-Zubayr, August 6, 2010.
161. PDF-000931, Mukhtar Abu al-Zubayr to Atiya, January 26, 2011.
162. Ibid.
163. PDF-003636, Atiya to Mukhtar Abu al-Zubayr, March 20–22, 2011.
164. PDF-003672, Usama bin Laden to Hajji Uthman, January 2010. For background reading about the Syrian Muslim Brotherhood experience and the Hama uprising, see Patrick Seale, *Asad of Syria*, California: University of California Press, 1989, particularly ch. 20.
165. SOCOM-2012-0000019, Usama bin Laden to Atiya, May–June 2010.
166. Ibid.
167. Ibid.
168. PDF-003133, Usama bin Laden to Atiya, September 25, 2010.
169. SOCOM-2012-0000019.
170. Ibid.
171. PDF-003159, Usama bin Laden to Atiya, October 16, 2010.
172. "Undated Letter 3," ODNI, May 20, 2015.
173. PDF-003159.
174. PDF-011131, Usama bin Laden to Ayman al-Zawahiri, December 3, 2010.

Chapter 8: The "First Martyr"

1. This section of the book draws, in part, on Nelly Lahoud, "What the Jihadis Left Behind," *London Review of Books*, vol. 42, no. 2, January 23, 2020. This was the first article to document the contributions of Usama bin Laden's wives and daughters to his public statements.
2. PDF-017471, Siham to Daoud, December 16, 2007.
3. Najwa bin Laden, in Jean Sasson, Najwa bin Laden, and Omar bin Laden, *Growing Up Bin Laden: Osama's Wife and Son Take Us Inside Their Secret World*, New York: St Martin's Griffin, 2009, pp. 74, 104. According to the Commission conducted by the Pakistani government, investigating the Abbottabad raid, Usama's wives related that the Bin Ladens lived in Haripur before they moved to Abbottabad in 2005. This is possible. But it is clear from the letters that the information they confessed was not entirely truthful. Hence, it is also possible that the wives did not disclose their true pre-2005 location to protect the security of those who had hosted them. *Bin Laden Dossier [Abbottabad Commission Report on Killing of Osama bin Laden]*, 2013, p. 42, https://dataspace.princeton.edu/handle/88435/dsp01jq085k07t.
4. Nelly Lahoud, "The Neglected Sex: The Jihadis' Exclusion of Women from Jihad," *Terrorism and Political Violence*, vol. 26, no. 5, pp. 780–802, at p. 788.
5. IMG-032990, notes and draft of a poem by Siham. We know from Najwa's account that both Fatima (her daughter) and Khadija were getting engaged on the same day.
6. His actual name is Abdallah. He is also known by his aliases Daoud, Abd al-Latif, and Abu Abdallah al-Halabi. I chose to use Daoud here, to avoid confusion with other Abdallahs.
7. IMG-034493, IMG-016349, notes and draft of a poem by Siham.

8. IMG-016349. Note that my rendering involves some guesswork as it is based on a draft of Siham's poem and some words are hardly legible.
9. IMG-017653, draft of a poem by Siham.
10. Peter Bergen, *Manhunt: The Ten-Year Search for Bin Laden from 9/11 to Abbottabad*, New York: Crown, 2013, pp. 6–7.
11. PDF-001093.
12. PDF-023382, Daoud to Siham, November 1, 2007.
13. PDF-023389, Daoud to Khaled, November 20, 2007.
14. "Press Briefing by Senior Administration Officials on the Killing of Osama bin Laden," *The White House*, May 2, 2011.
15. PDF-004974, Usama bin Laden to Muhammad Aslam, February 3, 2011.
16. PDF-009895, Sumayya to Khairiah, January 7, 2011. Sumayya relates the ages of the children in this letter.
17. PDF-018232, Khaled to Daoud, December 16, 2007.
18. VID-000313, video of many chickens.
19. VID-009968, video of the cow and her calf.
20. PDF-004974, Usama bin Laden to Muhammad Aslam, February 3, 2011.
21. PDF-001135, Usama Bin Laden to Atiya, April 26, 2011.
22. PDF-002419, Khairiah/Umm Hamza to Hamza, 2011.
23. PDF-000820, Khadija to Umm Ibrahim/Amal, 2005.
24. PDF-004270, Usama bin Laden to an "intermediary," probably January 3, 2011.
25. Khadija had written to her family in May 2005, but that letter was not recovered. Perhaps they had not moved to Abbottabad by then.
26. PDF-000377, Khadija to Usama bin Laden, 2005. It appears that at some point they made plans to travel to Abbottabad. See PDF-000823, Daoud to Usama bin Laden.
27. PDF-000126. Mariam's letter is one of several in this batch, September 27, 2005.
28. PDF-000126. Sumayya's 2005 letter is one of several letters in this batch.
29. IMG-058052, a poem praising Sumayya.
30. For background on Bin Laden's father, see Steve Coll, *The Bin Ladens: An Arabian Family in the American Century*, New York: The Penguin Press, 2008, Part One, esp. pp. 83–7.
31. IMG-058052, a poem praising Sumayya.
32. "Letter to Mom", ODNI, January 19, 2017. Khadija's letter was most likely written in July, August, or early September 2005. PDF-000126. Siham's letter, September 27, 2005, is one of several in this batch.
33. PDF-000126.
34. PDF-001673, Umm Hamza/Khairiah to Hamza/Abu Mu'adh, 2011.
35. PDF-016822, Khaled to Abd al-Rahman al-Maghrebi, August 7, 2010.
36. Some documents include track changes; others include handwritten comments in red on printed pages of draft statements. See IMG-041161; IMG-052523; IMG-058792; IMG-010487; IMG-071101; IMG-047092; IMG-057733; IMG-071875; IMG-042030; IMG-012483; IMG-010671; IMG-007731; IMG-063519; IMG-052971; IMG-047043; IMG-028150.
37. PDF-000126, Siham to Khadija, September 2005.
38. PDF-003604, PDF-002879. It is not clear if Hajar was Ayman's stepdaughter or the stepdaughter of a certain Muhammad Salah who was likely dead by then. Ayman was either looking after Hajar and her sister (*de facto*) or he adopted them (*de jure*).
39. PDF-000126, Siham to Khadija, September 2005.
40. PDF-001772, Khairiah/Umm Hamza to Hamza, 2011. She didn't list all the books read in Abbottabad by Siham's children, but they include: "Nadrat al-Na'im" (twelve volumes); "al-Shawqiyya"; "al-Riyad" (perhaps a reference to Tabari's *al-Riyad al-Nadir fi Manakib al-Ashab al-'Ashara*); "al-Rahiq" (perhaps a work of poetry, *al-Rahiq al-Makhtum*), in addition to the collection of *Sahih al-Jami'*, *Sunan Abi Daoud, Silsilat al-Ahadith al-Sahiha*.
41. PDF-016822.
42. https://archive.org/details/All-talks-by-Shiekh-Osama-Ben-Laden.
43. Robert Windrem and Victor Limjoco, "Was Bin Laden's Last Video Faked?" *NBC*, October 29, 2010, http://www.nbcnews.com/id/21530470/ns/nbc_nightly_news_with_brian_williams/t/was-bin-ladens-last-video-faked/.
44. PDF-018232, Khaled to Daoud, December 16, 2007.

45. PDF-002045. In a revised letter that was likely to be read by Siham, she rephrased her description of Khaled to "his contributions should not to be underestimated" (PDF-002419).
46. VID-009968.
47. PDF-000685, PDF-000516, Khadija to Siham, 2005.
48. PDF-017076, several short letters, from Siham to al-Halabi; from Siham to her brother Saad; from Usama bin Laden to his daughter Khadija; and from Siham to her daughter Khadija. They were composed in November 2005.
49. PDF-017076, Siham, November 2005.
50. Ibid.
51. Ibid.
52. Bergen, *Manhunt*, p. 7.
53. PDF-017076, Siham, November 2005.
54. PDF-018232, Khaled to Daoud, December 16, 2007.
55. PDF-023371, Umm Abd al-Rahman to Siham, 2007.
56. Ibid.
57. PDF-023389, Daoud to Khaled, November 20, 2007.
58. PDF-023382, Daoud to Siham, November 1, 2007.
59. Ibid.
60. Ibid.
61. David Cook, "Contemporary Martyrdom: Ideology and Material Culture," in Thomas Hegghammer (ed.), *Jihadi Culture: The Art and Social Practices of Militant Islamists*, Cambridge: Cambridge University Press, 2017, pp. 154–7.
62. PDF-017471, Siham to Daoud, December 16, 2007.
63. PDF-023374, Daoud to Usama bin Laden and Siham, 2007.
64. PDF-017471, Siham to Daoud, December 16, 2007.
65. Ibid.
66. See E. Kohlberg's entry "Shahid," *Encyclopaedia of Islam* (2), vol. 9, pp. 203–7, at p. 206. My thanks to Michael Cook for drawing this reference to my attention.
67. PDF-017244, Siham to Umm Khaled (who breastfed Fatima), 16 December 2007.
68. PDF-017471.
69. Coll, "The Unblinking Stare."
70. PDF-023382, Daoud to Siham, November 1, 2007.
71. The herb is *al-habba al-sawda'* (black seed). There is a mention of it in the Hadith, and it is said that it is a cure for all ailments. (See Fatwa 62318 on Isamweb.net.)
72. PDF-023407, Umm Khaled al-Habib to Siham, November 4, 2007.
73. PDF-023389. Fatima is also referred to as Siham. The second woman is Umm Khaled al-Habib, whose husband (perhaps the grandson of Khaled al-Habib?) was killed around 2009 (see PDF-003871).
74. Lings, *Muhammad*, p. 23.
75. Daoud notes that Abdallah had memorized "up to Sura al-Zalzala," which means 99 out of 114 chapters, while Aisha and Usama had memorized "up to Sura al-Ikhlas," which means 112 chapters. This is doubtful, and they may not have been memorizing them in order. In 2010, Abdallah wrote to his father that he had memorized "Sura al-Isra' and al-Kahf" (chapters 17 and 18).
76. PDF-023382, Daoud to Siham, November 1, 2007.
77. PDF-010966, "Daily Schedule."
78. PDF-018232, Khaled to Daoud, December 16, 2007. Based on the evidence in the videos recovered, there were many cats in the compound.
79. VID-007714.
80. AUD-000303.
81. VID-009969.
82. AUD-005846.
83. VID-004413.
84. VID-002617.
85. PDF-018232, Khaled to Daoud, 16 December 2007.
86. PDF-023827, Siham to Daoud.
87. AUD-005129, AUD-005057, AUD-003821

88. AUD-006160.
89. IMG066064. All three letters are on one page. By that time, the little Usama was going by the name Hamza.
90. PDF-023854, Daoud to Siham, 2010.
91. Lahoud, "The Neglected Sex."
92. PDF-023783, Daoud to Siham. We learn that she is "the daughter of Abu Hamza al-'Iraqi, who used to be with Sheikh Abdallah Azzam in Peshawar."
93. PDF-023783, Daoud to Siham.
94. IMG-029064, Umm Saad/Sarah to Siham, December 20, 2010.

Chapter 9: The Escapes

1. PDF-004992, Saad bin Laden to Usama bin Laden, August 5, 2008.
2. PDF-002879, Usama bin Laden to Tawfiq, December 9, 2004.
3. T. Fahd, "Ru'ya," *Encyclopaedia of Islam* (2).
4. PDF-000770, PDF-000852, PDF-017029, Usama bin Laden to Bakr bin Laden, 2007 (most likely the last one was the final letter he sent). Usama's dreams about political events are also discussed in Bergen, *The Osama bin Laden I Know*, pp. 400–1; Coll, *The Bin Ladens*, chs. 19 and 25.
5. PDF-017029. In sectarian parlance, the "Rafida" is a reference to those who rejected the legitimacy of the first three caliphs who succeeded the Prophet Muhammad, the founder of Islam, and whom Sunnis consider to be among the four "rightly guided caliphs." As far as the Shia are concerned, the line of legitimacy starts with the fourth caliph. For the origin and usage of the term "Rafida," see E. Kohlberg, "al-Rafida," *Encyclopaedia of Islam* (2). On how the first four caliphs came to be considered the rightly guided caliphs in the ninth century, see Crone, *God's Rule*, pp. 27–8.
6. PDF-017029.
7. Ibid.
8. Iman also goes by the name Asma'.
9. Cited in Coll, *The Bin Ladens*, p. 401.
10. PDF-017029.
11. Bergen, *The Osama bin Laden I Know*, p. 401; Coll, *The Bin Ladens*, pp. 278–9.
12. PDF-017029.
13. PDF-017471, Siham to Daoud, December 16, 2007.
14. PDF-023474.
15. PDF-004992, Saad bin Laden to Usama bin Laden, August 5, 2008.
16. Muhamad al-Shafi'i, "Muhamad Shawqi al-Islambuli (Abu Khaled) shaqiq qatil al-Sadat waffara li-A'da' 'al-Qaeda' maladhan aminan fi janubi Iran," *al-Sharq al-Awsat*, issue 8942, May 23, 2003, https://archive.aawsat.com/details.asp?article=172395&issueno=8942#.X-DKUeTsElQ.
17. Atiya, "al-Liqa' al-Maftuh ma' al-Sheikh 'Atiyatullah fi 'Shabakat al-Hisba al-Islamiyya'," November 2006, in *al-A 'mal al-Kamila li-al-Sheikh al-Imam al-Shahid al-Mujahid 'Atiyatullah al-Liby*, p. 227.
18. Ibid.
19. PDF-023392, February 2007. The letter consists of information from the "trusted intermediary" as well as information he learned from the cleric Bishr al-Bishr, one of the few clerics who supported al-Qaeda in the kingdom, and who was under house arrest at the time when the letter was composed.
20. PDF-003874, Usama bin Laden, 2004.
21. PDF-023383, Atiya to Usama bin Laden, November 2007.
22. PDF-003710, Arif Abu Shadia to Usama bin Laden, 2007.
23. PDF-023513, Hajji Uthman to Usama bin Laden, April 16, 2008.
24. Ayman al-Zawahiri, "al-Liqa' al-Maftuh," part II, April 2008. "Letter to Shaykh Azmarai," ODNY, 2016.
25. Laden is also referred to by the family as Bakr and on rare occasions as Hamid.
26. Sasson, Bin Laden, and Bin Laden, *Growing Up Bin Laden*, p. 64.
27. Judging by the map, Saad's trajectory makes sense.
28. PDF-004992, Saad's letter to his father, August 5, 2008.
29. PDF-010240, Abu Abd al-Rahman Uns al-Subay'i to Usama, 2010.

30. PDF-004992, Saad bin Laden, August 5, 2008.
31. Fatima got engaged on the same day as Khadija, and became a widow at the age of fifteen when her husband was killed in October 2001 during the U.S. bombing of Afghanistan.
32. Note that I am referring to the 2009 edition. When the 2010 edition was published, Iman had escaped and the detention of Usama's family had become a matter of public knowledge.
33. My thanks to Hassan Ahmadian, who shared with me that prisoners in Iran can be given a stipend if they prove that they need financial support to help their families.
34. Jane Perlez, "An Iranian Diplomat Is Abducted by Gunmen in Pakistan," *The New York Times*, November 13, 2008, https://www.nytimes.com/2008/11/14/world/asia/14envoy.html.
35. PDF-023570, Atiya to Usama bin Laden, November 6, 2009.
36. Ibid.
37. It is used as a supererogatory addition to the obligatory prayers. See A.J. Wensinck, "Subha," *Encyclopaedia of Islam* (2).
38. PDF-001582.
39. Ibid.
40. Ibid.
41. PDF-002195, PDF-011055, Abu Sahl al-Misri to Usama bin Laden. He was released from Iran in 2010.
42. Sasson, Bin Laden, and Bin Laden, *Growing Up Bin Laden*, pp. 301–2.
43. "Mutalabat Iran bi-Itlaq Usrat bin Laden," *Al Jazeera*, March 15, 2010.
44. At that time, Usama knew that he had ten grandchildren in Iran (based on Saad's letter); by April 2010, he had twelve grandchildren (based on Abu Sahl al-Misri's letter).
45. See the two letters with slight variations: PDF-002736 and PDF-002813.
46. PDF-003128.
47. PDF-010898, Daoud to Usama bin Laden, latter part of 2010. See also SOCOM-2012-0000019, pp. 42–3.
48. PDF-002195, PDF-011055, Abu Sahl al-Misri to Usama bin Laden.
49. PDF-010240, Abu Abd al-Rahman al-Subay'i to Usama bin Laden, October 13, 2010.
50. "Sulaiman Abu Ghaith Sentenced to Life in Prison," September 23, 2014, *BBC*, https://www.bbc.com/news/world-us-canada-29331395.
51. Benjamin Weiser, "Abu Ghaith, a Bin Laden Adviser, Is Sentenced to Life in Prison," *The New York Times*, September 23, 2014, https://www.nytimes.com/2014/09/24/nyregion/abu-ghaith-a-bin-laden-adviser-is-sentenced-to-life-in-prison.html.
52. Eric Schmitt, "U.S. Officials Say a Son of Bin Laden may be Dead," *The New York Times*, July 23, 2009.
53. IMG-047297, Saad's will to his wife, August 15, 2008.
54. Ibid.
55. Ibid.
56. IMG-047913, Saad's will to his wife, August 15, 2008.
57. Saad actually specified that "if you have someone else to look after you," i.e., if she did not need to be supported by their son.
58. Abu Burhan was in Usama's circle in the 1980s and was part of the meeting that saw al-Qaeda separate from Maktab al-Khadamat.
59. "Habs al-Madin fi qabrihi bi-daynihi," dorar.net. It is based on several Hadiths (Abu Daoud, 3341; al-Nisa'i, 7/315; Ahmad 5/20)
60. T.H. Weir and A. Zysow, "Sadaka," *Encyclopaedia of Islam* (2).
61. February 16, 2012, https://www.govinfo.gov/content/pkg/CHRG-112shrg79855/html/CHRG-112shrg79855.htm; it is worth noting that the 9/11 Commission Report claimed that al-Qaeda had sent some of its operatives to "Hezbollah training camps in Lebanon" to develop "tactical expertise" before the 1998 East Africa attacks (p. 68). I found nothing in the letters (or in other primary sources) to support this claim. In view of the dreams/nightmares that Usama was having about Iran, as discussed in this chapter, it is highly unlikely that he would have approved such training.
62. "Remarks by President Trump on the Joint Comprehensive Plan of Action," *The White House*, May 8, 2018.
63. Michael R. Pompeo, "The Iran-al-Qa'ida Axis," January 12, 2021, https://www.state.gov/the-iran-al-qaida-axis/.

64. PDF-002161, Hamza bin Laden to Usama bin Laden, December 4, 2010.
65. IMG-046353, Usama bin Laden notes.
66. PDF-001833, Ahmad Hasan Abu al-Khair to Mustafa Hamid, 22 August 2009.
67. Mustafa Hamid and Leah Farrall (in conversation), *The Arabs at War in Afghanistan*, London: Hurst, 2015, p. 214. Hamid and Farrall began their correspondence in 2009 when Hamid was still in Iran (see p. 16), which suggests that he enjoyed a special kind of "detention" that was not extended to others in al-Qaeda.
68. I reached out to Mustafa Hamid by email and requested an interview, but he politely declined "due to conditions that prevent me from doing so."
69. IMG-046353, Usama bin Laden notes.
70. Ibid.
71. See MAFA World, https://www.mafa.world/mustafa-hamed/.
72. About the 2015 deal, see Cole Bunzel, "Why Are Al Qaeda Leaders in Iran?" *Foreign Affairs*, February 11, 2021.
73. "Al Qaeda's No. 2, Accused in U.S. Embassy Attacks, Was Killed in Iran," *The New York Times*, November 14, 2020.

Chapter 10: The Final Chapter

1. PDF-004591, Usama bin Laden to Khairiah, January 3, 2011.
2. In addition to Khairiah and the four children, Usama had thirteen grandchildren in Iran. Also, since his daughter Fatima was married to Sulaiman Abu Ghaith, Usama optimistically assessed that "it would be unfair for Iran to separate women from their husbands." On that basis, he reasoned that Sulaiman and his other wife, Umm Hafs, and their daughter would also be released.
3. SOCOM-2012-0000019, draft letter from Usama bin Laden to Atiya, June–July 2010.
4. PDF-002746, Usama bin Laden to Atiya, January 6, 2011.
5. PDF-023765, Hajji Uthman to Usama bin Laden, undated/2009–2010.
6. PDF-002753, Atiya to Usama bin Laden, December 9, 2010.
7. PDF-010241, Atiya to Usama bin Laden, November 23, 2010.
8. SOCOM-2012-0000019, draft letter from Usama bin Laden to Atiya, June–July 2010.
9. "Letter to Sons Uthman, Muhammad, Hamza, Wife—Umm Hamza," September 26, 2010, ODNI, 2015.
10. PDF-023884, Atiya to Usama bin Laden, August 28, 2010.
11. PDF-002195, Abu Sahl al-Misri to Usama bin Laden, April 1, 2010.
12. PDF-002195. Saif al-Adl and Abu Hafs al-Mauritani were specifically named in this letter.
13. See previous chapter on the fate of Sulaiman.
14. PDF-010675, Khaled to Abdallah and Abu al-Harith, October 5, 2010.
15. PDF-023953, Atiya to Usama bin Laden, January 24, 2011.
16. PDF-002753, Atiya to Usama bin Laden, December 9, 2010. Khairiah may have departed on December 10.
17. Ibid. and PDF-023953, Atiya to Usama bin Laden, January 24, 2011.
18. "Letter to Sons Uthman, Muhammad, Hamza, Wife—Umm Hamza," September 26, 2010, ODNI, 2015.
19. "Letter to My Caring Family," Usama bin Laden to Khairiah, February 3, 2011, ODNI, March 2016.
20. PDF-004591, Usama bin Laden to Khairiah, January 3, 2011.
21. Ibid.
22. Ibid.
23. "Undated Letter 3," ODNI, May 20, 2015, Usama bin Laden to Khairiah, late December 2010– January 3, 2011.
24. Ibid.
25. PDF-004591, Usama bin Laden to Khairiah.
26. If he did, it would have been for a medical emergency, but the letters do not hint that this happened.
27. PDF-004270, Usama bin Laden to an unknown brother, most likely the first week of January, 2011.
28. PDF-009953, Khaled to Munir/Abd al-Rahman al-Maghrebi, November 4, 2010.

29. PDF-010568, Khaled's notes, most likely January 6, 2011.
30. PDF-011199, Siham to Umm Abd al-Rahman, January 7, 2011.
31. Ibid. See also "Muhammad," in Muhammad b. Sirin and Abd al-Ghani al-Nabulsi, *Mu'jam Tafsir al-Ahlam*, ed. Basil al-Baridi, Beirut: al-Yamama, 2008, p. 1021.
32. PDF-011199. This is a nationalist reference; one might have expected a reference about the *umma* instead?
33. The poetry of Qays b. al-Muluh can be accessed on https://adabworld.com; Ruqayya Yasmine Khan, *Bedouin and 'Abbasid Cultural Identities: The Arabic Majnun Layla Story*, London/New York: Routledge, 2021, pp. 1-15.
34. PDF-009895, Khaled to Khairiah, January 7, 2011.
35. PDF-003594, Usama bin Laden to Abu Muhammad and Abu Khaled, January 14, 2011.
36. Ibid. See Qur'an 5:2.
37. PDF-003594.
38. PDF-004993, Usama bin Laden to Abu Muhammad, January 19, 2011.
39. SOCOM-2012-0000019.
40. PDF-011177, Usama bin Laden to Muhammad Aslam, February 3, 2011.
41. See Qur'an 16:91.
42. We don't have the letter in which Khairiah described her condition.
43. "Letter to My Caring Family," ODNI, February, 2016.
44. "Letter to My Caring Family," February 3, 2011, ODNI, 2016.
45. PDF-009917, Umm Khaled to Umm Abd al-Rahman, February 2011.
46. PDF-002045, Khairiah to Hamza/Abu Mu'adh, 2011.
47. CIA, November 1, 2017, https://www.cia.gov/library/abbottabad-compound/index.html.
48. Ibid.
49. This is a challenging notebook to read, and it is not always coherent. In addition to the transcribed conversations, the notebook also includes summaries of the news, and on occasion it is used to draft letters (between father and daughter), and to record the thoughts and ideas of the daughter.
50. See PDF-023910 and PDF-023911, Abd al-Rahman al-Maghrebi to Usama bin Laden and his son Khaled, 2010.
51. C.E. Bosworth, "Tulaka,'" *Encyclopaedia of Islam* (2). Note that Bosworth is referring to the plural *tulaqa'*.
52. PDF-001042, PDF-001306, PDF-001381, PDF-002842, PDF-002847, PDF-003664, PDF-003991, PDF-004091, PDF-004278, PDF-004728, PDF-023598, PDF-023612, PDF-023629, PDF-023635, PDF-023636, PDF-023646
53. IMG-064408, Abd al-Qayyum (also known as Uns al-Subay'i al-Libi) to Abu Yahya, March 20, 2011.
54. PDF-023690, Atiya to Usama bin Laden, April 4, 2011.
55. Resolution 1973, March 17, 2011, https://www.nato.int/nato_static/assets/pdf/pdf_2011_03/20110927_110311-UNSCR-1973.pdf.
56. PDF-000939, Usama bin Laden to Atiya, April 26, 2011.
57. As translated by James Howarth, in Lawrence, *Messages to the World*, p. 229.
58. PDF-000952, notes in the form of a "to-do list."
59. 220-page notebook.
60. SOCOM-2012-0000019.
61. Ibid., draft letter from Usama bin Laden to Atiya, June–July 2010. See also AFGP-2002-600046, "List of Names of Al-Qa'ida Members." This internal al-Qaeda document, available through the CTC, shows that Hamza's brothers—Saad, Uthman, Muhammad, Omar, and Abd al-Rahman—were members of al-Qaeda: https://ctc.usma.edu/harmony-program/list-of-names-of-al-qaida-members-original-language-2/.
62. PDF-001673, Khairiah to Hamza, 2011.
63. "Letter Dtd November 24, 2010," ODNI, May 2015.
64. Sarah Westwood, Evan Perez, and Ryan Browne, "Trump Confirms Osama bin Laden's Son Hamza Killed in US Counterterrorism Operation," *CNN*, September 14, 2019, https://www.cnn.com/2019/09/14/politics/hamza-bin-laden-al-qaeda-dead/index.html.
65. Robert O'Neill, *The Operator: Firing the Shots That Killed Osama Bin Laden and My Years as a SEAL Team Warrior*, New York: Scribner, 2017, p. 308.
66. Ibid.

Chapter 11: The Real Courier

1. Ahmad al-Naysaburi, cited in Heinz Halm, *The Fatimids and Their Traditions of Learning*, New York: I.B. Tauris & Co. Ltd, 1997, p. 65. I am grateful to Michael Cook for drawing this nugget to my attention.

2. President Barack Obama, "Osama bin Laden Dead," May 2, 2011, https://obamawhitehouse. archives.gov/blog/2011/05/02/osama-bin-laden-dead.

3. McRaven, *Sea Stories*, 325–7.

4. Ibid.

5. Ibid, and 113th Congress, 2d Session, Senate Report 113-288, Report of the Senate Select Committee on Intelligence Committee Study of the Central Intelligence Agency's Detention and Interrogation Program, December 9, 2014, https://www.intelligence.senate.gov/sites/default/files/publications/CRPT-113srpt288.pdf, p. 379.

6. Carol Rosenberg, "What the C.I.A.'s Torture Program Looked Like to the Tortured," *The New York Times*, December 4, 2019, https://www.nytimes.com/2019/12/04/us/politics/cia-torture-drawings.html.

7. "Press Briefing by Senior Administration Officials on the Killing of Osama bin Laden," *The White House*, May 2, 2011, https://obamawhitehouse.archives.gov/the-press-office/2011/05/02/press-briefing-senior-administration-officials-killing-osama-bin-laden. This began on August 27th, 2010. See also Chris Wallace with Mitch Weiss, *Countdown bin Laden: The Untold Story of the 247-Day Hunt to Bring the Mastermind of 9/11 to Justice*, New York: Simon & Schuster, 2021.

8. "Revealed: The Hunt for Bin Laden," 9/11 Memorial & Museum https://www.911memorial. org/visit/museum/exhibitions//revealed-hunt-bin-laden.

9. Ibid.

10. Seymour M. Hersh, "The Killing of Osama bin Laden," *London Review of Books*, vol. 37, no. 10, May 21, 2015. Hersh's Pakistani source about this is General Ahmed Shuja Pasha, who was the director of the ISI during the Abbottabad raid. Since Usama was hiding from Pakistani authorities, the letters reveal nothing about the inner workings of the Pakistani government.

11. PDF-004974, Usama bin Laden to Muhammad Aslam, February 3, 2011.

12. Abu Khaled's first name was Amer; the first name of Abu Muhammad was not mentioned. According to media reports, the two brothers were married. One of the wives was killed during the raid. The letters do not mention the wives, nor do they disclose the full names/identities of the brothers.

13. PDF-004974, Usama bin Laden to Muhammad Aslam, February 3, 2011.

14. In late 2005, they vetoed the visit of Usama's daughter Khadija and her family, as they wanted to spend Ramadan *en famille*. After Khadija died in 2007, they allowed her four orphaned children to be raised in Abbottabad. When the widower Daoud married Khadija's sister Mariam, they did not allow him to visit (2008–09). For several months, they vetoed Khairiah's journey to Abbottabad (late 2010–early 2011).

15. PDF-023853, Hajji Uthman to Usama bin Laden, August 4, 2009.

16. PDF-010238, Atiya to Usama bin Laden, November 23, 2010. Atiya remarked that the Pakistani "brother" he suggested was not Pashtun, "but" Punjabi. It is not clear from the letter what this "but" is about. Other letters suggest that "allegiance" (*bay'a*) was a big deal for the Pashtun, which meant that Usama and his security guard shared an incorruptible bond.

17. PDF-003874, Usama bin Laden, draft letter, late 2004.

18. SOCOM-2012-0000019, Usama bin Laden, most likely July 2010.

19. The word for SIM cards is *shara'ih*, and the word *istikhraj* suggests that they were not simply dropped in an envelope and that some technical procedure was required to remove them.

20. PDF-010241, Atiya to Usama bin Laden (Atiya's answers in brackets), November 23, 2010.

21. PDF-023953, Atiya to Usama bin Laden, January 24, 2011.

22. PDF-002926, Usama bin Laden to Muhammad Aslam, February 12, 2011.

23. Ibid.

24. PDF- 002746, Usama bin Laden to Atiya, January 5, 2011.

25. Usama wanted Atiya to send him a large lump sum in euros, but Atiya declined and insisted that the intermediary should only carry local currency in case he was searched.

26. PDF-004058, Daoud to Khaled, August 25, 2010. See also PDF-010238, Atiya to Usama bin Laden, November 23, 2010.
27. SOCOM-2012-0000019, draft letter from Usama bin Laden to Atiya, June–July 2010.
28. "Letter to My Caring Family," ODNI. Khairiah's letter was not recovered, but its contents can be reconstructed from Usama's letter.
29. PDF-010241, Atiya to Usama bin Laden, November 23, 2010.
30. PDF-023953, Atiya to Usama bin Laden, January 24, 2011.
31. PDF-002753, Atiya to Usama bin Laden, December 9, 2010.
32. 220-page handwritten notebook.

Epilogue

1. PDF-002143, Siham to Hamza, 2011.
2. In a 220-page document consisting of transcription of family conversations.
3. See below, Appendix One: Usama bin Laden's Will.
4. Usama bin Laden press conference in late 2000. Released by al-Sahab in May 2021, using previously unavailable footage: https://archive.gnews.bz/index.php/s/kg2NbAXaf6kGSbx.
5. See above, Chapter Six.
6. Philip Alston, "The CIA and Targeted Killings Beyond Borders," *Harvard National Security Journal*, vol. 2, 2011, pp. 283–446, esp. section IV.
7. Greg Thielman, "The Missile Gap Myth and Its Progeny," *Arms Control Association*, 2011, https://www.armscontrol.org/act/2011-05/missile-gap-myth-its-progeny.

Appendix 1: Usama Bin Laden's Will

1. See Coll, *The Bin Ladens*, esp. Part I.
2. Ibid., p. 493.
3. Ibid., pp. 371, 383.
4. Ibid., p. 493.
5. PDF-000915, Usama bin Laden to Hajji Uthman, August 17, 2007.
6. Ibid. The phrase "*amwal khassa bina*" suggests that Usama was referring to private/family transfers, but it's not necessarily conclusive. See also Hajji Uthman's May 2007 letter to Usama, "Respected Brother, kind Shaykh, Zamrai, Sahib," ODNI, 2016.
7. PDF-003128, Atiya to Usama bin Laden, June 19, 2010.
8. PDF-004260, Usama bin Laden to Atiya, latter part of 2010.
9. PDF-023960, PDF-023961, Riyad al-Husayni, January 2011.
10. ODNI, 2016. Usama bin Laden's *wasiyya*.
11. J. Schacht, "Mirath," *Encyclopaedia of Islam* (2). See also A. Layish, "Mirath," section on Modern Islamic Countries, *Encyclopaedia of Islam* (2).
12. R. Peters, "Wasiyya," *Encyclopaedia of Islam* (2).
13. ODNI, 2016. As mentioned in the Epilogue, it is of note that Usama did not write "jihad in God's path." He probably chose "*fighting* in God's path" in case his law-abiding heirs in Saudi Arabia decided to donate his money to charitable organizations. The term "jihad" encompasses a wide range of activities: It refers to offensive and defensive warfare, and it also refers to spiritual activities.
14. It is difficult to estimate the amount of gold, because I don't know how many cousins Usama had.
15. I did not include in my calculations the $12 million invested by the Saudi Bin Laden Group, since Usama explicitly referred to "cash" (*al-amwal al-naqdiyya*); I also did not include the $2 million he received in Sudan and Jalalabad, because, judging by his bank account, he had spent it.

Appendix 2: *Dramatis Personae*

1. Sasson, Bin Laden, and Bin Laden, *Growing Up Bin Laden*, p. 282.

GLOSSARY OF ARABIC TERMS

'Ahd
Agreement (the fulfillment of which is legally binding).

Aman
Pledge of security.

Al-'amal al-khariji
Literally, "external work." In al-Qaeda's parlance, it refers to international terrorism.

Amir al-Mu'minin
Commander of the Faithful—the head of the *umma*, the global community of Muslims.

Ansar and muhajirun
"Helpers" and "emigrants" respectively. The historical context is necessary to understand their meanings: In A.D. 622, the Prophet Muhammad and his followers—consisting of men, women, and children—performed the *hijra*, "emigration," from Mecca to Yathrib in modern-day Saudi Arabia, escaping religious persecution. In support of their faith, these emigrants or *muhajirun* left their homes and properties behind. In Yathrib, they were welcomed by the *ansar*, the "helpers," who embraced the new religion. Muhammad went on to establish the first Islamic community in Yathrib, and it has since acquired the name Medina, Arabic for "city." In the case of al-Qaeda, Usama bin Laden and his associates referred to themselves as *muhajirun* and to the

	locals (Afghans or Pakistanis) as *ansar*. But since the term *muhajirun* is associated with those who have greater precedence in Islam (like the Prophet Muhammad and his companions), the Afghans refer to the Arabs as *ansar*.
Asiya	Afflicted. It is the name given by Qur'anic commentators to the wife of Pharaoh who adopted Moses.
Bay'a	Giving allegiance to a leader, thereby promising to obey his orders.
Istanfara	Call to arms.
Jama'a	Community.
Jihad	Struggle.
Jihad al-daf'	Defensive jihad/warfare.
Fard 'ayn or al-jihad al-muta'ayyin	Individual obligation. In the case of defensive jihad, this means that when a territory under the sovereignty of Islam is invaded, a call to arms follows, and all Muslims are obligated to take up jihad to repel the invaders.
Jihad al-talab	Offensive jihad/warfare.
Fard kifaya	Communal obligation. In the case of offensive jihad, this means that some Muslims can fulfill the obligation of jihad on behalf of others.
Kumun	Hiding.
Mahram	A male blood relative whom it is unlawful to marry, such as a son, father, or brother.
Muhajirun	See *ansar*.
Murafiq	Bodyguard or security guard.
Qital	Fighting.
Shahid/Shahida	Martyr (male and female terms).
Shura/Majlis al-Shura	Consultation/Consultative Council.

Al-shura mulzima   The leader is obligated to accept the counsel given by the Shura/Consultative Council.

Al-shura mu'lima   The counsel given by the Shura Council is to support the leader on an informational basis before he makes his decisions.

Tafsir al-Ahlam   Interpretation of dreams.

Tthuwwar (sing. tha'ir) Revolutionaries.

Umma   Global community of Muslims.

Wasit   Intermediary.

BIBLIOGRAPHY

Primary Sources

The Bin Laden Papers

PDF-000126, Letters from Siham, Mariam, and Sumayya to Khadija, September 2005.

PDF-000377, Khadija to Usama bin Laden, 2005.

PDF-000516, PDF-000685, Khadija to Siham, 2005.

PDF-000820, Khadija to Umm Ibrahim/Amal, 2005.

PDF-000823, Daoud to Usama bin Laden, 2005/6.

PDF-000915, Usama bin Laden to Hajji Uthman, August 17, 2007.

PDF-000931, Mukhtar Abu al-Zubayr to Atiya, January 26, 2011.

PDF-000939, Usama bin Laden to Atiya, April 26, 2011.

PDF-000952, Notes in the form of a "to-do list," 2011.

PDF-001042, PDF-001306, PDF-001381, PDF-002842, PDF-002847, PDF-003664, PDF-003991, PDF-004091, PDF-004278, PDF-004728, PDF-023598, PDF-023612, PDF-023629, PDF-023635, PDF-023636, PDF-023646, Drafts of Usama bin Laden's Arab Spring public statement, 2011.

PDF-001093, Curriculum 2001–02 (Bin Laden household).

PDF-001135, Usama bin Laden to Atiya, April 26, 2011.

PDF-001292, Atiya to Abu Basir, March 27, 2011.

PDF-001582, Hamza to Usama bin Laden, 2009.

PDF-001673, Khairiah to Hamza, 2011.

PDF-001772, Khairiah to Hamza, 2011.

PDF-001833, Ahmad Hasan Abu al-Khair to Mustafa Hamid, 22 August 2009.

PDF-002045, Khairiah to Hamza, 2011.

PDF-002143, Siham to Hamza bin Laden, 2011.

PDF-002161, Hamza bin Laden to Usama bin Laden, December 4, 2010.

PDF-002195, PDF-011055, PDF-002736, PDF-002813, Abu Sahl al-Misri to Usama bin Laden, April 1, 2010.

PDF-002419, Khairiah/Umm Hamza to Hamza, 2011.

PDF-002653, Usama bin Laden, addendum to PDF-004000, December 2004.

PDF-002655, Salah/possibly al-Wadud to Atiya, December 21, 2010.

PDF-002659, Atiya to Usama bin Laden, July 17, 2010.

PDF-002730, Atiya to Usama Bin Ladin (with Atiya's responses in brackets), October 11, 2010.

PDF-002746, Usama bin Laden to Atiya, January 6, 2011.

PDF-002753, Atiya to Usama bin Laden, December 9, 2010.

PDF-002772, Usama bin Laden to Younis al-Mauritani, July 6, 2010.

PDF-002879, Usama bin Laden to Abu Fatima/Ayman al-Zawahiri and Tawfiq, December 9, 2004.

PDF-002926, Usama bin Laden to Muhammad Aslam, February 12, 2011.

PDF-002935, Usama bin Laden notes, middle of 2010.

PDF-003128, Atiya to Usama bin Laden, June 19, 2010.

PDF-003133, Usama bin Laden to Atiya, September 26, 2010.

BIBLIOGRAPHY

PDF-003157, Usama bin Ladin to Ayman al-Zawahiri, October 16, 2010.
PDF-003159, Usama bin Laden to Atiya, October 16, 2010.
PDF-003181, Usama bin Laden to Younis al-Mauritani, March 17, 2010.
PDF-003212, Letter addressed to Hafiz Sultan/Hajji Uthman, March 28, 2007.
PDF-003213, Atiya and Abu Yahya al-Libi to Hakimullah Mahsud, December 3, 2010.
PDF-003223, Usama bin Laden to Atiya (and notes to Mukhtar Abu al-Zubayr), 2010.
PDF-003592, Usama bin Laden to Tawfiq, late 2004.
PDF-003594, Usama bin Laden to Abu Muhammad and Abu Khaled, January 14, 2011.
PDF-003596, Two letters: the original text by Abu al-'Abbas, the deputy leader of Ansar al-Sunna, and, in brackets, the responses from Raja' from al-Qaeda.
PDF-003600, Abu Musab al-Zarqawi to al-Qaeda leaders, 2004.
PDF-003604, Wakil Khan to leaders of al-Qaeda, October 18, 2004.
PDF-003636, Atiya to Mukhtar Abu al-Zubayr, March 20–22, 2011.
PDF-003672, Usama bin Laden to Hajji Uthman, January 2010.
PDF-003702, Usama bin Laden to Younis al-Mauritani, 2010.
PDF-003710, Arif Abu Shadia to Usama bin Laden, 2007.
PDF-003732, Ayman al-Zawahiri to Usama bin Laden, October 20, 2004.
PDF-003740, Abu Abdallah al-Shafii to Abu Hamza al-Muhajir, 2007.
PDF-003742, Abu Musab Abd al-Wadud to Usama bin Laden and Ayman al-Zawahiri, March 16, 2010.
PDF-003774, Usama bin Laden to Ayman al-Zawahiri, May 7, 2008.
PDF-003775, Usama bin Laden to Younis al-Mauritani, September 25, 2010.
PDF-003776, Muhammad Ilyas Kashmiri to Usama bin Laden, May 31, 2010.
PDF-003871, Usama bin Laden to Ayman al-Zawahiri, 2009.
PDF-003874, Usama bin Laden notes, late 2004.
PDF-003928, Usama bin Laden notes, late 2004.
PDF-003967, Usama bin Laden to his sons Uthman and Muhammad, January 7, 2011.
PDF-004000, Usama bin Laden to Hamza al-Rabia, December 2004.
PDF-004029, Atiya to Usama bin Laden, July 8, 2010.
PDF-004058, Daoud to Khaled, August 25, 2010.
PDF-004119, Jargh al-Din to Abd al-Rahman al-Maghrebi, most likely early 2005.
PDF-004225, PDF-003959, Usama bin Laden draft letter to Hajji Uthman and Atiya, early 2010.
PDF-004260, Usama bin Laden to Atiya, latter part of 2010.
PDF-004270, Usama bin Laden to an unknown brother/intermediary, most likely the first week of January, 2011.
PDF-004325, Abu Musab al-Zarqawi, 2004.
PDF-004345, Atiya to jihadis in Yemen and Somalia, June–July 2010.
PDF-004350, Younis al-Mauritani to Usama bin Laden, March 25, 2010.
PDF-004384, Usama bin Laden to Atiya, July 5, 2010.
PDF-004402, Security Committee Report, May 17, 2010.
PDF-004413, Hajji Uthman to Usama bin Laden, April 14, 2010.
PDF-004433, Majlis Shura—Islamic State of Iraq, 2010.
PDF-004436, Report by Younis al-Mauritani, August 14, 2007.
PDF-004555, Atiya to Usama bin Laden, October 6, 2010.
PDF-004588, PDF-003627, PDF-023584, Usama bin Laden to Atiya and Abu Yahya al-Libi, December 5, 2010.
PDF-004591, Usama bin Laden to Khairiah, January 3, 2011.
PDF-004648, Unknown, related to Abu Musab al-Zarqawi, 2004.
PDF-004740, Usama bin Laden to Atiya, December 3, 2010.
PDF-004835, Usama bin Laden to Mullah Omar, September 24, 2010.
PDF-004928, Usama bin Laden to Ayman al-Zawahiri, 2007.
PDF-004946, Notes about and excerpts from Bob Woodward's book *Obama's Wars*, 2010.
PDF-004974, Usama bin Laden to Muhammad Aslam, February 3, 2011.
PDF-004992, Saad bin Laden to Usama bin Laden, August 5, 2008.
PDF-004993, Usama bin Laden to Abu Muhammad, January 19, 2011.
PDF-005032, Atiya to Usama bin Laden, January 26, 2011.
PDF-005666, Usama bin Laden to Mukhtar Abu al-Zubayr, August 6, 2010.

BIBLIOGRAPHY

PDF-009341, Unknown, about Abu Omar al-Baghadi.

PDF-009895, Khaled and Sumayya's letters to Khairiah, January 7, 2011.

PDF-009917, Umm Khaled to Umm Abd al-Rahman, February 2011.

PDF-009953, Khaled to Munir/Abd al-Rahman al-Maghrebi, November 4, 2010.

PDF-010238, Atiya to Usama bin Laden, November 23, 2010.

PDF-010240, Abu Abd al-Rahman al-Subay'i to Usama bin Laden, October 13, 2010.

PDF-010241, Atiya to Usama bin Laden (Atiya's answers in brackets), November 23, 2010.

PDF-010568, Khaled's notes, most likely January 6, 2011.

PDF-010675, Khaled to Abdallah and Abu al-Harith, October 5, 2010.

PDF-010805, Abu-Salih al Somali, "Terror Franchise: The Unstoppable Assassin Techs Vital role for its success," 2009/2010.

PDF-010898, Daoud to Usama bin Laden, latter part of 2010.

PDF-010966, "Daily Schedule"/homeschooling.

PDF-011006, Letter from Younis al-Mauritani to Usama bin Laden, March 18, 2010.

PDF-011131, Usama bin Laden to Ayman al-Zawahiri, December 3, 2010.

PDF-011177, Usama bin Laden to Muhammad Aslam, February 3, 2011.

PDF-011199, Siham to Umm Abd al-Rahman, January 7, 2011.

PDF-016822, Khaled to Abd al-Rahman al-Maghrebi, August 7, 2010.

PDF-017029, PDF-000770, PDF-000852, Usama bin Laden to Bakr bin Laden, December 2007.

PDF-017043, Usama bin Laden draft letter to Ayman al-Zawahiri.

PDF-017045, Usama Bin Laden to Hajji Uthman, December 17, 2007

PDF-017076, Siham, November 2005.

PDF-017143, Usama bin Laden to Ayman al-Zawahiri, December 17, 2007.

PDF-017164, Usama bin Laden to Abu al-Laith and Abu Yahya, 2007.

PDF-017244, Siham to Umm Khaled (this person breastfed little Fatima), 16 December 2007.

PDF-017471, Siham to Daoud, December 16, 2007.

PDF-017785, Letter from Ayman al-Zawahiri to Abu Abdallah al-Shafii, January 26, 2006.

PDF-017949, Most likely Atiya to Usama bin Laden and Hajji Uthman, 2006.

PDF-018232, Khaled to Daoud, December 16, 2007.

PDF-018260, Hajji Uthman to Usama bin Laden, March 1, 2006.

PDF-023371, Umm Abd al-Rahman to Siham, 2007.

PDF-023374, Daoud to Usama bin Laden and Siham, 2007.

PDF-023376, Ayman al-Zawahiri to Abu Musab Abd al-Wadud, October 18, 2007.

PDF-023382, Daoud to Siham, November 1, 2007.

PDF-023383, Atiya to Usama bin Laden, November 2007.

PDF-023388, Atiya to Bishr al-Bishr through a "trusted intermediary."

PDF-023389, Daoud to Khaled, November 20, 2007.

PDF-023392, "Trusted Intermediary" from Saudi Arabia to Atiya.

PDF-023401, Exchange between Atiya and someone in the jihadi media outlet Markaz al-Fajr, June–July 2007.

PDF-023404, Atiya to Jaysh al-'Usra, September 2007.

PDF-023405, Hajji Uthman to Usama bin Laden, October 2007.

PDF-023407, Umm Khaled al-Habib to Siham, November 4, 2007.

PDF-023425, Ayman al-Zawahiri to Abu Omar al-Baghdadi, March 6, 2008.

PDF-023429, Abu Abdallah al-Halabi/Daoud to Abu Sulaiman, December 18, 2007.

PDF-023438, Unknown (most likely Atiya, who had contacts in the kingdom) to Abu Yahya al-Libi, 2010.

PDF-023447, Atiya to Usama bin Laden, March/April/May/June 2008.

PDF-023454, Ayman al-Zawahiri to Usama bin Laden, March 5, 2008.

PDF-023485, Abu Musab Abd al-Wadud to Ayman al-Zawahiri, March 28, 2008.

PDF-023513, Hajji Uthman to Usama bin Laden, April 16, 2008.

PDF-023514, Abu al-Tayyib to Usama bin Laden, February 25, 2008.

PDF-023532, Muhammad Khalil al-Hakayma to Ayman al-Zawahiri, February 11, 2008.

PDF-023566, Internal Report, June 2008.

PDF-023567, Ayman al-Zawahiri to unknown, June 20, 2009.

PDF-023568, List of names to be read alongside PDF-023566.

PDF-023570, Atiya to Usama bin Laden, November 6, 2009.

BIBLIOGRAPHY

PDF-023579, Abu Yahya al-Libi to Abu Musab Abd al-Wadud, October 7, 2010.

PDF-023625, Abu Basir to Atiya, February 10, 2011.

PDF-023642, Usama bin Laden to Abu Basir, most likely 2010.

PDF-023690, Atiya to Usama bin Laden, April 4, 2011.

PDF-023740, Abu Hurayra/Qasem al-Raymi to the leaders of al-Qaeda, undated.

PDF-023741, Abu Basir—letter in response to Hajji Uthman, most likely late 2009.

PDF-023749, Several letters from different leaders in AQIM addressed to Raja' (most likely Atiya), January 20–May 6, 2009.

PDF-023750, Hajji Uthman to Usama bin Laden, October 18, 2009.

PDF-023765, Hajji Uthman to Usama bin Laden, undated/2009–10.

PDF-023772, Muhannad al-Abyani/Tufan, "Arhibuhum" (meaning "Terrorize Them") February 13, 2010.

PDF-023767, Hajji Uthman to Usama bin Laden, March 8, 2010.

PDF-023783, Daoud to Siham, 2010.

PDF-023799/ PDF-023816, Abu Musab Abd al-Wadud to Shekau, August 31, 2009.

PDF-023811, Jaysh al-'Usra, 2007.

PDF-023821, Salah Abu Muhammad to Atiya, January 22, 2010.

PDF-023827, Siham to Daoud, 2010.

PDF-023842, Saleh, Report Concerning the External Work, 2009.

PDF-023844, Elisabeth Anna Windischmann to Usama bin Laden.

PDF-023850, Ayman al-Zawahiri to Usama bin Laden, March 12, 2009.

PDF-023853, Hajji Uthman to Usama bin Laden, August 4, 2009.

PDF-023854, Daoud to Siham, 2010.

PDF-023883, Atiya to Mukhtar Abu al-Zubayr, July 15, 2010.

PDF-023884, Atiya to Usama bin Laden, August 28, 2010.

PDF-023888, Atiya to Abu Basir, July 18, 2010.

PDF-023900, Ayman al-Zawahiri to Usama bin Laden, May 16, 2010.

PDF-023908, Ayman al-Zawahiri to Usama bin Laden, May 31, 2010.

PDF-023910, PDF-023911, Abd al-Rahman al-Maghrebi to Usama bin Laden and his son Khaled, 2010.

PDF-023935, Hajji Uthman and Atiya to Usama bin Laden, January 25, 2010.

PDF-023945, Ayman al-Zawahiri to Usama bin Laden, January 13, 2011.

PDF-023950, Abu Yahya al-Libi, 2009.

PDF-023953, Atiya to Usama bin Laden, January 24, 2011.

PDF-023956, Atiya to Mukhtar Abu al-Zubayr, December 27, 2010.

PDF-023960, PDF-023961, Riyad al-Husayni, January 2011.

PDF-023962, Atiya to Abu Muhammad Salah, December 11, 2010.

PDF-023983, Mukhtar Abu al-Zubayr to the General Leadership and the Sheikhs in Khurasan, March 5, 2010.

PDF-123763, A detailed report prepared by "Your brothers in the Ministry of Legal Affairs, Islamic State of Iraq," 2007.

IMG-040538, Usama bin Laden's notes, "The Birth of the Idea of 11 September," September 2002 (1/).

IMG-052993, Usama bin Laden's notes, September 2002 (1/7).

IMG-046353, Usama bin Laden's notes, September 2002 (2/7).

IMG-007097, Usama bin Laden's notes, September 2002 (3/7).

IMG-038618, Usama bin Laden's notes, September 2002 (4/7).

IMG-025138, Usama bin Laden's notes, September 2002 (6/7).

IMG-053149, Usama bin Laden's notes, September 2002 (7/7)

IMG-030337 (1/4), Abu al-Hasan al-Saidi/Tawfiq, September 8, 2004.

IMG-033568 (2/4), Abu al-Hasan al-Saidi/Tawfiq, September 8, 2004.

IMG-046447 (3/4), Abu al-Hasan al-Saidi/Tawfiq, September 8, 2004.

IMG-004960 (4/4), Abu al-Hasan al-Saidi/Tawfiq, September 8, 2004.

IMG-058732 (1/5), Khaled al-Habib to Usama bin Laden, 2004.

IMG-065081 (2/5), Khaled al-Habib to Usama bin Laden, 2004.

IMG-000667 (3/5), Khaled al-Habib to Usama bin Laden, 2004.

IMG-000468 (4/5), Khaled al-Habib to Usama bin Laden, 2004.

IMG-063395 (5/5), Khaled al-Habib to Usama bin Laden, 2004.

BIBLIOGRAPHY

IMG-063213, IMG-020402, IMG-063801, IMG-024865, IMG-031841, IMG-010391, IMG-040552, IMG-018029, IMG-037939, Abu Hammam al-Gharib to Usama bin Laden, undated, most likely around 2009.

IMG-019664, Iraq-related.

IMG-067996, Abu Hamza al-Muhajir to Abu Abdallah al-Shafii, April 29, 2007 (1/3).

IMG-053227/052915, Abu Hamza al-Muhajir to Abu Abdallah al-Shafii, April 29, 2007 (2/3).

IMG-051717/009822, Abu Hamza al-Muhajir to Abu Abdallah al-Shafii, April 29, 2007 (3/3).

IMG-059923, Abu Haidara Abd al-Razzaq Amari al-Awrasi (?), eader of the 5th Region, to Usama bin Laden, February 12, 2004.

IMG-064408, Abd al-Qayyum/Abu Abd al-Rahman Uns al-Subay'i to Abu Yahya, March 20, 2011.

IMG-047297 (1/2), Saad bin Laden, will addressed to his wife, August 15, 2008.

IMG-047913 (2/2), Saad bin Laden, will addressed to his wife, August 15, 2008.

IMG-021277, Saad bin Laden, will addressed to his father, August 15, 2008.

IMG-029064 (1/2), Umm Saad/Sarah (Daoud's wife) to Siham, December 20, 2010.

IMG-036096 (2/2), Umm Saad/Sarah (Daoud's wife) to Siham, December 20, 2010.

IMG-031090 (1/5), Uthman to Tawfiq, August 8, 2004.

IMG-057702 (2/5), Uthman to Tawfiq, August 8, 2004.

IMG-004980 (3/5), Uthman to Tawfiq, August 8, 2004.

IMG-057660 (4/5), Uthman to Tawfiq, August 8, 2004.

IMG-031009 (5/5), Uthman to Tawfiq, August 8, 2004.

IMG-032990, Siham's notes and draft poems.

IMG-034493, Siham's notes and draft poems.

IMG-016349, Siham's notes and draft poems.

IMG-017653, Siham's notes and draft poems.

IMG-038895, Siham's notes and draft poems.

IMG-063579, Siham's notes and draft poems.

IMG-058052, Poem praising Sumayya.

IMG-066064, Three letters by Daoud and Khadija's children to Daoud.

VID-007714, "Ana al-Bandoura al-Hamra."

VID-009969, "Unshudat al-Huruf al-Hija'iyya."

VID-004413, "Ya Qittati."

VID-002617, "7 Days in a Week – Song for Young Children."

VID-000313, Video of chickens in the Abbottabad compound

VID-009968, Video of the cow and her calf in the Abbottabad compound.

AUD-000303, "Ana Sirtu Saminan Ya Mama."

AUD-005846, "Ramadanu Ata wa-l-Qalbu Hafa."

AUD-005129, Aisha elocuting poetry.

AUD-005057, Abdallah elocuting poetry.

AUD-003821, Usama elocuting poetry.

AUD-006160, Fatima elocuting poetry.

"Bin Ladin's Journal" (inaccurate description by the CIA—it is a transcription of family conversation during the last two months of Usama bin Laden's life), https://www.cia.gov/library/abbottabad-compound/index.html.

SOCOM-2012-0000004, Adam Gadhan to al-Qaeda's leaders, January 2011.

SOCOM-2012-0000007, Atiya and Abu Yahya to Hakimullah Mehsud, December 3, 2010.

SOCOM-2012-0000011, Letter to Hafiz Sultan/Hajji Uthman, March 2007.

SOCOM-2012-0000012, Letter from 'Atiyatullah al-Libi, https://ctc.usma.edu/app/uploads/2013/09/Letter-from-Atiyahtullah-Al-Libi-Original.pdf.

SOCOM-2012-0000015, Usama bin Laden to Atiya, October 21, 2010.

SOCOM-2012-0000016, Usama bin Laden notes, 2010.

SOCOM-2012-0000019, Usama bin Laden to Atiya, May–June 2010.

"Letter to Sons Uthman, Muhammad, Hamza, wife—Umm Hamza," ODNI, 2015.

"Letter to Shaykh Abu Muhammad 17 August 2007," ODNI, 2016.

"Letter to Mawlawi 'Abd al-'Aziz," ODNI, 2016.
"To our respected Shaykhs," ODNI, 2016.
"Please Give Me Your News," ODNI, 2016.
"AQ Accounting Ledger," ODNI, 2017.
"Letter from Abu Yahya," ODNI, 2017.
"Letter to Haj 'Uthman," ODNI, 2017.
"Letter to Shaykh Mahmud 2," ODNI, 2017.
"Letter to My Caring Family," ODNI, 2016.
"Undated Letter 3," ODNI, 2015.
"Letter Dtd November 24, 2010," ODNI, May 2015.
"Dear Brother Shaykh Mahmud," ODNI, 2016.
"From Abu Ma'adh," ODNI, 2016.
"In Regard to the Money That Is in Sudan—Bin Laden's Will," ODNI, 2016.
"Draft of a Letter to Subordinates," ODNI, 2017.
"Letter to Abdallah and 'A'sisha," ODNI, 2016.
"Letter to Karim," ODNI, 2016.
"To Abu al-Faraj and 'Abd al-Hadi," Abu Saad, November 19, 2002, ODNI, 2016.
Letter from Atiya to Usama bin Laden, 22 August 2009, ODNI, March 2016.
"Jihad in Pakistan," ODNI, 2016.
"Letter Addressed to Shaykh," ODNI, 2015.
"Letter to My Dear Brother, Muhammad Aslam," ODNI, 2016.
"Letter to Our Honorable Shaykh," ODNI, 2015.
"Letter to Shaykh Azmarai," ODNI, 2016.
"Mujahidi Shura Council in Iraq," ODNI, 2016.
"Letter Dtd 7 August 2010," ODNI, 2015.
"Respected Brother, Kind Shaykh, Zamrai, Sahib," ODNI, 2016.
"Letter Dtd 5 April 2011," ODNI, 2015.
"Praise Be to God the Lord of All World," ODNI, 2016.
"Summary of the Points Session," ODNI, 2016.
"Undated Letter 3," ODNI, 20 May 2015.
"Letter to Mom", ODNI, 19 January 2017.
"My Generous Brother Tawfiq," ODNI, 2016 (1/2); "Letter from Hafiz," ODNI, 2015 (2/2).
"Letter Dtd 21 May 2007," ODNI, 2015.
"Letter Dtd 30 October 2010," ODNI, 2015.
"The Leadership of the Organization," ODNI, 2016.
"Letter Dtd 5 April 2011," ODNI, 2015.
"Letter from Khalid to Abdullah and Abu al-Harish," ODNI, 2015.
"Letter Dtd 18 July 2010," ODNI, 2015.
"Tehrik-e Taliban Pakistan (TTP) Charter," ODNI, 2016.
"To Emir Al-Mo'mineen," ODNI, 2016.
"Some Reactions to the Speech of al-Hafiz Abu Talhah al-Almani," ODNI, 2016.

Other Primary Sources

Al-Qaeda Internal Documents

AFGP-2002-600321, "Letter to Mullah Muhammed 'Umar from Bin Laden," undated, pre-2001, CTC, https://ctc.usma.edu/harmony-program/letter-to-mullah-muhammed-umar-from-bin-laden-original-language-2/.
AFGP-2002-003251, Abu Hudhayfa to Abu 'Abdallah (i.e., Usama bin Laden), June 21, 2000, CTC, https://ctc.usma.edu/wp-content/uploads/2013/09/A-Memo-to-Sheikh-Abu-Abdullah-Original1.pdf.
AFGP-2002-000112, "Al-Qa'ida Staff Count Public Appointments," CTC, https://ctc.usma.edu/harmony-program/al-qaida-staff-count-public-appointments-original-language-2/.
AFGP-2002-600046, "List of Names of Al-Qa'ida Members," https://ctc.usma.edu/harmony-program/list-of-names-of-al-qaida-members-original-language-2/.
Tarikh al-Ma'sada, CTC.

BIBLIOGRAPHY

Atiya to Abu Musab al-Zarqawi, December 12, 2005, https://ctc.usma.edu/wp-content/uploads/2013/10/Atiyahs-Letter-to-Zarqawi-Original.pdf.

Jihadi Literature

Al-Adnani, Abu Muhammad, "Udhran Amir al-Qaeda," May 2014.

Bin Laden, Usama, "Declaration of Jihad," "Muslim Bomb," "Among a Band of Knights," "To the Allies of America," "The Towers of Lebanon," "Depose the Tyrants," "Resist the New Rome," in Bruce Lawrence (ed.), *Messages to the World: The Statements of Osama bin Laden*, trans. James Howarth, New York: Verso, 2005.

—, https://archive.org/details/Qasam-Benladen.

—, "Hayya 'ala al-Jihad—Kalima ila Ahli Pakistan," August 2007.

—, "al-Nizal, al-Nizal, Ya Abtal al-Sumal," *al-Sahab*, March 2009.

—, "Risala ila Ikhwanina fi Pakistan—wa-Qatiluhum," May 2009.

—, "Min Usama bin Laden ila al-Sha'b al-Faransi," November 2010.

Al-Bishr, Bishr, http://www.tarhuni.org/i3teqal/olama/beshr.htm, and http://www.ilmway.com/site/maqdis/MS_5647.html.

Fadl, Dr. *al-Ta'riya* (1), *al-Masri al-Yawm*, November 18, 2008, https://www.almasryalyoum.com/news/details/1930360.

Harun, Fadil, *al-Harb 'ala al-Islam: Qissat Fadil Harun*, vols. 1 and 2, CTC, https://www.ctc.usma.edu/harmony-program/the-war-against-islam-the-story-of-fazul-harun-part-1-original-language-2/; https://www.ctc.usma.edu/harmony-program/the-war-against-islam-the-story-of-fazul-harun-part-2-original-language-2/.

Al-Jarbu', Abd al-'Aziz, *al-Mukhtar fi Hukm al-Intihar Khawfa Ifsha' al-Asrar*, http://www.ilmway.com.

Al-Libi, Abu Yahya, *al-Mu'lim fi Hukm al-Jasus al-Muslim* (A Guide to the Legal Judgement Concerning a Muslim Spy), Markaz al-Fajr al-I'lami, 2009.

—, "Al-Jaza'ir: Bayna Tadhiyat al-Aba', wa-Wafa' al-Abna'," June 2009.

—, "Usama: Masiratu 'Izzin wa-Khatimatu Sharaf," 2011.

Al-Libi, Atiya, *al-A'mal al-Kamila li-al-Sheikh al-Imam al-Shahid al-Mujahid 'Atiyatullah al-Libi* (Collected Works).

Al-Mauritani, Abu Hafs, Interview with Yusuf al-Shawli, "Mahfouz wuld al-Walid.. al-Qaeda wa-harakat Taliban," *Al Jazeera*, November 30, 2001.

Al-Rashid, Abu al-Hasan, "Butlan Muhadanat al-Murtaddin," http://www.ilmway.com/site/maqdis/MS_11240.html.

Al-Shamrani, Muhammad Saeed, "Ayyuha al-Sha'b al-Amriki," December 6, 2019.

Al-Siba'i, Hani, "al-Harakat al-Islamiyya al-Jihadiyya," http://www.albasrah.net/moqawama/maqalat/sba3iansar_140304.htm.

Al-Suri, Abu Musab, *Da'wat al-Muqawama al-Islamiyya* (*c.* 2005).

—, *Afghanistan wa-al-Taliban wa-Ma 'rakatu al-Islami al-Yawm*, 1998.

Al-Wuhayshi, Abu Basir, *al-Masra*, part 1, issue 3, January 30, 2016; part 2, issue 4, February 9, 2016. Accessed at https://jihadology.net/wp-content/uploads/_pda/2016/01/al-masracc84-newspaper-3.pdf.

Al-Zawahiri, Ayman, *al-Hiwar ma' al-Tawaghit: Maqbarat al-Da'wa wa-al-Du'at*.

—, Interview with al-Sahab, 2002.

—, "Qadaya Sakhina," Interview with al-Sahab, August 2006.

—, "al-Liqa' al-Maftuh," parts I (2006) and II (2008).

—, "Min Kabul ila Mugadishu," February 2009.

—, "Ikhwani wa-Akhawati al-Muslimin fi Pakistan," June 2009.

—, "Fursan tahta Rayat al-Nabi."

—, "Nasihat al-Umma al-Muwahhida bi-Haqiqat al-Umam al-Muttahida," November 23, 2021.

Al-Sahab, Qanadil min Nur (8), Usama bin Laden press conference in early 2001. Released in May 2021, https://archive.gnews.bz/index.php/s/kg2NbAXaf6kGSbx.

Nasa'ih wa-Tawjihat Shar'iyya min al-Sheikh Abi al-Hasan Rashid li-Mujahidi Nigeria (released by AQIM).

Sada al-Malahim (released by AQAP), issue 1, 2008.

"Tahni'at al-Umma al-Islamiyya 'ala Nasri Allah fi Afghanistan al-Abiyya," *al-Sahab*, August 2021.

BIBLIOGRAPHY

Other Primary Sources

Bush, George, W., "Presidential Address to the Nation", *The White House*, October 7, 2001, https://georgewbush-whitehouse.archives.gov/news/releases/2001/10/20011007-8.html.

—, "President Delivers State of the Union Address," January 29, 2002. https://georgewbush-whitehouse.archives.gov/news/releases/2002/01/20020129-11.html

Musharraf, Pervez, "Frontline," *PBS*, May 14, 2002, https://www.pbs.org/wgbh/pages/frontline/shows/campaign/interviews/musharraf.html.

Obama, Barack, "Osama Bin Laden Dead," May 2, 2011, https://obamawhitehouse.archives.gov/blog/2011/05/02/osama-bin-laden-dead.

Pompeo, Michael R., "The Iran-al-Qa'ida Axis," January 12, 2021, https://www.state.gov/the-iran-al-qaida-axis/.

Powell, Colin, "U.S. Secretary of State Colin Powell Addresses the U.N. Security Council," February 5, 2003, https://georgewbush-whitehouse.archives.gov/news/releases/2003/02/20030205-1.html.

Trump, Donald, "Remarks by President Trump on the Joint Comprehensive Plan of Action," *The White House*, May 8, 2018, https://uy.usembassy.gov/remarks-by-president-trump-on-the-joint-comprehensive-plan-of-action/.

"Press Briefing by Senior Administration Officials on the Killing of Osama bin Laden," *The White House*, May 2, 2011, https://obamawhitehouse.archives.gov/the-press-office/2011/05/02/press-briefing-senior-administration-officials-killing-osama-bin-laden.

"Joint Resolution to Authorize the Use of the United States Armed Forces Against Those Responsible for the Recent Attacks Launched Against the United States," Public Law 107-40-Sept. 18, 2001, https://www.congress.gov/107/plaws/publ40/PLAW-107publ40.pdf.

Senate Hearing 112-741, Current and Future Worldwide Threats to the National Security of the United States, February 16, 2012, https://www.govinfo.gov/content/pkg/CHRG-112shrg79855/html/CHRG-112shrg79855.htm.

United Nations Security Council, Resolutions 1189 (1998); 1193 (1998); 1267 (1999); 1333 (2000), https://www.un.org/securitycouncil/sanctions.

Resolution 1973, March 17, 2011, https://www.nato.int/nato_static/assets/pdf/pdf_2011_03/20110927_110311-UNSCR-1973.pdf.

Eleventh Report of the Analytical Support and Sanctions Monitoring Team, United Nations Security Council, May 27, 2020, https://www.securitycouncilreport.org/atf/cf/%7B65BFCF9B-6D27-4E9C-8CD3-CF6E4FF96FF9%7D/s_2020_415_e.pdf.

"Agreement for Bringing Peace to Afghanistan Between the Islamic Emirate of Afghanistan Which Is Not Recognized by the United States as a State and Is Known as the Taliban and the United States of America," February 29, 2020, https://www.state.gov/wp-content/uploads/2020/02/Agreement-For-Bringing-Peace-to-Afghanistan-02.29.20.pdf.

"Tora Bora Revisited: How We Failed to Get Bin Laden," A Report to Members of the Committee of Foreign Relations, United States Senate, November 30, 2009, https://www.govinfo.gov/content/pkg/CPRT-111SPRT53709/html/CPRT-111SPRT53709.htm.

Senate Report 113-288, Report of the Senate Select Committee on Intelligence Committee Study of the Central Intelligence Agency's Detention and Interrogation Program, 113th Congress, 2d Session, December 9, 2014, https://www.intelligence.senate.gov/sites/default/files/publications/CRPT-113srpt288.pdf.

The 9/11 Commission Report: Final Report of the National Commission on Terrorist Attacks Upon the United States (9/11 Report), July 22, 2004, https://www.govinfo.gov/app/details/GPO-911REPORT.

Bin Laden Dossier [Abbottabad Commission Report on Killing of Osama bin Laden], 2013, https://dataspace.princeton.edu/handle/88435/dsp01jq085k07t

Secondary Sources

Articles, Books, Encyclopedias

Alston, Philip, "The CIA and Targeted Killings Beyond Borders," *Harvard National Security Journal*, vol. 2, 2011, pp. 283–446.

Barfield, Thomas, *Afghanistan: A Cultural and Political History*, Princeton: Princeton University Press, 2012.

BIBLIOGRAPHY

—, "Problems in Establishing Legitimacy in Afghanistan," *Iranian Studies*, vol. 37, no. 2, June 2004, pp. 263–93.

Barnes, Cedric, and Hassan, Harun, "The Rise and Fall of Mogadishu's Islamic Courts," *Journal of Eastern African Studies*, vol. 1, no. 2, July 2007, pp. 151–60.

Bergen, Peter, *The Osama bin Laden I Know: An Oral History*, New York: Free Press, 2008.

—, *Manhunt: The Ten-Year Search for Bin Laden from 9/11 to Abbottabad*, New York: Crown, 2013.

—, *United States of Jihad: Who are America's Homegrown Terrorists, and How Do We Stop Them?*, New York: Crown Publishers, 2016.

—, *The Rise and Fall of Osama bin Laden*, New York: Simon & Schuster, 2021.

Beschloss, Michael, *Presidents of War: The Epic Story, from 1807 to Modern Times*, New York: Broadway Books, 2019.

Bosworth, C.E., "Tulaka,'" *Encyclopaedia of Islam* (2).

Coll, Steve, *The Bin Ladens: An Arabian Family in the American Century*, New York: The Penguin Press, 2008.

—, "The Unblinking Stare: The Drone War in Pakistan," *The New Yorker*, November 17, 2014.

Cook, David, "Contemporary Martyrdom: Ideology and Material Culture," in Thomas Hegghammer (ed.), *Jihadi Culture: The Art and Social Practices of Militant Islamists*, Cambridge: Cambridge University Press, 2017.

Cook, Michael, *Muhammad*, Oxford: Oxford University Press, 1983.

—, *The Koran: A Very Short Introduction*, Oxford: Oxford University Press, 2000.

—, *Commanding Right and Forbidding Wrong in Islamic Thought*, Cambridge: Cambridge University Press, 2000.

Crenshaw, Martha, "The Causes of Terrorism," *Comparative Politics*, vol. 13, no. 4, July, 1981, pp. 379–99.

Crone, Patricia, *God's Rule: Government and Islam*, Columbia: Columbia University Press, 2004.

Fahd, T., "Ru'ya," *Encyclopaedia of Islam* (2).

—, "Firasa," *Encyclopaedia of Islam* (2).

Farrall, Leah, and Hamid, Mustafa, *The Arabs at War in Afghanistan*, London: Hurst, 2015.

Fouda, Yosri, *Fi Tariq al-Adha: Min Ma'aqil al-Qa 'ida ila Hawadini Da'ish*, Cairo: Dar al-Shuruq, 2015.

Halm, Heinz, *The Fatimids and Their Traditions of Learning*, New York: I.B. Tauris & Co. Ltd, 1997.

Hastings, Max, *Vietnam: An Epic Tragedy, 1945–75*, New York: Harper Perennial, 2019.

Heck, Paul, L., "Jihad Revisited," *Journal of Religious Ethics*, vol. 32, no. 1, 2004, pp. 95–128.

Hegghammer, Thomas, *The Caravan: Abdallah Azzam and the Rise of Global Jihad*, Cambridge: Cambridge University Press, 2020.

Henze, Paul B., *Layers of Time: A History of Ethiopia*, New York: Palgrave, 2000.

Hussein, Fuad, *al-Zarqawi: al-Jil al-Thani li-al-Qa'ida*, Beirut: Dar al-Khayal, 2005.

Ibn al-Jawziyya, *Jami' al-Fiqh*, vol. 5, ed. Yusri al-Sayyid Muhammad, Dar al-Wafa' li-al-Tiba'a wa-al-Nashr, 2000.

Ibn Rushd, *The Distinguished Jurist's Primer*, vols. 1 and 2, trans. Imran Ahsan Khan Nyazee and Mohammad Abdul Rauf, Reading, UK: Garnet Publishing, 2000.

Ibn Sirin, Muhammad, b., and al-Nabulsi, Abd al-Ghanis, *Mu'jam Tafsir al-Ahlam*, ed. Basil al-Baridi, Beirut: al-Yamama, 2008.

Jordan, Robert W., with Fiffer, Steve, *Desert Diplomat: Inside Saudi Arabia Following 9/11*, Potomac Books, 2015.

Jordheim, Helge, "Philology and the Problem of Culture," in Harry Lonnroth (ed.), *Philology Matters!: Essays on the Art of Reading Slowly*, Leiden: Brill, 2017.

Karnow, Stanley, *Vietnam: A History*, 2nd edn., New York: Penguin Books, 1997.

Khadduri, Majid, *Shaybani's Siyar*, (trans.) *Islamic Law of Nations*, Baltimore: The Johns Hopkins Press, 1966.

Kohlberg, E., "Shahid," *Encyclopaedia of Islam*, 2nd edn., ed. P. Bearman, Th. Bianquis, C.E. Bosworth, E. van Donzel and W.P. Heinrichs, Leiden: E. J. Brill (online).

—, "al-Rafida, *Encyclopaedia of Islam* (2).

Lahoud, Nelly, *The Jihadis' Path to Self-Destruction*, London/New York: Hurst/Columbia University Press, 2010.

—, "The Evolution of Modern Jihadism," *Oxford Research Encyclopedia, Religion*, August 2016.

BIBLIOGRAPHY

—, "The Neglected Sex: The Jihadis' Exclusion of Women from Jihad," *Terrorism and Political Violence*, vol. 26, vol. 5, 2014, pp. 780–802.

—, "What the Jihadis Left Behind," *London Review of Books*, vol. 42, no. 2, January 23, 2020.

—, and Collins, Liam, "How the CT Community Failed to Anticipate the Islamic State," *Democracy and Security* (August 2016), pp. 199–210.

—, "Bin Laden's Catastrophic Success: Al Qaeda Changed the World—But Not in the Way It Expected," *Foreign Affairs*, September–October 2021. https://www.foreignaffairs.com/articles/afghanistan/2021-08-13/osama-bin-ladens-911-catastrophic-success

Lawrence, Bruce (ed.), *Messages to the World: The Statements of Osama bin Laden*, New York: Verso, 2005.

Layish, A., "Mirath," *Encyclopaedia of Islam* (2).

Lia, Brynjar, *The Architect of Global Jihad*, London/New York: Hurst/Columbia University Press, 2008.

Lings, Martin, *Muhammad: His Life Based on the Earliest Sources*, Cambridge: The Islamic Texts Society, 2002.

Al-Mawardi, *The Ordinances of Government*, trans. Wafaa H. Wahba, Reading, England: Center for Muslim Contribution to Civilization, 1996.

McRaven, William H., *Sea Stories: My Life in Special Operations*, New York/Boston: Grand Central Publishing, 2019.

—, *Spec Ops: Case Studies in Special Operations Warfare: Theory and Practice*, New York: Presidio Press, 1996.

—, Lecture at the Special Operations Policy Forum, New America, September 2019, https://www.newamerica.org/conference/special-ops-2019/.

Menkhaus, Ken, "Governance Without Government in Somalia," *International Security*, Vol. 31, no. 3, 2006–07, pp. 74–106.

—, "Somalia: A Country in Peril, a Policy Nightmare," Enough Strategy Paper, September 2008.

O'Neill, Robert, *The Operator: Firing the Shots That Killed Osama bin Laden and My Years as a SEAL Team Warrior*, New York: Scribner, 2017.

Perri, Timothy J., "The Evolution of Military Conscription in the United States," *The Independent Review*, vol. 17, no. 3, Winter 2013, pp. 429–39.

Peters, R., "Wasiyya," *Encyclopaedia of Islam* (2).

Sasson, Jean, Bin Laden, Najwa, and Bin Laden, Omar, *Growing Up Bin Laden: Osama's Wife and Son Take Us Inside Their Secret World*, New York: St Martin's Griffin, 2009 and 2010.

Schacht, J., "Mirath," *Encyclopaedia of Islam* (2).

Scott-Clark, Cathy, and Levy, Adrian, *The Exile: The Stunning Inside Story of Osama bin Laden and Al Qaeda in Flight*, New York: Bloomsbury, 2017.

Seale, Patrick, *Asad of Syria*, California: University of California Press, 1989.

Silber, Mitchell D., *The Al Qaeda Factor: Plots Against the West*, Philadelphia: University of Pennsylvania Press, 2012.

Stenersen, Anne, *Al-Qaida in Afghanistan*, Cambridge: Cambridge University Press, 2017.

Wallace, Chris, with Weiss, Mitch, *Countdown bin Laden: The Untold Story of the 247-Day Hunt to Bring the Mastermind of 9/11 to Justice*, New York: Simon & Schuster, 2021.

Warrick, Joby, *Black Flags: The Rise of ISIS*, New York: Penguin, 2015.

Weir, T.H., and Zysow, A., "Sadaka," *Encyclopaedia of Islam* (2).

Wensinck, A.J., "Asiya," *Encyclopaedia of Islam* (2).

—, "Subha," *Encyclopaedia of Islam* (2).

Williams, Brian Glyn, *Predators: The CIA's Drone War on al Qaeda*, Washington, D.C.: Potomac Books, 2013.

Woodward, Bob, *Obama's Wars*, New York: Simon & Schuster, 2010.

Yamskov, A.N., "Ethnic Conflict in the Transcaucasus: The Case of Nagorno-Karabakh," *Theory and Society*, vol. 20, no. 5, October 1991, pp. 631–60.

Yihdego, Zeray W., "Ethiopia's Military Action Against the Union of Islamic Courts and Others in Somalia: Some Legal Implications," *The International and Comparative Law Quarterly*, vol. 56, no. 3, July 2007, pp. 666–76.

Zaeef, Abdul Salam, *My Life with the Taliban*, ed. Alex Strick van Linschoten and Felix Kuehn, London: Hurst & Company, 2010.

BIBLIOGRAPHY

Zenn, Jacob, *Unmasking Boko Haram: Exploring Global Jihad in Nigeria*, Denver: Lynne Rienner Publishers, 2020.

Magazines, Newspapers, Reports

Benotman, Noman, "An Open Letter to Osama bin Laden," *Foreign Policy*, September 10, 2010.

Bergen, Peter, "The Man Who Wouldn't Hand Over bin Laden to the U.S.," *CNN*, July 29, 2015, https://peterbergen.com/the-man-who-wouldnt-hand-over-bin-laden-to-the-u-s-cnn-com/.

—, Cruickshank, Paul, "The Unraveling," *The New Republic*, June 11, 2008.

—, Sterman, David, and Salyk-Virk, Melissa, "America's Counterterrorism Wars: Tracking the United States' Drone Strikes and Other Operations in Pakistan, Yemen, Somalia, and Libya," *New America*, https://www.newamerica.org/international-security/reports/americas-counterterrorism-wars/.

Bunzel, Cole, "Why Are Al Qaeda Leaders in Iran?" *Foreign Affairs*, February 11, 2021.

Biswas, Soutik, "Mumbai 26/11 Attacks: Six Corpses, a Mobile Phone Call and One Survivor," BBC, November 26, 2018, https://www.bbc.com/news/world-asia-india-46314555.

Coll, Steve, "The Unblinking Stare: The Drone War in Pakistan," *The New Yorker*, November 17, 2014, https://www.newyorker.com/magazine/2014/11/24/unblinking-stare.

Dabashi, Hamid, "Who Is the 'Great Satan'?", *Al Jazeera*, September 20, 2015, https://www.aljazeera.com/indepth/opinion/2015/09/great-satan-150920072643884.html.

Dorronsoro, Gilles, "The World Isolates the Taliban," *Le Monde Diplomatique*, June 2001, https://www.globalpolicy.org/the-dark-side-of-natural-resources-st/water-in-conflict/41438.html.

Flaman, Annasofie, "Yemen's al-Qaeda Want Toxic Bombs," *PRI*, August 15, 2011.

Flissi, Lutfi, "al-Wasit al-Tijari li-Bin Ladin fi Qabdat al-Aman al-Jaza'iri," October 16, 2007.

Frantz, Douglas, "U.S.-Based Charity Is Under Scrutiny," *The New York Times*, June 14, 2002.

Hasan, Syed Shoaib, "Islamabad's Red Mosque," BBC News, July 27, 2007.

Hersh, Seymour M., "The Killing of Osama bin Laden," *London Review of Books*, vol. 37, no. 10, May 21, 2015.

Jackson, Kevin, *Abu al-Layth al-Libi*, in Nelly Lahoud (ed.), Jihadi Bios Project, February 15, 2015, CTC.

Jenkins, Brian M., "The New Age of Terrorism," The RAND Corporation, https://www.rand.org/content/dam/rand/pubs/reprints/2006/RAND_RP1215.pdf.

Khan, Zahid Ali, "Military Operations in FATA and PATA: Implications for Pakistan," ISSI-Islamabad, 2014, http://www.issi.org.pk/wp-content/uploads/2014/06/1339999992_58398784.pdf.

Koehler-Derrick, Gabriel (ed.), *A False Foundation? AQAP, Tribes and Ungoverned Spaces in Yemen*, CTC, October 3, 2011.

Lahoud, Nelly, *Beware of Imitators: Al-Qa'ida Through the Lens of Its Confidential Secretary*, CTC, June 4, 2012.

—, *Al-Qa'ida's Contested Relationship with Iran: The View from Abbottabad*, New America, September 2018.

—, Caudill, Stuart, Collins, Liam, Koehler-Derrick, Gabriel, Rassler, Don, and al-'Ubadydi, Muhammad, "Letters from Abbottabad: Bin Laden Sidelined," CTC, May 3, 2012, https://ctc.usma.edu/letters-from-abbottabad-bin-ladin-sidelined/.

Malnic, Eric, Rempel, William C., and Alonso-Zaldivar, Ricardo, "EgyptAir Co-Pilot Caused '99 Jet Crash, NTSB to Say," *Los Angeles Times*, March 15, 2002.

Mazzetti, Mark, "Officer Failed to Warn C.I.A. Before Attack," *The New York Times*, October 19, 2010, https://www.nytimes.com/2010/10/20/world/asia/20intel.html.

McCants, William, "The Believer: How an Introvert with a Passion for Religion and Soccer Became the Leader of the Islamic State," *Brookings*, 2015, http://csweb.brookings.edu/content/research/essays/2015/thebeliever.html.

Mellah, Salima, and Rivoire, Jean-Baptiste, "El Para, the Maghreb's Bin Laden," *Le Monde Diplomatique*, February 2005, https://mondediplo.com/2005/02/04algeria.

Miller, John, "Greetings, America. My Name Is Osama Bin Laden . . .," *Esquire*, February 1, 1999, https://www.pbs.org/wgbh/pages/frontline/shows/binladen/who/miller.html.

Mohamed, Ahmed, "Mauritani Sentences Alleged al-Qaida Leader to 20 Years," *Associated Press*, April 21, 2015.

BIBLIOGRAPHY

Orden, Erica, "Najibullah Zazi, who plotted to bomb the New York subway, gets a second chance," *CNN*, September 28, 2019, https://www.cnn.com/2019/05/01/us/najibullah-zazi-new-york-subway-bomb-plot-sentencing/index.html.

Pantucci, Raffaello "A Biography of Rashid Rauf: Al-Qa'ida's British Operative," *CTC Sentinel*, July 2012, Vol. 5, Issue 7.

Perlez, Jane, "An Iranian Diplomat Is Abducted by Gunmen in Pakistan," *The New York Times*, November 13, 2008, https://www.nytimes.com/2008/11/14/world/asia/14envoy.html.

Petraeus, David, "How We Won in Iraq," *Foreign Policy*, October 29, 2013.

Riedel, Bruce, "Al Qaeda's Latest Loss," *Brookings*, June 4, 2011, https://www.brookings.edu/opinions/al-qaedas-latest-loss/.

Rosenberg, Carol, "What the C.I.A.'s Torture Program Looked Like to the Tortured," *The New York Times*, Dec. 4, 2019, https://www.nytimes.com/2019/12/04/us/politics/cia-torture-drawings.html.

Rosenberg, Matthew, "C.I.A. Cash Ended Up in Coffers of Al Qaeda," *The New York Times*, March 14, 2015, https://www.nytimes.com/2015/03/15/world/asia/cia-funds-found-their-way-into-al-qaeda-coffers.html.

Schmitt, Eric, "U.S. Officials Say a Son of Bin Laden May Be Dead," *The New York Times*, July 23, 2009.

Al-Shafi'i, Muhamad, "Muhamad Shawqi al-Islambuli (Abu Khaled) shaqiq qatil al-Sadat waffara li-A 'da' "al-Qaeda" maladhan aminan fi janubi Iran," *al-Sharq al-Awsat*, issue 8942, May 23, 2003, https://archive.aawsat.com/details.asp?article=172395&issueno=8942#.X-DKUeTsElQ.

Smucker, Philip, "How Bin Laden Got Away," *Christian Science Monitor*, March 4, 2002.

Thielman, Greg, "The Missile Gap Myth and Its Progeny," *Arms Control Association*, 2011, https://www.armscontrol.org/act/2011-05/missile-gap-myth-its-progeny.

Tucker, Eric, and Balsamo, Michael, "US to Send Home Some Saudi Military Students After Shooting," *Associated Press*, January 12, 2020, https://apnews.com/726126ca1c1e0afb752b33234201137c.

Al-'Ubaydi, Muhammad, *Khattab* (Jihadi Bios Project, ed. Nelly Lahoud), CTC, March, 2015.

Walsh, Declan, "Pakistan's Spymaster Hamid Gul: Angel of Jihad or Windbag Provocateur," *Guardian*, May 31, 2011.

Weiser, Benjamin, "Abu Ghaith, a Bin Laden Adviser, Is Sentenced to Life in Prison," *The New York Times*, September 23, 2014, https://www.nytimes.com/2014/09/24/nyregion/abu-ghaith-a-bin-laden-adviser-is-sentenced-to-life-in-prison.html.

Westwood, Sarah, Perez, Evan, and Browne, Ryan, "Trump Confirms Osama bin Laden's Son Hamza Killed in US Counterterrorism Operation," *CNN*, September 14, 2019, https://www.cnn.com/2019/09/14/politics/hamza-bin-laden-al-qaeda-dead/index.html.

Windrem, Robert, and Limjoco, Victor, "Was Bin Laden's Last Video Faked?" *NBC*, October 29, 2010, http://www.nbcnews.com/id/21530470/ns/nbc_nightly_news_with_brian_williams/t/was-bin-ladens-last-video-faked/.

Whitlock, Craig, and Khan, Kamran, "Blast in Pakistan Kills Al Qaeda Commander: Figure Reportedly Hit by U.S. Missile Strike," *Washington Post*, December 4, 2005, https://www.washingtonpost.com/wp-dyn/content/article/2005/12/03/AR2005120301473_pf.html.

—, and DeYoung, Karen, "Senior Al-Qaeda Commander Believed to Be Dead," *Washington Post*, April 10, 2008, https://www.washingtonpost.com/wp-dyn/content/article/2008/04/09/AR2008040901793.html?hpid=moreheadlines.

Wojtanik, Andrew, "Mokhtar Belmokhtar: One-Eyed Firebrand of North Africa and the Sahel," Jihadi Bios Project, ed. Nelly Lahoud, CTC, February 2015.

"Al-Qaeda Chief Younis al-Mauritani Held, Says Pakistan," *BBC*, September 5, 2011.

"Mutalabat Iran bi-Itlaq Usrat Bin Laden," *Al Jazeera*, March 15, 2010.

"Sulaiman Abu Ghaith Sentenced to Life in Prison," *BBC*, September 23, 2014, https://www.bbc.com/news/world-us-canada-29331395.

"Al Qaeda's No. 2, Accused in U.S. Embassy Attacks, Was Killed in Iran," *The New York Times*, November 14, 2020.

"Austria Denies Ransom in Qaeda Hostage Release," *France24*, November 2, 2008.

"Timeline: Saudi Attacks," *BBC News*, http://news.bbc.co.uk/2/hi/middle_east/3760099.stm.

"Senior Afghan Taliban Leader, Mullah Obaidullah, Is Dead," *BBC*, February 13, 2012, https://www.bbc.com/news/world-asia-17011844.

BIBLIOGRAPHY

"Guantanamo Inmates Say They Were 'Sold,'" *Associated Press*, May 31, 2005, http://www.nbcnews.com/id/8049868/ns/world_news/t/guantanamo-inmates-say-they-were-sold/.

"U.S. Tells Taliban to Close New York Office," *The New York Times*, February 10, 2001.

"US-Taliban Talks: Who Is Mullah Baradar?" *Al Jazeera*, May 1, 2019, https://www.aljazeera.com/news/2019/05/us-taliban-talks-mullah-baradar-190501184035063.html.

"Baghdad Church Hostage Drama Ends in Bloodbath," *BBC*, November 1, 2010.

"Taliban Leader Mullah Akhtar Mansour Killed, Afghans Confirm," *BBC*, May 22, 2016, https://www.bbc.com/news/world-asia-36352559.

"Obituary: Hakimullah Mehsud," *BBC*, November 1, 2013, https://www.bbc.co.uk/news/world-asia-24464506.

"Syria Backs 'Iraqi People' in War," *CNN*, March 31, 2003, https://www.cnn.com/2003/WORLD/meast/03/31/sprj.irq.us.syria/.

"Zarqawi Beheaded US Man in Iraq," *BBC*, May 13, 2004, http://news.bbc.co.uk/2/hi/middle_east/3712421.stm.

"Iraqis Welcome Exiled Cleric Home," *BBC*, May 12, 2003, http://news.bbc.co.uk/2/hi/middle_east/3019831.stm.

"Ansar al-Islam," *Al Jazeera*, February 9, 2004, https://www.aljazeera.net/encyclopedia/movementsandparties/2014/2/9/%D8%A3%D9%86%D8%B5%D8%A7%D8%B1-%D8%A7%D9%84%D8%A5%D8%B3%D9%84%D8%A7%D9%85.

"Ansar al-Islam' al-Kirdiyya .. Min al-Ta'sis hatta 'Daesh,'" December 21, 2019, http://www.islamist-movements.com/32212.

BBC timeline of the Madrid attacks, http://news.bbc.co.uk/2/shared/spl/hi/guides/457000/457031/html/.

"Al Qaeda No. 3 Dead, But How?" *CNN*, December 4, 2005, http://www.cnn.com/2005/WORLD/asiapcf/12/03/pakistan.rabia/.

"Deadly Attacks Rock Baghdad, Karbala," *CNN*, March 2, 2004, http://edition.cnn.com/2004/WORLD/meast/03/02/sprj.nirq.main/.

"US Judge: Saudi Royals Must Answer Question in 9/11 Lawsuit," *Associated Press*, September 11, 2020, https://apnews.com/article/lawsuits-archive-courts-ac77fbfb343c5133019153eb864a820d.

"Abubakar Shekau: Nigeria's Boko Haram Leader Is Dead, Say Rival Militants," *BBC*, June 7, 2021, https://www.bbc.com/news/world-africa-57378493.

"Freed French Hostages Return amid Ransom Speculation," *BBC*, October 2013, https://www.bbc.com/news/world-europe-24739716.

"Al Qaeda Blamed for U.S. Embassy Attack," *CNN*, September 17, 2008.

"Al Qaeda Blamed for Yemen Attack," *CNN*, 2009.

"Al Qaeda Leader Behind Northwest Flight 253 Terror Plot Was Released by U.S.," *ABC News*, December 28, 2009.

"Key Afghanistan Taliban Commander Killed in US Air Strike," *BBC*, December 2, 2018, https://www.bbc.com/news/world-asia-46418776.

"The Guantanamo Files—Abdullah Khan," *WikiLeaks*, https://wikileaks.org/gitmo/prisoner/950.html.

Websites

The 9/11 Memorial & Museum, https://www.911memorial.org/visit/museum/exhibitions/in-memoriam.

9/11 Commission Report, https://govinfo.library.unt.edu/911/report/911Report.pdf.

UNESCO, https://whc.unesco.org/en/list/208/.

FBI, https://www.fbi.gov/history/famous-cases/east-african-embassy-bombings.

DIA, https://www.dia.mil/News/Articles/Article-View/article/567026/attacks-on-uss-cole-spurred-dias-counterterrorism-mission/.

United Nations – Zia-ur-Rahman Madani –https://www.un.org/securitycouncil/sanctions/1988/materials/summaries/individual/zia-ur-rahman-madani.

America's Navy, https://www.navy.com/seals.

Air Combat Command, "RQ-1/MQ-1 Predator Unmanned Aerial Vehicle," November 5, 2008, https://www.acc.af.mil/About-Us/Fact-Sheets/Display/Article/199130/rq-1mq-1-predator-unmanned-aerial-vehicle/.

BIBLIOGRAPHY

Air Force Technology, "Predator RQ-1/MQ-1/MQ-9 Reaper UAV," https://www.airforce-technology.com/projects/predator-uav/.

U.S. Air Force, "MQ-1B Predator," September 23, 2015, https://www.af.mil/About-Us/Fact-Sheets/Display/Article/104469/mq-1b-predator/.

Air Force Technology, "Predator RQ-1/MQ-1/MQ-9 Reaper UAV," https://www.airforce-technology.com/projects/predator-uav/.

U.S. Air Force, "MQ-9 Reaper," https://www.af.mil/About-Us/Fact-Sheets/Display/Article/104470/mq-9-reaper/.

EIA—US Energy Information Administration, https://www.eia.gov/dnav/pet/hist/LeafHandler.ashx?n=PET&s=MCRIMUS1&f=M.

CENTCOM, https://www.centcom.mil/ABOUT-US/COMPONENT-COMMANDS/.

The Hall of Valor Project, Kent G. Solheim, https://valor.militarytimes.com/hero/5554.

See more about the blood chit on https://www.airforcemag.com/article/1098chit/.

Isamweb.net, Fatwa 62318.

https://adabworld.com – Qays b. al-Muluh.

MAFA World, https://www.mafa.world/mustafa-hamed/.

dorar.net – "Habs al-Madin fi qabrihi bi-daynihi."

Sunnah.com – *Jami' al-Tirmidhi* 3604f, Bk 48, Hadith 240; *Musnad* Ahmad 628/Bk 5, Hadith 65.

INDEX

Note: Personal names prefixed with al- are filed under the second element of the name.
Names of organisations prefixed with al- are filed in the A sequence.
Page numbers in italic denote illustrations or maps and in bold indicate the *Dramatis Personae*
in Appendix 2, which gives background information, aliases, and alternative names.

INDEX

INDEX

INDEX

INDEX

INDEX

INDEX